Offend, Shock, or Disturb

Offend, Shock, or Disturb

Free Speech under the Indian Constitution

Gautam Bhatia

OXFORD
UNIVERSITY PRESS

OXFORD
UNIVERSITY PRESS

Oxford University Press is a department of the University of Oxford.
It furthers the University's objective of excellence in research, scholarship,
and education by publishing worldwide. Oxford is a registered trademark of
Oxford University Press in the UK and in certain other countries.

Published in India by
Oxford University Press
2/11 Ground Floor, Ansari Road, Daryaganj, New Delhi 110 002, India

First Edition published in 2016
Oxford India Paperbacks 2018

ISBN-13: 978-0-19-948864-3
ISBN-10: 0-19-948864-9

Typeset in Minion Pro 10.5/14
by Tranistics Data Technologies, New Delhi 110 044
Printed in India by Repro Knowledgecast Limited, Thane

To my parents, the first dissenters I knew.

[The freedom of expression] *is applicable not only to 'information' or 'ideas' that are favourably received or regarded as inoffensive or as a matter of indifference, but also to those that offend, shock or disturb...*

Handyside v. *United Kingdom*, European Court of Human Rights (1976), quoted in
Islamic Unity Convention v. *The Independent Broadcasting Authority*, Constitutional Court of South Africa (2002) and
S. Rangarajan v. *P. Jagjivan Ram*, Supreme Court of India (1989)

Contents

· ·

Preface

This book was written in 2014, which was a year of great ferment in Indian free speech law. On 3 February, the Supreme Court handed down its judgment in *Aveek Sarkar* v. *State of West Bengal*,[1] formally repudiating the 'Hicklin test' for determining obscene content. The Hicklin test (England, 1868), which was a product of the famously squeamish Victorians, had already been repudiated in the country of its birth by the time Justice Hidayatullah decided to incorporate it into Indian constitutional law in *Ranjit Udeshi* v. *State of Maharashtra*.[2] Subsequent decisions relentlessly chipped away at the foundations of *Ranjit Udeshi*, but it was only fifty years later, in *Aveek Sarkar*, that the ghost of Hicklin was finally laid to rest. The alternative, however, is far from satisfactory. The Court replaced Hicklin with the American standard in *Roth* v. *United States*,[3] which was itself subsequently abandoned by the US Supreme Court. Apart from that, *Roth* is predicated upon a federal model that finds few parallels in India, and its incorporation into Indian law raises some interesting questions about the direction that our obscenity jurisprudence will take in the coming years.

[1] (2014) 4 SCC 257 (hereinafter *Aveek Sarkar*).
[2] AIR 1965 SC 881: [1965] 1 SCR 65 (hereinafter *Ranjit Udeshi*).
[3] 354 U.S. 476 (1957) (hereinafter *Roth*).

Obscenity law is one prominent method of cultural regulation. Hate speech legislation is the other. India's hate speech laws were brought firmly into the spotlight in February 2014, when Penguin Books decided to withdraw and 'pulp' all copies of Wendy Doniger's book on Hinduism, in the teeth of a four-year-long criminal case. Section 295A of the Indian Penal Code, our own variant of a blasphemy law, was the legal provision used against the publisher and the writer. Penguin's capitulation was not entirely surprising. The Supreme Court's interpretation of Section 295A had in the past accorded great solicitude to religious feelings and beliefs, and taken a dim view of tracts that caused 'offence'. However, the very next month, in *Pravasi Bhalai Sangathan* v. *Union of India*,[4] the Court signalled a shift in its hate speech jurisprudence that could yet prove to be as significant as the change in its understanding of obscenity. In *Pravasi*, the Court dismissed a petition asking it to issue orders regulating hate speech in the context of elections. Consequently, its observations do not have precedential value. Nonetheless, the Court embarked upon a detailed analysis of existing hate speech legislation, before providing a philosophical justification for regulating hate speech. For the first time in its history, the Court grounded the offence not in hurt sentiments or wounded feelings, but in ideas of *equality*. Drawing upon the jurisprudence of the Canadian Supreme Court, it focused on the potential of hate speech to exclude, to discriminate, and to marginalize. If this understanding takes root in our constitutional jurisprudence, it will entirely transform the way in which hate speech laws are applied.

Towards the end of 2013, the Supreme Court controversially decided to recriminalize homosexuality in *Koushal* v. *Naz*.[5] In April 2014, however, the Court arrived at an opposite conclusion in a petition seeking legal and constitutional recognition for the transgender community (*NALSA* v. *Union of India*).[6] Among other things, the Court held that under Article 19(1)(a) of the Constitution, the transgender community had the right to 'express' its identity through dress, speech, and other mannerisms. Here again, the Court

---

[4] AIR 2014 SC 1591 (hereinafter *Pravasi*).

[5] *Suresh Kumar Koushal* v. *Naz Foundation*, (2014) 1 SCC 1.

[6] (2014) 5 SCC 438 (hereinafter *NALSA*).

broke new ground. Symbolic forms of expression, such as the flying of the Indian flag or the act of voting, have long been held to be protected under Article 19(1)(a). This was the first time, though, that the Court advanced an understanding of the freedom of speech that was linked to the right of cultural expression, and the right of communities to contribute on an equal footing to the public sphere.

While the Supreme Court's decisions in *Aveek Sarkar, Pravasi Bhalai Sangathan*, and *NALSA* overturn established judicial wisdom and open up possibilities for a new, evolving jurisprudence, 2014 is also notable for crucial issues that were brought before the Court, and now await decision. Section 66A of the Information Technology Act, 2000, is the legal provision that regulates online censorship. With the recent spate of arrests for Facebook posts and political satire, it has achieved a special degree of notoriety. The regime for regulation of online speech is completed by other provisions in the Information Technology Act that regulate website blocking and intermediary liability. Although these provisions have not attracted the media glare that Section 66A has, their impact upon online speech is every bit as pervasive. At the end of 2014, the Supreme Court began to hear a constitutional challenge to all these provisions. At the time I finished writing this book, at the end of 2014, oral arguments were in progress. The decision was delivered in March 2015, and has been analysed in a separate postscript at the end of the book.

Two other developments remain to be noted. In late 2014, the political leader Subramanian Swamy moved the Supreme Court challenging the constitutionality of criminal defamation laws. The hearings commenced in July 2015. Criminal defamation laws are alleged to be the weapon of choice used by powerful groups, such as politicians and corporates, to muzzle critical speech and investigative reporting.

Lastly, in 2011, the Supreme Court delivered a hugely important judgment in *Arup Bhuyan* v. *State of Assam*,[7] holding that an individual could not be punished for being a member of an unlawful association unless he was guilty of inciting others to imminent violence. In *Arup*

---

[7] (2011) 3 SCC 377 (hereinafter *Arup Bhuyan*).

Bhuyan, the Court adopted the American test in *Brandenburg* v. *Ohio*,[8] which is arguably amongst the most speech-protective standards in the world. In the perennial conflict between the right to free expression and concerns of public order and national security, *Arup Bhuyan* swung the pendulum significantly towards the former. Therefore, it is perhaps unsurprising that the State now asks the Court to review its judgment. At the time I finished writing this book, the review was pending.

All these cases—and more—are discussed in this book. There has perhaps never been a more exciting time to be studying free speech issues in India. The political discussion around Article 19(1)(a) and its attendant restrictions has gained intensity over the past few months. Constitutionally, the debate has been joined in the halls of the Supreme Court (and the High Courts). This book seeks to enter the conversation by subjecting Indian free speech jurisprudence to a thorough and critical scrutiny, and by suggesting possible pathways for the future.

[8] 395 U.S. 444 (1969).

Acknowledgements

. . . .

This book arose out of a series of seminars on the freedom of speech and the Indian Constitution, at the National Law School of India University, Bangalore, in July–August 2014. Thanks are due to my students, keen and critical interlocutors, who questioned me upon some of my more outlandish views, compelled me to think more deeply about the freedom of speech and expression, and challenged me to interrogate my own unacknowledged assumptions. The book owes much to their interventions.

The chapter on hate speech benefited from a talk at the Alternative Law Forum, Bangalore, in August 2014, and an informal round table discussion in November 2014 with Jawahar Raja, Siddharth Narrain, Arudra Burra, Rajat Gupta, and Rinku Lamba. The chapter on obscenity and pornography was discussed at the seminar on Philosophy in the Public Sphere, at the Jindal Global Law School in November 2014, where I received several important inputs, especially about my ideas regarding constitutional morality as a framework for understanding Article 19(2) restrictions.

Friends and colleagues read all or various parts of the manuscript, and bore my frequent and ungentle reminders with good grace. Sahana Manjesh worked her way through it all, and offered some very valuable suggestions. Lawrence Liang, Danish Sheikh, V. Niranjan,

Krishnaprasad K.V., Pranesh Prakash, and Madhav Khosla were all polite, yet uncompromising, reviewers. Rajendra Bhatia was my first and most exacting critic, bringing a mathematician's trained mind to an unfamiliar discipline with enviable fortitude.

Ever since I first began to think through the minefield of free speech, I have been lucky enough to have passed through institutions that have consistently granted me that rarest of gifts: colleagues and teachers who have provided constant intellectual encouragement, support, and challenges. This book, in large part, is a product of how my thinking on issues of free speech has been shaped through discussions and arguments with many outstanding individuals. At the National Law School of India University, when I was a callow undergraduate, Arghya Sengupta, Madhav Khosla, Mihir Naniwadekar, Shantanu Naravane, Ashutosh Kumar, Venugopal Mahapatra, Prahalad Bhat, and Krishnaprasad K.V. helped me through my first baby steps into constitutional law, theory, and interpretation, while Sudhir Krishnaswamy's lectures on fundamental rights made me fall in love with the subject irrevocably.

My interest in understanding the philosophical underpinnings of the free speech law, and of constitutional law in general, which I attempt to explore in this book at some length, was fuelled by two years of studying legal theory at the University of Oxford, first through seminars with John Gardner, Leslie Green, and Tony Honore, and then in the company of Nicos Stavropoulos, my MPhil advisor. Sandra Fredman's seminars on comparative human rights first awakened me to the fascinating complexities of studying constitutional law in a comparative context. Along the way, Shiv Swaminathan, Chris McConnachie, Max Harris, and Shreya Atrey were wonderful interlocutors. To Omar Shweiki, Benjamin Kindler, Gregory Lehman, and Thomas Moller-Nielsen, my companions at Balliol College, I owe my understanding of the need to always approach the law from a critical and interdisciplinary perspective.

The most direct inspiration for this book came from Jack Balkin's astounding free speech seminars at the Yale Law School, which revealed the architecture, contents and discontents, and hilarities and frustrations of the freedom of speech in a delightful and inimitable manner. Simultaneously, Lincoln Caplan, both in class and by personal example, taught me the rudiments of approaching the law with the soul of a writer. Bo Tojianco and Rebecca Wexler, fellow free speech insomniacs, were always on hand to listen to my incoherent thoughts, and questioned me until I achieved at least a vestige of clarity. I was also fortunate to meet Carey Shenkman, whose rigorous engagement and love for the First Amendment was the ideal mirror to which I could hold up my own struggles with Article 19(1)(a).

Malavika Prasad's interrogations during the tail-end of the writing of this book compelled me to repeatedly revisit my ideas about the connections between obscenity, hate speech, and equality, and rewrite my 'final' drafts long after I had determined to cease all tinkering. I am perhaps no closer than I was to discovering an equality standard that can take into account the complex and intersectional social stratifications of our society, and perhaps there is not one. Hopefully, however, the book now reflects a more thoughtful and contextual approach to the problem than it would otherwise have.

My thanks are also due to two anonymous peer reviewers, whose forthright criticisms have substantially improved this book, and saved me committing more than one embarrassing blunder. I am, of course, responsible for any remaining embarrassment.

In structure, method, and style, this book draws deeply from the work of the late Ronald Dworkin, whose writings have never failed to infuse an unlikely romance into constitutional law, and whose idea of integrity provides the most inspiring template that a young academic, approaching a new area of law, could wish for.

My intellectual and personal debt to three persons is beyond reckoning. V. Niranjan first taught me to love the law, to think and to feel it, and to read and write it, and in the long years of our friendship, has never failed to cast a keen, critical, and sympathetic eye upon my stumbling encounters with legal writing. Jordan Laris Cohen, eternal travelling companion and lately fellow-lawyer, has shaped my perspectives in ways too profound to describe. And Justice Ravindra Bhat, with whom I was privileged to spend six months at the Delhi

High Court, taught me to seek humanity in the law without ever losing sight of the intellectual rigour that is the prerequisite for making any good legal argument. I know that there is much they will find in this book to disagree with—but nothing, I hope, that would offend, shock, or disturb!

Above all else, this book owes its existence to my parents, who have never imposed restrictions—whether reasonable or unreasonable—upon my speech.

Table of Cases

- -

INDIA

AUSTRALIA

CANADA

ENGLAND AND PRIVY COUNCIL

EUROPEAN COURT OF HUMAN RIGHTS

MISCELLANEOUS

SOUTH AFRICA

UNITED STATES

Note on the Text

. . . .

For ease of online referencing, paragraph numbers of cited Indian cases correspond with their Manupatra equivalents.

The judgment in *Shreya Singhal* v. *Union of India*, which struck down Section 66A of the Information Technology Act, was delivered on 24 March 2015, well after the completion of this book. Consequently, I have left the text of the book unchanged, but added a Postscript at the end, briefly explaining the significance of the judgment.

Article 19(1): All citizens shall have the right—
(a) to freedom of speech and expression.

Article 19(2): Nothing in sub-clause (a) of clause (1) shall affect the operation of any existing law, or prevent the State from making any law, in so far as such law imposes reasonable restrictions on the exercise of the right conferred by the said sub-clause in the interests of the sovereignty and integrity of India, the security of the State, friendly relations with foreign States, public order, decency or morality or in relation to contempt of court, defamation or incitement to an offence.

Introduction

The freedom of speech and expression is a problem for all ages and for all societies. When, if ever, can the speech of individuals or groups be curtailed because those in power deem it necessary or expedient to do so? Ever since John Milton addressed the issue as a legal and philosophical problem, in his seventeenth-century tract, *The Areopagitica*, it has remained at the forefront of the modern political landscape. Societies all over the world have censored, in various forms and to various extents, the speech of artists and writers, political dissidents, cultural critics, anarchists, students, labour unions, and many other voices of dissent.

India is no exception. Salman Rushdie and Wendy Doniger are two of the more famous writers to have had their books banned or withdrawn under speech-restricting laws, and similar incidents are numerous and common. In recent times, we have seen the arrest of two girls in Bombay, for a Facebook post questioning the violent public reaction to the demise of a political leader.[1] We have seen the banning of the documentary film *No Fire Zone* for its realistic depiction of war crimes committed by the Sri Lankan army during its long civil war.[2]

---

[1] PTI (2012).
[2] Seervai (2014).

And we have seen defamation proceedings being used to gag journalists writing critical accounts of large and powerful corporations.[3] The struggle for free speech in India is a live and ongoing one.

Of course, the freedom of speech is not contingent only upon the laws of a nation. The dull compulsion of social relations, and the informal pressures of conformity, exerted in a pervasive, almost unconscious way, perhaps determine to a much greater extent, the limits of permissible speech in a society.[4] It is laws, however, through their own unique methods of coercion, which reinforce social sanctions. It is laws that are the most visible guarantors of—and impediments to—personal freedoms. This is a book about the laws that govern the freedom of speech and expression in India, and how those laws have been understood and applied by the wing of the State that is responsible for their interpretation: the Indian courts.

Contemporary liberal democracies normally guarantee to their citizens a 'right' to the freedom of speech and expression, before hedging it in with a series of restrictions. Some of the most important legal battles of the last few decades have been fought around the scope and ambit of these restrictions. In India, Article 19(1)(a) of the Constitution contains the right to freedom of speech and expression, while Article 19(2) permits the government to impose, by law, reasonable restrictions upon this right, in the interests of the sovereignty and integrity of India; the security of the State; friendly relations with foreign States; public order, decency, or morality; or in relation to contempt of court, defamation, or incitement to an offence. The Constitution is the fundamental law of the land, and the touchstone upon which the validity of all other laws is measured. This is a book about how the Indian courts have understood the myriad limitations of Article 19(2), and how they have adjudicated the validity of India's proliferating speech-restrictive laws in relation to its grand, constitutional guarantee of the freedom of speech and expression.

---

[3] See Chapter Eight.

[4] For a political and social history of free speech and censorship in India, see Dhavan (2008).

However, this is not just a book about the Indian Constitution, Indian laws, and Indian courts. The problems that our judges have had to grapple with—the banning of books and films, the use of defamation laws to silence criticism, issues of hate speech and pornography—are not problems unique to India. They have been considered and adjudicated upon by constitutional courts the world over, many with established free speech traditions. Sometimes, there is a striking similarity in decisions and analyses but more often than not, other judges have come to different conclusions about the value of free speech and the scope of its restrictions. This book is also a comparison: a comparison of how Indian courts understand free speech with how courts in the United States, Canada, South Africa, England, and others understand it.

The use of foreign law as a mirror to which we can hold up our own jurisprudence should be unexceptionable, for we are analysing a Constitution that is a smorgasbord of parts of other basic laws. To take just a few examples: we have a bill of rights drawn (with certain important departures) from the United States, Japan, and many other nations; a set of directive principles based upon Ireland; a commerce clause borrowed from Australia; and a Westminster system of parliamentary government lifted from the United Kingdom. Cosmopolitanism is part of the warp and woof of our Constitution, and has always played a constitutive role in the development of our jurisprudence.

But why the constitutional courts named above, among so many? Space necessitates selection, and any selection must ultimately be subjective and arbitrary, but there are a few reasons for paying specific attention to the jurisdictions that I have chosen. The first is that over the years, the Indian Supreme Court has often looked to these jurisdictions for guidance. As early as the Constituent Assembly Debates, when Ambedkar cited the American Supreme Court decision in *Gitlow* v. *New York*[5] to justify placing restrictions upon the freedom of speech, Indian free speech doctrine has engaged continuously with the

[5] 268 U.S. 652 (1925). See Chapter Three.

decisions of other constitutional courts. In attempting to formulate a
test for obscenity, the Court has, at varying times, invoked *R* v. *Hicklin*
(England),[6] *Roth* v. *United States*,[7] and *R* v. *Butler* (Canada).[8] The
evolution of the public order limitation has been strongly influenced
by its analogous development in the United States right until 2011,
when a two-judge bench of the Supreme Court adopted the highly
speech-protective standard of *Brandenburg* v. *Ohio*.[9] *R. Rajagopal* v.
State of Tamil Nadu,[10] India's seminal defamation law case, borrowed
heavily from the American *New York Times* v. *Sullivan*,[11] and the
English *Derbyshire Council* v. *Times*.[12] The influence of these decisions
upon our own is undeniable, and so it becomes necessary to pay close
heed to the conceptual foundations that underlie and justify them.

Even apart from the tangible role played by such foreign cases in
the development of Indian free speech law, there are independent
reasons why they repay close study. Apart from South Africa, the
legal systems of these countries are grounded in the common law of
England, which makes references and comparisons apposite. English
law itself—and its subsequent constitutionalization under the influence of the European Convention on Human Rights—is an obvious
point of reference because of its pervasive influence upon the codi-
fication and subsequent evolution of Indian law. The United States'
First Amendment remains the ultimate benchmark for a robust,
free speech libertarianism, and over the last 100 years, its judges
have developed an intricate, subtle, and philosophically complex
jurisprudence that is worth studying closely. The Canadian Supreme
Court provides a mirror to the American, its judgments equally well
thought out and complex, but following a different philosophical
path, one that does not cleave to a libertarian philosophy (and, in that
sense, is closer in spirit to the text of the Indian Constitution, with its

[6] L.R. 3 Q.B. 360 (1868).
[7] 354 U.S. 476 (1957).
[8] [1992] 1 SCR 452.
[9] 395 U.S. 444 (1969). See Chapter Three.
[10] (1994) 6 SCC 632 (hereinafter *R. Rajagopal*).
[11] 376 U.S. 254 (1964).
[12] [1992] UKHL 6. See Chapter Eight.

inbuilt restrictions). And South African jurisprudence is always illuminating for the shared postcolonial experiences of the two nations which—despite all their differences—throw up some fascinatingly similar constitutional conundrums. Reading all these cases together provides us with a critical perspective within which we can examine our Supreme Court's jurisprudence on analogous issues.

Lastly, this is not just a book about what the law says and what judges have said about the law. The freedom of speech and expression has always been closely linked with the political ideas that constitute the foundation of modern democracies: ideas of republican governance, personal freedoms, and equality. Many of these ideas are written into the text of the Indian Constitution, and permeate its structure. This book is an investigation into whether the understanding of our courts is compatible with these ideas; and if not, what *is* the philosophical foundation of Indian free speech jurisprudence? The question matters because, ultimately, law is about *justification*. If the Court upholds the law of sedition as being consistent with free speech, then there is a particular understanding of sedition, and of free speech, that is operating to justify that decision. This book asks whether the justifications that the Court has advanced, or which constitute the unarticulated premises of its decisions, are consistent with our Constitutional text, structure, and history, and with the foundational principles of our republic.

To maintain simplicity and clarity in structure, the book is divided into six parts. The first part of the book establishes the background framework by laying out its philosophical foundations in the opening two chapters. The first chapter outlines the major theoretical justifications for the freedom of speech and expression, and discusses their strengths and weaknesses. In the jurisprudence of constitutional courts all over the world, three arguments have found particular resonance: freedom of speech is essential for determining truth, it is an integral part of self-fulfilment and self-determination, and it is important in sustaining a democracy. The second chapter discusses some of the conceptual tools that constitutional courts have used to understand and analyse free speech cases. These tools include concepts such as overbreadth and vagueness, which are often used to strike down speech-regulating statutes; content neutrality, that aims to protect the communicative message behind expressive conduct, especially if there is a risk of persecuting dissidents; the chilling effect, which is used to neutralize the perils of self-censorship, and so on.

The doctrinal part of the book, which follows, is grounded within this framework. While analysing the Supreme Court's (and High Courts') decisions, we must ask: which idea of free speech explains or justifies this particular judgment? Have the courts been consistent in their application of theory in other judgments within the same area of free speech law? Have they also applied this theory in *other* areas of free speech law? Have they taken into account the possibility of overbreadth or of the chilling effect? How might the decision have been different if they had? And how have other constitutional courts dealt with the same issue?

The doctrinal part closely tracks the structure of the constitutional text. I begin with Article 19(2), which lists the permissible restrictions upon the freedom of speech. Within the broad heading of 'public order', the courts have had to grapple with various forms of subversive speech over the years. Whether it is speech that incites people to violence or speech that sparks violent reactions in others, the courts have struggled to find a workable balance between protecting the rights of the speaker and permitting the government enough latitude to maintain public order. In the public order chapter, we see for the first time a theme that will be repeated throughout this book: Indian free speech jurisprudence cleaves along two distinct and irreconcilable lines. One set of cases, marked by a sceptical judicial attitude towards the State's claims that subversive speech will cause public disorder and a keen solicitude towards the freedom of expression, requires the State to discharge a high burden before it can legitimately shut down speech on public order grounds. The other, characterized by a higher prioritization of public order and the means necessary to achieve it, allows the State much greater leeway in deciding when and how to curtail speech to that end. It is this second vision of the relationship between free speech and public order that was at work when the Supreme Court upheld the law of sedition in 1962, which is of enough historical and contemporary importance to merit a stand-alone chapter.

At the heart of the public order cases are the following questions: to what extent are the courts willing to treat citizens as autonomous, morally responsible agents who can be trusted to listen to whatever speech or expression that they wish to, and trusted to make up their own minds about the content of what they hear? And to what extent are the courts willing to close off channels of communication because of the harm that they fear individuals might cause if they are allowed to hear, unrestricted, any speech that comes their way? We find that the same questions are at play when the courts are called upon to interpret the 'decency and morality' prong of Article 19(2), in the context of obscenity and hate speech. While in cases such as *Ranjit Udeshi* v. *State of Maharashtra*[13] in 1964, the Supreme Court takes upon itself the task of protecting the 'most vulnerable' sections of society from moral depravity and corruption, by the time the hourglass runs to 2014, the Court—in *Aveek Sarkar*[14]—seems to suggest that the correct perspective is that of strong-willed, healthy-minded individuals. While in some of their decisions, the courts strongly proscribe texts and speeches that might offend or hurt religious sentiments, in others they advise the offended constituencies to grow a thick skin and look away if they must. Under the broad heading of the freedom of speech and cultural regulation, the courts struggle—once again—to find an interpretation of 'decency and morality' that can adequately reconcile speakers' rights to challenge dominant cultural and social mores, to utter words that might offend, shock, or disturb, with the rights of communities or groups to be free from hostility or discrimination. Many of these considerations are visible most clearly in the courts' cases dealing with film censorship which—like sedition law—deserve a separate chapter of their own.

While my examination of the Supreme Court's public order jurisprudence is largely reconstructive, teasing out the conceptual underpinnings latent within the cases themselves, my approach to issues of cultural regulation is more normative. I will attempt to demonstrate that the Court's approach, which largely follows Anglo-American free

[13] AIR 1965 SC 881: [1965] 1 SCR 65.
[14] (2014) 4 SCC 257.

speech law, and is grounded in an idea of 'public morality' constituting a threshold of permissible speech, is a legal and philosophical mistake. A constitutionally more justifiable standard takes *equality* as the threshold and basis of speech regulation. For the framers of our Constitution, who were concerned not just with political independence from alien rule, but also the progressive reform of a deeply riven and stratified society, equality was a foundational value, one that finds an important place in the bill of rights. Apart from a familiar equal protection guarantee,[15] the Indian Constitution has specific prohibitions dealing with discrimination,[16] the equality of opportunity in employment,[17] affirmative action,[18] the prohibition of untouchability,[19] the abolition of bonded labour,[20] and the rights of minorities.[21] On the occasion when it departs from the classic liberal model of fundamental rights being limited to enforcement against State action, and guarantees fundamental rights against private parties, it does so in the interests of social equality and the eradication of pervasive social discrimination against certain classes.[22] When it places limits upon liberal rights such as the freedom of religion, it does so in the interests of equality.[23] I will argue that equality provides a useful and normatively justified framework in thinking through issues such as obscenity and hate speech.

Article 19(2) also includes reasonable restrictions in the interests of preventing defamation and contempt of court. In recent times, defamation law is emerging as a particularly potent weapon of choice for powerful actors—whether politicians or companies—to silence critical speech. Such critical speech, which challenges the most

---

[15] Article 14, Constitution of India.

[16] Article 15(1), Constitution of India.

[17] Article 16(1), Constitution of India.

[18] Articles 15(4), 15(5), and 16(4), Constitution of India.

[19] Article 17, Constitution of India.

[20] Article 23, Constitution of India.

[21] Articles 29 and 30, Constitution of India.

[22] Article 15(2), Constitution of India.

[23] See the proviso to Article 25(2)(b) of the Constitution of India, which authorizes the government to make provisions for throwing open certain Hindu religious institutions to all classes.

dominant players in society, is at the heart of any constitutional free speech guarantee. Therefore, it is scarcely surprising that around the world, courts have begun the process of 'constitutionalizing' defamation law, and bringing its stringent requirements in line with the preservation and protection of the freedom of speech and expression. In India, notwithstanding the seminal judgment in *R. Rajagopal*, this development is in its protean stage. Numerous high courts have struggled with balancing the competing claims of freedom of speech, individual reputation, and individual privacy, and have often come to starkly differing conclusions.

And what about Article 19(1)(a) itself? What does 'the freedom of speech and expression' protect? What is the relationship between the freedom of speech and the economic structure of a society, in which control over the 'infrastructure' of speech—newspapers and television—is irrevocably linked to economic power? The penultimate part of the book addresses these questions. Under the rubric of 'the freedom of speech', the Supreme Court has included commercial advertisements, elections, the right to know, and certain 'expressive activities' like the flying of a flag and—most recently—the dress and conduct of the transgender community. What is the best way of conceptualizing these very diverse forms of expression? Ought we to understand them not in terms of some etymological meaning of 'speech and expression', but rather as a certain kind of contribution to public discourse? And if the core vision of a free speech guarantee is a thriving public discourse, then may the government attempt to make the discourse more participatory and egalitarian? May it do so by redistributive economic or regulatory measures that place a burden upon entrenched or privileged entities in order to allow others to enter the conversation? Such controversies, which arose most sharply in the Supreme Court's newspaper regulation cases, will be the focus of our discussion. We shall see how, unlike in the cases of cultural regulation, the Supreme Court has been far more attuned to the call of equality when issues of infrastructure and access are before it. And we will conclude with a brief foray into new areas—such as mass surveillance and copyright law—which have not yet been examined under the rubric of Article 19(1)(a), but are rapidly growing in importance.

Three overlapping themes, then, are at the heart of my analysis of Indian free speech law. The first is personal autonomy as a framework for deciding upon the regulation of subversive speech (whether political or cultural). The second is equality as a value for understanding issues of free speech, culture, and offensiveness on the one hand, and infrastructure and access on the other. And the third is the democratic role of speech in interrogating centres of power, in the context of defamation, contempt of court, and privacy. In each discussion, I will attempt to demonstrate how these values are not only latent in the constitutional text, structure, and history, but have often constituted the unarticulated premises of important judgments. I do not mean to argue that my understandings are the only, or even the best, understandings of the foundations of Indian free speech law, but I do hope to convince you that at the very least, they are constitutionally justifiable and normatively attractive understandings.

So much for law, doctrine, and philosophy. Any book on constitutional law in India faces a unique burden of justification. This is because of the yawning, almost insurmountable gap between law and practice, created by a serious breakdown of the rule of law.[24] An example brings out this stark reality: the Supreme Court's decision in *Kedar Nath Singh* v. *State of Bihar*,[25] upholding the constitutionality of sedition, was based upon the understanding that 'sedition' is limited to speech that can cause harm to public order. In other words, sedition was left upon the statute books upon *this* express understanding. In the fifty years since *Kedar Nath Singh* was decided, the executive and lower judicial authorities have acted as if that judgment never existed. People have been arrested (and often charged) for protesting against a nuclear power plant, for failing to stand up during the national anthem, and for publishing a mocking cartoon of the founding fathers. There has not even been an attempt to explain how any of these actions are remotely connected to public disorder.

---

[24] *See*, for instance, the discussion in Dhavan (2007).
[25] [1962] SCR Supp. (2) 769 (hereinafter *Kedar Nath Singh*).

Thus, the reality of how free speech works in India is vastly different from what the courts have said, or what the law actually says. Consider another example. In November 2014, students and activists across Indian cities staged public events labelled 'the kiss of love', to protest against moral policing carried out by cultural organizations. Radio Mirchi, a private radio station, decided to schedule an event at the DLF Place Mall in Saket, New Delhi—the heart of the national capital—to 'express solidarity with those demanding the right of expression'.[26] After a week of promotions, when the radio station reached the mall to set up for the event, they were told that the police had 'disallowed' the event. On speaking with the police, the organizers were warned—verbally—to expect no support from the authorities if they ran into 'problems'. It turned out that the 'Hindu Sena', a private vigilante group, had warned the police to take action, and threatened to do it themselves, 'in Hindu Sena style', if the police did not.[27]

Did it matter to the police that in judgment after judgment, the Supreme Court had decried the heckler's veto, clarified that the task of maintaining law and order rested with the authorities, and that the risk of vigilante-caused disturbances could not be a ground for curtailing the freedom of speech? Evidently not. Was Radio Mirchi in any position to approach the court for an immediate lifting of this 'informal' ban? Anyone with a rudimentary knowledge of the Indian legal system would laugh at the idea. This is how the freedom of speech is actually curtailed: not by grand Supreme Court decisions upholding (while restricting) the law of sedition, or prior restraints upon the cinema, but by a thousand tiny cuts, on a daily basis—until the heckler's veto becomes a part of the fabric of lived reality, whatever the Supreme Court might say.

Such issues are exacerbated by the fact that a large number of speech-restricting provisions in our penal laws are classified as cognizable offences under the Code of Criminal Procedure. This means that the police are authorized to arrest suspected offenders without

[26] Times News Network (2014).
[27] Times News Network (2014).

the requirement of a judicially sanctioned warrant. Consequently, whatever construction the Supreme Court places upon speech-based offences, their implementation, at the first instance, is in the hands of executive authorities. Most of these cases never come to trial, but the damage they inflict upon the actual working of the freedom of speech in India is obvious.

What then, it might be asked, is the purpose of a book focusing on the Supreme Court and the High Courts, on jurisprudence, and on comparative law, when none of that has any resonance with what *really* happens?

This is, of course, a problem with the operation of the legal system in India, and not unique to Article 19(1)(a). Two answers can be made, however. One is that whatever abuse of law and process happens, it is made possible *because laws exist*. The fact that sedition is on the statute books is what allows the police to persecute people. The existence of Section 295A in the Indian Penal Code was what allowed Dinanath Batra to file a case against Wendy Doniger, which ultimately resulted in Penguin Books withdrawing the book. And both, the sedition law and Section 295A of the Indian Penal Code, exist because the Court has, in its history, rejected constitutional challenges to them. It therefore becomes important to understand why the Court has done so, and whether those decisions are justifiable. If they are not, then it is always to be hoped that a future Court will correct the error of its predecessors. But even that correction is impossible without an understanding of what went wrong.

Second, it is by no means necessary that the rule of law will always remain in the state that it is now. The problems with India's legal system are manifold, but they are not irremediable. A thorough understanding of the law of free speech is essential for those situations—rare now, but perhaps more common in the future—in which the gap between law and practice is not quite as cavernous.

Ultimately, the story of free speech in India consists of not one but many overlapping narratives. For a nation whose independence struggle was shaped, in part, by resistance against a colonial police-State, and which has never quite forgotten the excesses of Indira Gandhi's Emergency, free speech, the freedom of the press, and the politics of censorship have always been closely connected. This story has been told admirably by Dhavan and Sorabjee, among others.[28] Another story revolves around the legal architecture, processes, and judicial decisions that govern the nuts-and-bolts workings of specific aspects of free speech law, described in painstaking detail by Divan,[29] Sathe,[30] and many more.[31] Still another explores the interface between free speech law and exploding technologies, in the age of an ever-changing, ever-expanding Internet. This is a story that has only just begun, and remains to be told. This book, while attempting to remain aware of and build upon all these realities, adds another story: a story of ideas, the ideas that ground and justify the courts' understanding and, as critics and interlocutors, our understanding, of the constitutional right to freedom of speech and expression in India.

For all its importance, and its impact upon peoples' lives on an almost daily basis, this story has not yet been told. This book, therefore, is an attempt to be a point of departure for discussion and analysis. If it can contribute, in whatever way, to deepening the constitutional debate, its central purpose will have been served.

---

[28] See Dhavan (1982); Dhavan (2008); Sorabjee (1976). In this book, I do not examine the numerous issues of censorship that arose at the time of the Emergency.

[29] Divan (2013).

[30] Sathe (1970: 1741)

[31] See, for example, Sethi (1980); Bhatia (1997); Desai and Gonsalves (1989).

PART ONE

Background

· ·

CHAPTER ONE

Understanding Free Speech

. . . .

The freedom of speech and expression occupies a central place in contemporary political thought and practice. International and regional human rights conventions, ratified by most nations, are committed to guaranteeing free speech and expression to all. Constitutional democracies worldwide have enshrined it as an individual right, often enforceable against the government in a court of law. Today, it would be difficult to imagine a State that calls itself a democracy and does not, at the very least, pay lip service to the ideal of free speech and expression.

This is hardly surprising. We are communicative beings. We use language and other forms of symbolic conduct to construct the world around us, to make ourselves intelligible to others, and to shape our own personalities. Therefore, the freedom to speak and to express oneself understandably ranks high in the list of core human interests. But while free expression is understood and accepted as a vital liberty in the abstract, its application to concrete situations has always been contested and controversial. To start with, it is clear that not *all* communicative acts are, or ought to be, protected under the rubric of free expression. We probably all agree that laws prohibiting and punishing murder, which prevent a nihilist from 'expressing' his philosophy through action, are justified. To take a more familiar example, we probably also agree that punishing a doctor who knowingly provides false information to a patient regarding a life-threatening drug presents no free speech concerns. Yet these, like others, are communicative acts, and we need to explain why we believe that some—but not all—communicative acts ought to be protected, and where the difference lies.

Not all instances are as intuitively obvious as the aforementioned two examples. Most constitutional democracies have witnessed bitter controversies over the nature and scope of the free speech principle. Should hate speech be protected? Should people be free to consume pornography? Should enthusiastic anarchists be allowed to encourage others to disobey the law? Should we punish people for slandering and defaming others? To what extent should the norms of copyright law prevent people from copying others' expression? To even begin to answer these questions—as topical in India as everywhere else—we need a *theory*, or theories, of free speech. What is valuable about free speech? What are we trying to protect, why are we trying to protect it, and which threats are we trying to protect it from? The enquiry cannot avoid questions of deep political and moral philosophy—of the meaning of democracy, of individual rights, and of the human self.

If controversial questions about free speech cannot be answered without recourse to theory, and if constitutional texts, which do no more than guarantee 'the freedom of speech and expression' in abstract terms provide little assistance, it is clear that in deciding a free speech case, courts are applying theory (whether they are aware of it or not). 'Jurisprudence', as Ronald Dworkin famously wrote, 'is the silent prologue to any decision at law'.[1] Therefore, understanding theory is important not simply to achieve clarity on contested issues, but also to appreciate the underlying foundations of judicial decisions that have a direct and far-reaching impact upon our polity, such as those on book bans, defamation suits, copyright litigation, and so on.

Consider, for example, one of the first free speech cases decided by the Indian Supreme Court: *Sakal Papers* v. *Union of India*.[2] Under

---

[1] Dworkin (1986b: 90).
[2] [1962] 3 SCR 842 (hereinafter *Sakal Papers*).

the Newspaper Act of 1956 and the Daily Newspaper Order of 1960, the government required newspapers to set their prices in accordance with the number of pages in a paper, and limited the number of supplements as well as the area allowed to advertisement space. The newspapers challenging the law under Article 19(1)(a) of the Constitution argued that either they would have to raise their prices if they wished to keep their size constant, and thus lose circulation—*or* they would have to reduce their size and thus provide less news than they wished to. In either event, their free speech rights were violated.

In response, the government argued that its objective was to prevent the rise of monopolies within the newspaper industry. Due to existing economies of scale, big, established newspapers were able to keep their prices down to a very low level, rendering smaller newspapers unable to compete. This would force existing smaller newspapers to exit the market by selling to a bigger one, and would prevent new papers from entering the market at all. Thus, the effect of the regulations was to free up the market and promote *more* speech.

How is the Court to decide a case like *Sakal Papers*? The constitutional text merely guarantees the right to freedom of speech and expression, subject to certain reasonable restrictions. The issue of newspaper monopolies was not really discussed by the framers during the Constituent Assembly Debates while drafting the free speech clause. So what should the Court do? Should it side with the established newspapers in holding that the State's restrictions on circulation violate their free speech rights? Or should it uphold the law as a valid measure aimed at breaking up the monopoly of big newspapers over the production and dissemination of information? What reasons could be advanced to support either view?[3]

Keeping these questions in mind, consider the following— impressionistic account of some of the dominant theories of free speech. My task in this chapter is not to adjudicate between the theories of speech, but to create a conceptual framework within which to understand and critique the actualities of free speech law in India. The following

---

[3] I will deal with *Sakal Papers* in detail in Chapter Eleven.

sample overview is not meant to be exhaustive. It is only a survey of the accounts that hold the field today, that have been invoked by lawmakers and courts the world over, and—pertinently—have been referred to by the Indian Supreme Court in its free speech judgments.

FREE SPEECH AS A MEANS TO TRUTH

> *And though all the winds of doctrine were let loose to play upon the earth, so Truth be in the field, we do injuriously, by licensing and prohibiting, to misdoubt her strength. Let her and Falsehood grapple; who ever knew Truth put to the worse, in a free and open encounter?*
> —John Milton, *Areopagitica*, quoted by the Indian Supreme Court in
> *Bennett Coleman v. Union of India*[4]

In 1992, Anand Patwardhan, the well-known documentary film-maker, approached the Bombay High Court, asking it to direct Doordarshan to broadcast his award-winning film on violence and terrorism in Punjab.[5] In its counter-affidavit before the Court, Doordarshan argued—among other things—that the film was one-sided and wrong because it advocated communism as the only solution to communal violence. Rejecting this argument, the Court noted that Patwardhan had the right to put his particular views before the public, and the public had the right to inform itself about issues of general concern from any legitimate source and form its own opinion on the subject. Unsurprisingly, at the very beginning of its judgment, the Court foregrounded its analysis by quoting the nineteenth-century English thinker, John Stuart Mill[6]—because, as it was well aware, the intellectual fount of its argument could, in significant part, be traced back to Mill.

In fact, it was Mill who provided the first sustained philosophical defence of free speech in modern times, which still bears a ring of familiarity today.[7] In a chapter titled 'On the Liberty of Thought and

---

[4] (1972) 2 SCC 788: [1973] 2 SCR 757, para 157.
[5] *Anand Patwardhan v. Union of India*, AIR 1997 Bom 25 (hereinafter *Anand Patwardhan*).
[6] *Anand Patwardhan*, para 1.
[7] Mill (1869).

Discussion', Mill argued that a free exchange of ideas and opinions was the only method of arriving at 'the truth'. If, on the one hand, a particular opinion were true, its suppression would only serve to perpetuate the existing error under which society laboured. The multiplicity of opinions in the past, which once had the force of undisputed axioms but were now entirely discarded, bore witness to this. How many decades was truth set back, for instance, when the Catholic Church forced Galileo to publicly repudiate his heretical beliefs about the earth moving around the sun?

On the other hand, even if an opinion was false, its airing was necessary in order to strengthen the force of the truth by having it prevail in a fair and open contest. Without being forced into a constant defence of the truth by having it tested on the whetstone of contrary arguments, men and women would soon reduce it to the level of a 'dead dogma'. Mill was unperturbed by the possibility that the contest could sometimes result in the triumph of falsehood. Like Milton before him, he believed that 'when an opinion is true, it may be extinguished once, twice, or many times, but in the course of ages there will generally be found persons to rediscover it...until it has made such head as to withstand all subsequent attempts to suppress it'.[8]

Mill's last argument was a dialectical one. Often, competing opinions split the truth between them. Certain aspects of the truth were invariably excluded by the 'common opinion', and could be obtained only by hearing all sides of a contested issue.

While Mill's writings continue to be invoked by the courts, the core of his theory is difficult to justify. Even if we accept his philosophical premise that 'opinions' can be 'right' or 'wrong', 'true' or 'false', his argument seems somewhat light on evidence. Indeed, if the time span is 'the course of the ages', the argument is virtually impossible to prove or to falsify. Let us assume, for the purposes of argument, that racism and neoliberalism—one discredited and the other dominant—are 'false' opinions. We can argue that the defeat of (the false idea of) racism in the contest of ideas vindicates Mill's thesis, while the triumph

---

[8] Mill (1869), Chapter II.

of (the false idea of) neoliberalism does not disprove it. Eventually, neoliberalism too will be defeated in 'the course of the ages'. Thus, agreement with Mill seems predicated upon an unsubstantiated faith in an indeterminate future. And second, eventual self-correction in the course of the ages will probably be of scant comfort to the present victims of false ideas. If it took a few thousand years to defeat the idea of legitimate slavery, then we perhaps need to ask ourselves whether there is not a better way of going about things.

Mill's argument was subtly—and most famously—reformulated by the famous American judge, Oliver Wendell Holmes.[9] It is this version of the argument that has gripped the imagination of courts ever since.[10] Dissenting against the prosecution of certain anti-war protesters, Justice Holmes argued 'that the best test of truth is the power of the thought to get itself accepted in the competition of the market'.[11] In common parlance, this is known as the *marketplace of ideas* argument.

Yet understanding free speech in the language of the market, for all its popularity, runs into a series of well-recorded difficulties. The first is the problem of access. Access to existing markets is determined by one's resources. In this sense, markets are exclusionary. Holmes' blithe confidence that the 'best test of truth' is its acceptance in the market seems undermined if many ideas never enter the marketplace because their propagators are blocked by resource-determined entry barriers. This is particularly true in today's world, when effective speech depends upon access to, and skillful use of, an entire economic infrastructure such as television, newspapers, and the Internet.

Second, all governments regulate markets in the interests of public welfare. At a basic minimum, we have statutory rules against fraud and misrepresentation, aimed at preventing market distortion.

[9] For the manner in which Holmes' version differs from Mill's, see Barendt (2007: 12).

[10] For example, see *S.* v. *Mamabolo*, 2001 (5) BCLR 449 (CC) (South African Constitutional Court); *R.* v. *Keegstra*, [1990] 3 SCR 697 (Supreme Court of Canada) (hereinafter *Keegstra*); *Raghu Nath Pandey* v. *Bobby Bedi*, (2006) ILR 1 Delhi 927 (High Court of Delhi).

[11] *Abrams* v. *United States*, 250 U.S. 616, 630 (1919) (dissenting opinion of Holmes J.).

Most governments, of course, go well beyond, often seeking to miti-
gate the undesirable consequences arising out of unregulated markets
by enacting labour laws, consumer protection laws, and other welfare provisions. Free market libertarians might object to this as bad
policy, but almost everyone agrees that governments are *entitled* to
regulate the market, and (barring extreme cases of uncompensated
property expropriation) nobody's rights are violated when they do so.
Free speech, on the other hand, is universally understood as a *right*,
one that is often set off against arguments of the common good, especially when governments aim to suppress unpopular speakers on the
ground that they offend or insult the majority. The language of the
marketplace sits uneasily with this vision of free speech.

We must remember, of course, that the Mill–Holmes line of
thought is best understood not in absolute, but in relative terms.
Holmes does not argue that truth will *necessarily* emerge from the
marketplace of ideas, but that the marketplace is the *best* (available)
mechanism for arriving at truth. It is better, at any rate, than the State
deciding which ideas are good and ought to be promoted, and which
are bad and ought to be suppressed. Put this way, the thesis becomes
both stronger and more interesting, and its objectors must meet
a greater burden of justification. They must demonstrate that their
arguments for regulation have independent merit, which outstrip
Holmes' market-based vision.

FREE SPEECH AS INDIVIDUAL SELF-FULFILMENT

On entering one of the many inner lanes of New Delhi's Connaught
Place, one's gaze is promptly arrested by a gigantic Indian flag atop a
207-feet flagpole. The storied history of this unmistakable fixture of
central Delhi's landscape involves, among other things, Article 19(1)
(a) and a visit to the Supreme Court. In *Union of India* v. *Naveen
Jindal*, the Court was asked to decide whether a citizen of the country
had a constitutional right to fly the flag.[12] The Court answered the

---

[12] (2004) 2 SCC 510: AIR 2004 SC 1559 (hereinafter *Naveen Jindal*).

question in the affirmative, and in a lengthy disquisition upon the value of the freedom of expression, noted that freedom of speech 'assure[s] individual self-fulfillment',[13] perhaps the most accurate justification for grounding Jindal's right within the contours of Article 19(1)(a).

Free speech scholars and constitutional courts have long argued that communication is an integral part of individual self-fulfilment.[14] It is through speech and expression that we grow and develop as human beings, and create a meaningful life for ourselves. Through expression, we receive and impart ideas, construct our personality, and project it onto the world. Put another way, autonomous self-determination is possible only through an 'untrammeled exercise of capacities central to human rationality'[15]—such as speech and expression.

This argument, while undoubtedly correct, is not an argument for protecting *speech*. It is an argument for the value of all activities that are integral to self-fulfilment, and that list goes far beyond what we conventionally understand to be 'speech and expression'. As the American scholar Robert Bork pointed out, 'an individual may develop his faculties or derive pleasure from trading on the stock market, [working] as a barmaid, engaging in sexual activity, [or] in any of thousands of other endeavours...[One] cannot, on neutral grounds, choose to protect speech [on this basis] more than [one] protects any other claimed freedom.'[16] The self-fulfilment rationale, therefore, which justifies Naveen Jindal's right to fly the Indian flag, but would also justify the constitutional right to gamble, cannot be a stand-alone argument for the freedom of speech and expression. Let us consider some more specific arguments.

[13] *Naveen Jindal*, para 46.
[14] Emerson (1970: 6); *Gardener v. Whitaker*, 1995 (2) SA 672, 687 (South Africa); *Irwin Troy v. Quebec (Attorney-General)*, [1989] 1 SCR 927 (Canada).
[15] Richards (1974: 62).
[16] Bork (1971: 25). Interestingly, in 2014, the Indian Supreme Court held that sexual conduct is protected under Article 19(1)(a). *See NALSA v. Union of India*, (2014) 5 SCC 438 (hereinafter *NALSA*).

Autonomy

The organs of the Indian State have often been hostile towards films that deal with historically 'sensitive' issues, such as those concerning communal violence. In 2009, for instance, the Central Board of Film Certification asked the director of the film *Had Anhad*, which dealt with the demolition of the Babri Masjid, to make four excisions in order to receive clearance. When the film-makers approached the Delhi High Court, the Board argued that the offending scenes would hurt the sentiments of certain communities, and provoke public disorder. Rejecting this argument, Justice Muralidhar observed that '[the] right of the viewer to think autonomously while reacting to the speaker or the film maker, and *to make informed choices, without being controlled by the State* ...constitutes an integral part of the freedom of speech and expression.'[17]

In focusing upon the right to make an informed choice without State control over the channels of communication, Justice Muralidhar was invoking an ideal that has played a central role in liberal political thought since the time of the Enlightenment. As far back as 1784, Immanuel Kant established the motto of the Enlightenment to be '*Have courage to use your own reason!*'[18] Although Kant himself was no great defender of free speech, his basic idea—that one must be free of 'tutelage', or having the use of one's understanding determined by another, remains relevant today (its echoes in Justice Muralidhar's opinion are evident), and has been invoked by free speech scholars. It has special resonance when the State seeks to curtail speech and expression on the ground that it would lead to the moral (or some other manner of) corruption and degradation of its citizens. These arguments fall within the broad head of 'paternalism': the State justifies regulation of speech on the ground that it knows and decides what is best for its citizens in any given area, without according them the opportunity to make up their own minds about it. Autonomy-based

---

[17] *Srishti School of Art, Design and Technology* v. *The Chairperson, Central Board of Film Certification*, 178 (2011) DLT 337, para 25; emphasis mine.
[18] Kant (1784).

objections to paternalism argue that questions about individual tastes, preferences, ideologies, and ways of living must be decided by individuals themselves.

One prominent exposition of the autonomy theory is provided by the philosopher Thomas Scanlon. Examining cases where free speech is restricted or punished on the ground that it is in some way dangerous or leads to consequences that we all agree are harmful (such as successfully persuading someone to commit a violent crime), he argues that censorship is impermissible 'where the connection between the acts of expression and the subsequent harmful acts consists merely in the fact that the act of expression led the agents to believe...these acts to be worth performing'.[19] This is because 'the harm of coming to false beliefs is not one that the autonomous man could allow the State to protect him through restrictions on expression'.[20] The 'autonomous man' is presumed to apply his own canons of rationality and sense, and weigh up the evidence in order to come to his own conclusions about the desirability or undesirability of performing an act—the consequences of which *he* and not anybody else—is responsible for. This principle has also found particularly prominent judicial application in the American and Indian laws of commercial speech. Judges have struck down regulations of advertising insofar as they are motivated by governments' desire to protect or prevent customers from making choices that they consider are harmful for customers.[21]

The argument from autonomy provides us with an elegant framework to think about a whole host of issues related to free speech and public order, dangerous and subversive speech, the regulation of sexually explicit material, and so on. Yet there are other cases where it seems to fail utterly. Consider medical malpractice and consumer protection laws. It is nobody's case that laws aimed at enforcing medical standards by punishing doctors for knowingly or negligently prescribing harmful and inappropriate medicine to their patients

---

[19] Scanlon (1972: 213).

[20] Scanlon (1972: 217).

[21] *Virginia Citizens' Consumer Council* v. *Virginia State Board of Pharmacy*, 425 U.S. 748 (1976).

somehow violates the patients' autonomy by not permitting *them* to make up their own minds about the information that is given to them. The same considerations apply to consumer legislation prohibiting false or misleading information about products. Clearly, some relationships are relationships based not on autonomy, but on *dependency*. It therefore follows that even if autonomy is the correct conceptual framework to examine *some* aspects of free speech, we need a deeper principle that tells us *when* that is so; or, in other words, we need a principle that helps us classify relationships that are defined by autonomy, and those defined by dependency.[22]

Pluralism

In 2014, the Supreme Court handed down an important judgment extending legal and constitutional protection to members of the transgender community.[23] One of the constitutional rights that the Court identified was Article 19(1)(a). Transgender persons, it held, had a fundamental right to 'express' their self-identified gender through dress, words, action, or behaviour. The Court's opinion represents an extension of the self-fulfilment argument, in the direction of the idea of pluralism.

As Joseph Raz argues, in modern societies, 'pluralism'—that is, respect (or at least, toleration) for diverse and often antagonistic sets of thoughts, beliefs, and ways of life—is a core value. Communicative acts, as we discussed above, are important—albeit non-exclusive—means through which individuals create and live meaningful lives. Raz agrees that meaning is created through all expressive conduct, both communicative and non-communicative. However, he also argues that since public expression of a way of life often serves as a source of validation, it is particularly important for its practitioners. The existence, availability, and circulation of gay magazines, for instance, where gay lifestyle is discussed and explored openly, is important in securing the overall well-being of the gay community.[24] Correspondingly, State

---

[22] See, for instance, the examples given by Robert Post in Post (1997:1521).

[23] *NALSA* v. *Union of India*, (2014) 5 SCC 438.

[24] For an account of Raz's ideas, see Barendt (2007: 32).

censorship of gay magazines not only makes that literature unavailable, but also takes the form of a public insult towards, or contempt of, that entire way of life. This is distinctly anti-pluralistic. And, the position is similar—as the Supreme Court recognized—with respect to the dress, words, or actions of the transgender community.

While this seems similar in form to the self-fulfilment argument, there is a crucial difference. Self-fulfilment is centred upon the *individual* developing her own faculties and form of life. Razian pluralism, on the other hand, is a *social good*—that is, according to Raz, all things considered, a society that endorses pluralism is *better for everyone* than an intolerant society. And tolerance, as the South African Constitutional Court has pointed out, 'requires the acceptance of the public airing of disagreements and the refusal to silence unpopular views'.[25] Strong free speech protection, insofar as it protects the public expression of diverse ways of life, is integral to building a pluralist and tolerant society.

FREE SPEECH AS A MEANS OF DEMOCRATIC SELF-GOVERNANCE

The first significant agitation for free speech in colonial India can be traced back to the 1820s. On 14 March 1823, the Governor-General in Council passed a Press Ordinance, which required a government licence to be obtained for every newspaper or periodical, revocable at pleasure. One of the foremost objectors to the Ordinance was Raja Rammohun Roy. In a famous Memorandum, addressed to the Supreme Court (which was tasked with deciding whether or not to allow the Ordinance), Roy argued that without a free press, 'natives' would no longer be able to inform the government of the 'errors and injustices' that its executive officers might be committing across India.[26] In making this argument, Roy would draw a connection that was implicit in the structure of the American First Amendment, which places the

---

[25] *South African National Defence Union* v. *Minister for Defence*, 1999 (6) BCLR 615 (CC), para 8.
[26] Collett (1914: 102).

guarantee of the freedom of speech and the press next to the right of the people to petition the government for a redress of grievances:[27] the connection between free speech and *responsive* government.

Although Roy was no democrat, his protean arguments focusing on a responsive government anticipated, in part, what has now become the most popular justification for a strong right to free speech: the argument from democracy.[28] The word 'democracy' has come to mean different things to different people. To fix ideas, let us take the following as our working definition, and bracket the problems that it entails: we understand democracy to be a political system in which ultimate governing power rests in the hands of the people. Where this power is exercised indirectly through a representative government, that government must be chosen by the will of, and be accountable and responsive to, the people (for example, through periodic elections).

The democratic justification for free speech was most famously propounded by Alexander Meiklejohn, whose writings have had a tremendous influence upon courts worldwide.[29] Meiklejohn argued that democratic *self-government* requires citizens to judge for themselves the wisdom or fairness of any governmental policy. And an informed judgment is possible only if citizens are acquainted with any 'information or opinion...relevant to the issue'.[30] In other words, self-government (by the people) requires that the people be acquainted with all sides of all issues of governing importance. Free speech is indispensable to the dissemination and propagation of political information. Meiklejohn's vision of the polity was that of one large town hall, where issues of public importance are brought to the table, discussed, debated

---

[27] First Amendment, Constitution of the United States.

[28] *Ranjit Udeshi v. State of Maharashtra*, AIR 1965 SC 881: [1965] 1 SCR 65; *Keegstra; Islamic Unity Convention v. The Independent Broadcasting Authority*, 2002 (5) BCLR 433 (CC) (South Africa); *New York Times v. Sullivan*, 376 U.S. 254 (1964).

[29] See, for instance, *S. Rangarajan v. P. Jagjivan Ram*, (1989) 2 SCC 574: [1989] 2 SCR 204; *Anand Patwardhan; N.V.S.J. Rama Rao v. Broadcasting Corporation of India*, AIR 2013 AP 165; *Khushwant Singh v. Maneka Gandhi*, AIR 2002 Del 58.

[30] Meiklejohn (1948: 26).

and argued over, and ultimately decided upon, by the people. Thus, he was adamant that 'no suggestion *of policy* shall be denied a hearing because it is on one side of the issue rather than another. [Citizens] may not be barred [from speaking] because their views are thought to be false or dangerous.'[31]

But there are two problems with Meiklejohn's original position, as it stands. The first is that it is radically indeterminate. The question of what constitutes a public issue, or an issue of governing importance, is a bitterly contested one. For example, until the middle of the twentieth century, marital and sexual relationships were considered to lie entirely within the private domain. As the feminist movement argued, however, that the 'private' was itself a political category, and was used to mask relations of domination and subordination between the sexes.[32] Today, many of those issues—domestic violence, marital rape, and so on—are inescapably public. Meiklejohn provides us with no conceptual framework to settle disputes about the dividing line between the public and the private.

Even if we could successfully bracket that problem, Meiklejohn's theory proves too little. For instance, if only explicitly *political* speech is protected, it would leave literature and the arts to the whims of majoritarian politics and the blunt club of the government censor. This runs counter to our intuitions. We do think that book bans raise free speech concerns; that they impact the rights of authors, publishers, and readers; and that artists should be protected against politically powerful and too-easily offended religious or political groups. A theory of free speech that fails to address this seems incomplete.[33]

Faced with this criticism, Meiklejohn expanded his account. In his subsequent writing, he argued that '[free speech] protects the freedom of *those activities of thought and communication by which we govern*'.[34] While the ultimate expression of self-governance

---

[31] Meiklejohn (1948; emphasis mine).

[32] See, for example, MacKinnon (1988).

[33] A critique that has been made by innumerable scholars since the time that Meiklejohn first wrote.

[34] Meiklejohn (1961: 255; emphasis mine).

is the casting of the ballot, voting is only the culmination of a lengthy deliberative process that involves *understanding* the issues that face a nation, *judging* the decisions that representative agents make about those issues, and *constructing* methods to revise, modify, or substitute those decisions in order to better achieve public welfare. To do this effectively, one would need to protect all communication from which voters could derive 'knowledge, intelligence and sensitivity to human values'.[35] For Meiklejohn, this included education, discussions about philosophy and science, literature and the arts, and public issues. It did not include libel, slander, conspiracy, and so on.

If Meiklejohn's first argument proved too little, his second argument seems to prove too much. Virtually every experience in life contributes towards deriving *some* kind of knowledge of human values. That is the very meaning of 'experience'. As the free speech scholar C. Edwin Baker pointed out, 'restriction on experience-generating conduct [would] stunt the progressive development of understanding as well'.[36] We now simply seemed to have arrived at self-fulfilment by another name.[37]

---

[35] Meiklejohn (1961: 256).

[36] Baker (1978: 975).

[37] Nonetheless, there seems to be a crucial kernel of truth in Meiklejohn's argument. Successive scholars have taken his basic idea, and constructed their theories upon its foundations. Cass Sunstein, for example, defends the position that it is *political* speech that ought to be protected, and tries to take the objectors head on. Political speech is different from other kinds of speech, he argues, because 'restrictions on political speech have the distinctive feature of impairing the ordinary channels for political [change]'. Sunstein (1992: 306). If the government bans a book or prohibits certain kinds of advertising, citizens can argue against those actions in a political forum. This is what is known as the 'democratic corrective'. If political speech *itself* is barred, however, the democratic corrective is foreclosed. Consequently, Sunstein would place the government under 'a special burden of justification when it seeks to control speech *intended and received as a contribution to public deliberation*' (Sunstein 1992; emphasis mine). The rest would be left to the normal democratic process.

Sunstein's argument suffers from three shortcomings. First, the democratic corrective is majoritarian in nature. Unpopular minorities (of whom, historically, radical and unconventional artists and writers have been regular members) are protected outside of the majoritarian process precisely because it is structurally closed off to them.

Cognizant of these issues, a number of scholars have expanded Meiklejohn's core concept (that of democratic justification) by taking, as their starting points, very different conceptions of democracy. I briefly consider two important accounts.

Jack Balkin and Cultural Democracy

In 2005, the famous Tamil actress Khushboo remarked to the *India Today* magazine that the Indian society should stop expecting women to be virgins at the time of marriage. In response, twenty-three criminal complaints were filed against her at various places. Khushboo approached the Supreme Court, which quashed all the proceedings. Focusing upon the importance of free and unimpaired communication as a constitutional right, the Court observed that 'communication prompts a dialogue within society wherein people can choose to either defend or question the existing social mores'.[38]

The Court's affirmation that the freedom of speech includes the right not just to political dissent, but cultural dissent as well, is crucial.

Second, we have a repeat of the Meiklejohnian problem: what about speech that is *intended* as a contribution to public deliberation, but not *received* as such? As Nancy Fraser tells us, 'until quite recently, feminists were in the minority in thinking that domestic violence against women was a matter of common concern and thus a legitimate topic of public discussion. The great majority of people considered this issue to be a private matter between what was assumed to be a fairly small number of heterosexual couples' (Fraser 1997: 86). The danger with limiting free speech protection to what is expressly defined as political at any given moment risks an 'improper bias in favour of presently dominant groups' Baker (1989: 16). It is an open question, however, whether *any* theory of free speech can adequately address this concern.

And third, speech that is not intended or received as a contribution to *public deliberation* can nonetheless be a unique and distinctive way of addressing issues of public concern. Which anti-slavery political speech would have the same power and force of *Uncle Tom's Cabin*? Can newspaper columnists ever speak about caste violence in the manner of Meera Kandasamy's *The Gypsy Goddess*, or discuss partition quite like Deepa Mehta's *1947: Earth*? Leaving these works to the vagaries of majoritarian politics would, it seems, deeply impoverish the political discourse. If we define these works as contributing to public deliberation, on the other hand, we are back on the same slippery slope that the Meiklejohnian position suffered from.

[38] *Khushboo v. Kanniammal*, 2010 (4) SCALE 467, para 18.

As the free speech scholar Jack Balkin argues, taking the focus beyond Meiklejohnian deliberation of public issues, the purpose of free speech is to 'promote a democratic culture...[which is] a culture in which individuals have a fair opportunity to participate in the forms of meaning-making that constitute them as individuals'.[39] Communication and communicative conduct are the means through which we can participate in the production and distribution of culture.[40] Free speech is thus both individual and inescapably social. It is characterized by a social process in which individuals interact with one another and with the existing corpus of cultural material, in order to appropriate and transform it, and thus create meaning in their lives.

This vision of free speech unambiguously protects writers and artists like Khushboo, but it does two other things as well: it places the issue of copyright squarely within the domain of free speech, since the entire *raison d'être* of copyright law is to wall off artistic creations from certain forms of appropriation. It also places a heightened emphasis on the issue of *access*. If cultural participation is dependent upon access to an infrastructure that makes effective communication possible, then free speech laws should be solicitous to any action that could act as a barrier to access. For instance, under this vision, concentrated corporate control over the media is a core free speech issue. Another topical example is that of net neutrality. One of the most prominent arguments against abandoning net neutrality and creating 'fast lanes' on the Internet, access to which is dependent upon the ability to pay, is that it will kill the next garage-invention like Facebook or Twitter in the womb. While this is normally framed as a technology/innovation debate, the argument from cultural democracy treats it as a vital free speech issue.

It is clear that on this account, *equality* is a foundational value that is meant to structure and give shape to a robust right of free expression. The connections may not immediately be obvious, since we intuitively think of free speech as raising issues of *liberty*, which are sometimes regarded as conflicting with—or at least, orthogonal to—equality. As

[39] Balkin (2004: 3).
[40] Balkin (2004: 1).

Ronald Dworkin argues, however, part of what it means for a democratic polity to accord equal respect and concern to all its members, is to accord to each person an equal opportunity (*via* communication) to shape the moral, political, and cultural environment in which they live, something that can happen only by embracing a wide, almost untrammelled right to freedom of speech and communication.[41] Put this way, the deep linkages between free speech and equality—a theme that we will return to often in this book—no longer seem quite so far-fetched.

Robert Post and Deliberative Democracy

Both Balkin and Dworkin place emphasis, as we have seen, upon the idea of *authorship*: authorship over culture, or over the moral and political environment. The idea that we are only bound by something that we have authored—given to ourselves, as it were—is one of the foundational ideas of post-Enlightenment political philosophy, again going back to Kant. Models of political legitimacy and political obligation since then have repeatedly drawn upon this basic idea of *self-legislation* as the moral foundation of a political community (Rawls' theory of justice is one of the best-known examples). Since the 1960s, following the work of the influential German philosopher Jürgen Habermas, self-legislation has formed the basis of another school of democratic thought, broadly known as *deliberative* or *dialogic* democracy.

What sets Habermas apart from others is the centrality of *actual* speech and communication to his theory of legitimacy. Simply put, Habermas argues that a norm mandating a particular course of action is valid and binding upon its subjects only if it is agreed upon by all possibly affected persons participating in a rational discourse.[42] A rational discourse, in turn, is defined as a discussion in which 'participants *genuinely* want to convince one another...[allowing themselves] to be influenced solely by the force of the better argument.'[43]

---

[41] See, for example, Dworkin (1981: 177).
[42] Habermas (1996: 107).
[43] Habermas (1994: 31).

In order to achieve this, Habermas places a series of structural constraints upon the discourse. Two of these are particularly important: the principles of *inclusion* and *equality*. The Inclusion Principle stipulates that 'every subject with the competence to speak and act is allowed to [participate]'.[44] The Equality Principle requires that 'no speaker may be prevented, by *internal or external* coercion, from exercising his rights as laid down above'.[45] It is only when the two principles are satisfied—that is, when everyone can both freely enter and participate in the discourse, *and* do so on an equal, non-coercive footing, that the results of the discourse enjoy a presumption of validity.

To work out the full implications for free speech, we will need to excavate Habermas' concrete construction of the structural conditions for legitimate discourse in a political community, which is based upon a vision of equal participants communicating with each other in the 'public sphere'. This is an enterprise that will lead us far afield. For the moment, we only need to note that the free speech scholar Robert Post has expressly made the connection between Habermas' conception of democratic legitimacy through an equal discourse, and a strong free expression right. Following Habermas, Post argues that 'the value of democratic legitimation occurs through processes of communication in the public sphere'.[46] Consequently, 'speech', for the purposes of democratic legitimacy, refers to all 'acts and media of communication that are socially regarded as the necessary and proper means of participating in the formation of public opinion'.[47] Call this the 'public discourse'. As long as individuals are participating in public discourse, the Inclusion and Equality principles require that they be included (through providing them access to the public sphere) and that their voices be heard on equal terms with those of others. Naturally, much turns upon the meaning of 'public discourse' and 'public sphere' (which Post concedes is a normative question), terms

---

[44] Habermas (1990: 89).
[45] Habermas (1990; emphasis mine).
[46] Post (2011: 483).
[47] Post (2011).

that are controversial and tend to raise problems similar to those that
we have noticed elsewhere. Post's argument, however, is much more
flexible, open, and potentially inclusive than Meiklejohn's definition
of the 'political', and is sensitive to issues such as access.

WHY DOES IT MATTER? THE CASE OF *SAKAL PAPERS* CONSIDERED

We have seen how the three dominant theories discussed so far have
been regularly invoked by the courts to ground and justify their decisions on the scope and limitations of the constitutional guarantee of
the freedom of speech and expression. Let us now investigate, in a
little more detail, the role that theory could play in the *process* of an
actual decision.

Recall *Sakal Papers*, which we discussed at the beginning of this
chapter. Was the government entitled to regulate the circulation of
established newspapers in order to free up the market? The Supreme
Court held that it was not, and struck down the regulations. Justice
Mudholkar held that the regulations directly limited circulation, and
consequently infringed the Article 19(1)(a) rights of the petitioners.[48]
Permissible restrictions upon Article 19(1)(a), enumerated under
Article 19(2), were limited to public order, decency, or morality, and
did not cover the government's unfair competition argument, which
the Court characterized as a 'public interest' justification.[49]

According to the Court, the point of guaranteeing an individual
free speech right was precisely that the government would not be
able to override it by making claims about the larger common good.
And the Court ended by highlighting the importance of the freedom
of speech 'under a *democratic Constitution* which envisages changes
in the composition of legislatures and governments...',[50] emphasizing that any regulation that would necessarily 'undermine...

---

[48] *Sakal Papers*, paras 27, 31.
[49] *Sakal Papers*, para 40.
[50] *Sakal Papers*, para 45 (emphasis mine).

power to influence public opinion' *was* 'capable of being used against democracy as well'.[51]

The nature of the case, and the manner of the Court's decision, should make clear the role of theory. *Sakal Papers* raises many of the issues that we have discussed in this chapter. At the heart of the dispute is a question about infrastructure and access. The contested regulations were aimed at equalizing access to the infrastructure of communication by redistributing the resources that made such access possible. The Court held that to be constitutionally irrelevant, choosing to focus only on the fact that the established newspapers would be able to—so to say—speak less. In so doing, it invoked democracy, which—crucially—it located *within* the Constitution. But it invoked a particularly cribbed Meiklejohnian version of democracy that is insensitive to prior distributional arrangements, as opposed to its potentially richer Dworkinian, or Postian versions.

What if the Court, instead, had chosen a Dworkinian or deliberative vision of democracy? Perhaps it might have justified this more substantive idea of democracy by going back to the Constituent Assembly Debates, where many of the framers had spoken of 'economic democracy', and famously declared that the new Constitution was based not just on the principle of 'one man, one vote', but also on the principle of 'one man, one value'.[52] Preventing monopolistic control over the means of access to speech would then not be a public-interest based 'restriction' upon speech, but an element of the freedom of speech itself. Creating an economic environment that would be conducive to the entry and survival of smaller newspapers, with diverse and varying viewpoints, would amount not to a violation of free speech by the government, but to a fulfilment of its obligation to ensure the freedom of speech.

We shall have occasion to examine *Sakal Papers* in much greater detail at a subsequent point in this book. For now, I hope only to have

---

[51] *Sakal Papers*, para 45.

[52] See, for example, speech of Shibban Lal Saksena, 22 November 1948, Indian Constituent Assembly (Vol. VII).

convinced you that a careful engagement with the philosophies of free speech is crucial in developing a deep understanding of the issues that come up in important free speech cases, and in appreciating what assumptions the Court is relying upon when it decides those cases one way or another. That is an indispensable starting point for any full-blooded critique of our Supreme Court's free speech jurisprudence.

As we progress through the book, we will have many opportunities to observe how rival theories come together and part ways, clash and complement each other, in cases as diverse as those involving film censorship, newspaper regulation, book bans, hate speech, defamation, and so on. And by the end of the book, we shall—hopefully—be in a position to effectively critique the Court's approach to free speech *as a whole*, from the point of view of both legal consistency and fidelity, and constitutional–political theory.

CHAPTER TWO

Common Concepts

· · · · · · · · · · ·

Throughout this book, we shall discuss the constitutionality of a number of statutes that regulate or prohibit various kinds of speech. While issues such as subversive speech, pornography, and defamation, all raise their own unique set of concerns, there are also a number of interpretive concepts that apply to many areas of free speech law. In this chapter, I briefly set out some of those concepts, and illustrate their working.

THE PATHOLOGICAL PERSPECTIVE ON FREE SPEECH

'*Amid the clash of arms, the laws are not silent.*'[1] When the famous British judge Lord Atkin wrote these words, he was writing them in dissent, at the height of the Second World War, protesting against his brother judges' reading of a law that allowed the executive almost untrammelled powers of preventive detention. The very fact that he was dissenting illustrates a simple point: free speech in democratic countries often tends to follow a certain historical pattern. However liberal and tolerant of different viewpoints a nation might generally be, times of normalcy are invariably punctuated by periods of

---

[1] *Liversidge* v. *Anderson*, [1942] AC 206, 244 (dissenting opinion of Atkin L.J.).

persecution. War is an obvious example of a time when free speech effectively ceases to exist, but there are other occasions as well, when the demands of extreme ideological conformity lead to the passing of repressive laws. In colonial India, for example, it was the rise of the Wahabi movement that led to the passage of the law of sedition, and the rise of the organized nationalist movement that prodded the British government into passing a series of restrictive press laws.[2]

While colonial India lacked a written constitution, in other nations it has been seen that constitutional courts, subject to the same pressures and stresses as the rest of society, often uphold speech-restrictive laws in times of supposed fear. Consider the case of the United States, widely accepted to be the most speech-protective of democracies. At the height of the First World War, the State persecuted anti-war activists—a ten-year prison sentence for socialist leader Eugene V. Debs is the most glaring example—and the courts acquiesced.[3] In the 1950s, the State used the Smith Act to launch a witch-hunt of suspected communist sympathizers—and the courts acquiesced.[4] With the benefit of decades of hindsight, these periods are considered to represent governmental overreach and the decisions of the courts are now widely accepted as incorrect (subsequent cases have overruled them).[5] However, the crucial point is that *at the time*, neither the constitutionally guaranteed right to freedom of speech, nor the courts entrusted with protecting it against majoritarian excesses, ended up being of any use to persecuted dissidents or minorities. In independent India as well, we are familiar with the excesses of the Emergency, and laws such as the Unlawful Activities Prevention Act, which severely restrict civil liberties on the grounds of national security.

In response to this, the free speech scholar Vincent Blasi has proposed that courts ought to have a 'pathological perspective' on free speech law. This means that 'the overriding objective at all times should

---

[2] See Chapters Three, Four.
[3] *Debs v. United States*, 249 U.S. 211 (1919).
[4] *Dennis v. United States*, 341 U.S. 494 (1951) (hereinafter *Dennis*).
[5] *Brandenburg v. Ohio*, 395 U.S. 444 (1969) (hereinafter *Brandenburg*).

be to equip [free speech law] to do maximum service in those historical periods when intolerance of unorthodox ideas is most prevalent
and when governments are most able and most likely to stifle dissent
systematically'.[6] One method of doing so is by 'confining the range
of discretion left to future decision makers who will be called upon
to make judgments when pathological pressures are most intense'.[7]
Cabining discretion through the use of rigid, narrowly defined standards makes it more difficult for the legislature or the courts, as the
case may be, to give in to the temptation of unjustifiably curtailing
speech in disturbed times.

An example will illustrate the point. During its convictions of
anti-war and other left-wing activists in the 1920s and 1930s, the
American Supreme Court was often faced with dissenting opinions by
the two famous judges, Oliver Wendell Holmes and Louis Brandeis.
In an attempt to take the Court in a more speech-protective direction,
and protect the free speech rights of unpopular dissidents, Holmes
proposed a test of 'clear and present danger' for determining when
the State could legitimately suppress speech that it believed was leading to harmful consequences.[8] When the Court eventually came to
accept this test, it was widely seen to be a move that would prevent the
recurrence of wartime excesses. However, during the communist per-
secutions of the 1950s, the flexibility and indeterminacy of the phrase
'clear and present danger' allowed the Court to uphold the Smith Act
convictions simply by finding that there *was* a clear and present danger to the United States from internal communist conspiracies.[9] Once
a normal climate had returned, the Court in 1969 abandoned the clear
and present danger test, and shifted to a more stringent requirement
that the speech be directed towards incitement to *imminent* lawless
action, and be likely to produce such action.[10] The twin requirements
of imminence and probability have meant that since that judgment,

[6] Blasi (1985: 449–50).
[7] Blasi (1985: 474).
[8] *Schenck v. United States*, 249 U.S. 47 (1919).
[9] *Dennis*.
[10] *Brandenburg*.

only once—in 2012—has the Court upheld a conviction or a statute that is aimed at prohibiting speech on the ground of its dangerous consequences.[11]

We should keep the pathological perspective on free speech in mind when, later in the book, we examine widely worded provisions like Section 66A of the Information Technology Act, which criminalizes 'offensive speech', in light of the Court's public order jurisprudence.

The pathological perspective is closely connected with the question of judicial deference. Typically, when assessing the constitutionality of a statute, the Court defers to the legislature's findings of fact. For example, if the basis of a reservation policy is the legislature's judgment that a particular group is not adequately represented in public employment, then the Court will not—barring extreme circumstances—substitute its own opinion about the group's representation quotient, even though it might believe that the legislature has got it wrong. This is because the legislature possesses the institutional capacity to make these kinds of calls (which the Court does not), and also because ultimately, the nuts-and-bolts of policymaking ought to be the prerogative of the elected representatives of the people.

The argument from deference, however, is much weaker in certain kinds of free speech cases, especially those that involve anti-government dissidents. Here, when the government evaluates the public order threat from speech that is hostile or opposed to it, it is—in the classic sense of the phrase—acting as a judge in its own cause. Like any other institution, the government possesses limited foresight, actual bias, and an overriding interest in self-preservation. A combination of these factors makes it highly likely that the government will overestimate the threat from hostile speech, and tend towards overregulation. This is something we should keep in mind when we examine issues of sedition, public order, anti-terror, other national security legislation, and—analogously—contempt of court law.

---

[11] *Holder* v. *Humanitarian Law Project*, 561 U.S. 1 (2010).

OVERBREADTH, VAGUENESS, AND THE CHILLING EFFECT

Speech-regulating statutes often suffer from two infirmities: overbreadth and vagueness. A statute is overbroad when its wording is such that it could potentially be used to prohibit *both* speech and expression that the State is constitutionally entitled to prohibit, as well as speech and expression that it is not. For instance, Section 16(2) of the South African Constitution withholds free speech protection from '...advocacy of hatred that is based on race, ethnicity, gender or religion, and that constitutes incitement to cause harm'.[12] In *Islamic Unity Convention v. The Independent Broadcasting Authority*,[13] Section 2(a) of the Code of Conduct for Broadcasting Services, which prohibited broadcasting material that was 'likely to prejudice...relations between sections of the population' was challenged. The South African Constitutional Court found that 'likely to prejudice' encompassed a much wider range of material than that which only advocated hatred; and 'sections of the population' included categories that went beyond the specifics of 'race, ethnicity, gender or religion'.[14] Nor was there a requirement of incitement to harm.[15]

Consequently, although admittedly advocacy of race-based hatred would be likely to prejudice relations between sections of the population, not all material likely to do the latter would constitute advocacy of hatred. Yet, this material would come within the ambit of Section 2(a), and be proscribed. Therefore, because Section 2(a) permitted *both* restrictions on freedom of speech and expression that the government was authorized to impose (advocacy of certain kinds of hatred), *and* restrictions that it was not (other ways of prejudicing relations), it suffered from the vice of 'overbreadth'.

Overbreadth is a problem that all laws can potentially suffer from. For example, in *Chintaman Rao v. State of Madhya Pradesh*, the Indian Supreme Court struck down a law authorizing the prohibition of

---

[12] Section 16(2)(c), Constitution of South Africa.
[13] 2002 (5) BCLR 433 (CC) (hereinafter *Islamic Unity Convention*).
[14] *Islamic Unity Convention*, para 36.
[15] *Islamic Unity* Convention, para 36.

the manufacture of *bidis* during the agricultural season, which was ostensibly passed to ensure that an adequate supply of agricultural labour was maintained in bidi-producing areas. While acknowledging that this purpose was a valid measure in public interest, a legitimate ground for restricting the Article 19(1)(g) freedom of trade, the Court nonetheless struck it down because of its blanket nature. 'The language employed', it held, 'is wide enough to cover restrictions both within and without the limits of constitutionally permissible legislative action affecting the right. So long as the possibility of its being applied for purposes not sanctioned by the Constitution cannot be ruled out, it must be held to be wholly void.'[16]

Constitutionally, overbreadth is closely connected with the reasonableness requirement under Article 19(2) (a connection explicitly made in *Chintaman Rao*). In the jurisprudence of the Indian courts, the interpretation of the phrase 'reasonable restrictions' has received scant scrutiny over the years. Its clearest exposition remains the 1952 case of *State of Madras* v. *V.G. Row*, which was about the freedom of association. In that case, the Supreme Court drew a link between reasonableness and proportionality. It held that in judicially reviewing a restriction for its reasonableness, 'the nature of the right alleged to have been infringed, the underlying purpose of the restrictions imposed, the extent and urgency of the evil sought to be remedied thereby, *the disproportion of the imposition*, the prevailing conditions at the time, should all enter into the judicial verdict'.[17] An overbroad statute, which would empower the State to restrict the freedom of speech on grounds covering a wider scope than those specifically listed under Article 19(2), would arguably—by that reason—upset the requirement of proportionality between the constitutionally permissible, 19(2)-based goals of the State, and the extent of the restriction.

On the other hand, a statute suffers from the vice of vagueness when persons 'of ordinary intelligence...have no reasonable opportunity to

[16] *Chintaman Rao* v. *State of Madhya Pradesh*, AIR 1951 SC 118, para 9 (hereinafter *Chintaman Rao*).

[17] *State of Madras* v. *V.G. Row*, AIR 1952 SC 196 (emphasis mine).

know what is prohibited'.[18] Vagueness thus defeats one of the basic purposes of law: providing citizens with fair warning of what is permitted and what is not, so that they can plan their affairs with a degree of security and certainty, leaving them instead—as the Indian Supreme Court observed—'in a boundless sea of uncertainty'.[19] For instance, in *State of Madhya Pradesh* v. *Baldeo Prasad*, the Central Provinces and Berar Goondas Act authorized a district magistrate to pass an order restricting the movements of 'goondas', in the interests of public order, but failed to define who a 'goonda' was. Noting that 'sufficient safeguards should be provided by the Act to protect the fundamental rights of innocent citizens and to save them from unnecessary harassment',[20] the Court struck it down.

The European Court of Human Rights provides an interesting example of vagueness as applied to the freedom of speech. In an English case, two people who disrupted a hunting expedition were found liable for engaging in acts that were *contra bono mores*, that is, behaviour considered to be wrong by a 'majority of contemporary fellow citizens'.[21] The European Court of Human Rights found that this was a violation of the European Convention's free speech guarantee, since the concept of *contra bono mores* was so vague that it gave the applicants no guidelines on how they should behave in the future.

Additionally, one direct result of vagueness—as the Indian Supreme Court held in *Kartar Singh* v. *State of Punjab*, citing the American Supreme Court's opinion in *Grayned* v. *City of Rockford*—is that it delegates to an impermissible degree 'basic policy matters to policemen, judges, and juries for resolution on an ad hoc and subjective basis, with the attendant dangers of arbitrary and discriminatory application'.[22] Thus, implementing power—with the accompanying risk of arbitrary application—ends up vested in the hands of non-elected bodies, such as the police.

---

[18] *Grayned* v. *City of Rockford*, 408 U.S. 104, 108 (1972).
[19] *K.A. Abbas* v. *Union of India*, AIR 1971 SC 481: [1971] 2 SCR 446, para 47.
[20] *State of Madhya Pradesh* v. *Baldeo Prasad*, AIR 1961 SC 293, para 11.
[21] *Hashman and Harrup* v. *United Kingdom*, (2000) 30 EHRR 241.
[22] (1994) 3 SCC 569, para 77, citing *Grayned*, p. 109.

In addition to being constitutionally problematic at a general level, overbreadth and vagueness are specifically problematic when it comes to free speech because of something that courts the world over—including India—have identified as the 'chilling effect'.[23] The chilling effect refers to a practice of self-censorship that citizens engage in to avoid being penalized for illegal speech. The fear of punishment will invariably push citizens to stay well within the border that separates legal from illegal speech, so much so that they will often refrain from even exercising their *legitimate* free speech rights in order to ensure that they remain unambiguously upon the right side of the law. In this way legitimate speech is 'chilled', thus ensuring the impoverishment of the political discourse.

If one of the functions of free speech is to keep open the channels for effective democratic politics and public accountability—as Raja Rammohun Roy pointed out almost 200 years ago—then the chilling effect is something that statutes should aim to avoid, and courts should be sensitive towards. Notice the connections between the chilling effect and overbreadth, the end result of both of which is that legitimate speech is proscribed. Consequently, the chilling effect—much like overbreadth—implicates the reasonableness requirement of Article 19(2). Thus, to the extent that statutes prohibit or regulate expression, they must be both clear and narrowly drawn.

The chilling effect is not limited to overbreadth and vagueness, but occurs throughout free speech jurisprudence. It has featured prominently in the area of defamation. The common law of defamation is designed to protect people's public reputation by creating a legal regime in which the publishers of defamatory statements must compensate the persons whom they have defamed. While truth is a defence to a claim for defamation, the burden of proving that the defamatory statement was true in all material respects lies upon its

[23] *Petronet LNG Ltd.* v. *Indian Petro Group*, 158 (2009) DLT 759: [2009] 95 SCL 207 (Del). *Grant* v. *Torstar Corp.*, [2009] 3 SCR 640: [2009] SCC 61; *Case* v. *Minister of Safety and Security*, 1996 (5) BCLR 608, para 55 (South Africa): 1996 (3) SA 617.

publishers. Furthermore, defamation plaintiffs invariably ask for astronomically high sums of compensation known as exemplary damages, which are ostensibly meant to deter future violations. A combination of the high burden of proof (even a single inadvertent, unintentional mistake could be fatal) and the possibility of crippling damages (even though Indian courts are not known for granting them) has made defamation law the tool of choice of governments and corporations intent on stifling critical speech, primarily emanating from the press. Indeed, defamation law's potential to chill vital speech was recognized by the American Supreme Court in one of its most famous decisions on press freedom: *New York Times* v. *Sullivan*,[24] decided in 1964.

In *New York Times*, the officials of the state of Alabama attempted to stop the New York Times from reporting on the civil rights protests in the deep South by bringing a heavy defamation claim against it on the ground of some minor factual inaccuracies that had crept into an advertisement about police brutality against students and other civil rights activists. The Alabama courts had decided the case against the *Times*, with other similar cases waiting in the wings, and the total sum of money claimed—three million dollars—would have possibly bankrupted it, and certainly cast a chill over other newspapers reporting the events in the South. Recognizing this fact, the Court unanimously held in favour of the newspaper, holding that in libel cases brought to court by public officials, false statements were not punishable unless their falsehood was either known to the publisher, or if the publisher proceeded with reckless disregard for their veracity. In a famous opinion, Justice Brennan observed that 'the [prized] right to speak one's mind about public officials and affairs...needs *breathing space* to survive'.[25] And in his concurring opinion, Justice Goldberg noted, expressly, 'the *chilling effect* that Alabama's libel laws have on First Amendment

---

[24] *New York Times* v. *Sullivan*, 376 U.S. 254 (1964) (hereinafter *New York Times*).

[25] *New York Times*, p. 272 (emphasis mine).

freedoms'.[26] In the opinion of Anthony Lewis, the great historian of free speech, a major reason for the eventual success of the civil rights movement was its winning over public opinion due to the extensive press coverage it received throughout the nation, which in turn was made possible by the *New York Times* v. *Sullivan* decision.[27] How far-reaching and impactful the chilling effect can be—and how important the role of the court is in guarding against it—can hardly be overstated.

CONTENT NEUTRALITY AND THE POWER TO IMPOSE TRUTH

In the first chapter, we discussed two cases of film censorship: *Anand Patwardhan*[28] and *Srishti School.*[29] In these cases, censorship was defended on the ground that the film-makers had presented a biased and ideologically slanted perspective of controversial historical events. The corollary of this argument is that the government possesses the authority and legitimacy to decide the balanced, correct, or most acceptable way of portraying an event. In rejecting this argument, and emphasizing the liberty of the film-makers to choose the message they wished to convey to their audience and the concomitant liberty of the audience to watch and hear it, the High Courts of Bombay and Delhi were tapping into a crucial idea: whether it is fear of excessive conformity, distaste for paternalism, or any other reason, the government's attempts to impose *its* version of the truth upon all its citizens as a *universal truth* is regarded with deep suspicion.

'*Doubting is happiness*',[30] as Brecht's Galileo might say, and the legal point was put particularly eloquently by Justice Muralidhar: '[the] right of the viewer to think autonomously while reacting to the speaker or the film maker, and to make informed choices, without

[26] *New York Times*, p. 300 (Goldberg J., concurring); emphasis mine.
[27] Lewis (1992).
[28] *Anand Patwardhan* v. *Union of India*, AIR 1997 Bom 25.
[29] *Srishti School of Art, Design and Technology* v. *The Chairperson, Central Board of Film Certification*, 178 (2011) DLT 337 (hereinafter *Srishti*).
[30] Brecht (1986: 79).

being controlled by the State…constitutes an integral part of the freedom of speech and expression.'[31]

The specific form that this idea takes in free speech jurisprudence
goes by the name of 'content neutrality'. Content neutrality bars the
government from regulating or prohibiting speech *solely* because of its
communicative content, or its message. Content-based restrictions are
distinguishable from restrictions based on the 'time, place and manner'
of the speech. For instance, the case of *Nova ADS* v. *Secretary* involved
a challenge to the validity of the Chennai City Municipal Corporation
Rules, which regulated the erection of hoardings throughout the City
of Chennai. The Rules prohibited hoardings at places of aesthetic or
historical importance, popular places of worship, hospitals, educational
institutions, and others. They also regulated the size, width, and spac-
ing of the hoardings. In rejecting the challenge, the Supreme Court
observed that 'the Advertisement Rules in essence constitute a Code
for regulating erection of hoardings and *do not deal with content except
where it is found to be obscene or objectionable*…there can be cases where
because of the size and the height, it can be dangerous to [the] public
and also be hazardous. There is no structural safeguard in respect of
such hoardings. There have to be regulatory measures'.[32]

In *Nova ADS*, the restrictions were upheld because, as the Court
pointed out, they were not content-based restrictions. Their justification
did not turn upon what the hoardings were saying, but rather, upon
ancillary considerations such as road safety and access to important
public sites, which are entirely independent of the message that the
hoardings might have been communicating. Of course, the distinction is not a firm one. While it is possible to spin most content-based

[31] *Srishti*, para 25. The most famous exposition remains Justice Jackson's, in
West Virginia Board of Education v. *Barnette*, 319 U.S. 624, 642 (1943). Upholding
the right of school students *not* to salute the American flag, the judge observed: 'If
there is any fixed star in our constitutional constellation, it is that no official, high
or petty, can prescribe what shall be *orthodox* in politics, nationalism, religion,
or other matters of opinion or force citizens to confess by word or act their faith
therein' (emphasis mine).

[32] *Nova ADS* v. *Secretary, Department of Municipal Administration and Water
Supply*, AIR 2008 SC 2941, paras 48, 51 (hereinafter *Nova ADS*); emphasis mine.

restrictions as content-neutral ones, there are genuinely hard cases, and much of the analysis comes down to common sense.[33]

Content neutrality is most vividly (and controversially) illustrated in the case of *American Booksellers* v. *Hudnut*.[34] At issue was a constitutional challenge to an anti-pornography ordinance passed by the city of Indianapolis. The ordinance defined pornography as the 'graphic sexually explicit *subordination* of women', which occurred (among other things) through their presentation as 'sexual objects who enjoy pain or humiliation'. The City argued that it was trying to combat the various ways in which pornography socialized men and women into accepting gender discrimination as normal, or even desirable. Judge Easterbrook accepted the premise of the argument: 'depictions of subordination tend to perpetuate subordination. The subordinate status of women in turn leads to affront and lower pay at work, insult and injury at home, battery and rape on the streets.'[35] Nonetheless, he struck down the ordinance because it 'discriminates on the ground of the content of the speech. Speech treating women in the approved way—in sexual encounters "premised on equality" is lawful…speech treating women in the disapproved way—as submissive in matters sexual or as enjoying humiliation—is unlawful…the state may not ordain preferred viewpoints in this way. The Constitution forbids the state to declare one perspective right and silence opponents.'[36] What particularly worried Judge Easterbrook was that—despite the intuitive desirability of the City's position—it was arrogating to itself the power to decide and impose a position on sexual

---

[33] Content neutrality is a specific aspect of political liberalism, one of the dominant philosophies at the foundations of modern constitutional democracies. Political liberalism requires the State to be neutral between competing conceptions of the good. The State cannot choose to endorse—or condemn—any particular 'comprehensive theory'—that is, theories about what is good, true, or beautiful, and how one ought to live one's life. See Rawls (1993). Thus, a close examination of the Indian free speech law will also give us an interesting window into examining the extent to which our Constitution is committed to the principles of political liberalism.

[34] 771 F.2d 323 (7th Cir. 1985) (hereinafter *American Booksellers*).

[35] *American Booksellers*, p. 329.

[36] *American Booksellers*, p. 325.

relations that it had identified as the 'true' one. As he noted, 'a power to limit speech on the ground that truth has not yet prevailed and is not likely to prevail *implies the power to declare truth*'.[37]

There is much to disagree with in Judge Easterbrook's opinion. Indeed, brief reflection will reveal that content neutrality is hardly a pervasive aspect of free speech: copyright law, laws against fraud and blackmail, and insider trading regulations are all examples of content-based speech regulation. Non-American jurisprudence does not follow content neutrality even in explicit domains, like that of public order. For instance, the International Covenant on Civil and Political Rights prohibits propaganda for war,[38] and Section 16(2) of the South African Constitution incorporates the same restriction.[39] The German Constitution subscribes to the concept of 'militant democracy': for instance, political parties whose platform violates the basic tenets of liberal democracy may justifiably be banned under the Constitution.[40]

Following a similar line of argument, the European Court of Human Rights upheld the ban of a Turkish political party whose mandate involved abolishing secular law and establishing sharia courts if it came to power. It held that 'a political party may promote a change in the law or the legal and constitutional structures of the State on two conditions: first, the means used to that end must be legal and democratic; second, the *change proposed must itself be compatible with fundamental democratic principles*'.[41]

At the same time, the rhetorical force and intuitive plausibility of Judge Easterbrook's words are undeniable. Therefore, content neutrality tracks the ambivalent argument that we made about autonomy in the previous chapter: governmental imposition of orthodoxy, or truth, seems tolerable in some cases but not in others. As we go through the cases in the next section of the book, that is one important idea to keep in mind. At

[37] *American Booksellers*, pp. 330–31; emphasis mine.
[38] Article 20, International Covenant on Civil and Political Rights, *United Nations Treaty Series, 1966*, 999: 171.
[39] Section 16(2)(a), Constitution of South Africa.
[40] Article 21, Basic Law for the Federal Republic of Germany.
[41] *Refah Partisi* v. *Turkey*, [2003] ECHR 87; emphasis mine.

this point, we may note that Article 19(2) contains an eclectic mix of content-neutral and content-based restrictions, the precise nature of which depends heavily upon judicial interpretation: public order, decency and morality, contempt of court, defamation, incitement to an offence— all of these can occupy any number of spaces on the neutrality spectrum. One important critique of the Court's jurisprudence is to identify the areas and extents to which it has upheld the government's determination of truth or orthodoxy, and how well that fits with our more considered convictions about neutrality. In doing so, it is also important to develop a normative vision of the content-based restrictions of Article 19(2), on lines similar to what Germany and the European Court of Human Rights have done: what *principles* determine the content—or communicative messages—that may be legitimately regulated by the government?

VALUING SPEECH

Is some speech more valuable than other speech? Should certain kinds of speech be given greater protection than other kinds? How do we know? The answer depends—once again—on what we believe free speech is for, or our theory of free speech. Is there a central purpose to free speech, so that speech fulfilling this purpose is entitled to maximum protection, while other kinds of speech are relegated to the background? A self-fulfilment/autonomy theorist would rank all expressive conduct as equally worthy of protection. A marketplace-of-ideas theorist might make a difference between 'opinions' (ideas) and 'facts'. Naturally, it is in democracy-based theories that the issue of ranking speech becomes most acute. One form that this has taken— with a particularly interesting dynamic in India, as we shall see—is the lower standard of protection that is accorded to 'commercial speech' (advertisements) than, say, political speech. Another example is defamation where constitutional courts have established different standards—and consequently, different levels of protection—for the criticism of public officials and private persons. Examining the Indian Supreme Court's approach to judging the 'worth' or 'value' of different kinds of speech across a series of cases will be important in developing a holistic account of its free speech jurisprudence.

Note: The Changing Faces of the Free Speech Clause

. . . .

Draft Clause 8 of the Fundamental Rights Sub-Committee was first debated by the Constituent Assembly on 29 and 30 April 1947. It read:

> Clause 8: There shall be liberty for the exercise of the following rights subject to public order and morality or to the existence of grave emergency declared to be such by the Government of the Union or the Unit concerned whereby the security of the Union or the Unit, as the case may be, is threatened:-
>
> (a) The right of every citizen to freedom of speech and expression: Provision may be made by law to make the publication or utterance of seditious, obscene, blasphemous, slanderous, libellous or defamatory matter actionable or punishable.

When introducing Clause 8 to the Assembly on 30 April 1947, Sardar Patel, the Chairman of the Sub-committee, dropped the proviso. An amendment proposed by Somnath Lahiri seeking to replace the word 'security' with 'defence', on the ground that 'security' was too vague a term, was rejected.

In the Draft Constitution of February 1948, Draft Article 13(1)(a) guaranteed the freedom of speech and expression, and Draft Article 13(2) read:

> (2) Nothing in sub-clause (a) of clause (1) of this article shall affect the operation of any existing law, or prevent the State from making any law

relating to libel, slander, defamation, sedition or any other matter which offends against decency or morality or undermines the authority or foundation of the State.

Draft Article 13(2) after debate and amendment (December 1948) read:

> (2) Nothing in sub-clause (a) of clause (1) of this article shall affect the operation of any existing law in so far as it relates to, or prevent the State from making any law relating to libel, slander, defamation or any matter which offends against decency or morality or which undermines the security of, or tends to overthrow, the State.

Draft Article 13(2) after the Second Reading (17 October 1949) came to state:

> (2) Nothing in sub-clause (a) of clause (1) shall affect the operation of any existing law in so far as it relates to, or prevent the State from making any law relating to, libel, slander, defamation, contempt of Court or any matter which offends against decency or morality or which undermines the security of, or tends to overthrow, the State.

The notable addition was the phrase 'contempt of court', which was adopted after a fractious debate. Ultimately, draft Article 13 became Article 19 of the Constitution. Consequently, the final wording of Articles 19(1)(a) and 19(2) was as follows:

> 19. (1) All citizens shall have the right—
> (a) to freedom of speech and expression;
>
> ...
>
> (2) Nothing in sub-clause (a) of clause (1) shall affect the operation of any existing law in so far as it relates to, or prevent the State from making any law relating to, libel, slander, defamation, contempt of court or any matter which offends against decency or morality or which undermines the security of, or tends to overthrow, the State.

After the Supreme Court's decisions in *Romesh Thappar* v. *State of Madras*[1] and *Brij Bhushan* v. *State of Delhi*,[2] interpreting the term

---

[1] [1950] 1 SCR 594.
[2] [1950] SCR Supp. 245.

'undermines the security of, or tends to overthrow, the State', in a speech-protective manner, the first Parliament amended Article 19(2) via the First Amendment to the Constitution. The final wording of Article 19(2) was:

> (2) Nothing in sub-clause (a) of clause (1) shall affect the operation of any existing law, or prevent the State from making any law, in so far as such law imposes reasonable restrictions on the exercise of the right conferred by the said sub-clause in the interests of the security of the State, friendly relations with foreign States, public order, decency or morality, or in relation to contempt of court, defamation or incitement to an offence.

The notable changes were substituting the security-and-overthrow clause with 'public order', substituting 'relates to' with 'in the interests of', removing 'libel and slander', adding 'friendly relations with other States', and—perhaps most importantly—adding a requirement of reasonableness for the restrictions (something that had been the object of deep disagreement during the Constituent Assembly Debates).

The Sixteenth Amendment, in 1963, made one last change to Article 19(2). In a bid to promote 'national integration', Parliament added 'sovereignty and integrity' to Article 19(2). Article 19(2)'s language, which it retains today, finally became:

> (2) Nothing in sub clause (a) of clause (1) shall affect the operation of any existing law, or prevent the State from making any law, in so far as such law imposes reasonable restrictions on the exercise of the right conferred by the said sub clause in the interests of the sovereignty and integrity of India, the security of the State, friendly relations with foreign States, public order, decency or morality or in relation to contempt of court, defamation or incitement to an offence.

PART TWO

Subversive Speech

. . . .

CHAPTER THREE

Public Order

. . . .

> ALL. *Revenge! About! Seek! Burn! Fire! Kill! Slay!*
>   *Let not a traitor live!*
> ANTONY. *Stay, countrymen.*
> FIRST CITIZEN. *Peace there! hear the noble Antony.*
> SECOND CITIZEN. *We'll hear him, we'll follow him, we'll die with him.*
> ANTONY. *Good friends, sweet friends, let me not stir you up*
>   *To such a sudden flood of mutiny.*
>   *They that have done this deed are honourable:*
>   *What private griefs they have, alas, I know not,*
>   *That made them do it: they are wise and honourable,*
>   *And will, no doubt, with reasons answer you.*
>   *I come not, friends, to steal away your hearts:*
>   *I am no orator, as Brutus is;*
>   *But, as you know me all, a plain blunt man...*
>
>   —*Julius Caesar*, Act III, Scene 2

When the Fundamental Rights Sub-Committee (and subsequently, the Constituent Assembly) met to debate the fundamental rights chapter of independent India's Constitution, there was little doubt that the freedom of speech and of the press would occupy an important space. Right from 1823, when the colonial government passed the Press Ordinance,[1] the press was one of the important sites upon which the colonial–nationalist struggle played out. The nationalists regarded a thriving, free press as serving at least two distinct functions. The first, as Rammohun Roy stressed in his *Memorandum*, was as a vehicle of disseminating information and education for the advancement of the masses.[2] But as the nationalist movement began to gather steam towards the end of the nineteenth century, newspapers—and especially the vernacular press—came to be seen as an important instrument for rallying public opinion around the nationalist cause.[3] This was something the British were keenly aware of, and passed a number of legislations to counter. The Licensing Act of 1857, the Vernacular Press Act of 1878, the Newspapers Act of 1908, and the Indian Press Act of 1910 are examples of some of the laws that conferred sweeping pre- and post-publication censorial powers upon the authorities, such as registration requirements (with large security deposits), powers of confiscation, and so on. In periods of relative calm, some of these laws were repealed, but whenever it seemed that the nationalist movement was gaining ground, they made a prompt re-entry.[4]

Due to this, the freedom of the press—and the freedom of speech more generally—was always a central plank of nationalist demands. As early as 1895, the Constitution of India Bill (which is the first recorded 'bill of rights' emerging out of the nationalist movement) guaranteed the right of every citizen to 'express his thoughts by words or writings, and publish them in print without liability to censure... but they shall be answerable to abuses, which they may commit in

---

[1] The subject of Rammohun Roy's *Memorandum*, which we have discussed before. See Chapter One.

[2] Collett (1914).

[3] We shall consider some specific examples in the chapter on sedition.

[4] For instance, Lord Metcalfe repealed the 1823 Ordinance in 1835, but it was largely brought back in 1857. Lord Ripon repealed Lord Lytton's Vernacular Press Act in 1882, but in 1910, its worst features were rewritten into law via the Indian Press Act. This, in turn, was repealed on the recommendations of the Sapru Press Committee, before making a re-entry in 1931.

the exercise of this right, in the cases and in the mode the Parliament shall determine.'[5] In the teeth of proliferating sedition prosecutions and deep colonial hostility towards the press following the Press Act of 1910, the nationalist movement stepped up its demands. Under the guidance of Annie Besant, a 1917 Congress resolution demanded 'the removal of all hindrances to free discussion',[6] and called for an immediate repeal of laws, regulations, and ordinances to the contrary. The Commonwealth of India Bill, demanding dominion status for India, which was introduced (and defeated) in the British Parliament in 1925, called for 'free expression of opinion'.[7] Three years later, in the *Motilal Nehru Report*, the guarantee was rendered more concrete, making it subject to 'public order or morality'[8] (words that would echo through the annals of post-Independence Indian free speech law).

As Arun Thiruvengadam points out, in an astute summary of the evolution of the free speech guarantee through the numerous bills of rights put forth by the Congress over the years, 'what is striking…is the near absence of language on restrictions that could be imposed on the right',[9] bringing the nationalist understanding of free speech very close to its American counterpart. This is hardly surprising, considering the crucial role of the press in building and sustaining the national movement.

The framing of India's Constitution, however, would take free speech along a very different path. Even as Draft Article 13(1)(a), guaranteeing the freedom of speech and expression to all citizens was proposed, it was hedged in with restrictions. These restrictions were staunchly opposed in the Assembly. It was the Founding Fathers, the likes of Nehru, Patel, Ambedkar, and Alladi Krishnaswami Iyer, who

---

[5] Clause 16, the Constitution of India Bill, 1895, c.f. Shiva Rao (1967: 5, 7). For a brief account of this history, see Sorabjee (2000: 334–35).

[6] Clause 2(a), Congress Resolution on Self-Determination, 1918, c.f. Shiva Rao (1967: 31).

[7] Clause 4, the Commonwealth of India Bill, 1925, c.f. Shiva Rao (1967: 43, 44).

[8] Clause 4(iv), *The Nehru Report*, 1928, c.f. Shiva Rao (1967: 58, 59).

[9] Thiruvengadam (n.d.).

defended and ultimately pushed them through, to the consternation of early liberal critics.[10] What is particularly interesting is how the Constituent Assembly Debates saw a curious reversal of roles. In the pre-Independence days, as we have just seen, it was the nationalists who argued for untrammelled freedom of expression, while the colonial authorities claimed the right to restrict that freedom to prevent subversion and threats to law and order. But during the time of the Constituent Assembly Debates, perhaps driven by the imperatives of constructing a nation out of fragmentary and dissentient parts, and alarmed by the communal violence surrounding them, those very same stalwarts of the independence movement began to speak in the voices of their erstwhile rulers, warning against the perils of allowing unrestricted freedom of expression.[11]

In fact, in one of history's many ironies, Dr. Ambedkar justified[12] the Drafting Committee's proposed restrictions by extensively citing from the case of *Gitlow* v. *New York*.[13] *Gitlow* was decided by the American Supreme Court in 1925, at the height of the First Red Scare. In that case, the Supreme Court held that speech with a 'bad tendency' towards causing public disorder was punishable. Yet surely Dr. Ambedkar knew that by 1948, the very Supreme Court that had spawned *Gitlow* had begun to move away from it. Surely Dr. Ambedkar was also aware that by that time, instead of the majority opinion that he chose to quote from, it was Justice Oliver Wendell Holmes' dissent—defining a 'clear and present danger' test—that was largely applied.[14] Indeed, Justice Holmes' opinion in *Gitlow*, dealing with the conviction of certain Socialist Party members for putting out

[10] See, for example, Shastri (1949).

[11] In fact, the final wording of Article 19(1)(a) had no express press freedom clause. It has never seriously been suggested, however, that the 'freedom of expression' does not include the freedom of the press, and the point is now of little more than historical interest.

[12] Speech of B.R. Ambedkar, 4 November 1948, Indian Constituent Assembly (Vol. VII).

[13] 268 U.S. 652 (1925) (hereinafter *Gitlow*).

[14] *Thornhill* v. *Alabama*, 310 U.S. 88 (1940).

their manifesto, is the ideal point of departure for our discussions in this chapter:

> It was said that this manifesto was more than a theory, it was an incitement. *Every idea is an incitement.* It offers itself for belief and if believed it is acted on...the only difference between the expression of an opinion and incitement in the narrower sense is the speaker's enthusiasm for the result. Eloquence may set fire to reason...[15]

Ideas, and ideas expressed in words or in symbolic conduct, as Shakespeare so strikingly demonstrated in *Julius Caesar*, can and invariably do cause people to act in certain ways. Some of those acts might be illegal or harmful. But if we are not to descend to the levels of the thought police, on the lines of colonial restrictions upon speech and the press that the nationalists tirelessly fought against, we need a clear idea of the *causal connection* between words and deeds that might justify prohibiting or punishing the words themselves.

Consider the following hypothetical questions. What if my academic treatise on a certain community's much-loved historical leader 'causes' members of that community to take to the streets and destroy public property? What if I publish a newspaper editorial advocating all material support to the Naxalites to back their stated goal of overthrowing the Indian State? What if I stand on a pulpit before an enraged crowd, recite to them a litany of the historical wrongs they have suffered at the hands of a certain religious community, and then encourage them to destroy that community's religious building, located nearby? What if I shout 'fire' in a crowded theatre? Each example assumes some causal relationship between expression and (harmful) action, but our intuitions seem to distinguish between these cases when it comes to justifying an interference with the *expression*. We probably all agree that it would be entirely unjustified to ban the book (Example 1), and entirely justified to prohibit or punish shouting 'fire' (Example 4). There might be some degree of disagreement over Examples 2 and 3.

---

[15] *Gitlow*, p. 673 (dissenting opinion of Holmes J.); emphasis mine.

When can speech and expression be curtailed on grounds of public order, public safety, or other analogous legitimate governmental
interests in maintaining peace and security? What principle—or
principles—can we use to distinguish between Examples 1 and 4, and
help us in deciding Examples 2 and 3? In this chapter, we shall discuss
these issues, by understanding and critiquing what the courts and
Parliament have done.

EARLY DAYS AND THE FIRST AMENDMENT

Notwithstanding the robust speech guarantees in pre-Independence
nationalist bills of rights, the free expression clause that finally
emerged out of the birth-pangs of the original Constitution had
endured a tumultuous drafting history. The Fundamental Rights
Sub-Committee's strategy of declaring a broadly worded right
(Article 19(1)(a)) and curtailing it with almost equally broad restrictions (Article 19(2)) was vehemently opposed at every stage of the
Constituent Assembly Debates: at the presentation of the fundamental rights draft in the early days of 1947, and at both the first and the
second readings of the Draft Constitution of 1948. Opponents repeatedly raised the fear of an overbearing State riding roughshod over
the liberties guaranteed in Article 19, and were repeatedly rebuffed.
That Articles 19(1)(a) and 19(2) appear to be reasonably similar to the
original Clause 8 of the 1947 Sub-Committee draft, despite passing
through three rounds of fractious debate, is probably testament to the
influence of Patel, Ambedkar, Nehru, and Alladi Krishnaswami Iyer,
each of whom rose to assure the Assembly that the State would not
misuse its 19(2) powers. Ultimately, their libertarian opponents on the
left and the right lost heavily, failing both to get a last-minute insertion
of 'contempt of court' removed, and to have a reasonableness requirement inserted into 19(2). Perhaps their only notable victory was the
removal of 'sedition' from the list of permissible restrictions on free
speech, although judicial history has long nullified that achievement
as well.

Almost immediately after the birth of the Constitution, the
Supreme Court was called upon to determine the meaning of the

term 'undermines the security of, or tends to overthrow, the State'. The Court's judgments, and the government's response, shaped (most of the) Article 19(2) that we know today. The impact of this early Court–legislature clash, though, was much more far-reaching than a simple constitutional amendment because, as we shall see, its legacy is still with us.

During the days of the Raj, the press had been the most important battleground of free speech. Continuing the role-reversal that we first saw in the Constituent Assembly, while the battleground remained the same, it was the new government of independent India that replaced the colonial authorities as one of the contestants. *Romesh Thappar* v. *State of Madras*[16] and *Brij Bhushan* v. *State of Delhi*[17] were decided by the Supreme Court in 1950. In *Romesh Thappar*, the constitutionality of Section 9(1-A) of the Madras Maintenance of Public Order Act was at issue. That provision authorized the state government to regulate the entry and circulation within the state, of any 'set of documents' (read: newspapers), for the purposes of 'securing public safety and maintaining public order'. The Madras government used this provision to prohibit the entry and circulation of the leftist magazine, *Cross Roads*. The ban—and the provision authorizing it—were challenged.

The Court was called upon to examine the relationship between the terms 'public safety' and 'public order' on the one hand (the words of the statute), and 'undermin[ing] the security of, or tend[ing] to overthrow the State' on the other (the words of the Constitution). The majority's opinion (Justice Fazl Ali dissented) is a classic example of overbreadth analysis. It defined 'public order' as 'that state of tranquility which prevails among the members of a political society'.[18] 'Undermining the security of the State', on the other hand, meant 'nothing less than endangering the foundations of the State or threatening its overthrow'.[19] Obviously, undermining the security of the State was an act against public order and public safety as well, but not

---

[16] [1950] 1 SCR 594 (hereinafter *Romesh Thappar*).
[17] [1950] SCR Supp. 245 (hereinafter *Brij Bhushan*).
[18] *Romesh Thappar*, para 5.
[19] *Romesh Thappar*, para 8.

every instance of public disorder reached the level of undermining the security of the State. Consequently, the terms 'public safety' and 'public order' were overbroad. They covered instances of free expression that the government could legitimately prohibit, as well as instances that it could not.

The State contended that the banning of books and journals was such a drastic step that it would only be used in extreme situations, where the security of the State was actually undermined. Again, following overbreadth analysis to the letter, the Court simply noted that 'there [is no] guarantee that those authorised to exercise the powers under the Act will in using them discriminate between those who act prejudicial to the security of the State and those who do not'.[20]

The Court buttressed its conclusion by noting the removal of 'sedition' from the list of permissible restrictions during the Constituent Assembly Debates. This indicated that the drafters intended to permit only 'very narrow and stringent limits' because 'freedom of speech... [lies] at the foundation of all democratic organisations...without free political discussion no public education, so essential for the proper functioning of the processes of popular government, is possible'.[21] Section 9(1-A) was accordingly held unconstitutional.

Brij Bhushan v. *State of Delhi* was a similar case, although this time the attack was upon a right-wing journal.[22] Section 7(1)(c) of the East Punjab Public Safety Act authorized the government to pre-censor material 'prejudicial to public safety or the maintenance of public order'. *The Organiser*, which was (and still is) the in-house magazine of the RSS (Rashtriya Swayamsevak Sangh), was required to submit, for pre-publication scrutiny, all news and views relating to Pakistan. The prior restraint was challenged. Invoking Blackstone, the majority followed its decision and reasoning in *Romesh Thappar*, and held the section to be void, since it imposed a prior restraint upon publication. Justice Fazl Ali dissented in both cases, and gave

---

[20] *Romesh Thappar*, para 6.

[21] *Romesh Thappar*, para 6.

[22] It is quite interesting that the first two Supreme Court cases on 19(1)(a) involved bans upon a communist journal, and an RSS magazine.

his reasons in *Brij Bhushan*. He argued that 'public order', 'public safety', 'sedition', and 'undermining the security of the State' essentially amounted to the same thing. Sedition, according to Fazl Ali J., undermined the security of the State *through* public disorder.[23] Consequently, public disorder was clearly a matter that undermined the security of the State.

Readers will note something of a *non sequitur* in Fazl Ali J.'s chain of reasoning. More interesting, though, is the substantive disagreement between the majority and the dissent over the consequences of removing 'sedition' from the draft free speech article. The majority saw it as evidence of the framers' intent to expand freedom of speech, and narrow possible restrictions. Fazl Ali J., on the other hand, simply understood the Constituent Assembly to have substituted one concept (sedition) by its equivalent (undermining the security of, or tending to overthrow, the State). We will return to this dispute when we discuss the law of sedition.

The Court's decisions, reading Article 19(2) restrictively, were highly speech-protective, and did not last. The Parliament's response was swift and direct. Via the First Amendment to the Constitution, it replaced the undermine/overthrow wording with 'public order', added 'incitement to an offence', and introduced a reasonableness requirement. The breadth of these terms, and their potential for abuse, was immediately noticed and criticized.[24] In any event, the relevant part of the provision now read:

> (2) Nothing in sub clause (a) of clause (1) shall...prevent the State from making any law, in so far as such law imposes reasonable restrictions... in the interests of...public order...or incitement to an offence.

In its Statement of Objects and Reasons, Parliament justified the amendment by observing that 'the citizen's right to freedom of speech and expression guaranteed by article 19(1)(a) has been held by *some courts* to be so comprehensive as not to render a person culpable

---

[23] *Brij Bhushan*, para 10.
[24] Bindra (1954).

even if he *advocates murder and other crimes of violence*.[25] There is, of course, a distinction between 'advocacy' and 'incitement', and it is not clear how the amended 19(2) responds to the problem identified by the Statement of Objects and Reasons. In any event, what is clear is that the legislature accepted the distinction between 'public order' and 'undermining the security of the State', and wrote the former concept into Article 19(2).

At this point, we have a working definition of 'public order', which the Court provided in *Romesh Thappar*. That alone, however, does not take us too far. The key questions must turn upon the scope of 'reasonable restrictions' and 'in the interests of'. It is the interpretation of these terms that will establish the causal relationship between expression and public order necessary to justify State interference. Over three cases spanning three years—*Ramji Lal Modi* (1957), *Virendra* (1957), and *Lohia* (1960)—the Court tried to do just that.

THE SCOPE OF THE PUBLIC ORDER RESTRICTION

The first of these cases—*Ramji Lal Modi* v. *State of UP*[26]—involved a constitutional challenge to Section 295A of the Indian Penal Code, which criminalizes insulting (or attempting to insult) religious beliefs, when such insult is delivered with the 'deliberate and malicious intention' of outraging the religious feelings of any class of citizens of India'.[27] The case was about the prosecution of an editor of a cow-protection magazine for writing an article that allegedly hurt the sentiments of Muslims. As in *Romesh Thappar*, the petitioner raised an overbreadth argument. He contended that the relationship between

---

[25] Statement of Objects and Reasons, The Constitution (First Amendment) Act, 1951, http://indiacode.nic.in/coiweb/amend/amend1.htm (accessed on 24 July 2014); emphasis mine. The Courts in question were the Patna and Punjab High Courts. See *In Re: Bharati Press*, AIR 1951 Pat 12; *Amer Nath v. State*, AIR 1951 Punj 18.

[26] [1957] 1 SCR 860 (hereinafter *Ramji Lal Modi*).

[27] Section 295A will be discussed in detail in the chapter on hate speech. See Chapter Six.

the expression and the breach of public order must be 'proximate, not remote'. Outraging a community's religious feelings might in some cases lead to public disorder, but would not do so in all cases. Consequently, Section 295A covered both instances that the government could legitimately regulate (proximate) and those that it was not permitted to regulate (non-proximate). Section 295A was, therefore, overbroad and unconstitutional.

Rejecting this contention, the Court noted that the phrase 'in the interests of public order' was of very wide ambit (as opposed to the narrower 'for the maintenance of public order'[28]). Therefore, it covered all cases where the acts in question had a '*tendency*'[29] to cause public disorder.[30] The Court understood such acts to be those that take an 'aggravated form of insult to religion when [they are] perpetrated with the deliberate and malicious intention of outraging the religious feelings of that class…the calculated tendency of this aggravated form of insult [is] clearly to disrupt the public order'.[31] On this ground, the overbreadth challenge was rejected. The First Amendment, according to the Court, had simply expanded the boundaries of what the State could permissibly regulate, and Section 295A remained within those boundaries.

This decision is curious. In particular, the Court seems to shift back and forth between a subjective and an objective test for interpreting Section 295A. The petitioners' argument challenging the constitutionality of Section 295A rested upon the objective likelihood of public disorder, in the form of a 'proximate connection' test. At first, the Court only appears to loosen the likelihood standard by substituting a

---

[28] *Ramji Lal Modi*, para 7.

[29] This is, of course, similar to the 'bad tendency' test that the American Supreme Court abandoned in the 1940s.

[30] The protest against a 'tendency' standard was registered most eloquently by G.D. Khosla. 'Anything may have a tendency for almost anything. A lamp post may be taken as a phallic symbol, a convenient object for canine relief, a source of light, evidence of civilization, something to lean against when waiting for a bus or something to demolish in order to demonstrate a sense of rebellion or discontent. So what is the tendency of a lamppost' (Khosla 1976: 122)?

[31] *Ramji Lal Modi*, para 9.

test of 'tendency' for 'proximity'. For example, due to heavy smoking, I might tend towards developing cancer, although cancer may not follow proximately—especially if I have just started smoking. This is still an objective standard.

Next, however, the Court restricts it to acts done deliberately or maliciously, and which have a 'calculated tendency' to disrupt public order. But what is a 'calculated tendency'? 'Calculation' refers to my subjective state of mind in making the statement, while 'tendency' simply has to do with the objective relationship between act and consequence. The only solution is to presume that intentional or malicious 'calculated' acts (aimed at outraging or insulting religious sentiment) *simply by virtue of being so* have a tendency to disrupt public order. Yet this is purely a legal fiction, and an entirely fact-free basis upon which to take the serious step of restricting an important constitutional right.

There is, however, a deeper problem with *Ramji Lal Modi*, which goes to the structure of the argument itself. And that is that *mere statistical probability ought not to be a ground for curtailing free speech*. This is because it provides a private privilege of censorship to anyone who has the ability to break the law with impunity. Suppose I offend some members of a powerful and prickly religious group, who immediately take to the streets and start setting fire to buildings. The likelihood test (whether you look at it as one of proximity or tendency) will justify the government in curtailing my speech, to prevent that outcome. On the other hand, if I offend some members of a peaceable or powerless group, the law will have nothing to say to me. This cannot be right. The Court gets around this problem by holding *all* intentional or malicious acts (within the scope of the section) to be illegal. But in so doing, as we have seen before, it adopts a boundlessly wide and empirically groundless understanding of the necessary connection between free speech and consequent public disorder (and eschews the reasonableness requirement under Article 19(2)). In the Court's analysis, it is intentional outrage and insult that is doing all the work now. As long as the intent requirement is fulfilled, it is simply assumed that there is a public order violation. Clearly, this is a very unsatisfactory conclusion.

In *Virendra* v. *State of Punjab*,[32] however, the Court saw little wrong with this. That case involved the Punjab Special Powers Act, which, in the interests of communal harmony or public order, allowed the state government to 'prohibit the printing or publication in any document or any class of documents of any matter relating to a particular subject or class of subjects for a specified period or in a particular issue or issues of a newspaper or periodical',[33] for a period of two months. In free speech law, this kind of restriction, on publication itself—which was held unconstitutional out of hand in *Brij Bhushan*—is known as 'prior restraint', and is considered to be so repressive that the English jurist Blackstone, writing as far back as 1769, was able to say that 'the liberty of the press consists in laying upon it *no prior restraint*'.[34]

We shall return to issues of prior restraint later.[35] In *Virendra*, an order was passed banning the magazine *Pratap* from publishing any material 'whatsoever relating to or connected with' the 'Save Hindi Agitation'. This overbroad order—that, on its face, covers the core of basic journalistic activity—was upheld by the Court, which cited *Ramji Lal Modi*'s broad definition of 'in the interests of'. Here, because the atmosphere in Punjab was communally charged, and because the Court felt that the press was a 'powerful institution in its ability to sway public opinion, the pre-emptive ban was justified because '*quite conceivably* this agitation *might at any time* assume a nasty communal turn and flare up into a communal frenzy and factious fight disturbing the public order of the State'.[36]

Applying the principles of judicial deference, the Court refused to go into whether the state's assessment of the situation was actually

---

[32] [1958] 1 SCR 308 (hereinafter *Virendra*).

[33] *Virendra*, para 4.

[34] Blackstone (1765–69; emphasis mine).

[35] The most notorious instances of prior restraint happened during the 1975 Emergency, a detailed analysis of which is beyond the scope of this book.

[36] *Virendra*, para 12; emphasis mine. While upholding Section 2 of the Act, which allowed prior restraint, the Court struck down Section 3, which authorized the government to prohibit the entry and circulation of journals into the state of Punjab, primarily because of the absence of safeguards such as a time limit and a right of representation.

warranted, holding that it was the state's institutional prerogative to make that determination on the basis of the materials available to it. Responding to a contention that state government officials could well abuse such discretionary power, the Court held—in sharp contradistinction to *Romesh Thappar* and *Brij Bhushan*—that 'no assumption ought to be made that the State Government or the authority will abuse its power'.[37] Recall our discussion, in the previous chapter, of the pathological perspective on free speech, and ideas of overbreadth and impermissible delegation. The *Virendra* decision, very obviously, contradicts these principles.[38]

In *Virendra*, the worst fears of the liberal opponents of 19(2) came true: the government was allowed a free hand to pre-censor political materials without any meaningful judicial scrutiny, *simply* by citing 'public order'. At this point, Article 19(1)(a) was in serious danger of becoming—to invoke James Madison's memorable turn of phrase—a 'parchment barrier'.[39] Just three years later, however, the Court would retreat from this understanding.

In 1947, it had been a socialist—Somnath Lahiri—who first raised a dissenting voice against the creeping encroachment of the Fundamental Rights' Sub-Committee's list of restrictions on free speech. Interestingly, it was another socialist who was responsible for the revival of Article 19(1)(a). Ram Manohar Lohia was brought to Court under the U.P. Special Powers Act of 1932, a colonial-era legislation. Simply put, Section 3 of that Act criminalized instigating people against paying taxes or other liabilities.[40] Lohia, the General

---

[37] *Virendra*, para 14.

[38] In 1961, the Supreme Court also upheld the much-maligned Section 144 of the Code of Criminal Procedure, which—to put it shortly—allows a magistrate to pass restraining orders on persons to prevent disturbances of public tranquility, riots, and others, holding that anticipatory prevention was justified under Article 19(2). *Babulal Parate* v. *State of Maharashtra*, AIR 1961 SC 884 (hereinafter *Babulal Parate*). The Court also limited its application to situations of 'emergency', although in the fifty years that have followed, this stricture has been honoured more in the breach than in the observance.

[39] Madison (1788).

[40] Clearly designed keeping in mind civil disobedience movements during the freedom struggle.

Secretary of the Socialist Party of India, was prosecuted for doing just that, and challenged the constitutionality of the Section.[41] The case went up to the Supreme Court, which delivered its judgment in 1960.

The Court commenced with an important observation that 'public order' was 'synonymous with public peace, safety and tranquility'[42] (and thus, narrower than simple law-breaking). And then, it took upon itself—again—the task of interpreting the phrase 'in the interests of'. While formally adhering to its previous observations in *Ramji Lal Modi*, the Court—in substance—broke with precedent. When *Ramji Lal Modi* was cited before it, it noted that

> [*Ramji Lal Modi*] was only making a distinction between an Act which *expressly and directly* purported to maintain public order and one which did not expressly state the said purpose but left it to be implied therefrom; and between an Act that directly maintained public order and *that indirectly brought about the same result*. The distinction does not ignore the necessity for *intimate connection* between the Act and the public order sought to be maintained by the Act.[43]

But this misreads *Ramji Lal Modi* entirely! In that case, the petitioners' contention for a relationship of proximity had been rejected *in favour of a test requiring 'tendency' to public disorder'*. Clearly, the Court had opted for a more relaxed relationship between speech and public disorder. *Lohia* thus performed a sleight of hand: it substituted an indirect relationship between *speech and consequence*, which was what *Ramji Lal Modi* held, with an indirect relationship between the *law and its goal of achieving public order*—which was *not* what *Ramji Lal Modi* held. In so doing, the Court changed the test entirely, while maintaining an ostensible fidelity to precedent.

---

[41] *The Superintendent, Central Prison, Fatehgarh* v. *Dr. Ram Manohar Lohia*, [1960] 2 SCR 821 (hereinafter *Lohia*).

[42] *Lohia*, para 11. This point was elaborated in great detail in *Ram Manohar Lohia* v. *State of Bihar*, AIR 1966 SC 740, where the Court elaborated its famous 'three concentric circles' theory: those of 'law and order' (widest circle), 'public order', and 'security of the State' (narrowest).

[43] *Lohia*, para 12; emphasis mine.

The Court buttressed its new proximity test by referring to the use of the word '*reasonable*', and holding that only a 'proximate connection or nexus with public order, but not one far-fetched, hypothetical or problematical or too remote in the chain of its relation with the public order'[44] could be upheld under 19(2). This brought it to the issue of deference. The State argued that even instigating one individual not to pay his taxes was a 'spark' that could, in the long run, 'ignite' a revolution. Following *Virendra*, the Court should have deferred to the government's assessment of proximity, since—going by its own prior dictum—it was the government that had the institutional competence and information to best make such assessments. Instead, it held that 'fundamental rights cannot be controlled on such hypothetical and imaginary considerations'.[45] The Section, being an unreasonable 19(1)(a) restriction, was struck down.

Lohia did two very important things. Substantively, it changed the test for the reasonableness of a public order restriction, making it much more speech-protective than before. In this, it departed from *Ramji Lal Modi*. And it changed the Court's role in the enquiry from one of passive deference to active interrogation of the reasonableness of the restriction. In this, it departed from *Virendra*. For all practical purposes, *Lohia* swung the pendulum back to the speech-protective pre-First Amendment era, albeit with a changed constitutional text. As Seervai points out, under the 'tendency' test upheld in *Ramji Lal Modi* and *Virendra*, the offending Sections in *Lohia* would have to be upheld because 'to say that an exhortation to disobey the law by refusing to pay taxes would not have a tendency to affect public order would be to run counter to the facts of

---

[44] *Lohia*, para 13. The Supreme Court relied upon the Federal Court judgment in *Rex* v. *Basudeva*, AIR 1950 FC 67, a case dealing with a challenge to preventive detention for black marketing, where Patanajali Sastri J. put the point starkly: 'It is true that black-marketing in essential commodities may at times lead to a disturbance of public order, but so may, for example, the rash driving of an automobile or the sale of adulterated food stuffs' (*Lohia*, para 7).

[45] *Lohia*, para 14.

history in not one, but in a number of countries'[46] (the Dandi March comes to mind).

However, if the difference between *Ramji Lal Modi* and *Lohia* is simply proximity as a test of statistical probability (how likely is the speech to lead to a public order violation?), then we are faced with the problem identified here: if I *always* riot when I am offended, and I am strong enough or brazen enough to do so, then I can effectively shut down your speech anytime I want to. The proximity test must also have an inbuilt moral, or normative, component. It is here that theory can help us.

THE IDEA OF AUTONOMY

In his famous defence of the freedoms of speech, press, and association, written in 1922, Gandhi argued that 'assemblies of people [ought to be able to] discuss *even revolutionary projects*, the State relying upon *the force of public opinion* and the civil police, not the savage military at its disposal, to crush any *actual outbreak of revolution* that is designed to confound public opinion and the State representing it [emphasis mine]'.[47] Gandhi's distinction between the discussion of revolutionary projects and the actual outbreak of revolution, and his focus on the use of public opinion as a countering force (while maintaining a role for the police in containing actual revolution), embody some crucial insights that can help us to arrive at a coherent and justified understanding of the public order limitation.

Recall that in Chapter One, we briefly discussed Scanlon's autonomy-based theory of free speech.[48] The autonomy argument is founded on a basic principle of our legal thinking, and more generally, our moral thinking as well: the idea of *responsibility*. We

[46] Seervai (2005: 790–91). Seervai takes this as a reason to have *Lohia* overruled.

[47] Gandhi (Vol. 22, 1958–1984: 176–7). For an analysis of Gandhi's understanding of the central importance of free speech and free association to *swaraj*, see Tripathi (1958).

[48] Scanlon (1972).

punish someone if we believe they are responsible for an illegal act or for causing a wrongful harm. Consequently, we are only permitted to use subsequent harm to prohibit someone's speech if they are *responsible*—in some meaningful way—for that harm.

The idea of responsibility leads Scanlon to make an important distinction: between causing people to act by giving them the *means* to do what they were looking to do already, and by giving them *reasons* to do so. We can explain this with the help of a concrete distinction. There is a difference between restraining a misanthropic inventor from distributing copies of his homemade nerve-gas recipe at the local street corner, and prohibiting 'seditious propaganda' challenging the authority of the government. The first is a case of providing means (nerve-gas recipe) and the second a case of providing reasons (seditious arguments). What distinguishes the second case is that the agent (in this case, the person who listens to the seditious propaganda and then acts upon it) 'comes to her own judgment' about the merits of the action (harmful acts). Our intuitions about autonomy impel us to attribute responsibility for that action upon *her* shoulders. Thus, as we pointed out in Chapter One, Scanlon's central argument is that you cannot prohibit speech where 'the connection between the acts of expression and the subsequent harmful acts consists merely in the fact that *the act of expression led the agents to believe (or increased their tendency to believe) these acts to be worth performing*'[49] because 'the harm of coming to have false beliefs is not one that an autonomous man could allow the State to protect him through restrictions on expression.'[50]

Therefore, by punishing someone for the considered actions of another autonomous individual, the State misattributes responsibility. And by prohibiting one person from listening to another for fear of what the listener might be persuaded to do, the State violates the listener's autonomy. To put it very simply: if I listen to your seditious propaganda and betake myself to assault the nearest policeman, the

[49] Scanlon (1972: 213); emphasis mine.
[50] Scanlon (1972: 217).

responsibility for that—as an autonomous, thinking person—should be attributed to me, and you should not be penalized either by being punished, or by having your speech censored. As Ronald Dworkin puts the point:

> ...morally responsible people insist on making up their own minds what is good or bad in life or in politics, or what is true or false in matters of justice or of faith. Government insults its citizens, and denies their moral responsibility, when it decrees that *they cannot be trusted to hear opinions that might persuade them to dangerous and offensive convictions.*[51]

Scanlon's argument (although incomplete in many respects) helps us to understand why—going back to the beginning of this chapter— Example 4 is punishable, Example 3 *probably* is, and Examples 2 and 1—arguably—are not. Creating a panic by shouting 'fire' in a crowded theatre is a classic example of a situation of *diminished responsibility*. A crowd, in a closed, dark space, faced with a call of 'fire' has neither the time nor the opportunity to assess the accuracy of the claim, and consider the reasons for and against an immediate stampede. It neither violates anyone's autonomy, nor disrespects anyone, to proscribe that kind of speech. The hypothetical can be extrapolated towards Example 3: arguably, inciting an already enraged mob to immediate violence is the kind of situation where autonomy concerns are, if not absent, much less weighty than other times.

A less technical way of looking at the issue was provided by the great American judge, Louis Brandeis (who, along with Justice Holmes, dissented from the Court in its red scare cases). In *Whitney v. California*, Justice Brandeis argued that when considering public order cases, 'if there be *time* to expose through discussion the falsehood and fallacies, to avert the evil by the processes of education, the remedy to be applied is *more speech*, not enforced silence.'[52] Echoing Gandhi's call to let public opinion counter

---

[51] Dworkin (1997: 200); emphasis mine.
[52] 274 U.S. 357, 377 (1927) (concurring opinion of Brandeis J.) (hereinafter *Whitney*); emphasis mine.

subversive speech (while accepting the role of the civil authorities in controlling *actual* disturbances of public order), this statement elegantly combines the proximity test with its normative component. After a point, the proximity between expression and consequence is of such a nature that the basis of the autonomy justification—that persons choose to act one way or another after weighing up the reasons for and against an action—simply does not exist. This is why we may justifiably prosecute the man who shouts 'fire' in a crowded theatre, and the man who incites an excited mob to immediate violence, but may not prosecute the man who writes a journal article calling for the overthrow of the State.

CONCEPTUAL FOUNDATIONS IN *RANGARAJAN* AND *SHAILABALA DEVI*

The lines outlined above will often be blurred, but I hope, at least, to have presented a workable and persuasive model, which justifies the proximity test. *Lohia* represented a step towards this framework, and was affirmed soon afterwards in *Kameshwar Prasad* v. *State of Bihar*, where a rule prohibiting government servants from participating in strikes or demonstrations pertaining to conditions of service, was challenged. Holding that demonstrations (but not strikes) fell within the ambit of Article 19(1)(a), the Court struck down the rule. The State argued that a body of disciplined public servants was essential for the maintenance of public order. If public servants were ill-disciplined, this would have a knock-on effect in ensuring a gradual, overall deterioration of public order. Rejecting this analysis, the Court quoted the *Lohia* test of proximity, and applied the overbreadth framework to hold that 'the vice of the rule…consists in this that it lays a ban on every type of demonstration…however innocent and however incapable of causing a breach of public tranquility and does not confine itself to those forms of demonstrations which might lead to that result'.[53]

---

[53] *Kameshwar Prasad* v *State of Bihar*, AIR 1962 SC 1166, para 20.

One year later, in *O.K. Ghosh* v. *E.X. Joseph*, the Court reiterated that 'a restriction can be said to be in the interests of public order only if the connection between the restriction and the public order is proximate and direct.'[54] However, the next significant development occurred only about thirty years later, in *S. Rangarajan* v. *P. Jagjivan Ram*.[55] This is a case we shall return to in detail when we discuss film censorship. Briefly, *Rangarajan* was about precisely the kind of private bully-censorship that we have discussed before. It involved the revocation, by the Madras High Court, of the 'U' certificate granted to a Tamil film. One of the stated reasons was the 'volatile' reaction that it would receive in Tamil Nadu because of its portrayal of caste and reservations. The reader will note that the facts resemble *Virendra* v. *State of Punjab*. Notwithstanding that, when the revocation was challenged before the Supreme Court, it firmly rejected the argument. It noted that 'the expression of thought should be intrinsically dangerous to the public interests. In other words, the expression should be inseparably locked up with the action contemplated like the equivalent of a *"spark in a powder keg"*.'[56]

It would seem that we have almost come full distance. From a 'tendency' to disturb public order and a justification for prior restraint, over thirty-two years, the Court came around to an 'inseparable' connection, as inevitable as a spark in a powder keg. The spark-in-a-powder-keg analogy is a euphemistic way of getting at the same idea that Gandhi and Justice Brandeis had in mind. The connection is proximate not only in the sense of statistical probability, but in a way that provides no scope for any different outcome that could have come about had the actor (the recipient of the expression) been able to meaningfully exercise her autonomous choice. Seervai seems to

---

[54] AIR 1963 SC 812, para 9. One year earlier, the Supreme Court had echoed *Lohia* in *Dalbir Singh* v. *State of Punjab*, AIR 1962 SC 1106, while nonetheless holding that an act which punished spreading 'disaffection' amongst the police forces did meet the test of proximity. See also *Madhu Limaye* v. *Sub-Divisional Magistrate, Monghyr*, AIR 1971 SC 2486 (hereinafter *Madhu Limaye*), where the Court adopted the same *Lohia* distinction, while upholding the constitutionality of Section 144 of the Code of Criminal Procedure.

[55] (1989) 2 SCC 574: [1989] 2 SCR 204 (hereinafter *Rangarajan*).

[56] *Rangarajan*, para 42; emphasis mine.

suggest something similar when he reads 'spark in a powder keg' to mean words that 'will *of necessity* lead to explosive action which may either threaten the security of the State or public order....'[57] The phrase 'of necessity', with its connotations of inevitability, seems to reflect the Brandeis observation we cited before: 'If there be time to expose through discussion the falsehood and fallacies, to avert the evil by the processes of education, the remedy to be applied is more speech, not enforced silence.'[58]

Before and between *Lohia–Rangarajan,* the Supreme Court had other—although not as conclusive—occasions to examine the public order restriction. Indeed, the judgments in *Ramji Lal Modi* and *Virendra* make no mention of the Court's holding in *State of Bihar* v. *Shailabala Devi,*[59] soon after the First Amendment, in 1952. *Shailabala Devi* concerned Section 4(1)(a) of the 1931 Indian Press Act, which defined objectionable matter to be 'words or signs or visible representations which incite to or encourage, *or tend to incite to or encourage* the commission of any offence of murder or any cognizable offence involving violence'.[60] Under Section 3(3) of the Act, the Government could order the printing press responsible for printing such matter to furnish a security. A pamphlet called 'Sangram', which called for revolution in colourful phrases such as 'break the proud head of the oppressors',[61] was the subject matter of an order for furnishing security. Section 4(1) was challenged. While the Court did not strike down the Section—thus upholding prior restraint *contra Brij Bhushan*—it read it narrowly to hold that the order was invalid, noting that 'rhetoric of this kind might in conceivable circumstances inflame passions as, for example, if addressed to an *excited mob,* but if such exceptional circumstances *exist it was for the State Government to establish the fact'.*[62] In a 'normal' atmosphere, what was written in 'Sangram' was not punishable.

---

57 Seervai (Vol. 2, 2005: 786); emphasis mine.
58 *Whitney,* p. 377 (concurring opinion of Brandeis J.).
59 [1952] 1 SCR 654 (hereinafter *Shailabala Devi*).
60 *Shailabala Devi,* para 6.
61 *Shailabala Devi,* para 28.
62 *Shailabala Devi,* para 14; emphasis mine.

In making context paramount—and more so, in its reference to the excited mob—the Court itself anticipated the conceptual argument that we used to ground the reasoning in *Lohia*. The 'excited mob' is the example, par excellence, of a situation of diminished rationality, where autonomy concerns are not as weighty as they might otherwise be. Unfortunately, however, subsequently in the judgment,[63] as well as in the concurring opinion of Mukherjea J., much of this good work was undone through observations that a more cleverly worded pamphlet could even affect 'reasonable readers' in an adverse way.[64] As we have discussed before, autonomy and responsibility concerns render that fact—even if true—irrelevant. It is the reasonable reader who 'reasonably' weighs up the reasons for and against any action, and then chooses—and assumes responsibility for—her decision. If the reasonable reader, on perusing a pamphlet, is convinced that she had rather be off *that very moment* to engage in violently overthrowing the State, then it is perhaps the State that needs to take a long, hard look in the mirror! In any event, the observation in *Shailabala Devi* concerns a hypothetical case, and it is *Lohia* that—presumably—continues to hold the field.

The *Rangarajan* test—if applied correctly—has some important implications. Foremost among them is a constriction in the scope of prohibitory orders under Section 144 of the Code of Criminal Procedure. The constitutionality of Section 144 was upheld in *Babulal Parate*[65] and *Madhu Limaye*,[66] with the Court stressing that there must be a situation of emergency or urgency for the Magistrate to impose anticipatory, prohibitory orders. *Rangarajan's* requirement of 'spark-in-a-powder-keg' proximity between speech and public disorder implies that Section 144 can be validly applied only in those circumstances where a person, for instance, is about to make an incendiary speech in an already-inflamed situation. In other words, prior restraint under Section 144 cannot be imposed without

---

[63] *Shailabala Devi*, para 17.
[64] *Shailabala Devi*, para 31 (concurring opinion of Mukherjea J.).
[65] *Babulal Parate.*
[66] *Madhu Limaye.*

demonstrating a very close proximity between the prohibitory order, the persons whose freedom it restricts, and the State's goal of maintaining public order.

THE EVOLUTION TOWARDS *BRANDENBURG*

The path that the Court took is strikingly similar to the path of the American Supreme Court, which we briefly described in Chapter Two. The 'tendency to public disorder' test was what the Court used in its now-overruled free speech judgments from the late 1910s and 1920s, such as *Abrams* v. *United States*,[67] *Schenck* v. *United States*,[68] *Gitlow* v. *New York*, and *Whitney* v. *California*. Leftists of various persuasions, anarchists, and anti-war activists were routinely prosecuted and magazines were banned. In a series of cases that are now universally regarded as clearly wrong, the Court upheld the convictions and the bans on the ground of something very similar to the 'bad tendency' test, deferring to the government's judgment as it went along. Justices Holmes and Brandeis' relentless dissents, along with strong criticism from the academy, eventually succeeded in shifting the law to a more speech-protective 'clear and present danger' test. Yet in the Second Red Scare—the McCarthyism of the 1950s—the judges once again upheld the prosecutions and convictions of suspected communists under the Smith Act. In a series of cases which, like their precursors of the 1920s, are now discredited, the Court held that the clear and present danger test required it to take into account the likelihood of the feared consequence coming to pass in consonance with the extent of harm. Here, the extent of harm was so great—the overthrow of the State itself—that even a miniscule possibility of it coming about through the activities of the communists justified their suppression. In *Dennis* v. *United States*,[69] for instance, the accused were not even alleged to have called for specific acts of violence, but that the Communist Party

---

[67] 250 U.S. 616 (1919).
[68] 249 U.S. 47 (1919).
[69] 341 U.S. 494 (1951).

of U.S.'s *general philosophy* was to overthrow government by violence (Karl Marx's *Communist Manifesto* was produced as evidence). Their convictions were upheld by using the 'balancing test' outlined before.[70]

Clear and present danger, thus, proved to be little defence for advocates of unpopular causes in a politically charged climate. Finally, it was in 1969—in *Brandenburg* v. *Ohio*[71]—that the Court moved to its most speech-protective test yet, and one that has stood the test of time. *Brandenburg* limited punishment to speech that is directed at inciting—and likely to incite—'*imminent* lawless action'. In so doing, it held unconstitutional Ohio's criminal syndicalism statute, which had criminalized 'advocacy' of violence. The test of imminence is, evidently, similar to *Lohia's* proximity test. Indeed, in his concurring opinion, Justice Douglas expressly invoked the fire-in-the-crowded theatre analogy, which is not too far, in meaning and effect, from the 'spark in a powder keg' of *Rangarajan*.[72]

The journey of the United States Supreme Court from *Schenck* to *Brandenburg* is thus, in some ways, similar to the journey of our Supreme Court from *Ramji Lal Modi* to *Rangarajan*. And most interestingly, in 2011, a two-judge Bench of the Supreme Court in *Arup Bhuyan*[73] directly incorporated the *Brandenburg* test into Indian free speech law. Reversing the conviction of an individual for his membership in the banned organization, ULFA, the Court distinguished between 'passive' and 'active' membership, before going on to hold:

> In [*Brandenburg* v. *Ohio*] the U.S. Supreme Court...held that mere 'advocacy or teaching the duty, necessity, or propriety' of violence...is not per se illegal. It will become illegal only if it incites to imminent lawless action. *We respectfully agree with the above decisions, and are of the opinion that they apply to India too, as our fundamental rights are similar to the Bill of Rights in the U.S. Constitution.*[74]

---

[70] *See* Chapter Two.

[71] 395 U.S. 444 (1969) (hereinafter *Brandenberg*).

[72] *Brandenburg* (concurring opinion of Douglas J.)

[73] *Arup Bhuyan* v. *State of Assam*, (2011) 3 SCC 377 (hereinafter *Arup Bhuyan*).

[74] *Arup Bhuyan*, paras 13–15; emphasis mine.

At the heart of the *Brandenburg* test is a crucial distinction between *advocacy* and *incitement*. The distinction lies in the proximity, or imminence, between speech and consequence (which is not the same as a statistical likelihood). The ultimate justification—as we have discussed before—is grounded in concerns about individual autonomy and responsibility. The *Ramji Lal Modi* line of cases fall within the advocacy standard because they punish a person purely for the *content* of what that person says. The *Lohia* line of cases, ending with *Arup Bhuyan*, in adopting *Brandenburg*, adopt an incitement standard. Incitement, following *Brandenburg*, is autonomy-respecting, because it is limited to situations where (as Justice Brandeis pointed out) there is no opportunity for counter-speech, or where the audience is operating under conditions of diminished autonomy.

With the size and complexity of the Indian Supreme Court, *stare decisis*—or precedent—is a fragile thing at the best of times. It is unclear whether *Arup Bhuyan* and its incorporation of the *Brandenburg* test will go on to become an established part of the Indian Constitutional landscape. At the very least, though, in *Romesh Thappar, Lohia, Rangarajan*, and *Arup Bhuyan*, we have—over four generations of the Court—a line of outstanding cases that are both philosophically and legally sound, and in their outcomes, worthy of a great civil liberties tradition.

VOICES FROM ABROAD

Jurisdictions around the world have had to deal with broadly worded speech-restricting statutes which—according to the government—are necessary to maintain public order. *Hector* v. *Attorney-General*,[75] a case decided by the Privy Council on appeal from Antigua and Barbuda, is particularly important because Antigua's public order restrictions follow the exact wording of Article 19(2). At issue was Section 33B of Antigua's Public Order Act, which criminalized false statements 'likely to cause fear or alarm in or to the public or to disturb

---

[75] [1990] 2 AC 312 (hereinafter *Hector*).

the public peace, or to undermine public confidence in the conduct of public affairs'.[76] Antigua argued that 'in the interests of' included statements that had the tendency to eventually cause public disorder, and the State was entitled to step in at that 'early stage', to prevent future harmful consequences.

The argument echoes *Ramji Lal Modi*, and indeed, Antigua cited that very case in support![77] The Privy Council, however, declined to follow that line of reasoning and, instead, undertook an overbreadth analysis along the lines of *Romesh Thappar* and *Brij Bhushan*. Lord Bridge, writing for the Council, noted that if 'a particular false statement although likely to undermine public confidence in the conduct of public affairs is not likely to disturb public order, a law which makes it a criminal offence cannot be reasonably required in the interests of public order by reference *to the remote and improbable consequences that it may possibly do so'*.[78] Like in *Lohia*, the Court insisted that reasonableness required proximity between speech and consequence. It found that the proximity requirement was not satisfied through arguing that undermining the public confidence in the conduct of public affairs could *potentially* lead to breaches of public order.

Similar issues arose before the South African Constitutional Court in *Islamic Unity Convention* v. *The Independent Broadcasting Authority*,[79] which we briefly discussed in Chapter Two. South Africa's free speech clause explicitly withholds protection from 'advocacy of hatred that is based on race, ethnicity, gender or religion, and constitutes incitement to cause harm'.[80] Section 2(a) of the Code of Conduct for Broadcasting Services prohibited broadcasting material 'likely to prejudice...relations between sections of the population'.[81] The constitutionality of the Section was challenged, and the government

---

[76] *Hector*, p. 316.
[77] *Hector*, p. 315.
[78] *Hector*, p. 319; emphasis mine.
[79] 2002 (5) BCLR 433 (CC) (hereinafter *Islamic Unity Convention*).
[80] Section 16(2)(c), Constitution of South Africa.
[81] *Islamic Unity Convention*, para 2.

defended it by arguing that it was justified under Section 16(2) of the Constitution. Rejecting the argument on grounds of overbreadth, the Constitutional Court held that

> expression that makes propaganda for war (Section 16(2)(a)) may, depending on the circumstances, threaten relations between sections of the population, or produce a situation where these are likely to be prejudiced. *The converse is however not true.* Not every expression or speech that is likely to prejudice relations between sections of the population would be 'propaganda for war', or 'incitement of imminent violence' or 'advocacy of hatred'...*that also 'constitutes incitement to cause harm'.* *There may well be instances where the prohibition in clause 2(a) coincides with what is excluded from the protection of the right.*[82]

A narrow reading of the public order restriction has been preferred by the European Court of Human Rights as well. In a series of cases involving criminal prosecutions in Turkey,[83] the Court has repeatedly distinguished between speech that is hostile to the government and speech that incites violence or hatred. In fact, in *Karkin* v. *Turkey,* the fact that the impugned incendiary speech was made in a peaceful area, and far away from any 'conflict zone' played a decisive role— once again emphasizing, on the lines of *Brandenburg,* the importance of background context in any public order enquiry.[84]

OTHER LAWS

Speech-restricting provisions are scattered throughout different statutes. Earlier in this chapter, we discussed Section 295A of the Indian Penal Code in *Ramji Lal Modi*'s case, which criminalizes insulting

---

[82] *Islamic Unity Convention,* para 36; emphasis mine.

[83] *Seher Karatas* v. *Turkey,* (no. 33179/96), judgment of 9 July 2002; *Karkin* v. *Turkey,* Application no. 43928/98, judgment of 23 September 2003 (hereinafter *Karkin*); *Kizilyaprak* v. *Turkey,* Application no. 27528/95, judgment of 2 October 2003; *Abdullah Aydin* v. *Turkey,* Application no. 42435/98, judgment of 9 March 2004.

[84] *Karkin.*

religions and religious beliefs. In *Ramji Lal Modi*, the constitutionality of this provision was upheld on 19(2) public order grounds. Consider also Section 153A of the Indian Penal Code, which criminalizes promoting 'disharmony', 'enmity', 'ill-will', or 'hatred' between different religious groups, castes, communities, and so on,[85] or Section 153B, which punishes imputations or assertions that a certain class of people cannot be faithful to country and Constitution, or ought to be deprived of their rights.[86] In a similar vein, Section 123(2)(a)(ii) of the Representation of the People Act defines as a corrupt electoral practice 'induc[ing] or attempt[ing] to induce a candidate or an elector to believe that he, or any person in whom he is interested, will become or will be rendered an object of divine displeasure or spiritual censure'.[87] Section 508 of the Indian Penal Code extends this to using the threat of divine displeasure in causing or attempting to cause a person to commit any act that he is not legally bound to do, or to omit doing anything he is legally entitled to do.[88] Section 66A of the Information Technology Act criminalizes speech of a 'menacing' or 'offensive' character.[89] The Scheduled Castes and Scheduled Tribes (Prevention of Atrocities) Act criminalizes 'intentionally insulting' or 'intimidating, with intent to humiliate' any Scheduled Caste/Scheduled Tribe person.[90] And the Unlawful Activities Prevention Act criminalizes participation even in *meetings* of associations that have been declared unlawful.[91]

Quite evidently, these are all free speech restrictions, and must be justified—and interpreted—in light of Article 19(2). One plausible justification is public order. Hatred between different groups, offensive speech, and caste-based insults certainly bear some relationship

---

[85] Section 153A, Indian Penal Code, 1860.

[86] Section 153B, Indian Penal Code, 1860.

[87] Section 123(2)(a)(ii), Representation of the People Act, 1951.

[88] Section 508, Indian Penal Code, 1860.

[89] Section 66A, Information Technology Act, 2000.

[90] Section 3(1)(x), Scheduled Castes and Scheduled Tribes (Prevention of Atrocities) Act, 1989.

[91] Section 10, Unlawful Activities Prevention Act, 1967.

with maintaining public order and public tranquility.[92] For example, in *Manzar Sayeed Khan* v. *State of Maharashtra*—a case about James Laine's academic book on Shivaji, which infuriated people enough for them to vandalize the Bhandarkar institute—the Supreme Court made it clear that 'the intention to cause disorder or incite the people to violence is the sine qua non of the offence under Section 153A of IPC.'[93] Similarly, when in *Chandanmal Chopra* v. *State of West Bengal*, the Koran was memorably impugned under Section 153A, the Calcutta High Court responded by observing that 'because of the Koran no public tranquility has been disturbed up to now and there is no reason to apprehend any likelihood of such disturbance in future.'[94]

If public order is the relevant 19(2) restriction at stake, then two options are available to us. One is to accept the logic of *Ramji Lal Modi*—that the phrase 'in the interests of' is of wide and compendious meaning. In that case, there is nothing more to be said. All these provisions are constitutionally valid because they clearly have *some* nexus to public order.

There are many reasons, however, why we should *not* accept the logic of *Ramji Lal Modi*. It ignores the reasonableness prong of Article 19(2), and the requirement of proportionality laid down in *V.G. Row*.[95] Doctrinally, there is an alternative line of argument, represented by *Lohia* and beyond. Philosophically, we have argued that this interpretation respects individual autonomy better. And perhaps most importantly, at a pragmatic level, it is the lack of any determinable standards that go with a wide and compendious understanding of 'in the interests of' that permits the well-documented abuse of Section 144 of the Code of Criminal Procedure, Section 153A of the Indian Penal Code, Section 66A of the Information Technology Act,

---

[92] The case of the Representation of the People Act is slightly more difficult to fit within this heading; perhaps unsurprisingly, constitutional challenges to the Representation of the People Act on free speech grounds have been rejected under other heads, as we shall shortly see.

[93] (2007) 5 SCC 1, para 11.

[94] AIR 1986 Cal 104, para 37.

[95] *State of Madras* v. *V.G. Row*, AIR 1952 SC 196.

and the like. The wordings of these provisions are vague, and open to boundless expansion, without any analytical constraints. The *Ramji Lal Modi* standard simply vests far too much power and discretion in implementation at the local level, thus permitting and authorizing the erosion of a meaningful right to free speech and expression.

If, on the other hand, we accept *Lohia* and its progeny as laying down the correct test of public order, it is immediately evident that all the statutes under consideration are overbroad. It should be obvious, beyond cavil, that disharmony between classes, or offensive speech, or insult and intimidation, are all undesirable things, but they do not have a 'spark-in-the-powder-keg' relationship with public order.

Having established these alternatives, there is little more to discuss about these provisions, as far as public order is concerned. On one interpretation, they are obviously constitutional. On the other, there are strong arguments to suggest that they are unconstitutional—or, at the very least, their scope must be drastically curtailed, and limited to the 'spark-in-the-powder-keg' situations that *Rangarajan* contemplates.

But are these cases about public order at all? As Siddharth Narrain points out, Indian cases on 'hate speech' cleave along two distinct lines: speech that could incite violence (that is, speech that is a threat to public order), but also speech that could 'harm' its listeners by causing hurt or emotional distress.[96] Furthermore, in his assessment of the Andhra Pradesh High Court's opinion in *N. Veerabrahmam* v. *State of Andhra Pradesh*,[97] where a majority of the Court upheld a ban on a 'rationalist critique' of the Bible (which, among other things, questioned Christ's legitimacy and challenged the Bible's divine origins), Pratap Bhanu Mehta points to the absence of any analysis on the part of the Court *actually* demonstrating an existing threat to public order.[98] Although the Court did pay lip-service to the ideal of public order, the judgment itself focused on the

---

[96] Narrain (2014: 7).
[97] AIR 1959 AP 572 (hereinafter *Veerabrahmam*).
[98] Mehta (2009: 311).

argument that 'no citizen could claim a right to insult the religion or religious beliefs of another section of the population. The right which one citizen claims should be consistent with *the rights of the other citizens.*'[99] The idea of balancing the rights of citizens is particularly interesting, and provides an ideal segue into an alternative line of argument.

This is because public order, of course, does not, limit the 19(1)(a) enquiry. Article 19(2) also permits reasonable restrictions in the interests of 'decency and morality', and this is where the Andhra Pradesh High Court's reference to the rights of others bears particular resonance. If we examine the justifications for prohibiting hate speech, criminalizing holocaust denial, and for other similar speech-restricting laws in Canada, Europe, and South Africa, we find that more often than not, arguments are couched in the language of moral principle, and focused on a balancing of rights. In the next part of this book, I will argue that many of the provisions we have discussed before, along with anti-pornography and obscenity laws, are best understood, interpreted, and—importantly—limited, through a particular reading of the 'decency and morality' clause (as opposed to public order exceptions).

It must be noticed, however, that the highly controversial anti-terror legislation, the Unlawful Activities Prevention Act, bears a quite different logic. The Unlawful Activities Prevention Act was first enacted in 1967, following the Sixteenth Amendment (and has recently been amended after the repeal of the Prevention of Terrorism Act and the Terrorist and Disruptive Activities (Prevention) Act). Recall that by virtue of the Sixteenth Amendment, the term 'sovereignty and integrity of India' was added to the list of permissible grounds for imposition of reasonable restrictions under Article 19(2). Pursuant to this, the Unlawful Activities Prevention Act defines an 'unlawful activity' as, inter alia, 'support[ing] any claim, to bring about, on any ground whatsoever, the cession of a part of the territory of India or the secession of a part of the territory of India from the Union, or [which]

---

[99] *Veerabrahmam*, para 8; emphasis mine.

disclaims, questions, disrupts or is intended to disrupt the sovereignty and territorial integrity of India'.[100]

During the debates over the First Amendment, Shyama Prasad Mookerjee asked: 'If I hold that this Partition [of India, in 1947] has been a mistake and has to be annulled some day or the other, why should I not have the right to agitate for it?'[101] This seems a rather basic point. The nation and its borders are not possessed of sacred qualities that allow the State to insulate them from public debate, criticism, or questioning. But the Unlawful Activities Prevention Act does so with almost breathtaking casualness.

Admittedly, 19(2) allows reasonable restrictions upon the freedom of speech, in the interests of the integrity of India. The Unlawful Activities Prevention Act, however, seems to have dispensed with the need for 'reasonableness' altogether. Under the striking breadth of its provisions, there is no requirement of proximity between the offending speech and damage to the integrity of India. Instead, it penalizes even 'disclaiming' or 'questioning' India's territorial integrity, torn from any manner of context. Even if we are to import the broad understanding of *Ramji Lal Modi*, and only require the government to demonstrate some kind of link between speech and consequence, it seems clear that penalizing *any* questioning of territorial integrity, in any form or forum, penalizes speech *purely* for its content, and must surely fail constitutional scrutiny.

Arup Bhuyan's distinction between active and passive membership in unlawful organizations, which was made in the context of the now-lapsed Terrorist and Disruptive Activities (Prevention) Act, assumes great importance in the context of the Unlawful Activities Prevention Act. Section 3(5) of the Terrorist and Disruptive Activities (Prevention) Act, which was at issue in *Arup Bhuyan*, criminalized membership of a 'terrorist gang or a terrorist organisation'.[102] To save it from unconstitutionality on the touchstone of Articles 19(1)(a), (c),

---

[100] Section 2(o), Unlawful Activities Prevention Act, 1967.
[101] Menon (2004: 1817).
[102] Section 3(5), Terrorist and Disruptive Activities (Prevention) Act, 1987.

and 21 grounds, Justice Katju read down Section 3(5) to refer only to *active membership*—that is, to a person who 'resorts to violence or incites people to violence or creates public disorder by violence or incitement to violence'.[103]

Section 10 of the Unlawful Activities Prevention Act deals with membership of associations declared unlawful under the Act. While various sub-clauses of Section 10 delineate aspects of *active* membership, such as soliciting funds or assisting operations, Section 10(a)(i) criminalizes membership *simpliciter*, like the Terrorist and Disruptive Activities (Prevention) Act did.[104] The logic of Justice Katju's reasoning in *Arup Bhuyan* applies squarely to Section 10 of the Unlawful Activities Prevention Act: 'membership' must be narrowly construed to be *active* membership which, in turn, must bear a proximate nexus with disorder and violence.

ADDENDUM: A NOTE ON THE GOONDA ACTS

On 4 August 2014, the *Bangalore Mirror* carried a report excoriating the Karnataka state government for amending its 'Goonda Act', and bringing in offences under the Copyright Act and the Information Technology Act within its ambit.[105] As the *Mirror* reported:

> If you are planning a digital 'offence'—which could be an innocuous opinion like the young girls' in Mumbai after the bandh declared on Bal Thackeray's death—that could attract the provisions of the Information Technology Act. You can even be taken into preventive custody like a 'goonda'. Even those given exceptions under the Indian Copyright Act can find themselves in jail for a year without being presented before a magistrate. Technically, if you are even planning to forward 'lascivious' memes and images to a WhatsApp group or forwarding a song or 'copyrighted' PDF book, you can be punished under the Goondas Act.[106]

---

[103] *Arup Bhuyan*, para 12. See also *State of Kerala* v. *Raneef*, 2011 (1) SCALE 8.

[104] S. 10(a)(i), Unlawful Activities Prevention Act, 1967.

[105] Prasad (2014).

[106] Prasad (2014).

The Goonda Act is one of those colonial oddities that anachronistically lives on in independent, democratic India. It was first enacted in 1923, by the colonial government, in Bengal, ostensibly to control petty and habitual offenders (although, as Kalyani Ramnath argues, it was used to target political activity).[107] It now exists in nine Indian states.[108]

Let us take a closer look at Karnataka's Goonda Act (or, the Karnataka Prevention of Dangerous Activities of Bootleggers, Drug-offenders, Gamblers, Goondas, Immoral Traffic Offenders, Slum Grabbers and Video or Audio Pirates Act, as it was before the amendment). The Goonda Act is ostensibly a public order legislation. Subject to confirmation by an Advisory Board within three weeks, it allows the government to detain a person for up to one year to '*prevent him from acting in any manner prejudicial to the maintenance of public order*'.[109] A goonda is deemed to be acting in any manner prejudicial to the maintenance of public order 'when he is engaged, or *is making preparations for engaging*, in any of his activities as a goonda which affect adversely or are likely to affect adversely the maintenance of public order'.[110] 'Goonda activities' include offences under Sections 153A and 295A of the Indian Penal Code, both of which are speech-restricting provisions. Under the July 2014 amendments, more speech-restricting provisions, such as parts of the Copyright Act and Section 67 of the Information Technology Act—which proscribes publishing 'any material which is lascivious or appeals to the prurient interest'[111]—have been brought within the ambit of this legislation.

Preventive detention finds a separate place in Part III of the Constitution, regulated by Article 22.[112] In *Ram Singh* v. *State of Delhi*,[113] the Supreme Court held that because Articles 19, 21, and 22 were separate codes, dealing with separate freedoms, a preventive

---

107 Ramnath (n.d.).
108 Chari (2014).
109 Section 13, Karnataka Act 12 of 1985.
110 Section 2(iv), Karnataka Act 12 of 1985; emphasis mine.
111 Section 67, Information Technology Act, 2000.
112 Article 22, Constitution of India.
113 AIR 1951 SC 270.

detention order could not be challenged under Article 19(1)(a) *even though* the order was made specifically to prevent the appellants (members of the Hindu Mahasabha) from making speeches allegedly prejudicial to public order. In other words, the executive could bypass Article 19(1)(a) and prevent individuals from speaking by simply preventively detaining them, as long as the procedural requirements of Article 22 were satisfied.[114] The judgment in *Ram Singh* followed *A.K. Gopalan* v. *State of Madras*, which propounded the position that Articles 14, 19, and 21/22 were complete and separate codes, and would be interpreted only on their own terms.[115] However, *A.K. Gopalan* was famously overruled in *Maneka Gandhi* v. *Union of India*[116] (via *R.C. Cooper* v. *Union of India*),[117] and the constitutional position now is that executive action must be subject to Articles 14, 19, and 21 if it directly impacts the exercise of those fundamental rights. Consequently, at the very least, executive action—that is, preventive detention orders—under the Goonda Act must survive Article 19(1)(a) scrutiny. Furthermore, in *A.K. Roy* v. *Union of India*, the Supreme Court subjected the preventive detention provisions under the National Security Act to Article 21 scrutiny, noting that 'the fundamental rights conferred by the different Articles of Part III of the Constitution are not mutually exclusive and that therefore *a law* of preventive detention which falls within Article 22 must also meet the requirements of Articles 14, 19 and 21'.[118] Therefore, it is not simply executive action under the Goonda Act, but the legal provisions themselves, that must pass constitutional muster under Article 19(1)(a).

[114] For a critique of this position, see Grossman (1956–57). Grossman predicted that this position might well be overturned in the course of time.

[115] *A.K. Gopalan* v. *State of Madras*, AIR 1950 SC 27.

[116] AIR 1978 SC 597.

[117] AIR 1970 SC 564 (this is known as the Bank Nationalization case).

[118] AIR 1982 SC 710, para 75; emphasis mine. Throughout its history, the Court has regularly upheld preventive detention laws. The argument that preventive detention laws that directly curtail *speech* need to be separately judged under Article 19(1)(a) has not yet been considered. For an example, see *Haradhan Saha* v. *State of West Bengal*, AIR 1974 SC 2154.

Let us, therefore, examine the speech-restricting provisions of the Goonda Act within the framework of Article 19(1)(a)'s public order jurisprudence. It is difficult to imagine what conceivable relation the Copyright Act and 'lascivious material' have with public order, even under *Ramji Lal Modi's* generous understanding of Article 19(2). In any case, the Act permits the government to *preventively detain persons* whom it suspects *might be making preparations* for engaging in speech that *could* constitute an offence under the Indian Penal Code, the Information Technology Act, or copyright law. Preventive detention, when applied to speech and expression, is an example par excellence of prior restraint. And unlike *Virendra's* case (or *Babulal Parate*), where the prior restraint was imposed in a (supposedly) volatile situation, limited to a specific topic in a specific magazine, and *upheld by the Court on that ground*, the Goonda Act imposes prior restraint across the board.

Prior restraint—as we discussed earlier in this chapter, and will discuss again subsequently—is considered to be one of the most serious infringements of the right to freedom of speech and expression. It vests censorial power in the hands of a non-judicial, administrative body. Unlike subsequent punishment for speech, prior restraint chokes off the marketplace of ideas at its very source. Instead of requiring the government to justify why it wishes to regulate or restrict speech, it places the burden of going to court and having the prior restraint lifted, upon the *speaker*, who wishes to exercise her constitutional rights. Prior restraint—as we have seen—was considered an anathema even in eighteenth-century England, which was not exactly known for its protection of the freedom of speech and expression.

Under the *Lohia* test of public order, it is clear that, insofar as they encompass speech-restricting provisions such as 295A and 153A of the Indian Penal Code, and Section 67 of the Information Technology Act, the Goonda Acts are unconstitutional. Even under the expanded version, however, the result is arguably the same. A *general* prior restraint was held unconstitutional in *Romesh Thappar* and *Brij Bhushan*, a position that need not necessarily have been overturned by the First Amendment, which only effected a change in the substantive part of Article 19(2). As discussed here, although *Virendra* did uphold prior restraint, it was in very specific circumstances, and *Babulal Parate*, another case that upheld prior restraint, specifically limited it to cases of emergencies. Even after *Virendra* and *Babulal Parate*, general prior restraints have been held unconstitutional in cases such as *R. Rajagopal v. State of Tamil Nadu*.[119] The prior restraints under the Goonda Acts—preventive detention for one year—are particularly severe, and cut at the very heart of our free speech guarantee. They ought to be struck down.

[119] (1994) 6 SCC 632.

CHAPTER FOUR

Sedition

. . . .

The law of sedition has gained a special degree of notoriety in recent times. Section 124A of the Indian Penal Code punishes anyone who 'brings or attempts to bring into hatred or contempt, or excites or attempts to excite disaffection towards, the Government established by law in India',[1] even though she might do so by speech, and speech alone. In the last few years, sedition charges (or arrests for sedition) have been made against Arundhati Roy[2] (voicing her support for an independent Kashmir), Binayak Sen[3] (for allegedly possessing Maoist literature), a Bombay cartoonist called Aseem Trivedi[4] (for an ill-advised parody), and—perhaps most egregiously—against villagers protesting a nuclear power plant in Kerala.[5] One would think that dissenting from a politically dominant narrative (Roy and Sen), mocking the powerful (Trivedi), and voicing peaceful opposition to a large-scale energy project by those most affected (the Kerala villagers) are activities that are central to the democratic project. It is the presence of non-violent,

---

[1] Section 124A, Indian Penal Code, 1860. For a detailed, early account, see Donogh (1911). See also Sastri (1964).

[2] PTI (2010).

[3] Jebaraj (2011).

[4] *The Hindu* (2012).

[5] Sudhakar and Vijay Kumar (2012).

oppositional, minority voices that accords legitimacy to democracy. But if that is true, then what is a provision that permits criminalizing, prosecuting, and harassing such voices still doing in our Penal Code, almost seventy years after we became a democratic republic?

To understand why this is so, it is important to understand the history of Indian sedition law. That history begins in the colonial epoch.

SEDITION IN THE COLONIAL ERA

The crime of sedition was originally conceptualized in monarchical England to insulate the King, and a largely unelected parliament, from public criticism. In 1704, Chief Justice Holt explained that 'if people should not be called to account for possessing an *ill opinion* of the government, no government can subsist. For it is necessary for all governments that people should have a *good opinion* of it'.[6] Consequently, unlike cases of ordinary defamation, 'truth' was not considered a defence. In fact, the greater the truth, the more harm it was likely to cause to the reputation of the government, the preservation of which—whether deserved or undeserved—was treated as the ultimate end.

With India serving as a laboratory for British legislators, it is unsurprising that sedition also found a way into our criminal law. Most of the ills of our Penal Code are commonly attributed to Macaulay, that doyen of Victorian moralizing and crude orientalism. Interestingly however, the sedition provision, while present in an early draft Bill, was absent from Macaulay's final version of the Code. It was inserted in 1870, at the instance of James Fitzjames Stephen (who also drafted the Indian Evidence Act), as a response to the rising Wahabi political movement.[7] Section 124A read:

> Whoever excites…or attempts to excite feelings of disaffection…to the Government…shall be punishable with transportation for life.[8]

---

[6] *Rex* v. *Tutchin*, 90 Eng. Rep. 1133, Holt 424 (Q.B. 1704); emphasis mine.
[7] Narrain (2011).
[8] For a history, see Ganachari (2009: 97).

Following this, a proviso stated that 'disapprobation of the measures of the Government as is compatible with a disposition to render obedience to the lawful authority of the Government' remains lawful.

The meaning of 'disaffection' (as opposed to 'disapprobation') was clarified by Petheram C.J. at the Calcutta High Court, in *Queen-Empress* v. *Jogendra Chunder Bose and Ors.*[9] As the editor of the magazine *Bangobasi*, Bose was prosecuted for an article that was highly critical of the Age of Consent Bill. The article accused the British of 'forced Europeanisation', while nonetheless disavowing open rebellion, on the ground that Hindus were incapable of it. Nevertheless, it was argued that the piece was aimed at stirring up thoughts of rebellion. Petheram C.J. instructed the jury on the meaning of 'disaffection', and his observations deserve to be quoted in full:

> Disaffection means a feeling contrary to affection, in other words, dislike or hatred. Disapprobation means simply disapproval. It is quite possible to disapprove of a man's sentiments or action and yet to like him. If a person uses either spoken or written words *calculated to create in the minds of the persons to whom they are addressed a disposition not to obey lawful authority of the Government, or to subvert or resist that authority,* if and when occasion should arise, and if he does so with the *intention of creating such a disposition* in his hearers or readers, he will be guilty of the offence of attempting to excite disaffection within the meaning of the section, *though no disturbance is brought about by his words or any feeling of disaffection, in fact, produced by them.*[10]

We may note some important aspects of this formulation. First, 'disaffection'—in order to separate it from (legitimate) 'disapprobation'—is defined as 'dislike or hatred' which, in turn, is connected with *disobedience* (of the government). Second, there is no need to demonstrate actual harm. All that matters is that the speaker (or writer, or publisher) *intends* to create a *disposition* in the minds of others to disobey or resist the government, and that the words be *calculated* to create that disposition. At first blush, the offence appears to consist of

---

[9] (1892) ILR 19 Cal 35 (hereinafter *Jogendra Chunder Bose*).

[10] *Jogendra Chunder Bose*, para 13; emphasis mine.

two components: subjective (that the author intend...) and objective (that the words be calculated to...). However, on closer scrutiny, the distinction dissolves. Intention, as Petheram C.J. pointed out, was to be gleaned from the words themselves—that is, from the objective import of what is spoken or written.

Justice Petheram's interpretation survived all of six years. In 1897, Bal Gangadhar Tilak was brought to court in the first of his sedition trials. The accusations turned upon his delivering lectures and singing patriotic songs at the Shivaji Coronation Ceremony. To get around the fact that Tilak's speeches made no mention of overthrowing (or otherwise disobeying) the government or the law, Justice Strachey widened the scope of Section 124A. If any writing was found to be 'attributing to [the government] every sort of evil and misfortune suffered by the people, *or dwelling on its foreign origin* and character, or imputing to it base motives, or accusing it of hostility or *indifference to the welfare* of the people...',[11] the writer had committed the offence of sedition. Gone was Justice Petheram's stress on 'disobedience'. Under Strachey J.'s formulation, one did not need to even attempt to excite rebellion or disturbance—all that was needed was an attempt to excite '*feelings* of enmity'. And a few months after *Tilak's* case, a full Bench of the Bombay High Court, in the Pratod Case, expanded the definition of 'disaffection' yet further, by implying it to mean 'alienation from [one's] allegiance'.[12] Under this version, what was effectively criminalized was any attempt to persuade Indians *not* to love their British rulers. Not until the passage of the Unlawful Activities Prevention Act in 1967 have we come so close to a law of thought-crimes.

The Tilak and Pratod prosecutions led to an amendment to Section 124A, specifically designed to counter the defence's arguments in those cases by codifying the Bombay judgments. The words 'hatred' and 'contempt' were added alongside 'disaffection'. An explanation was inserted that expressly defined 'disaffection' as including 'disloyalty...and all feelings of enmity'. And through the same amendment,

---

[11] *Queen-Empress* v. *Bal Gangadhar Tilak*, (1897) ILR 22 Bom 112, p. 151; emphasis mine.

[12] *Queen-Empress* v. *Ramchandra Narayan*, (1897) ILR 22 Bom 152.

Section 153A was also added to the Penal Code. Under these two new provisions, nationalist newspapers were pursued relentlessly.

Tilak was brought back to court in 1908, when British repression—following the partition of Bengal—was at its height. In the aftermath of a bomb attack in Muzaffarpur, the Tilak-edited magazine, *Kesari*, published articles strongly critical of the repression that was breeding acts of violence against the government. Tilak was found guilty by the jury, and Davar J. emphasized one part of Strachey J.'s gloss on Section 124A: nobody, he held, was permitted to 'attribute dishonest or immoral motives to Government'.[13] This language appears to dissolve the original distinction between 'disaffection' and 'disapprobation'. Presumably, it is possible to attribute immoral motives to government while remaining entirely loyal towards it—which was the point of the sedition law when it was first drafted, and interpreted by Petheram C.J. Under this framework, in 1927, Satyaranjan Bakshi was convicted for alleging that the British were pursuing policies of divide and rule. It was observed that nobody could '[attribute] base, improper or dishonest motives to those who carry on the work of the government of the country'.[14] Similarly, in *In Re Pothan Joseph* (which was a case that arose under the Press Act, bearing a similar—although, even narrower—definition of sedition), confiscation of deposits was upheld when an editor wrote an article alleging that the local government was misusing and abusing its powers.[15]

Nor did resort to allegory and myth-making do any good. In 1910, Ganesh Damodar Savarkar was convicted for publishing a series of allegorical poems, Chandavarkar J. remarking that,

> no doubt the writer has used several words, each having a double meaning, but that meaning only serves to emphasise the fact that the writer's main object is to preach war against the present Government, in the names of certain gods of the Hindus and certain warriors such as Shivaji.

[13] *Emperor* v. *Bal Gangadhar Tilak*, (1908) 10 Bom LR 848, para 2.

[14] *Satyaranjan Bakshi* v. *King-Emperor*, AIR 1927 Cal 698, para 10; for a rare case that held in the opposite direction, *see Kamal Krishna Sircar* v. *Emperor*, AIR 1935 Cal 636.

[15] (1932) 34 Bom LR 917.

Those names are mere pretexts for the text which is: 'Take up the sword and destroy the Government because it is foreign and oppressive.'[16]

In 1942, however, this relentless fifty-year expansion of the sedition law was brought to an abrupt halt by Sir Maurice Gwyer, writing for the Federal Court in *Niharendu Dutt Majumdar* v. *King Emperor*. In that case, departing from the existing line of precedent, and turning instead to English law, it was held that 'public disorder or the reasonable anticipation or likelihood of public disorder, is thus the gist of the offence. The acts or words complained of must either incite to disorder or must be such as to satisfy reasonable men that that is their intention or tendency.'[17] Suddenly, sedition was no longer about alienation of allegiances, imputation of base and immoral motives to the government, or feelings of enmity: the test had been radically altered to inciting disorder, or intending to do so. Expectedly, this state of affairs did not last long. In the last major decision before the new Constitution, the Privy Council, in *King-Emperor* v. *Sadashiv Narayan Bhalerao*, overruled Sir Maurice Gwyer's opinion, and restored Strachey's test.

THE CONSTITUENT ASSEMBLY AND THE EARLY CASES

This brief overview should make a few things clear. Section 124A was used almost exclusively by the British to contain and repress the freedom struggle. Nationalist politicians (such as Gandhi, Tilak, and Annie Besant), editors, and journalists were its most frequent targets. In addition, as the Ganesh Savarkar prosecution demonstrates, it was used not only in the domain of politics, but in that of culture as well. The force of the law was turned against attempted resistance *through* the means of culture. For instance, Aravind Ganachari lists thirty-nine dramas that were prosecuted for dissemination of sedition, as well as readings of *kirtan*s and the *Puranas*.[18]

With this ignominious history, one might have expected that consigning the sedition law to the dustbin of history would have been on

---

[16] *Emperor* v. *Ganesh Damodar Savarkar*, (1910) 12 Bom LR 105, para 5.
[17] *Niharendu Dutt Majumdar* v. *King-Emperor*, 1942 F.C.R. 38, para 16.
[18] Ganachari (2009: 106).

or near the top of the Constituent Assembly's priority list. Nonetheless, the Fundamental Rights Sub-Committee—comprising, for the most part, of veterans of the freedom movement, and chaired by Sardar Patel—in its first draft of a bill of rights, *expressly included sedition as a ground for restricting free speech*. When the draft came up for debate on 29 April 1947, it was trenchantly criticized by Somnath Lahiri. Did Patel, he asked sarcastically, think that the incoming, popularly elected government needed even *more* powers than the autocratic and alien British did, to protect itself?[19] Lahiri also warned—presciently enough—that sedition would be used to crush political dissent, as it had been used in colonial times. The next day, however, Patel himself moved for the deletion of the seditious speech proviso—only for it to make a reappearance in the Draft Constitution of 1948. Once again, there was strenuous opposition. Sardar Hukum Singh specifically pointed to the similarities with the Press Act, which we have discussed in the previous chapter, and warned about the scope of repression that blanket immunity for sedition law could provide an intolerant government[20] (recall that at this time, the free speech restrictions were not qualified by the word 'reasonable'). In the teeth of much resistance, the sedition proviso was withdrawn once more. The strength of feeling against this colonial provision is perhaps best illustrated in this anecdote, courtesy Seth Govind Das:

My great grandfather had been awarded a gold waist-band inlaid with diamonds. The British Government awarded it to him for helping it in 1857 and the words 'In recognition of his services during the Mutiny in 1857' were engraved on it. In the course of my speech during the Satyagraha movement of 1930, I said that my great-grandfather got this waist-band for helping the alien government and that he had committed a sin by doing so and that I wanted to have engraved on it that the sin committed by my great-grandfather in helping to keep such a government in existence had been expiated by the great-grandson by seeking to uproot it. For this I was prosecuted under section 124A and sentenced to two

[19] Speech of Somnath Lahiri, 29 April 1947, Indian Constituent Assembly (Vol. III).

[20] Speech of Sardar Hukum Singh, 1 December 1948, Indian Constituent Assembly (Vol. VII).

years' rigorous imprisonment. I mean to say that there must be many Members of this House who must have been sentenced under this article to undergo long periods of imprisonment. It is a matter of pleasure that we will now have freedom of speech and expression under this subclause and the word 'sedition' is also going to disappear.[21]

What are we to make of the Constituent Assembly's decision to consciously withdraw the word 'sedition' from its list of permissible restrictions upon free speech? Shibban Lal Saksena, for one, clearly felt that *only* laws relating to the remaining categories (morality, undermining the foundation of the State, defamation, and others) 'will remain on the *statute book*'.[22] Ananthasayaman Ayyangar provided the theoretical rationale, which was directly grounded in the shift from a colonial regime to one based upon principles of *self-government*: it was the fundamental right of citizens to non-violently overthrow an entrenched government by exposing its faults and persuading each other that it ought to be removed. Consequently, unless it rose to the level of 'the entire state itself [being] sought to be overthrown or undermined by force or otherwise, leading to public disorder...any attack on the government itself ought not to be made an offence under the law'.[23]

It therefore seems clear that in terms of the free speech clause that came into being with the Constitution, sedition was inconsistent with it.[24] The Constituent Assembly itself, of course, was not into the business of repealing legislation. Consequently, it inserted into Article 13 a proviso that rendered void all existing colonial laws that were inconsistent with the Constitution, from the moment the Constitution came into force. Common sense would dictate, therefore, that from early 1949, Section 124A became unconstitutional—a dead law on the

[21] Speech of Seth Govind Das, 2 December 1948, Indian Constituent Assembly (Vol. VII).

[22] Speech of Shibban Lal Saksena, 2 December 1948, Indian Constituent Assembly (Vol. VII).

[23] Speech of Ananthasayaman Ayyangar, 2 December 1948, Indian Constituent Assembly (Vol. VII).

[24] Soli Sorabjee comes to a similar conclusion on his reading of the Constituent Assembly Debates, focusing in particular on K.M. Munshi's speech (Sorabjee 2000: 336).

statute books, waiting to either be repealed by the first legislature, or be struck down by the courts. The legislature, however, seemed not to be interested, and so the battle moved to the courts.

Initially, there were signs heralding the end of sedition. In the previous chapter we discussed the Supreme Court's opinions in *Brij Bhushan*[25] and *Romesh Thappar*.[26] Referring to the Constituent Assembly Debates, and the deletion of sedition, the majority all but held that in the post-Article 19(1)(a) era, Section 124A was unconstitutional. Fazl Ali J. dissented, arguing that the framers had selected Maurice Gwyer's public-order based interpretation of sedition, as opposed to the consistent jurisprudence of the Indian courts between 1891 and 1947. Fazl Ali J. believed that sedition was an offence insofar as the impugned words incited disturbances against public tranquility, or tended to do so—which he then linked with undermining the security of the State.[27] In other words, his defence of sedition rested upon expressly equating it—*a la* Sir Maurice Gwyer—with disturbance of public tranquility, and equating that with the existing language of 19(2).

It is quite evident that the majority in *Brij Bhushan* and *Romesh Thappar* believed that Section 124A was unconstitutional. They were unable to strike it down simply because that issue was not before them in the two cases they were adjudicating. The Punjab High Court, however, had no such compunctions when it heard a sedition case that same year. In *Tara Singh Gopi Chand* v. *State*, Weston C.J., applying overbreadth analysis, tersely noted:

> India is now a sovereign democratic State. Governments may go and be caused to go without the foundations of the State being impaired. A law of sedition thought necessary during a period of foreign rule has become inappropriate *by the very nature of the change which has come about....* The unsuccessful attempt to excite bad feelings is an offence within the ambit of Section 124A. In some instances at least the unsuccessful attempt will not undermine or tend to overthrow the State. It is enough if

---

[25] *Brij Bhushan* v. *State of Delhi*, [1950] SCR Supp. 245 (hereinafter *Brij Bhushan*).

[26] *Romesh Thappar* v. *State of Madras*, [1950] 1 SCR 594.

[27] *Brij Bhushan*, paras 14, 16–17 (Dissenting opinion of Fazl Ali J.)

one instance appears of the possible application of the section to curtailment of the freedom of speech and expression in a manner not permitted by the constitution. The section then must be held to have become
void.[28]

For the same reason, the High Court held Section 153A to be void
as well.

In the previous chapter, we noted that Parliament responded to
Brij Bhushan and *Romesh Thappar* by amending the Constitution to
replace 'undermining the security of the State' with 'in the interests of
public order'. This alteration, significant as it is, clearly did not disturb
the logic of the Punjab High Court. Just as a successful—or unsuc-
cessful—attempt to excite bad feelings about the government would
not necessarily undermine the State, neither would it necessarily
undermine public order. Furthermore, the Statement of Objects and
Reasons to the First Amendment makes it rather clear that Parliament
did not even have sedition in mind: it was more concerned with preventing incitement to violent offences. In fact, as Siddharth Narrain
notes, during the debates, Nehru affirmed his desire to 'get rid' of the
sedition offence as soon as possible.[29] The (un)constitutionality of
Section 124A, therefore, ought not to have been affected by the First
Amendment.

The Patna High Court, however, disagreed. In *Debi Soren* v. *State*,[30]
it adopted Justice Fazl Ali's dissents in *Brij Bhushan* and *Romesh
Thappar* which, in turn, had adopted Maurice Gwyer's (overruled)
understanding of sedition. Arguing that the phrase '*in the interests of...
public order...*' was of very wide ambit, the Court held that Section 124A—
on Maurice Gwyer's interpretation—could easily be justified as a
reasonable restriction on free speech, in the interests of public order.
Notice, however, that Maurice Gwyer's test had no requirements of
proximity or imminence: as long as the words were either intended
to—or had a 'tendency' to disrupt public order, they were seditious.

---

[28] *Tara Singh Gopi Chand* v. *State*, 1951 Cr LJ 449, para 13; emphasis mine.
[29] Narrain (2011: 35).
[30] 1954 (2) BLJR 99.

The second part of the test—'tendency to disrupt...' was also similar—as we saw in the previous chapter—to the Supreme Court's public order jurisprudence in the 1950s.

At the turn of the 1950s, therefore, there were two conflicting High Court decisions on Section 124A. The Punjab High Court, taking the broad definition of sedition from the Privy Council, had declared it unconstitutional. The Patna High Court, taking the narrow definition from Sir Maurice Gwyer *via* Justice Fazl Ali's dissents, had found it to be constitutional. Between the two decisions lay the First Amendment. The stage was set for the Supreme Court to rule definitively on the issue, which it did in 1962, in *Kedar Nath Singh's* case.

KEDAR NATH SINGH AND BEYOND

Kedar Nath Singh was brought to court for making a somewhat intemperate speech against the government.[31] He had said something to the following effect:

> To-day the dogs of the C.I.D. are loitering round Barauni. Many official dogs are sitting even in this meeting. The people of India drove out the Britishers from this country and elected these Congress goondas to the gaddi and seated them on it. To-day these Congress goondas are sitting on the gaddi due to mistake of the people. When we drove out the Britishers, we shall strike and turn out these Congress goondas as well...[32]

before progressing in the same vein. He was booked for sedition, and ultimately, the constitutionality of Section 124A was challenged before the Supreme Court. His case was clubbed together with a number of other cases brought by assorted Muslims and communists, most of whom had been convicted of sedition.

Only recently, the Allahabad High Court had followed the Punjab High Court in holding that Section 124A was unconstitutional. In *Ram Nandan* v. *State*, employing a classic overbreadth analysis, the

---

[31] *Kedar Nath Singh* v. *State of Bihar*, [1962] SCR Supp. (2) 769 (hereinafter *Kedar Nath Singh*).

[32] *Kedar Nath Singh*, para 2.

High Court noted that 'harbouring a feeling of hatred, contempt or disaffection towards the Government does neither necessarily nor inevitably have an effect upon public order; a hearer may have this feeling in his mind but the public would not be affected if he does not do some act which disturbs the public or the peace or tranquillity in the public'.[33] Consequently, since there could be cases where 'disaffection' would lead to a public order breach, and cases where it would not, Section 124A, in making no distinction between the two and criminalizing 'disaffection' *simpliciter*, was overbroad and unconstitutional.

Thus, by the time the Supreme Court was called upon to decide *Kedar Nath Singh*, two High Courts, employing impeccable constitutional reasoning, had found that Section 124A violated the constitutional guarantee of freedom of speech and expression, and had struck it down. The Supreme Court, however, chose to disagree.

After going into an extensive history of sedition law in India, the Court made the following observation: 'Every State, whatever its form of Government, has to be armed with the power to punish those who, by their conduct, jeopardise the safety and stability of the State, or disseminate such feelings of disloyalty as have the tendency to lead to the disruption of the State or to public disorder.'[34] Readers will notice the first part of the test (actually jeopardizing the safety of the State) is relatively uncontroversial, while the second part more or less recapitulates Sir Maurice Gwyer's test for sedition. That is precisely what the Court proceeded to do. It noticed the two lines of contrary opinion

---

[33] AIR 1959 All 101, para 15 (Desai J.). Justice Gurtu's concurring opinion expressly invoked overbreadth. As it turned out, the Court had a reached a similar conclusion earlier, in *Sabir Raza* v. *The State*, Cri App No 1434 of 1955, D/-11-2-1958 (All). Interestingly, Desai J., who wrote one of the judgments in *Ram Nandan*, was responsible for the collapsing of *Ramji Lal Modi's* distinction between 'in the interests of public order' and 'for the maintenance of public order' that happened in *Lohia* (*The Superintendent, Central Prison, Fatehgarh* v. *Dr Ram Manohar Lohia*, [1960] 2 SCR 821). It was Justice Desai who wrote the *Ram Manohar Lohia* judgment in the Allahabad High Court, in *Dr Ram Manohar Lohia* v. *Supt Central Prison, Fatehgarh*, AIR 1955 All 193, which first introduced the direct/indirect distinction that was ultimately adopted by the Supreme Court, when the case went up in appeal.

[34] *Kedar Nath Singh*, para 18.

on sedition, the opinions in *Romesh Thappar* and *Brij Bhushan*, and argued that the First Amendment had accepted Fazl Ali's dissenting arguments by replacing 'security of the State' with 'public order'.[35] It then cited *Ramji Lal Modi*[36] and *Virendra*[37] for the proposition that the phrase '*in the interests of…*' had a very wide ambit. Consequently (and blithely dispensing with the reasonableness requirement, which is *expressly* a part of 19(2)), it held that '*any law* which is enacted in the interest of public order may be saved from the vice of constitutional invalidity'.[38] Insofar as the Maurice Gwyer–Fazl Ali–First Amendment view of sedition—limiting it to intention or tendency to create public disorder—was the correct one, Section 124A was indeed a law enacted '*in the interests of* ' public order, and therefore, it was constitutionally valid.

In the previous chapter, we discussed the problems with a 'tendency' test that dispenses with any notion of proximity. Historically, we saw that precisely this test was used in the United States to persecute dissidents for years. The reason is obvious. 'Tendency' is a boundlessly manipulable word. Just about anything, if construed in a certain way, can have a 'tendency' to eventually overthrow the State. That, indeed, was precisely the argument made in *Lohia*: encouraging people to break one law—even as innocuous as a minor tax could eventually lead to conflagration and revolution. The Court rejected the argument, and rightly so. To prevent complete arbitrariness, and to give effect to 19(2)'s requirement of reasonableness, there needs to be some test of causation, some understanding of proximity, which courts can use to hold a speaker responsible for the eventual consequences of his speech. The *Kedar Nath Singh* opinion fails entirely to develop such a test.

The curious thing is that it did not even need to because *Lohia* had done so already. *Kedar Nath Singh* (1962) cites *Ramji Lal Modi* (1957) and *Virendra* (1957), but ignores entirely *Lohia* (1960), which

---

[35] *Kedar Nath Singh*, para 32.
[36] *Ramji Lal Modi* v. *State of UP*, [1957] 1 SCR 860.
[37] *Virendra* v. *State of Punjab*, [1958] 1 SCR 308.
[38] *Kedar Nath Singh*, para 38; emphasis mine.

had reinterpreted *Ramji Lal Modi* to yield a strict test of proximity. It is difficult to see how Section 124A could have survived under the *Lohia* standard of proximate relationship, since all that the Gwyer formulation requires is either an intention or a tendency. By ignoring *direct* precedent on 19(2), it is submitted that the Supreme Court erred in upholding a statute that had caused—and would continue to cause—tremendous damage to the democratic fabric of the country.

At the very least, what *Kedar Nath Singh* does is to expressly link Section 124A with Article 19(2)'s public order test. In other words, Section 124A is constitutional only *because* and *insofar as* it fits within the meaning of Article 19(2), which *Kedar Nath Singh*, following *Ramji Lal Modi*, and ignoring *Lohia*, interprets in broad terms. Yet after *Lohia*, as we have seen, cases such as *Rangarajan*[39] and *Arup Bhuyan*[40] represent a further narrowing of the standard, gradually approaching something akin to a *Brandenburg* test[41] ('incitement to imminent lawless action'). Section 124A, however, must still be tested on the touchstone of 19(2).

This leads to one of the two conclusions. Either Section 124A itself must be interpreted to embody a *Brandenburg* level of proximity (although it is difficult to see how 'disaffection' and 'disloyalty' can be interpreted to resemble imminent incitement to public disorder, or as a spark in a powder keg). Alternatively, if Section 124A is still understood as embodying Gwyer's formulation of 'intention' or 'tendency' to public disorder, then it is at least *now* unconstitutional and violates 19(1)(a) and 19(2), even though it might not have been in 1957 (*Ramji Lal Modi*), or in 1962 (*Kedar Nath Singh*).

In 1995, the Supreme Court came close to connecting the dots. In *Balwant Singh v. State of Punjab*,[42] it reversed the convictions of some men who had raised a 'Khalistan Zindabaad!' slogan just outside a cinema, in the immediate aftermath of Indira Gandhi's assassination. If anything could have a 'tendency' to public disorder, then

---

[39] *S. Rangarajan v. P. Jagjivan Ram*, (1989) 2 SCC 574: [1989] 2 SCR 204.
[40] *Arup Bhuyan v. State of Assam*, (2011) 3 SCC 377.
[41] *Brandenburg v. Ohio*, 395 U.S. 444 (1969).
[42] (1995) 3 SCC 214 (hereinafter *Balwant Singh*).

surely chanting a separatist slogan in a crowded place immediately following the assassination of a Prime Minister must qualify! Yet the Court focused on the fact that the slogan—and others like it—were chanted just a couple of times, that the accused were not even leading a procession, and that—most importantly—there was no response, and no visible impact on law and order. Demonstrating harm has never been the test for sedition, however; sedition has always turned upon the *content* of the expression, with the courts analysing whether the words written or spoken, *qua* words, have the tendency (or have been said or stated with the intention) to create public disorder. Here, however, the Court evidently went into a host of factors surrounding the actual chanting of the slogans, and found the relationship between them and public disorder so attenuated, that it could afford to dismiss them as 'casual slogans',[43] not worthy of a sedition charge. This line of reasoning—shifting from what the words *say* (or, the message they communicate) to their proximate relationship with public disorder is *Brandenburg* reasoning, even though the Court was probably not aware of it.

Nonetheless, we are still waiting for a judgment to expressly analyse Section 124A in light of the *Lohia–Rangarajan–Bhuyan* line of public order cases. *If* that happens, there is no doubt that Section 124A can no longer survive. There is no guarantee, however, that it will happen. Quite the contrary: *Ramji Lal Modi* has never been overruled (only creatively reinterpreted), and the fragile nature of precedent in India indicates that it is almost equally likely that the 'tendency' test will make its return instead, and affect 19(2) public order jurisprudence *via* Section 124A. In the meantime, without parliamentary repeal, or any clear Supreme Court guidance on the issue, the provision, with its broad and compendious wording, continues to be abused in deeply anti-democratic ways. And what is perhaps most ironic in all of this is that the United Kingdom, which gave us the law of sedition, and upon whose common law precedents our present standard for sedition is based entirely, had no sedition prosecutions for many decades

---

[43] *Balwant* Singh, paras 7, 8, 12.

before entirely abandoning the concept in 2010, by expressly writing it out of the common law via statute.[44] Nor is this a Eurocentric issue: constitutional courts in countries such as Uganda have found sedition to be an unconstitutional violation of free speech, holding that the wording of the offence was so vague, that it had an 'endless catchment area'.[45] There is no reason why we cannot follow suit.

THE PARADOX OF LIBERAL NEUTRALITY

So far, our analysis has focused entirely on the meaning of words such as 'disaffection', 'contempt', and 'hatred', and their connection with public order. The sedition provision, however, has another important phrase: '*government established by law*'. In *Kedar Nath Singh*, the Supreme Court understood this term in the following way:

> ...the expression 'the Government established by law' has to be distinguished from the persons *for the time being engaged in carrying on the administration*. 'Government established by law' is the visible symbol of the State. The very existence of the State will be in jeopardy if the Government established by law is subverted.[46]

This is worded somewhat curiously. Presumably, if I incite disaffection against the ruling government, or attempt to bring it into hatred or contempt, that would not qualify as sedition, since my target is only persons 'for the time being engaged in carrying on the administration'. This is a crucial way in which the colonial and postcolonial scope of the sedition law must differ. Prior to 1947, there was no meaningful difference between government and State. The (British) ruling class embodied both, with no prospect of replacement *within* the existing legal framework. In a democratic republic, however, every government is transient. Consequently, 'government established by law' as referring to the party in power, and as referring to the 'symbol of the State', must be distinguished.

---

[44] Section 73, Coroners and Justice Act, 2009.
[45] *Andrew Mujuni Mwenda* v. *Attorney-General*, [2010] UGCC 5. The State of Uganda cited *Kedar Nath Singh* as international precedent.
[46] *Kedar Nath Singh*, para 36; emphasis mine.

But then, what does it mean to incite disaffection against government as the 'visible symbol of the State'? The last sentence in the excerpted quotation provides a clue: perhaps it is about replacing the government unlawfully. Yet that seems to be captured more accurately by 'disaffection', and its allied terms. 'Government established by law' seems rather to refer not to the *manner* of the outlawed speech, but to the entity (or set of ideas) which it is directed against.

Here is another possibility: considering that sedition began as an offence against the King, and the elements of the offence have changed along with changes in forms of governance, perhaps the target must now be the *institution* of governance, as practiced in India—that is, republican democracy, embodied by the various elements of the Constitution's basic structure.[47]

This brings us to an alleged contradiction at the heart of liberal political theory. Political liberalism—following Rawls—is committed to the idea of 'neutrality': neutrality between competing 'comprehensive theories' about what is good, true, or just. It is not for the State to impose its own vision of the good upon its citizens. Of course, one particular comprehensive theory is liberalism *itself*. Consequently, liberalism, according to its own tenets, cannot claim moral priority for its own principles over others, or ask that they be enforced by the State against the will of the people. So if I use existing liberal institutions to acquire political power, and then use that power to dismantle those very institutions, there is no argument from *within* liberalism that makes my doing so illegitimate.

The free speech law of the United States presently subscribes to this position, although it was not always like that. Cases affirming the convictions of communist party members were justified on the precise ground that they were attempting to use democratic institutions

---

[47] In *Kesavananda Bharati* v. *State of Kerala*, (1973) 4 SCC 225, the Supreme Court held that the Constitution possessed an immutable 'basic structure', which could not be 'damaged or destroyed' even by means of constitutional amendments. The Court clarified that the 'basic structure' included core constitutional values, such as republican democracy, the separation of powers, judicial review, and secularism.

to subvert democracy itself. Ever since *Brandenburg*, however, that position has been abandoned, and presently, Justice Holmes' original opinion holds sway: 'If in the long run the beliefs expressed in proletarian dictatorship are destined to be accepted by the dominant forces of the community, the only meaning of free speech is that they should be given their chance and have their way.'[48] The constitutional scholar Laurence Tribe agrees: 'It should be clear that no satisfactory theory of free speech can presuppose or guarantee the permanent existence of any particular social system. For example, a free speech theory must permit evolution from a society built on the ideals of liberal individualism to a society aspiring to more communitarian visions—just as it must permit evolution from communitarianism to individualism.'[49]

While Tribe's point is well-taken, it does not resolve the issue. Presumably, the communitarianism and individualism he has in mind are both compatible with fundamental liberal–democratic traditions, including guaranteed rights of free speech. It is not immediately obvious why a system of free speech should permit political manifestos that make it a point to abolish free speech should their proponents come to power. Legal systems in Europe have, indeed, taken the opposite view. The German Constitution subscribes to a concept of 'militant democracy'. Article 21.2 of its basic law states that political parties which 'seek to undermine or abolish the free democratic basic order'[50] are unconstitutional. This viewpoint was echoed by the European Court of Human Rights in *Refah Partisi* v. *Turkey*. Refah Partisi was a Turkish political party that was expressly committed to the abolition of secularism, imposing sharia law, and establishing a theocracy. After a string of electoral successes, the Turkish Constitutional Court ordered its dissolution. Refah Partisi appealed to the European Court, which upheld the dissolution. The Court held that any proposed change to a State's legal and constitutional structure 'must itself be compatible with fundamental democratic principles'.[51] Sharia law and the setting

---

[48] *Gitlow* v. *New York*, 268 U.S. 652, 673 (1925) (dissenting opinion of Holmes J.)
[49] Tribe (1978: 239).
[50] Article 21.2, Basic Law of Germany.
[51] *Refah Partisi* v. *Turkey*, [2003] ECHR 87.

up of sharia courts were not, in the opinion of the European Court of Human Rights, compatible with those principles. Consequently, it was permissible to forestall the party from implementing its resolutions even *before* it came to power, as long as the need was reasonably perceived to be urgent.

Philosophically, such a position is justified by scholars such as Rawls[52] and Popper,[53] who argue that in order to survive, a liberal society must set limits on what it is willing to tolerate. Where that limit is to be set, however, remains a complex issue. For example, as we have seen, when it comes to a refusal to tolerate mere *speech*, we have serious autonomy-based objections. One interesting way of thinking through the issue is by looking to Joseph Raz, whose entire political theory is based on the fundamental principle of autonomy (as opposed to neutrality). Raz understands autonomy as a range of worthwhile choices open to an individual to make towards the shaping of her life.[54] Since coercion in any form (for example, banning of free speech) restricts *some* choices, it leads to a loss of autonomy. Consequently, it can only be justified if there is a corresponding, greater autonomy *gain*. Thus, it might be argued that a thriving liberal democracy is the political system that provides maximal autonomy for all its members—and so, the autonomy loss in restricting speech for the purposes of preserving this order is justified.

The idea of anti-democratic speech—and whether, ultimately, that is what the sedition provision is—or ought to be—getting at, are issues yet to be considered seriously on the touchstone of the Indian Constitution. There are a number of other provisions, however, which can be read as attempting to protect certain fundamental aspects of the liberal–democratic political order against attempts at eroding them through speech. This will form one aspect of our analysis in the next part of this book, when we examine issues arising out of regulating hate speech, pornography, and other analogous forms of expression, under the 19(2) head of 'decency and morality'.

---

[52] Rawls (1993).
[53] Popper (1945).
[54] See Raz (1988).

Free Speech and Cultural Regulation

. . . .

CHAPTER FIVE

Obscenity and Pornography

. . . .

> *We appeared in court on the appointed day. Witnesses were pre-seated.*
> *They were to prove that Manto's 'Bu' (odour) and my 'Lihaf' were both*
> *obscene. My lawyer explained carefully that until I was questioned*
> *directly I was not to open my mouth. He would say whatever he deemed*
> *proper. 'Bu' was taken up first.*
> *'Is this story obscene?' asked Manto's lawyer. 'Yes sir,' the witness said.*
> *'What word indicates that it is obscene?'*
> *Witness: 'Bosom.'*
> *Lawyer: 'My Lord, the word "bosom" is not obscene.'*
> *Judge: 'Correct.'*
> *Lawyer: 'The word "bosom" is not obscene then?'*
> *Witness: 'No, but the author has used it for a woman's breasts.'*
> *Suddenly Manto rose to his feet.*
> *'What else did you expect me to call a woman's breasts—peanuts?'*
> *A loud laughter swept across the courtroom. Manto too started laughing.*
> *'If the accused indulges in this type of tawdry humour again he will be*
> *thrown out for contempt of court or be fined.'*
>
> —Ismat Chughtai, *Kaghazi Hai Pairahan*[1]

I smat Chughtai and Sadat Hasan Manto, now widely regarded as two of twentieth century's greatest Urdu writers, were both

---

[1] In 'An Excerpt from *Kaghazi Hai Pairahan* (The "Lihaf" Trial)', available at http://www.urdustudies.com/pdf/15/28naqviExerpt.pdf (accessed on 7 October 2015).

prosecuted (unsuccessfully) for obscenity under a colonial law that still remains upon the statute books: Section 292 of the Indian Penal Code. Chughtai and Manto repeatedly pushed the boundaries of the socially acceptable in their short stories, addressing proscribed themes of sexuality and the position of women in society and the home, with a frankness and candour that alarmed sections of the reading populace. *Lihaaf*, the story for which Chughtai was taken to court, detailed the homoerotic tendencies of an abandoned bride from the perspective of her eight-year-old niece, and can be taken to be a wider commentary upon the sexual repression prevalent in society at the time.

Ironically, Chughtai escaped punishment because the extant Section 292, in 1945, did not define 'obscenity'. Consequently, the prevalent law was the common law, which understood obscenity in terms laid down by the 1868 case of *R* v. *Hicklin*. In that case, Justice Cockburn defined the test to be 'whether the tendency of the matter charged as obscenity is to deprave and corrupt those whose minds are open to such immoral influences, and into whose hands a publication of this sort may fall'.[2] Importantly, the *Hicklin* test was *acontextual*: 'matter' was obscene if any part of it could be demonstrated, to the satisfaction of the judges, to have a tendency to deprave or corrupt. This explains the rather hilarious excerpt at the beginning of the chapter, detailing the floundering efforts of a witness to pick out the *specific* word or sentence that could be labelled obscene. Chughtai's story—like Manto's—traded upon allusion and reference to make its point. Homoeroticism was never explicit, but only hinted at through images of a shaking quilt. The prosecution failed to demonstrate that the *Hicklin* test had been satisfied.

Nonetheless, the context of the Manto–Chughtai trials should serve as an indicator that more often than not, obscenity is a weapon of *cultural regulation*. Under the gloss of moral corruption and perversion, it establishes the boundaries between what might and might not be said, which themes and topics are fit for public discussion and which are not. It is an attempt to establish and then police norms of

---

[2] *R* v. *Hicklin*, L.R. 2 Q.B. 360 (1868).

civility and behaviour that one section of a community conceives of, and then imposes upon, the rest of its members.

RANJIT UDESHI AND THE MEANING OF 'OBSCENITY'

These are strong claims, and they are best illustrated—as I will argue—in the 1965 case that upheld the constitutionality of Section 292, *Ranjit Udeshi v. State of Maharashtra*.[3] *Lady Chatterley's Lover*, D.H. Lawrence's sexually explicit novel about the extramarital relationship between an aristocratic woman and her gamekeeper, had already been banned—and become the subject of obscenity trials—all over the world. Published in 1928, it was legally unavailable for many years in the United Kingdom, Canada, United States, and Australia. In the first three of those countries, the years 1959–60 saw either a lifting of the ban via the court, or a verdict of 'Not Guilty' in an obscenity trial.[4]

It was under these circumstances that Ranjit Udeshi, a Bombay bookseller, appealed his Section 292 conviction for possessing an unexpurgated copy of the book, and took his case to the Supreme Court. Udeshi argued that after the coming into being of the Constitution, Section 292 violated Article 19(1)(a), and was not rescued by Article 19(2). In any event, he contended that *Lady Chatterley's Lover* was not an obscene text.

Article 19(2) permits reasonable restrictions upon the freedom of speech and expression in the interests of '*decency and morality*'. *Ranjit Udeshi* would be the Supreme Court's first attempt to directly engage with the import of these terms.

On the first question, the Court upheld the constitutional validity of Section 292. Justice Hidayatullah, writing for the Court, noted that Article 19(2):

...makes an exception in favour of existing laws which impose restrictions on the exercise of the right in the interests of *public decency or*

---

[3] AIR 1965 SC 881: [1965] 1 SCR 65 (hereinafter *Ranjit Udeshi*).
[4] See *R v. Penguin Books Ltd.*, [1961] Crim LR 176; *Grove Press Inc.* v. *Christenberry*, 175 F. Supp. 488 (SDNY 1959).

> *morality...*[Section 292] *does not go beyond obscenity which falls directly within the words 'public decency and morality' of the second clause of the article...*[Obscenity] denotes the quality of being obscene which means offensive to *modesty or decency*; lewd, filthy and repulsive. It cannot be denied that it is an important interest of society to suppress obscenity.[5]

Immediately after that, he observed:

> It can hardly be claimed that obscenity which is offensive to modesty or decency *is within the constitutional protection given to free speech or expression, because the article dealing with the right itself excludes it.* That cherished right on which our democracy rests is meant for the expression of free opinions to change political or social conditions or for the advancement of human knowledge. This freedom is subject to reasonable restrictions which may be thought necessary in the interest of the general public and one such is the interest of *public decency and morality.*[6]

Readers will immediately notice some confusion here. In one part of his opinion, Justice Hidayatullah seems to argue that while obscenity is protected under Article 19(1)(a), the 'decency and morality' clause permits restricting obscene expression. In another part, however, he seems to be arguing that the purpose of free speech and expression is to change political/social conditions or advance human knowledge, and consequently, obscenity is unprotected under Article 19(1)(a) itself—or, in his words, '*the article dealing with the right itself excludes it*'. Of course, if *that* is true, then the question of 19(2) never arises at all.

The difference is crucial because it tracks two very distinct ideas about the nature or purpose of free speech and has consequences beyond obscenity law. Recall that in Chapter One, we discussed the self-fulfilment, marketplace of ideas, and democracy theories of free speech. It is under the third—and arguably, the second—theories that obscene expression can be taken entirely outside the ambit of

---

[5] *Ranjit Udeshi*, para 8; emphasis mine.
[6] *Ranjit Udeshi*, para 9; emphasis mine.

free speech protection altogether. This has been the approach of the United States Supreme Court. Justifying the exclusion of various forms of speech (including obscenity) from First Amendment protection, the Court argued that 'such utterances are no essential part of *any exposition of ideas, and are of such slight social value as a step to truth* that any benefit that may be derived from them is clearly outweighed by the social interest in order and morality.'[7] As we can see, the Court ran together arguments from truth and democracy to deny protection to obscene speech. Such an argument would not, however, be open to it on the self-fulfilment theory because there is no obvious reason why indulging in obscene expression should be any less fulfilling than other forms. Yet whatever the underlying basis, Justice Hidayatullah's opinion appears internally contradictory.

There is, in addition, a second critical problem with the judgment. Four times in two paragraphs, Justice Hidayatullah argues that 19(2) permits reasonable restrictions in the interests of '*public* decency and morality' (and at one point, he even goes so far as to equate 'decency' with 'modesty'). But these are not the terms that Article 19(2) uses. The precise wording of 19(2) is '*public order*, decency or morality'. Public order, as we have discussed in the previous chapters, is a term of art and was introduced via the First Amendment. Draft Article 13(2), on the other hand, contained the terms '*decency and morality*', as did the original Article 19(2). This suggests that the word 'public' in present-day Article 19(2) qualifies *only* order, and not the compendious '*order, decency or morality*', as Justice Hidayatullah would have it.

The distinction is not a pedantic one because much depends, as we shall see, upon whether Article 19(2) is meant to protect *public* morality, or some other form of morality. For now, we may simply note that the constitutional text and history does not support Justice Hidayatullah's uncritical equation of '*decency or morality*' with '*public decency and morality*'.

Having established that Section 292 was constitutional, it then fell to the Court to define 'obscenity' (since the Section did not do so). Observing that the *Hicklin* test had been incorporated from common

---

[7] *Chaplinsky* v. *New Hampshire*, 315 U.S. 568, 572 (1942); emphasis mine.

law into Indian law, the Court declined the invitation to reconsider it in light of its abandonment not just in the United States, but in the United Kingdom as well, noting that *Hicklin* was justified because of its 'emphasis on the *potentiality* of the impugned object to deprave and corrupt by immoral influences'.[8] (This, of course, seems remarkably similar to the 'tendency' test we have discussed in the public order cases.) The Court disagreed with the proposition that *Hicklin* was only about stray passages or isolated sentences, and held that the correct test—insofar as it was applicable to India—was that 'obscenity *without a preponderating social purpose or profit* cannot have the constitutional protection of free speech'.[9] Nonetheless, it upheld the *other* part of *Hicklin*—namely that the purpose of the law was to protect 'not those who can protect themselves but those whose prurient minds take delight and secret sexual pleasure from erotic writings'.[10]

This, of course, leads to the following inevitable results: on the social-value prong, judges assume the mantle of literary critics, deciding upon the 'social purpose' of controversial works of art or literature. And the identification of the vulnerable constituency that the law is supposed to protect becomes little more than a foregone conclusion. The consequences are evident from the last part of the judgment:

> The poetry and music which Lawrence attempted to put into sex apparently cannot sustain it long and without them the book is nothing...the book is probably an unfolding of his philosophy of life and of the urges of the unconscious but these are unfolded in his other books also and have been fully set out in his Psychoanalysis and the Unconscious and finally in the Fantasia of the Unconscious. There is no loss to society if there was a message in the book. The divagations with sex are not a legitimate embroidery but they are the only attractions to the common man.[11]

And:

> The promptings of the unconscious particularly in the region of sex is suggested as the message in the book. But it is not easy for the *ordinary*

[8] *Ranjit Udeshi*, para 19.
[9] *Ranjit Udeshi*, para 22; emphasis mine.
[10] *Ranjit Udeshi*, para 26.
[11] *Ranjit Udeshi*, para 27.

reader to find it. The Machine Age and its impact on social life which is its secondary theme *does not interest the reader for whose protection, as we said, the law has been framed.*[12]

THREE VIEWS ON THE MEANING OF MORALITY

Ranjit Udeshi, I contend, is a deeply flawed judgment, and the heart of the error lies in its misunderstanding of what the term '*decency or morality*', under 19(2), really means (for ease of exposition, I shall refer only to '*morality*' hereafter, taking it to include both terms). The error is exposed by a close look at paragraph 9 of the judgment:

> This [19(1)(a)] freedom is subject to reasonable restrictions which may be thought necessary in the interest of the *general public* and one such is the interest of *public decency and morality*.[13]

I have already argued that constitutional history militates against this reading. More importantly, however, Justice Hidayatullah contends that protecting public decency and morality is a matter of 'public interest' (or 'interest of the general public'), which is permitted under Article 19(2). *But this is very clearly incorrect.* Article 19(2) has no public interest exception. Compare, for instance, Article 19(6), which provides for restrictions upon Article 19(1)(g):

> Nothing in sub clause (g) of the said clause shall…prevent the State from making any law imposing, *in the interests of the general public*, reasonable restrictions on the exercise of the right conferred by the said sub clause.[14]

This demonstrates that where the framers were of a mind to insert a public interest exception, they did so in categorical terms. In *Sakal Papers*, a case that we briefly discussed in Chapter One, a public interest argument was made and rejected in precisely these terms:

---

[12] *Ranjit Udeshi*, para 27; emphasis mine.
[13] *Ranjit Udeshi*, para 9; emphasis mine.
[14] Article 19(6), Constitution of India; emphasis mine.

some clauses of Article 19 provided for a public interest exception, while others did not, and 19(1)(a) belonged to the latter category.[15] Evidently, the founders viewed the rights of free expression, assembly, and association (19(1)(a), (b), and (c)) as far too important to be subjected to a general public interest exception.

Thus, the foundation of *Ranjit Udeshi* is built upon an identification of 'public decency and morality' with 'public interest', which is then read into Article 19(2). The second exercise involves, however, reading into 19(2) an expression that is not only absent, but was *clearly* intended by the framers not to be there, a fact that was acknowledged as such by the Supreme Court five years before the *Ranjit Udeshi* decision (in *Sakal Papers*).

So what, then, does '*morality*' really refer to? There are, I suggest, three possibilities: '*public morality*' (what we have been considering so far), '*individual morality*', and '*constitutional morality*'. By individual morality, I refer to the moral make-up of individual persons. Protecting individual morality might mean sheltering the individual from moral deterioration. Constitutional morality is a concept that is distinct from both public and individual morality, and refers to the set of abstract, unstated principles or values that underlies and justifies our bill of rights. Or, to put it another way, it refers to the elements of the political and moral philosophy that our Fundamental Rights chapter, taken as a whole, is committed to. The concept was referred to by Nani Palkhivala in his writings,[16] and the distinction was made expressly by the Delhi High Court in *Naz Foundation* v. *NCT*, where the Court quoted Ambedkar (albeit out of context) for the following proposition:

> Popular morality, as distinct from a constitutional morality derived from *constitutional values*, is based on shifting and subjecting notions of right and wrong.[17]

---

[15] *Sakal Papers* v. *Union of India*, [1962] 3 SCR 842.

[16] Sorabjee (2003).

[17] *Naz Foundation* v. *NCT*, 160 (2009) DLT 277, para 79 (hereinafter *Naz Foundation*); emphasis mine.

It shall be the burden of this chapter, and the next, to demonstrate that it is 'constitutional morality' that is the most justified interpretation of Article 19(2)'s morality clause, both in terms of constitutional law and philosophy. Understanding Article 19(2) to be referring to constitutional morality also provides us with a coherent and defensible interpretation not only of obscenity law, but also of a number of controversial statutory provisions which come under the rubric of hate speech (Section 295A and Section 153A of the Indian Penal Code, Section 123(2) of the Representation of the People Act, and so on).

MORALITY AS PUBLIC MORALITY

In the first section of this chapter,[18] it was argued that reading 19(2) as allowing restrictions in the interests of '*public morality*' is unjustified on a purely analytic understanding of the constitutional text and history. Let us now consider arguments from political and constitutional philosophy. The question of when the so-called 'moral majority' is justified in imposing its moral convictions upon all of society in the form of criminal law was famously debated in the 1960s by the legal philosophers Lord Devlin, H.L.A. Hart, and Ronald Dworkin. This was in the immediate aftermath of the *Wolfenden Committee Report* on homosexuality and prostitution in England. The Committee, in its conclusions, memorably declared: 'there is an area of private morality...that is none of the law's business,'[19] and called for the decriminalization of homosexuality.

In *The Enforcement of Morals*,[20] Lord Devlin rejected the Committee's position on two grounds. He argued, first, that every society had the right to protect itself against practices or modes of conduct that threatened its very existence. Second, he argued that society also had the right to preserve and protect its moral environment, by preventing (what it considered to be) adverse changes. Consider the

---

[18] '*Ranjit Udeshi* and the meaning of "Obscenity"', discussed earlier.
[19] Committee on Homosexual Offences and Prostitution (1957), c.f. Dworkin (1966: 988).
[20] Devlin (1959).

case of pornography. Let us assume that the institutions of marriage and the family are central features of our society, and ones that society considers vital to its existence. Now, the Devlin argument could be either that the prevalence of pornographic material will end up eroding marriage and the family (first prong), or that it will fundamentally transform the way people understand sex and relationships, in a way that society considers detrimental (second prong). In either case, society has the right to forestall such changes through criminal legislation.

Hart attacked the first prong of the argument. He argued that *'society'* could mean one of two things: a simple physical aggregation of people—in which case, it was difficult to see how 'society' could be destroyed by a mere change in practices. Alternatively, it could mean—somewhat anthropomorphically—a community having 'shared ideas on politics, morals and ethics', as Devlin had said.[21] But if—admittedly—these shared ideas were in a state of constant shift, change, and flux, on what principled basis could the majority *of a moment* justifiably assume the power to freeze a transient moral *status quo* into permanence?

Dworkin challenged the second prong of the argument, focusing on the meaning of *'moral conviction'*. Lord Devlin had defined the term to be 'a level of disgust, rising to intolerance'.[22] Dworkin, however, distinguished a moral conviction in the true sense (for example, 'homosexuality is immoral') from a matter of taste ('homosexuals make me sick'), prejudice ('homosexuals aren't real men'), rationalizations based on demonstrably incorrect facts ('homosexuality is physically debilitating'), and parroting ('everybody knows that homosexuality is immoral, so it must be!'). Dworkin argued that none of the four stated grounds could justifiably restrict forms of action of expression, because

> ...the principles of democracy we follow do not call for the enforcement of the consensus [against homosexuality], for the belief that prejudices, personal aversions and rationalizations do not justify restricting another's freedom *itself occupies a critical and fundamental position in our*

---

[21] See Hart (1963).
[22] Dworkin (1966: 989).

popular morality. Nor would the bulk of the community then be entitled to follow its own lights, for the community does not extend that privilege to one who acts on the basis of prejudice, rationalization, or personal aversion. Indeed, the distinction between these and moral convictions, in the discriminatory sense, exists largely to mark off the former as the sort of positions one is not entitled to pursue.[23]

Hart and Dworkin's arguments would require a very high burden—in most cases, an unachievable one—in order to justify restricting rights on the basis of the moral convictions of the majority. But should it be even a high burden? Recall, once again, that one of the basic purposes of an entrenched Bill of Rights is to *protect* minorities against the legislative power of an extant majority. There would be little meaning in having a fundamental right if majority sentiment was all that was required to override it. Once again, Justice Jackson's words in *West Virginia Board of Education v. Barnette* resonate most profoundly on this point:

> The very purpose of a Bill of Rights was to withdraw certain subjects from the vicissitudes of political controversy, to place them beyond the reach of majorities and officials and to establish them as legal principles to be applied by the courts. One's right to life, liberty, and property, to free speech, a free press, freedom of worship and assembly, and other fundamental rights may not be submitted to vote; they depend on the outcome of no elections.[24]

Consider, also, the following argument. We accept that the value of democracy lies in something more than a periodic referendum on the choice of our leaders. Cyclical elections embody a deeper principle: that of *collective self-determination*.[25] We have a political obligation to obey laws even when they are opposed to our immediate self-interest because democracy is a structure of organizing political power in a manner that allows us to treat ourselves as the *authors* of those laws. In a functioning democracy, therefore, the process by which citizens form their preferences and visions of the good, which ultimately translate into political

---

[23] Dworkin (1966: 1001); emphasis mine.
[24] *West Virginia Board of Education v. Barnette*, 319 U.S. 624, 638 (1943).
[25] Post (1991).

action, must be reasonably free from coercion. It is only in this way that we can truly say that we are the authors of the laws that govern us.

Now, one of the most important ways in which these preferences are formed is through the exchange of competing ideas that together constitute the public discourse. This demonstrates why there is a particular harm to democracy when free expression is curtailed in the name of public morality. By denying the people access to an entire set of ideas on the ground that the majority finds those ideas unacceptable or offensive, the government ensures that the public discourse is distorted and, consequently, people's preferences and choices are shaped in a directly coercive manner. 'Silence coerced by law', in the words of Justice Brandeis, is 'the argument of force in its worst form'.[26] In a society where an entire set of ideas is removed from the public discourse in this manner, there is a clear democratic deficit.

To put the matter in another way: if democracy is about '*self-government*', then there must be a 'self' that uses the majoritarian-democratic process in order to govern itself. But that must imply—logically—that the constitution of the 'self' must, in some fundamental way, be *independent* of that process. Again, accepting the simple truth that the self is constituted through exposure to a continuous stream of ideas, attitudes, and opinions, whose primary vehicle of transmission is expression, majoritarian control over free speech becomes deeply problematic.[27]

Even if all these arguments could be surmounted, there remains an overriding difficulty (which we shall examine at much greater length when we consider book bans for offending religious sentiment): the very *identification* of public morality. How does one know whether Indian public morality is against homosexuality? Is there even such a thing as a uniform *Indian* morality? Does one ask the man (or woman) on the New Delhi metro or the Bombay train? Take a random poll? Look at religious texts? But which religious texts, and written by whom? Arguments invoking the very idea of a single 'public morality'

---

[26] *Whitney* v. *California*, 274 U.S. 357, 376 (1927) (concurring opinion of Brandeis J.).

[27] This formulation is Meiklejohn's. See Post (1991).

make the mistake that cultural anthropologists and social theorists have been warning us about for decades: we cannot treat a society, a culture, or a community, as an indivisible whole.[28] The history of any aggregation of individuals contains relentless clashes and struggles over what is true, good, or just. Often, these struggles are violent, and what comes down to us as history is little more than victors' history. If, for example, we take the *Manusmriti* as our source of Indian culture (as some courts have done), must we not take into account the highly stratified nature of society at the time, and the violent silencing of the cultural contributions of lower castes (which, for all their disappearance from the public record, nonetheless continued to exist off-stage, as a 'hidden transcript'[29])—exemplified by a public burning of that text carried out by Dr. Ambedkar?[30] The problem of public morality is not only that it is indeterminate, but that any historically grounded investigation into its content will almost always privilege some voices over others because at no point have all members of society been able to contribute towards the formation of public culture.

MORALITY AS PERSONAL MORALITY

What if, however, 19(2) refers not to public morality, but to individual morality? Notwithstanding what Justice Hidayatullah says, this seems to be a far stronger underlying basis for the *Hicklin* test, which he actually adopts. *Hicklin* is predicated upon protecting the *individual* person from corruption or depravity. It is concerned with *her* morality, and with preserving its purity.[31] This raises an important question about the limits of law: is a supposed moral 'harm' caused by an individual to herself sufficient justification for State intervention?

---

[28] Benhabib (2002).

[29] Scott (1990).

[30] See Arundhati Roy's 'Introduction' in Ambedkar (2014).

[31] The personal corruption formula is also found in a number of other statutes. See, for example, The Young Persons (Harmful Publications) Act of 1956, which defines a 'harmful publication' as one that would 'tend to corrupt a young person into whose hands it might fall' (Section 2(a)). See also Section 67, Information Technology Act, 2000.

In the famous text *On Liberty*, John Stuart Mill memorably argued that it is not, laying down what is now known as the 'harm principle':

> The only purpose for which power can rightfully be exercised over any member of a civilised community against his will is to prevent harm to others. His own good, whether physical or moral, is not a sufficient warrant.[32]

Joel Feinberg expands upon the Millian principle by arguing that in certain circumstances, causing *offence* to others (the 'offence principle') is an adequate ground for legal regulation.[33] It is clear that neither the offence principle, nor the harm principle were motivating concerns of the Court in *Ranjit Udeshi*. Rather, it seems that one of two possible justifications underlay that decision. For the sake of convenience, let us refer to them as legal paternalism and legal moralism.[34]

Legal paternalism involves the use of law to prevent a person from causing harm to herself, whatever her own views on the matter (for example, laws against smoking, or laws requiring the wearing of seat belts). Legal paternalism assumes that in certain matters, it is the State that knows best what is in the interests of its citizens, and can therefore compel them to act in accordance with their own best interests, whether they know or agree with it or not. Legal moralism, on the other hand, justifies prohibiting action on the sole ground of immorality (public or private), regardless of harm.

Legal moralism is evidently inconsistent with the idea of liberal neutrality that we have discussed in the previous chapters because it involves the State in privileging certain ways of life over others, and enforcing that privilege through the criminal law. In any case, it does not seem that *Ranjit Udeshi* is a case that is concerned with *bare* immorality. The Court repeats its concern that the book would 'deprave and corrupt *by* immoral influence',[35] and clarifies that the law is meant to '*protect*...those whose prurient minds take delight and

[32] Mill (1869).

[33] Feinberg (1987b).

[34] For a discussion, see Stanton-Ife (2014). See also Feinberg (1971).

[35] *Ranjit Udeshi*, para 19.

secret sexual pleasure from erotic writings'.[36] This makes it clear that the Court considers moral depravity and corruption to be a tangible *harm* caused by the individual to herself, separate from immorality itself. *Ranjit Udeshi* is thus a case of legal paternalism.

Let us now introduce two further distinctions. Paternalism itself might be *soft* or *hard*.[37] Soft paternalism limits interference to cases of absent knowledge or imperfect volition. For example, a man about to cross a bridge without knowing that it will break under him (absent knowledge) or a drunk man about to fall into a manhole (imperfect volition) can be justifiably restrained from doing so. Hard paternalism, on the other hand, acknowledges no such limitations. We prevent the man from crossing the bridge or falling into the manhole even if he is perfectly aware of what he is doing, and specifically wishes to commit suicide *because*, in our opinion, suicide is not in his best interests. In other words, soft paternalism restricts interference to mistakes of *fact* (you are mistaken that the bridge will bear your weight), while hard paternalism permits interference to prevent acts based on mistaken *values* (you are wrong to believe that suicide is in your best interests).[38]

Second, there is a difference between *welfare paternalism*—which looks to improving the interests of persons, whether they would prefer such improvement or not—and *moral paternalism*, which aims at enhancing peoples' well-being by making them better persons *through* improving their moral character.[39] It should be clear that in *Ranjit Udeshi*, the Court adopts a version of hard moral paternalism: that is, the idea that the State is allowed to compel people to live a morally better life by prohibiting or proscribing certain activities.

It is, however, an open question whether moral compulsion is valuable to an individual's life in the first place. Dworkin, for instance, argues that it is not. According to his *endorsement thesis*, '[nothing]…may contribute to the value of a person's life *without his*

---

[36] *Ranjit Udeshi*, para 26; emphasis mine.
[37] See, for instance, Feinberg (1987a).
[38] Of course, the distinction between fact and value is not quite so facile.
[39] This discussion tracks that of G. Dworkin (2014).

endorsement.[40] Take two different cases: a smoker who is well aware that her life would be better if she were forced to give up smoking, but nonetheless insists on her *right* to smoke; and an atheist who rejects the idea that compelled faith will improve her moral life in any way. What matters to us is the second case because what is at stake in obscenity laws is a dispute between the State and the individual upon the moral *evaluation* of the activity or expression that the State seeks to prohibit. Whereas the smoker and the State both agree that her life would be better if the State forced her to stop smoking, here the atheist and the State *disagree* over whether a compelled course of action would make her life better or not.

There is another crucial way in which the smoker and the atheist occupy different positions, and that turns—once again—upon an (admittedly somewhat crude) distinction between fact and value. Arguably, a person who *rejects* the view that smoking is injurious to health is simply mistaken (for lack of information or inherent biases), and would accept being compelled not to smoke if she had full information, and was free of bias. This is arguable because smoking's effect on health is determined by a set of factual inferences, based upon rules of science, observation, and evidence that the person in question probably accepts in other areas of life (for example, driving without seat belts is dangerous). So she is simply being inconsistent in her standards of evaluating evidence. Such an argument is far more difficult to make in conflicts over value, however, because there it is the very ground rules of evaluation that are in dispute (for example, A believes that homosexuality is a sin on religious grounds, while B rejects the authority of religion altogether). Ultimately, therefore, hard moral paternalism of the *Ranjit Udeshi* type ends up requiring an external authority (legislature or court) to label one set of *values* as good, or true, or integral to wellbeing, notwithstanding whatever disagreement there may be with that perspective.

---

[40] R. Dworkin, *The Foundations of Liberal Equality*, cited in Dworkin (2005: 309); emphasis mine.

Apart from being clearly problematic from the point of view of a liberal constitution grounded upon individual rights, hard moral paternalism is also deeply suspect from the point of view of autonomy and personal freedoms. While discussing the public order cases in the previous Part, we had dwelt at some length on the basic idea that the very meaning of autonomy and responsibility lies in individuals determining *for themselves* what conceptions of well-being, and what ideas of truth or rightness they wish to adopt (as we can see, this is close to Dworkin's endorsement thesis). Moral paternalism denies them that.

This reveals a curious tension between the public order and the morality clause of Article 19(2). The *Lohia* line of public order cases, as we discussed previously, does indeed view the individual as an autonomous self, tasked with making up her own mind about how to act, and assuming responsibility for her actions. *Ranjit Udeshi*, on the other hand, views the individual to be in need of protection from corrupting moral influences, and by restricting the flow of information available to her based on this worry, *denies* her the autonomy—and accompanying responsibility—of making up her own mind, unhindered by external influences. This is a tension that pervades the Court's entire free speech jurisprudence, and one which we shall return to in subsequent chapters.

POST-*UDESHI* DEVELOPMENTS

The immediate impact of *Ranjit Udeshi* was an amendment to Section 292 of the Indian Penal Code, inserting a definition of 'obscenity'. Obscenity, under the amended Section, was defined as matter that is 'lascivious...or appeals to the prurient interest...or if its effect is...taken as a whole, such as to tend to deprave and corrupt persons who are likely, having regard to all relevant circumstances, to read, see or hear the matter contained or embodied in it'.[41] Apart

---

[41] Section 292, Indian Penal Code, 1860. Obscene publications on the Internet are now regulated by Section 67 of the Information Technology Act, which is largely similar to Section 292. Section 292 is supplemented by Section 294 of the Indian Penal Code, which renders punishable obscene acts done in public.

from inserting a specific requirement that the work must be viewed 'as a whole', the Amendment more or less followed *Udeshi* and *Hicklin* in focusing on moral 'depravity', and paternalistically targeting groups of (adult) people the State believes are most vulnerable or impressionable to being corrupted. The 1969 Amendment also followed *Udeshi* in specifying a 'public good' exception for works in the 'interest of science, literature, art or learning or other objects of general concern.'[42]

In the decade after *Udeshi*, the Supreme Court largely followed the reasoning of that case, although it came to the opposite conclusion. In *Chandrakant Kalyandas Kakoddar* v. *State of Maharashtra*[43] and *Samaresh Bose* v. *Amal Mitra*,[44] the Court adopted *Udeshi* but held, in both cases, that the literature in question was not obscene. The Court distinguished 'vulgarity' and 'bad taste' from a tendency to deprave or corrupt, and—in *Samaresh Bose*—tempered its own literary analysis by taking into account the evidence of writers and critics, but did little else. A few cases in the last decade, however, point to a possible change in the direction of obscenity law.

In *Khushboo* v. *Kanniamal*, criminal proceedings were initiated against a Tamil actress after an *India Today* interview in which she stated that 'our society should come out of the thinking that at the time of the marriage, the girls should be with virginity' [*sic*]. It was argued by the complainants that her statements would have a 'morally corruptive' influence upon the youth, 'obscure some basic moral values', and 'expose people to...bizarre ideas about premarital sex'. Quashing the criminal proceedings, the Court made two important departures from *Ranjit Udeshi*. First, it held that the test for obscenity must be based on 'contemporary community standards that reflect the sensibilities as well as the tolerance levels of an *average reasonable person*'[45]—not, it must be pointed out, people inherently prone to being corrupted. More importantly, however, the Court noted that

---

[42] Section 292, Indian Penal Code, 1860.

[43] [1970] 2 SCR 80.

[44] [1985] SCR Supp. (3) 17.

[45] *Khushboo* v. *Kanniamal*, 2010 (4) SCALE 467, para 18 (hereinafter *Khushboo*); emphasis mine.

...in the long run, such communication prompts a dialogue within society wherein people can choose to either *defend or question the existing social mores*...we must lay stress on the need to tolerate unpopular views in the socio-cultural space. The framers of our Constitution recognised the importance of safeguarding this right since the free flow of opinions and ideas is essential to sustain the collective life of the citizenry. While an informed citizenry is a pre-condition for meaningful governance in the political sense, we must also promote a culture of open dialogue when it comes to societal attitudes. Admittedly, the appellant's remarks did provoke a controversy since the acceptance of premarital sex and live-in relationships is viewed by some as an attack on the centrality of marriage. *While there can be no doubt that in India, marriage is an important social institution, we must also keep our minds open to the fact that there are certain individuals or groups who do not hold the same view*....If the complainants vehemently disagreed with the appellant's views, then they should have contested her views through the news media or any other public platform.[46]

These observations are crucial because in invoking Hart's objection to Lord Devlin's argument, they strike at the heart of the 'public morality' interpretation of Article 19(2). The whole point of free speech, the Supreme Court holds, is to enable people to question and challenge the dominant social mores and moral convictions that a majority of the society may hold at a particular time. The morality clause of Article 19(2) does not permit the choking off of free expression on the ground that it attacks institutions that a transient majority holds sacrosanct for the time being.[47] The only permissible

---

[46] *Khushboo*; emphasis mine.

[47] For other examples where courts have worked within the restrictive confines of the *Hicklin* test to reach liberal results consistent with such propositions, see for instance, *Raj Kapoor* v. *State*, AIR 1980 SC 258; *Maqbool Fida Husain* v. *Raj Kumar Pandey*, Crl. Revision Petition No. 114/2007. In dismissing an action against the painter M.F. Husain, the Delhi High Court fittingly invoked Swami Vivekananda: 'we tend to reduce everyone else to the limits of our own mental universe and begin privileging our own ethics, morality, sense of duty and even our sense of utility.' The M.F. Husain judgment repays close study, particularly because it draws out the values of pluralism and dissent—values at the heart of any system of free expression—from Indian sources (from Khajuraho to the Kamasutra); see also *T. Kannan* v. *M/s Liberty Creations*, W.P. No. 8780 of 2007 (Madras High Court).

answer to that kind of speech—in the words of Justice Brandeis—is 'more speech'.[48]

Aveek Sarkar v. *State of West Bengal*, decided in 2014, is equally important because of its *express* abandonment of *Hicklin*. In that case, the Supreme Court held that a 1993 photograph of Boris Becker and his fiancée, in the nude (a protest message against racism and in favour of inter-racial relationships), was not obscene within the meaning of Section 292. Citing the examples of a number of countries where *Lady Chatterley's Lover* had been held not to be obscene, the Court held that 'the Hicklin test is not the correct test to be applied to determine what is obscenity'.[49] Instead, the Court cited the 1957 American case of *Roth* v. *United States*,[50] understanding obscenity as related to sexual arousal, to be determined by a 'community standards' test:

> A picture of a nude/semi-nude woman, as such, cannot per se be called obscene unless it has the tendency to arouse feeling or revealing an overt sexual desire. The picture should be suggestive of deprave mind [*sic*] and designed to excite sexual passion in persons who are likely to see it, *which will depend on the particular posture and the background in which the nude/ semi-nude woman is depicted.* Only those sex-related materials which have a tendency of 'exciting lustful thoughts' can be held to be obscene, but the obscenity has to be judged from the point of view of an average person, *by applying contemporary community standards.*[51]

Aveek Sarkar represents a shift from the old 'tendency to deprave or corrupt' test to whether 'the work, taken as a whole, appeals to the prurient interest'. Repudiating an 1868, Victorian-era test to a 1957 American test probably represents progress of some sort. Also welcome is the focus on contemporary standards, which forecloses arguments invoking some timeless, eternal 'Indian' morality, rooted in ancient scriptures. Nonetheless, the test remains unsatisfactory for

[48] See also *Ajay Goswami* v. *Union of India*, (2007) 1 SCC 143; *D-G, Directorate-General of Doordarshan* v. *Anand Patwardhan*, (2006) 8 SCC 433.

[49] *Aveek Sarkar* v. *State of West Bengal*, (2014) 4 SCC 257, para 24 (hereinafter *Aveek Sarkar*).

[50] 354 U.S. 476 (1957).

[51] *Aveek Sarkar*; emphasis mine.

many reasons. To start with, *Roth* also required the obscene work to be 'utterly without social value', something the Court fails to reference. Of course, Section 292 itself has a public good exception, but that has gone virtually un-interpreted in the Court's history. More importantly, however, *Roth* itself was superseded twice over in the United States—in 1966, by *Memoirs* v. *Massachusetts*,[52] and in 1973, by *Miller* v. *California*,[53] neither of which is cited by the Court. *Miller*, in particular, is important. It refined the obscenity test, introducing the requirement of patent offensiveness as defined by the applicable *state* law, thus trying to take into account differing views about offensiveness across the country. As Divan correctly points out, in India, which is considerably more diverse than the United States,[54] 'contemporary *community* standards' beg the question about defining and delimiting the 'community' in question. Without substantial narrowing, this test will only serve as a foil for judges to insert their own moral values into obscenity judgments. Furthermore, *Miller* liberalized the social interest prong of the obscenity test, holding it to be a question of whether 'the work, taken as a whole, lacks serious literary, artistic, political or scientific value'.[55] This is considerably broader than Udeshi's '*preponderating* social purpose or profit', and provides less leeway for judges to act as literary critics.

Ultimately, while *Aveek Sarkar* represents progress, it also represents an opportunity missed. This is particularly stark in its acknowledgment and citation of—but failure to incorporate—the Canadian case of *R* v. *Butler*,[56] in its discussion of community standards. In *Butler*, the Canadian Supreme Court permitted the proscription of 'undue exploitation of sex', which it defined as either sex accompanied by violence, or sex that was 'degrading or dehumanising'. *Butler* thus made community standards relevant to the obscenity enquiry, but not dispositive, focusing, in addition, on certain other values. In the next section, we

[52] 383 U.S. 413 (1966),

[53] 413 U.S. 15 (1973) (hereinafter *Miller*).

[54] Divan (2003: 4).

[55] *Miller*.

[56] [1992] 1 SCR 452 (hereinafter *Butler*).

will discuss which, of such values, might provide a coherent and intel-
lectually defensible approach to regulating sexually explicit material.

MORALITY AS CONSTITUTIONAL MORALITY: JUSTIFIABLE REGULATION OF SEXUALLY EXPLICIT MATERIAL

To sum up: after *Aveek Sarkar*, the test for obscenity in India is
whether, on an application of 'contemporary community standards',
a piece of work has a tendency to 'excite lustful thoughts' (or, in
perhaps somewhat more felicitous phrasing, used in *Roth*, whether
the dominant theme of the work, taken as a whole, appeals to the
prurient interest). While this is considerably more speech-protective
than *Hicklin/Ranjit Udeshi*, it continues to suffer from the flaws
associated with an overtly moral–paternalistic approach discussed
before. The issue is important because a number of speech-regulating
statutes impose restrictions on the basis of the decency and morality
prong of Article 19(2). Apart from Section 292 of the Indian Penal
Code, these include the Cinematograph Act of 1952 (films), the
Dramatic Performances Act of 1876 (theatre), the Customs Act of
1962 and the Post Office Act of 1898 (transportation of material), the
Indecent Representation of Women (Prohibition) Act of 1896, the
Young Persons (Harmful Publications) Act of 1956, the Information
Technology Act of 2000 (online communication), and others.[57]

In this section, I will propose an alternative approach to the
regulation of sexually explicit material, one that is grounded in
an understanding of the morality clause as embodying 'constitutional morality', and tracks the arguments of legal scholars such as
Catherine MacKinnon, as well as the Canadian Supreme Court's
approach in *Butler*.

Admittedly, the 'decency and morality' prong of Article 19(2)
envisages restrictions upon free speech that are content-based,
and thus depart from principles of liberal neutrality. As we have
discussed here, restricting speech based purely upon its content also

---

[57] The list has been collated by Divan. See Divan (2003).

violates the principle of autonomy, which is at the bedrock of any constitution (such as ours), which is committed to core personal freedoms. The question then becomes: under what circumstances is such a departure justified? In the previous sections, we saw how justifications based on 'public morality' and 'personal morality' are deeply problematic. Here, however, is an alternative suggestion: when the State seeks to curtail a guaranteed constitutional right by invoking moral values, *then they must be limited to values grounded within the Constitution.* More broadly, if a constitutional right is to be restricted, then the restrictions themselves must be located in the Constitution.[58]

The moral values that can serve as content-based grounds of speech-restriction under the morality prong, therefore, must also be constitutional values. Let us call this set of values 'constitutional morality'. An argument to this effect was made by the Delhi High Court in *Naz Foundation*, which decriminalized homosexuality.[59] Rejecting the argument that public morals could justify the violation of constitutional norms of equal treatment and the right to privacy and dignity, the Court held that the scope of fundamental rights ought to be understood in terms of constitutional morality. The constitutional value that played a critical role in the Court's decision was the value of inclusiveness (or pluralism).[60]

Let us take the argument of the Delhi High Court further. Constitutional morality, as discussed, refers to the set of basic political principles that underlie and justify Part III of the Constitution. One possible method of identifying aspects of constitutional morality is through the lens of the basic structure doctrine: concepts of democracy, the rule of law, secularism, the Article 14-19-21 'triangle', and so on, have all been held to be part of the basic structure of the Constitution, beyond even the amending power of the Parliament.

---

[58] Of course, where restrictions are based on 'public interest', which expressly invites the legislature to travel beyond the Constitution itself, matters might be different.

[59] Subsequently overruled, although not on this point, by the Supreme Court in *Suresh Kumar Koushal* v. *Naz Foundation*, AIR 2014 SC 563.

[60] *Naz Foundation*, para 130.

For the purposes of the argument that follows, I assume that—as a principle—there is no controversy over the fact that *equality* is a part of our constitutional morality. Furthermore, it is not merely equality as an abstract principle of formally neutral classification ('colour-blindness'). Consider numerous provisions, which depart from a traditional liberal conception of personal rights enforceable against the State, such as Articles 15(2) (prohibition of horizontal discrimination in certain public spaces), 15(3) (special provisions for women and children), 17 (abolition of untouchability), 18 (abolition of titles), 23 (abolition of bonded labour), and 25(2)(b) (overriding the freedom of religion for the purposes of making Hindu religious institutions open to all classes and sections of Hindus). These provisions demonstrate the Constitution's commitment not just to treat all citizens equally in a classic, colour-blind manner, but also to locate sites and practices of historic discrimination, and take all necessary steps to eliminate them. This is hardly surprising. As the Constitutional framers were well aware, and as the Debates clearly indicate, it was always understood that inequality in India was—and is—complex, multilayered, and horizontal, and is accomplished as much by discrete, coercive acts of the State, as it is by traditions and practices of the society.

Consequently, let us label the principle that emerges out of a combined reading of all these provisions as the 'anti-subordination'[61] conception of equality: that is, the Constitution is committed to achieving equality by tackling practices of historical and present subordination, whether they are at the instance of the State, or at the instance of private individuals, groups, or communities. In the argument that follows, I will try to draw a connection between certain forms of sexually

[61] The phrase 'anti-subordination' is borrowed from American equal protection jurisprudence. See for instance, Reva Siegel, quoting Laurence Tribe: 'facially neutral state action [should] be analyzed in accordance with an antisubjugation principle, such that "strict judicial scrutiny would be reserved for those government acts that, given their history, context, source, and effect, seem most likely not only to perpetuate subordination but also to reflect a tradition of hostility toward an historically subjugated group, or a pattern of blindness or indifference to the interests of that group"' (Siegel 2004: 1473).

explicit material, and the historical and continued subordination of women. Such an understanding, I will contend, allows us to ground the 'decency and morality' prong of Article 19(2) within the constitutional value of equality as anti-subordination.

Now, it is common knowledge that certain forms of widely prevalent sexually explicit material (which, following Catherine MacKinnon, we can call 'pornography') involve representations that glorify or eroticize male sexual dominance and, correspondingly, female sexual submission. Scholars such as MacKinnon and Andrea Dworkin argue that by constructing a social reality of dominance and submission, pornography does not merely *depict* subordination, but *actually* subordinates women to men. MacKinnon observes, for instance, that 'the way pornography produces its meaning *constructs and defines men and women as such*. Gender is what gender means. It has no basis in anything other than the social reality that its hegemony constructs. The process that gives sexuality its male supremacist meaning is therefore the process through which gender inequality becomes *socially real*.'[62] Just as a 'Whites Only' sign in a racially segregated society does not merely represent the *idea* of apartheid, but is an *instance* of it, similarly, MacKinnon argues that pornography is to be understood not as representation of reality, but as reality itself.[63]

As we can see, the nature of the argument—as well as its target—is entirely different from traditional obscenity law. Whereas the justification for obscenity law relies upon moral argumentation, aimed at preventing the depravity and corruption of the individual, MacKinnon's critique is political in nature, and grounded in concerns of sexual equality. The focus is not upon prurience and offensiveness (patent or otherwise), but upon exploitation and subordination.

Closely connected with the argument from subordination is the argument from *silencing*. Pornography, it is claimed, in representing women as sex objects, and stripping them of agency, autonomy, and

---

[62] MacKinnon (1988: 149); emphasis mine.
[63] MacKinnon (1988: 156).

self-determination, creates an environment in which women's voices are systematically devalued, distorted, and stripped of significance. In this way, even as it is an exercise of the *pornographer's* right of free speech, pornography drowns out the speech of its *subjects*, that is, women.[64] Or, to put it another way, a pornography-soaked culture is one that impedes access to the public sphere for a certain set of people (women), by treating their voices as less important, or less worthy of respect, than that of men.[65] This argument is closely connected to Habermas' justification of free speech that we briefly discussed in the first chapter: if the validity of laws depends upon a free and open discourse in which everyone affected can participate on equal terms, then speech that acts against equal participation in the discourse is particularly problematic.

Based upon these two arguments—that of subordination and silencing—Catherine MacKinnon and Andrea Dworkin drafted an anti-pornography ordinance for the city of Indianapolis, in which they defined pornography as the 'graphic *sexually explicit subordination*'[66] of women through pictures or words that also includes women *dehumanized as sexual objects, things or commodities* (as distinguished from 'erotica', which was sexually explicit material premised on conditions of equality, and not covered by the ordinance). In *American Booksellers* v. *Hudnut*, the ordinance was struck down as unconstitutional. Judge Easterbrook, writing for the Ninth Circuit, accepted the premise that pornography perpetuated subordination, but nonetheless noted:

> Racial bigotry, anti-semitism, violence on television, reporters' biases— these and many more influence the culture and shape our socialization.

---

[64] Langton (1993); Hornsby (1995).

[65] MacKinnon compares the situation to one of group libel: '*it* [is] *understood that an individual's treatment and alternatives in life may depend as much on the reputation of the group to which that person belongs as on their own merit*'. (MacKinnon 1988: 192; emphasis mine).

[66] Section 16-3(q), Chapter 16, Code of Indianapolis and Marion County Indiana, available at http://www.nostatusquo.com/ACLU/dworkin/other/ordinance/newday/AppB1.htm (accessed 28 July 2015).

None is directly answerable by more speech, unless that speech too finds its place in the popular culture. Yet all is protected as speech, however insidious. *Any other answer leaves the government in control of all of the institutions of culture, the great censor and director of which thoughts are good for us*....A power to limit speech on the ground that truth has not yet prevailed and is not likely to prevail implies the power to declare truth. At some point the government must be able to say (as Indianapolis has said): 'We know what the truth is, yet a free exchange of speech has not driven out falsity, so that we must now prohibit falsity.' If the government may declare the truth, why wait for the failure of speech? *Under the First Amendment, however, there is no such thing as a false idea.*[67]

Or, in other words, a government that could decide to write its convictions about sexual equality into law by prohibiting pornography could also decide to enforce its convictions about science by silencing Galileo. If we are to guarantee the freedom of Galileo to voice his heretical opinions about the earth moving around the sun, then we have no choice but to also guarantee the freedom of the pornographer to undermine sexual equality.

Judge Easterbrook's opinion rests upon an absolutist conception of governmental neutrality (between ideas) that we have previously discussed as an aspect of political liberalism. As we have argued before, whatever the ultimate merits of that viewpoint, to the extent that Article 19(2) provides an express restriction on the grounds of 'morality', it is clear that absolute neutrality is not the conception of free speech that our Constitution is committed to. What we need to do is to take on board the philosophical merits of neutrality, and consider the situations in which a departure from that principle is justified. And, to emphasize again, the most potent justification is *that which is grounded in the principles of the Constitution itself*—that is, constitutional morality. This brings us back to the ideal of equality, and demonstrates how—if we understand pornography as the subordination and silencing of women—19(2)'s morality clause allows us to identify and

[67] *American Booksellers* v. *Hudnut*, 771 F.2d 323, 330–31 (7th Cir. 1985); emphasis mine.

regulate certain kinds of sexually explicit material on grounds that are located *within the Constitution*, as well as defensible philosophically.

One concrete instance of this is the Canadian Supreme Court's obscenity opinion in *R* v. *Butler* (which—as observed here—was referred to in *Aveek Sarkar*). In that case, the Court classified potentially obscene materials into those that depict 'explicit sex with violence', 'explicit sex without violence, but which subjects participants to treatment that is degrading or dehumanising', and 'explicit sex without violence that is neither degrading nor dehumanising'. It was the first two categories that could justifiably be outlawed consistent with freedom of speech guarantees. Notably, the Court stated that the objective was not to preserve morals, but to protect the community from harm—harm being defined as 'behaviour which society formally recognises as incompatible with its proper functioning'.[68] The Court identified gender equality as integral to the proper functioning of society, and drew the MacKinnon link between such pornography and equality: 'degrading or dehumanizing materials place women (and sometimes men) in positions of subordination, servile submission or humiliation. They run against the principles of equality and dignity of all human beings.'[69] The question of when a depiction of sex was degrading or dehumanising was where community standards came in. Community standards were used by the Court not to determine whether material was prurient or offensive, but whether its depiction of sex was degrading. In this way, community standards formed an ingredient of the obscenity analysis, but their application was very different—and based on a different set of principles—than the American obscenity test in *Roth* and subsequent cases.

Butler is a controversial case, and its analysis (especially the role of community standards) is open to criticism. Nonetheless, I suggest that it provides a helpful point of departure to change our constitutional thinking about sexually explicit material, whether it is the short stories of Chughtai, the novels of D.H. Lawrence, or the pornographic

[68] *Butler.*
[69] *Butler.*

films sold by the local DVD shop. Ultimately, the basis for regulation ought not to rest upon problematic conceptions of public morals or individual corruption, but upon constitutional fundamentals such as equality.[70]

Indeed, the South African Constitutional Court has followed a similar approach. In *Case*, which involved a challenge to the South African obscenity and indecency law, the Court thoroughly criticized the *Roth–Memoirs–Miller* line of cases in the United States. It emphasized that the distinction between the American and Canadian approaches lay in roles played by the amorphous conception of 'public morals' vis-à-vis constitutionally recognized harm.[71] The Court did not, however, uncritically accept *Butler* either. It warned that the Canadian approach could also be used to stifle 'marginalised discourses'[72] if 'harm' was interpreted too subjectively. Ultimately, it decided the case on overbreadth grounds, and did not incorporate a specific test. It was clear, however, that the Court favoured a variant of *Butler*, with strictly defined application. This was made clear in *De Reuck* v. *DPP*,[73] where a provision criminalizing the creation, distribution, or possession of child pornography (real or simulated) was challenged. Child pornography was defined as depiction of 'sexual conduct...which amounts to sexual exploitation, or participating in, or assisting another person to engage in sexual conduct which amounts to *sexual exploitation or degradation of children*.' Therefore—unlike the definitions in *Hicklin*, in *Roth*, and in *Aveek Sarkar*, where the focus was on the 'prurient interest' and/or the 'patent offensiveness' that the publication generates, the South African child pornography law required, in addition, 'exploitation or degradation'. In upholding the law, the South African Constitutional Court argued[74]—among other things—that the

---

[70] This by no means suggests that the conception of equality I propose here is the only one, or even the correct one.

[71] *Case* v. *Minister of Safety and Security*, 1996 (5) BCLR 608: 1996 (3) SA 617 (hereinafter *Case*).

[72] *Case*, para 47.

[73] *De Reuck* v. *DPP*, 2004 (1) SA 406 (hereinafter *De Reuck*).

[74] *De Reuck*, paras 61–63, 67.

objectification and sexualization of children violated their right to *dignity*, a specific Constitutional value.[75]

* * *

Let us briefly summarize. Our survey of international jurisprudence reveals two distinct arguments for regulating pornography and obscene material. The Anglo-American approach is public-morality based. It justifies regulation on the basis of the offensiveness of the impugned material. The Canadian and South African approach is harm-based, and it understands harm in the context of protecting established constitutional values, such as dignity and equality.

Indian obscenity law, shifting between *Hicklin* and *Roth* over fifty years, is loosely based upon a vague amalgamation of moral paternalism, which seeks to protect the individual from moral degradation and corruption by preventing access to 'prurient' materials, and public morality, which makes the 'community' the arbiter of what ought or ought not to be permitted by way of sexual depiction. It is broadly in line with the English and American approaches.

In this chapter, I have tried to criticize both these viewpoints: the first because it disrespects individual autonomy, and is inconsistent with the vision of the responsible, self-determining individual that the Court has (in my opinion, correctly) adopted in its public order decisions; and the second, both because of the impossibility of fairly determining the 'community' view in a country as heterogeneous and diverse as ours, and because of its unjustifiable imposition of one moral viewpoint to suffocate the expression of a dissenting minority.

---

[75] Section 10, Constitution of South Africa. Similarly, while the South African Constitutional Court was divided over the constitutional validity of a law prohibiting nude dancing in establishments that sold liquor, the judges who upheld the law were very clear that it was justified only because its objective was to prevent the harm that might flow from exhibiting such dances before intoxicated men. Justice Madala expressly held that 'there is no substance in the contention that the purpose of the provision is to force the morals of the majority onto the minority. If this were so, Parliament may have tried to prohibit erotic dancing all together' (*Phillips* v. *DPP*, 2003 (4) BCLR 357 (CC), para 50).

The alternative, I have suggested, is to read 19(2)'s morality clause as representing neither public morality nor individual morality, but *constitutional morality*, one aspect of which is equality. In the specific context of India and the Indian Constitution, equality is best understood as embodying a vision of anti-subordination. An equality–as–anti-subordination approach helps us to reorient our understanding of traditional obscenity laws, and provides a constitutionally-grounded, philosophically-justifiable argument for regulating certain kinds of sexually explicit material, as the Canadian Supreme Court did in *Butler*, and as the South African Court has done in *De Reuck*.

ADDENDUM: HOW OUGHT WE TO READ THE INDECENT REPRESENTATION OF WOMEN ACT?

The moral paternalism that formed the bedrock of the Court's analysis in *Ranjit Udeshi* has found legislative endorsement in the Indecent Representation of Women Act, passed by the Parliament in 1986. The Act prohibits the publication, distribution, circulation, and advertisement of any material that contains 'indecent representation of women in any form'[76] (there are boilerplate exceptions for material deemed to be in the 'public good', and religious representations). Indecent representation is defined as 'the depiction in any manner of…a woman… in such a way as to have the effect of being indecent, or derogatory to, or denigrating women, or is likely to deprave, corrupt or injure the public morality or morals'.[77]

Insofar as we understand 'indecency' to be determined by the effect of being derogatory towards (and further, understanding 'derogatory' in the language of dignity), or denigrating women ('denigration', one would assume, is denying someone an equal moral status), this legislation follows the Canadian–South African jurisprudence, and is grounded in constitutional morality. That, however, is entirely undone

---

[76] Sections 3 and 4, Indecent Representation of Women (Prohibition) Act, 1986.
[77] Section 2, Indecent Representation of Women Act (Prohibition), 1986.

by the next part of the definitional section, which echoes the *Ranjit Udeshi* language of depraving and corrupting public morals.

We have already discussed the flaws in such an approach. Here we may add that there is an obvious Article 14 problem with a law that privileges protecting public morality when it comes to depictions of women, but not men. Is it only women whose 'indecent' representation has the potentiality to corrupt the public morals? The paternalistic foundations of this legislation are clear: it rests upon a worldview that holds that women must be contained and confined within a narrow sphere of civility and respectability, if they are not to pose a threat to the morals of society.

The Canadian approach would require reading the public morals clause as *evidence* of something being derogatory to or denigrating women. The word 'or' between the two, however, rules out that interpretation under the constraints of maintaining fidelity to the text. Alternatively, 'public morality' itself could be understood as espousing the values of equality and dignity. Until—and unless—a judicial decision interprets the Act in that way, however, the Indecent Representation of Women Act remains a constitutionally unjustifiable restriction upon the freedom of speech and expression.

CHAPTER SIX

Hate Speech

. . . .

Police on Sunday arrested a 21-year-old girl for questioning the total
shutdown in the city for Bal Thackeray's funeral on her Facebook account.
Another girl who 'liked' the comment was also arrested.

The duo were booked under Section 295 (a) [sic] of the IPC (for hurting
religious sentiments) and Section 64 (a) [sic] of the Information Technology
Act, 2000. Though the girl withdrew her comment and apologised, a mob
of some 2,000 Shiv Sena workers attacked and ransacked her uncle's
orthopaedic clinic at Palghar.

'Her comment said people like Thackeray are born and die daily and one
should not observe a bandh for that,' said PI [Police Inspector] Uttam
Sonawane.[1]

—Mumbai Mirror, 19 November 2012

Over the years, the law has emerged as a weapon of choice for
groups or constituencies claiming to be offended or hurt by a
literary or artistic work.[2] A number of provisions constitute the back-
bone of the applicable legal regime, many of them from the colonial

---

[1] The correct account should read 'Section 295A' and 'Section 66A'.

[2] As Siddharth Narrain correctly notes in his detailed thesis on hate speech law
in India, groups making these claims include 'religious groups (Hindus, Muslims,
Christians), intra-religious groups (Shias), caste groups (Lingayats, Dalits),
occupation-based groups, which have strong caste associations (washermen,
cobblers), language groups (Oriya speakers), gender-based groups, intersecting

era, and one as recent as 2008. Sections 295A and 153A of the Indian Penal Code, and Section 66A of the Information Technology Act have been in the news in recent times, but the Indian Penal Code contains numerous variations.[3] Under these sections, books have been banned; books have been withdrawn; people arrested for political satire, for political critique, and for 'liking' someone else's political critique on Facebook.[4] Requirements of prior sanction and other safeguards ensure that not all cases come to trial. Nonetheless, a large part of the problem is the cognizable nature of these offences under the Code of Criminal Procedure, which grants the police the powers of arrest without the need for obtaining a judicially sanctioned warrant.[5]

If the entire raison d'être of free speech is the advocacy of political, social, and cultural change, if free speech 'best serves its high purpose when it induces a condition of unrest, creates dissatisfaction with conditions as they are, or even *stirs people to anger*',[6] if freedom of speech is nothing without the freedom to 'offend, shock or disturb'[7]—then the above examples seem to indicate that there is something problematic about the workings of free speech law in India today. Yet is the issue merely one of flawed process?

Let us examine the substantive law. Section 295A (insulting religious feelings) and Section 153A (causing disharmony or enmity between different castes and communities) of the Indian Penal

---

with language (Tamil women), nationalist based claims (Indians affected because Gandhi was disparaged)' (Narrain 2014).

[3] See, for instance, Section 298 (uttering words with deliberate intent to wound the religious feelings of a person); Section 509 (word, gesture, or act intended to insult the modesty of a woman); see also Section 508 (act caused by inducing a person to believe that he will be rendered an object of divine displeasure); Section 504 (intentional insult with intent to provoke a breach of peace). The latter two provisions sit somewhat uncomfortably within the conceptual domain of hate speech.

[4] See epigraph to this chapter.

[5] For a detailed account of how the process becomes the punishment in such cases, see Dhavan (2008: 175, 197–201).

[6] *Terminiello* v. *Chicago*, 337 U.S. 1, 4 (1949); emphasis mine.

[7] *Handyside* v. *The United Kingdom*, (no. 5493/72), [1976] ECHR 5 (7 December 1976).

Code, Section 66A of the Information Technology Act (offensive or 'menacing' speech) along with other provisions such as Section 123 of the Representation of the People Act (restricting certain kinds of speech during elections), and Section 3(1)(x) of the Scheduled Castes and Scheduled Tribes (Prevention of Atrocities) Act can be clubbed together under the compendious category of 'hate speech': speech that is, broadly speaking, derogatory towards someone else. Most democracies (the United States is the exception) have provisions regulating and curtailing hate speech. The challenge is to ensure that regulation is compatible with republican principles, the rule of law, and the overriding importance of the freedom of expression in a democracy. The implementation of various hate speech laws in India, as we have seen here, fails the challenge. The task remains, however, to reconcile hate speech legislation (as it stands) with free expression, and to provide an interpretation of these laws that is consistent with Article 19(2). That is the burden of this chapter.

At the outset—to briefly repeat a point made at the end of Chapter Three—we may note that hate speech restrictions can be justified under two 19(2) heads. *Ramji Lal Modi*[8] understood Section 295A to be about preserving public order by protecting religious feelings. Section 153A, similarly, has often been described in public order terms. Those arguments have been critiqued extensively during the discussion of public order. In this chapter, my concern is to examine hate speech on the touchstone of the 'morality' provision. When—if ever—can a democracy justifiably regulate or prohibit speech not because of any causal connection to public disorder, but simply because the *content* of that speech is in some way derogatory or offensive?

SECTIONS 295A AND 153A: ANTECEDENTS, INTERPRETATION, AND ABUSE

Section 295A criminalizes insulting or attempting to insult 'the religion or the religious beliefs' of a class of citizens, 'with deliberate and

[8] *Ramji Lal Modi v. State of UP*, [1957] 1 SCR 860.

malicious intention of outraging...religious feelings'. The antecedents of Section 295A lie in the communally charged atmosphere of North India in the 1920s. Tensions were exacerbated particularly when a tract—brought out by a Hindu publisher—made certain disparaging remarks about Prophet Muhammad's private life. The publisher was found not guilty by the Punjab High Court under Section 153A of the Indian Penal Code (promotion of hatred or enmity among different classes).[9] The Punjab High Court distinguished between an attack on a *community*, and an attack on a *deceased leader of that community*, holding that polemics against the latter did not come within the meaning of 153A. Consequently, there were calls for the judge to be replaced, and thinly veiled threats were issued by leaders of the Muslim community, intent on 'protecting the honour of the Prophet'.[10] Tensions worsened with the publication of a second, similar piece. This time, the Lahore High Court held that a 'scurrilous and foul attack'[11] on a religious leader would prima facie fall within Section 153A—*although not every criticism need do so.*

It was in this context—and responding to the resulting communal tensions stemming from the unsettled nature of the law—that the colonial government amended the Indian Penal Code to insert Section 295A. As Neeti Nair records, there was considerable controversy when the Bill was first introduced in the legislative assembly, and when it was discussed by a Select Committee. Dissenters were worried about an evident lack of protection for the press, for sceptical atheists, for humourists, and for social reformers.[12] The response was that 'fair comments' and 'honest views as regards religious beliefs' would continue to be protected, even under the new law.[13] Ultimately,

---

[9] Nair (2013). Section 295A is supplemented by Section 298, which punishes 'whoever, with the deliberate intention of wounding the religious feelings of any person, utters any word or makes any sound in the hearing of that person or makes any gesture in the sight of that person or places, any object in the sight of that person'.

[10] Nair (2013: 324).

[11] Nair (2013: 330).

[12] Nair (2013: 331).

[13] Nair (2013: 336).

Explanations to the Section, seeking to protect fact-based criticism of religious figures, especially in the course of 'historical or sociological or philosophical disquisitions', were also not moved.[14]

The historical context of Section 295A raises a few important points. First, contrary to *Ramji Lal Modi*, Section 295A was not only about public order. Although it arose out of a situation of communal tension, the objective ultimately was to 'protect religious feelings'. Whatever the validity of that objective for a colonial government, it must clearly be examined afresh in light of a Constitution that is premised on equality and the freedom of expression. Second, as the debate within the Select Committee demonstrates, the objective of the Section was never to cover scholarship or art, but rather, the 'scurrilous scribbler'.[15] The vague and overbroad framing of the Section, and the absence of clarifying Explanations have, however, led to precisely the consequences that the dissenting voices of the Select Committee feared: when it has come to ground-level implementation, it is precisely writers and artists that have been targeted. Instances are famous, and more recent ones include Taslima Nasreen and Dan Brown.[16]

The abuse of Section 295A is not limited to the executive.[17] *Sri Baragur Ramachandrappa* v. *State of Karnataka*[18] represents one of the more problematic moments of the Supreme Court's ambiguous engagement with free speech.[19] That case involved the ban of an award-winning Kannada novel that fictionalized the life of the twelfth-century Saint Basaveshwara. In this fictional account, the author suggested that Basaveshwara's nephew was born out of wedlock, and the public odium that followed his birth compelled the family to leave the town. These suggestions so infuriated people who revered Basaveshwara,

---

[14] Nair (2013: 338).

[15] Nair (2013: 330).

[16] A ban on Taslima Nasreen's book was overturned by the Calcutta High Court, primarily on the ground that it was aimed at social reform (*Sujato Bhadra* v. *State of West Bengal*, 2005 Cr LJ 368).

[17] See, for instance, *Baba Khalil Ahmed* v. *State*, AIR 1960 All 715; *State of Mysore* v. *Henry Rodriguez*, 1962 (2) Cr LJ 564.

[18] (2007) 3 SCC 11 (hereinafter *Baragur Ramachandrappa*).

[19] For more examples of a recent vintage, see Venkatesan (2014: 204–27).

that they moved for the book to be banned and forfeited. The state complied. The ban was challenged before the Supreme Court, which upheld it, in the following words: 'no person has a right to *impinge on the feelings* of others on the premise that his right to freedom of speech remains unrestricted and unfettered. It cannot be ignored that India is [a] country with vast disparities in language, culture and religion and *unwarranted and malicious criticism or interference in the faith* of others cannot be accepted.'[20]

The Court then decided to take it upon itself to resolve a historical disagreement about the actual parentage of Channabasaveshwara. What follows rivals *Ranjit Udeshi*,[21] and deserves to be quoted in full:

> Chennabasavanna was regarded as the son of Nagalambike, though the identity of the father was not known and several alternatives have thereafter been spelt out. *We find however that there is no suggestion whatsoever that Akkanagamma had conceived out of wedlock.* Reference has also been made to an Article written by Dr. B.V. Mallapur, Reader in Kannada, Karnataka University, Dharwad and published by the Department of Kannada and Culture, Bangalore, which refers to the speculation as to the circumstances leading to the birth of Channabasavanna and *several theories have been mooted but again without any suggestion of illegitimacy.* Our

---

[20] *Baragur Ramachandrappa*, para 8; emphasis mine. In adopting a supposedly 'pragmatic' approach to the freedom of speech and expression, the Court was following the opinion in *State of UP* v. *Lalai Singh Yadav*, where Krishna Iyer J. noted that 'essentially, good government necessitates peace and security and whoever violates by bombs or books societal tranquillity will become target of legal interdict by the State'. *State of UP* v. *Lalai Singh Yadav*, (1976) 4 SCC 213. Notwithstanding Krishna Iyer J.'s famed love for alliteration, the fact that the Indian Supreme Court, supposedly tasked with the protection of core fundamental rights, could think that 'books' and 'bombs' are interchangeable in this facile manner, reflects the deep pathology of our civil liberties jurisprudence. What is the difference between the Security State and the Supreme Court? Often, the answer seems to be: none. The broader point, of course, is that a 'pragmatic approach' to civil liberties is a contradiction in terms. We are guaranteed certain basic rights as matters of principle, and these rights are constitutionally entrenched *precisely* to place them beyond the domain of politics and pragmatism. A 'pragmatic' understanding of the freedom of speech renders the right as illusory as the rabbit in a magician's hat.

[21] *Ranjit Udeshi* v. *State of Maharashtra*, AIR 1965 SC 881: [1965] 1 SCR 65.

attention has then been drawn to an article by Dr. R.C. Hiremath, an expert in the history of the Veerashaivas, and he too refers to the speculation as to the birth of Channabasavanna, and to the belief amongst common folk of the region that if those who were childless were to sing a particular lullaby they would be endowed with children, and reference is made to the fact that Akkanagamma had inadvertently swallowed some 'prasada' and had become pregnant thereby, *but there is again no suggestion as to her conception out of wedlock.* The author has also cited the other instances like those of Shankaracharya, Seeta and Jesus who are believed to have taken birth in unusual circumstances. We notice from Annexure P8 that there is no indication in any of the articles that Akkanagamma was of low character to be equated with Jabala *or the slightest hint that Akkanagamma had conceived Channabasaveshwara outside her marriage and had left Bagewadi in shame for that reason.* We therefore endorse the suggestion made by the learned Advocate General and the counsel for the intervener that Chapter 12 is not in sync with the rest of the novel and has been deliberately designed to be hurtful and to bring the family to shame. *We also have no hesitation in observing that the novel with its complimentary passages in favour of Basaveshwara is merely a camouflage to spin and introduce a particularly sordid and puerile story in Chapter 12.*[22]

Only, Baragur Ramachandrappa was writing *fiction.*

In effect, the Supreme Court held that if the writer of *historical fiction* was unable to demonstrate to the satisfaction of a judge that some incident was not *absolutely settled* by scholarly consensus in his favour, and that incident offended people who 'revered' the subject of the book, it was clearly 'deliberately designed to be hurtful', and a fit subject for a ban.[23] This chain of reasoning, I would suggest, is unconvincing.

Section 153A—whose pernicious nature was well-recognized during the Constituent Assembly Debates[24]—bears a similar history.[25]

---

[22] *Baragur Ramachandrappa*, paras 22–23; emphasis mine.

[23] Compare *Baragur Ramachandrappa* with the Bombay High Court's famous decision in *Gopal Vinayak Godse* v. *Union of India*, AIR 1971 Bom 56 (hereinafter *Gopal Vinayak Godse*), where the Court held that the mere fact that the writer's claims were not completely borne out by history did not mean that Section 153A was attracted.

[24] See Narrain (2014: 18).

[25] For some early cases interpreting this Section, see *Rajpal* v. *Emperor*, AIR 1927 Lah 590; *Kali Charan Sharma* v. *King-Emperor*, AIR 1927 All 654.

One of the more recent instances of this was the controversy surrounding James Laine's book, *Shivaji: A Hindu King in Islamic India*. The writing of this historical work on Shivaji was followed by a Pune mob blackening the face of a Sanskrit scholar who was supposed to have assisted Laine in his research. Another mob ransacked the Bhandarkar Oriental Research Institute and destroyed a large number of manuscripts.[26] Soon after that, the Maharashtra government banned the book. The ban was challenged and struck down by the Bombay High Court. The government appealed. Ironically, before the Supreme Court, the ransacking of the Bhandarkar Institute was used *as evidence* of the fact that the book created feelings of enmity between classes (originally, it was argued that the enmity was between those who revere Shivaji and those who do not, although by the time the case came up to the Supreme Court, the groups became Marathas and Brahmins).[27] It was also argued that if a book caused enmity between classes, it could not be protected under Article 19(1)(a) *even if it contained historical truth*.[28]

Ultimately, the Court upheld the Bombay High Court's decision on the narrow, procedural ground that the government's banning order did not specify the classes or communities between which enmity had been created.[29] It added that the perspective from which the book ought to be judged must be that of 'the standards of reasonable, strong-minded, firm and courageous men, and not those of weak and vacillating minds, nor of those who scent danger in every hostile

[26] Mathur (2004).

[27] *State of Maharashtra* v. *Sangharaj Damodar Rupawate*, (2010) 7 SCC 398, para 8 (hereinafter *Rupawate*).

[28] *Rupawate*, para 10.

[29] In *Bilal Ahmed Kaloo* v. *State of Andhra Pradesh*, AIR 1997 SC 3483 (hereinafter *Bilal Ahmed Kaloo*), the Supreme Court likewise reversed a 153A conviction. The accused was alleged to have been fomenting 'communal hatred' by spreading the news that army personnel were committing atrocities against Kashmiri Muslims. The Court focused on the phrase 'between different...communities', and held that 'merely inciting the feeling of one community or group without any reference to any other community or group cannot attract either of the two sections' (*Bilal Ahmed Kaloo*, para 15).

point of view'.[30] However, it *also* upheld the contention that historical truth was *not* a complete defence to a Section 153A charge.[31]

This is a pyrrhic victory because it takes history out of the hands of the historians, and puts it into the clutches of offended constituencies. Will Section 153A be attracted if a book about the Holocaust holds the German nation historically responsible for genocide against the Jews? Or if a book on the caste system holds the Brahmins responsible for systematic violence against lower castes? The debilitating impact of the Supreme Court's stance was illustrated recently, when the Orient Blackswan publishing house withdrew a whole host of academic texts for 'review'. One of the texts was the historian Megha Kumar's account of the impact of communal riots in Ahmedabad upon women. Kumar was asked to 'excise' certain paragraphs which, apparently, would have violated Section 153A. On asking for legal advice, she was told by former Attorney-General Soli Sorabjee that historical truth was not a defence under Section 153A.[32]

While the Court's own attempt at historical analysis in *Baragur Ramachandrappa* is almost a parody, the position of the law is concerning. The parallels with sedition should also be obvious. Sedition is based on the premise that the people must bear goodwill towards the government, and not be disaffected with it, whether or not it deserves their goodwill or affection. Similarly, Section 153A seems to require that good relations be maintained among different 'classes', even when it comes to indisputably genuine historical scholarship. That the Indian past (and indeed, the present) was, and remains, hierarchical, oppressive, and frequently violent is undeniable. Its suppression under Section 153A is even more problematic.

SECTIONS 153A, 295A, AND THE PROBLEM OF BURDENS

In addition to the substantive issues with the Supreme Court's understanding of Sections 295A and 153A, there is also an acute problem

[30] *Rupawate*, para 25.
[31] *Rupawate*.
[32] Joshua (2014).

with the procedure under which books may be banned. The procedure is contained in Section 95 of the Code of Criminal Procedure,
which reads:

> Where…any newspaper, or book, or…any document, wherever printed,
> *appears* to the State Government to contain any matter the publication of
> which is punishable under section 124A or section 153A or section 153B
> or section 292…of the [Indian Penal Code], the State Government may,
> by notification, stating the grounds of its opinion, declare every copy
> of…[such] document to be forfeited.[33]

The key word in Section 95 is 'appears'. This word was the subject of
dispute in both *Baragur Ramachandrappa* and the James Laine case.
In *Baragur Ramachandrappa*, the Court held that the meaning of the
word 'appear' placed upon the government a lighter burden of justification than the word 'proved' because Section 95 was of a 'preventive
nature'.[34] Or, in other words, there is no need for any evidence that
the requirements of Section 153A (enmity between classes) or 295A
(insulting religious feelings) have *actually* been satisfied. All that is
required is that it '*appear*' to the government that they have. In *State of
Maharashtra* v. *Sangharaj Damodar Rupawate* (the James Laine case),
the Supreme Court accepted this interpretation, and also followed
Baragur Ramachandrappa in holding that the burden of *dislodging the
government's prima facie opinion lay on the applicant!*[35]

We have discussed before the unique problems attendant upon a
regime of prior restraint. It is noteworthy that Section 95, in permitting the executive to ban and confiscate books *without the need for an
actual legal violation*, exhibits some of the more pernicious features
of prior restraint. Equally noteworthy is the Court's failure to engage
with the severe dangers to free speech that prior restraint poses. Recall
that as far back as 1769, in a time not exactly known for the freedom of speech, the great English jurist William Blackstone was able
to write that 'the liberty of the press is indeed essential to the nature

---

[33] Section 95, Code of Criminal Procedure 1973; emphasis mine.
[34] *Baragur Ramachandrappa*, para 18.
[35] *Rupawate*, para 25.

of a free state...[and] consists in laying *no previous restraints upon publications*'.[36] In America, prior restraint was held unconstitutional, subject to very narrow exceptions, by the Supreme Court in *Near v. Minnesota*.[37] In another case, the Court noted that it is impermissible to 'vest restraining control over the right to speak in an *administrative official* where there are *no appropriate standards to guide his action*'.[38]

The dangers that accompany a system of prior restraint are discussed by the free speech scholar, Emerson. Emerson points out that a system of prior restraint involves far more pervasive governmental involvement in censorship than a system of subsequent punishment. It makes it much easier for the government to suppress free expression, than it would be if it had to approach the court for subsequent punishment; the procedure is administrative rather than judicial; and so on.[39] The most potent danger, in addition, is the placement of burden. In a system of subsequent punishment, it is the *State* that must approach the court, and prove its case. Under Section 95 of the Code of Criminal Procedure, however, it is the *individual* who bears the burden of going to court and attempting to get the State ban lifted.[40]

This being the case, and in light of the fact that free speech is a crucially important constitutional right, one would at least expect that in court proceedings, it is the *State* that must justify the ban. It is the State that must explain, to the satisfaction of the court, why it has decided to curtail the freedom of speech. According to *Baragur*

---

[36] Blackstone (1765–69); emphasis mine.

[37] 283 U.S. 697 (1931).

[38] *Kunz v. New York*, 340 U.S. 290, 295 (1951); emphasis mine.

[39] Emerson (1955). See also Sorabjee (2000: 342), who draws an important distinction between prior restraint and a licensing regime, such as that found in the 1867 press registration law.

[40] Unfortunately, the perils of such partial prior restraint to a thriving system of free speech were not even considered by the Bombay High Court in *Gopal Vinayak Godse* where the constitutionality of Section 99A of the old Code of Criminal Procedure (which would go on to become Section 95 of the 1973 Code of Criminal Procedure) was challenged. Rejecting the challenge, the Court simply noted that since Sections 124A, 153A, and 295A covered issues of 'national importance', Section 99A's forfeiture provisions were constitutionally valid.

Ramachandrappa and *Rupawate*, however, it is the *individual* (writer or artist) who not only bears the burden of approaching the court to get the ban lifted, but also of proving to the court that he ought to be allowed to exercise his constitutionally guaranteed liberty of expression!

It is important to note that—*contra* the Supreme Court's analysis, there is nothing in the text of Section 96 of the Code of Criminal Procedure that allocates burdens in this manner. Section 96 entitles individuals having an interest in the banned material to appeal an order of forfeiture under Section 95, to a Special Bench of the jurisdictional High Court. It authorizes the High Court to set aside the order of forfeiture if it is not satisfied that the material actually violates the stated laws. Section 96 is entirely silent upon the evidentiary burdens at issue. In light of this ambivalence, the Supreme Court effectively interpreting it to require anyone wishing to exercise their fundamental right under Article 19(1)(a) to establish that their writing has *not* broken the law is, it is submitted, incorrect.

Section 95 of the Code of Criminal Procedure: The Fault in Our Standard

The construction of Section 95 of the Code of Criminal Procedure, as provided by *Baragur Ramachandrappa* and the James Laine case, I contend, rests upon an incorrect premise. The argument that under Section 95, the government only needs to demonstrate a prima facie 'appearance' that a book might violate Sections 124A, 153A, 295A, and so on, is somewhat analogous to judicial review standards in administrative law. In a challenge to an administrative decision, the court will not concern itself with the merits of the decision, but will restrict itself to examining whether there existed any grounds on which the decision was taken, and whether these grounds were *relevant* to the decision. Similarly, the effect of the James Laine case seems to be that the government's obligation under Section 95 is limited to specifying the groups between whom disharmony will be created (grounds), and why that might 'appear' to be the case (prima facie determination of relevance).

A hands-off judicial approach in administrative law cases is quite obviously sound. Administrative decisions involve weighing and balancing a host of (often complex) policy questions. Both in terms of competence and legitimacy, this is an exercise best left to the government (or its delegate). The situation is completely different, however, when the government's decision deprives individuals of their fundamental rights, rights that it is the court's constitutionally mandated task to safeguard. In such cases, a deferential administrative law standard is entirely inappropriate.

Contra Baragur Ramachandrappa and the James Laine case, in a series of precedents, the courts had actually been acutely aware of their role while construing Section 95 (or Section 99A in the pre-1973 Code of Criminal Procedure). In *Harnam Das* v. *State of Uttar Pradesh*, a Constitution Bench of the Supreme Court made it clear that 'it is the duty of the High Court to set aside an order of forfeiture if it is not satisfied that the grounds on which the Government formed its opinion…could justify that opinion.'[41] In holding the government to a strict standard in such cases, the Gujarat High Court specifically noted that 'the State is dealing with the fundamental rights of its citizens and therefore, great amount of caution, prudence and care is expected.'[42]

What emerges out of these cases is that under Section 95, the government's confiscation order must state the communities that the book will allegedly alienate from one another, and explain how that will happen. This is an essential, liberty-protecting procedural requirement, which the courts have correctly laid great stress upon, and thrown out cases because of the government's failure to comply. Beyond that, the waters are somewhat muddy. According to *Baragur Ramachandrappa* and the James Laine case, the government need only show that there was an 'appearance' of the confiscated material causing such harms, and then the burden shifts to the individual to demonstrate the contrary. According to *Harnam Das* and its progeny, however, there must be a full-blooded enquiry into whether the offending tract actually violates Section 153A, 295A, or the other provisions mentioned in

---

[41] AIR 1961 SC 1662, para 16.
[42] *Manishi Jani* v. *State of Gujarat*, AIR 2010 Guj 30, para 10.

Section 95 of the Code of Criminal Procedure, in light of the fact that fundamental rights are at stake. In light of all our previous discussion, it should be evident that it is the second approach that is far more consistent with our constitutional free speech principles.[43]

CAUSING OFFENCE: DEMOCRACY, PRIVATE CENSORSHIP, AND CULTURAL DISSENT

> …[impurities] *give rise to changes, in other words, to life.…In order for the wheel to turn, for life to be lived, impurities are needed, and the impurities of impurities in the soil, too, as is known if it is to be fertile. Dissension, diversity, the grain of salt and mustard are needed.*
>
> —Primo Levi, *The Periodic Table*

In light of the Supreme Court's lukewarm approach towards restricting the scope of Sections 153A and 295A, Penguin Books' controversial withdrawal of Chicago professor Wendy Doniger's book on Hinduism is hardly surprising.[44] Faced with 295A proceedings, and the prospect of interminable legal proceedings with an uncertain outcome, Penguin's decision was, ultimately, an indictment of the 153A–295A regime, and the courts' failure to extend meaningful protection to writers and artists.

---

[43] Section 95 of the Code of Criminal Procedure has an even more stringent, analogous set of provisions: Section 111(d) of the Customs Act authorizes the confiscation of goods that have been brought within Indian customs waters, contrary to any provision of the Customs Act or any other law in force. Under its predecessor—the 1878 Sea Customs Act—there was a government notification that prohibited bringing into the territory of India any newspaper, news-sheet, book, or other document that was likely to—inter alia—incite violence or sabotage, promote feelings of enmity or hatred between sections of the people, or was grossly indecent, scurrilous, or obscene. *Gajanan Vishweshwar* v. *Union of India*, (1994) 5 SCC 550, was a case where books containing the writings of Mao Zedong were confiscated. The Court struck down the confiscation orders, on the ground that—much like the Section 95 (Code of Criminal Procedure) cases—they did not explain the grounds on which the government notification was attracted. The Court ended by handing down a few choice remarks about thought control in a democratic society. For an account of censorship and its discontents under the Customs Act, see Dhavan (2008: 148–51).

[44] Burke (2014).

The Doniger case is important because it brings together two crucial questions that are individually and separately present in *Baragur Ramachandrappa* and *Rupawate*, and require a detailed analysis: first: *what* ought Section 295A protect; and second: *who* ought it protect? *Baragur Ramachandrappa's* invocation of the 'reasonable, strong-willed man' standard is an attempt to clarify that not every instance of hurt feelings can suffice to attract 295A. *Rupawate's* insistence on showing the existence of identifiable *classes* between whom enmity must be generated is a similar attempt to focus on the question of the subjects of protection. Let us consider both issues.

The Court's reasonable man standard—without more—is really nothing but an invitation for judges to fill in their own opinions into a more or less empty vessel of subjectivity (as *Baragur Ramachandrappa* itself shows). It does, however, illustrate an important point: *mere subjective feelings of hurt or offence cannot be a ground for curtailing the freedom of speech.* This should be immediately obvious. If every single person has a private right to prevent somebody else from speaking on the basis of hurt feelings, the freedom of speech is entirely meaningless. The Bombay High Court put the point particularly eloquently in its discussion of the State's ban on the play '*Mee Nathuram Godse Boltoy*', when it observed: 'The right of the playwright, of the artist, writer and of the poet will be reduced to husk if the freedom to portray a message—whether it be in canvas, prose or verse—is to depend upon the *popular perception of the acceptability of that message.* Popular perceptions, however strong cannot override values which the constitution embodies as guarantees of freedom in what was always intended to be a free society.'[45]

In *Baragur Ramachandrappa*, therefore, the Court is incorrect when it claims that speakers can be prevented from '*impinging*' upon others' feelings. It would be absurd, for instance, if as a devout believer I could claim that my feelings were outraged by the publication of tracts defending evolution—and get all books on evolution banned on that ground—no matter how genuine, sincere, or deeply felt my

---

[45] *Anand Chintamani Dighe* v. *State of Maharashtra*, (2002) 1 Bom LR 671, para 19; emphasis mine.

outrage is. In technical terms, this is known as the 'heckler's veto', and has been widely decried by constitutional courts.[46]

More troublingly, however, Section 295A privileges certain kinds of offence, or insult, or outrage, which are grounded in *religion*, over others, which are not. Correspondingly, it accords to religious believers a right to suppress offending material that is not accorded to non-religious people. My belief in Basaveshwara, apparently, justifies the State in banning a book that questions whether his nephew was born out of wedlock because I find that offensive and insulting. My deeply held conviction in atheism, however, gives me no right to ask the State to ban the Bible and the Qu'ran, which inform me that I will spend an eternity in hell for my opinions, no matter how offensive *I* might find that. My sincere belief in pacifism and deep revulsion to armed conflict give me no right to demand the banning of books that glorify war. How can a Constitution committed to equality before law (Article 14) and non-discrimination on the basis of religion (Article 15) justify placing a higher value upon religious believers' feelings than upon the feelings of all others?

This should be enough to demonstrate that what is at stake cannot be simply subjective hurt feelings. The text of 295A itself makes that clear. It does not use the word 'offence', but makes the gravamen of the offence the causing of *insult*. Insult, as distinguished from 'offence', indicates an objective component to the utterance that goes beyond the subjective reaction of its target. Yet what, precisely, is the objective component that we ought to read into Section 295A? Since the ultimate touchstone of the validity and interpretation of all legislation is the Constitution, Section 295A—like all other laws—must be consistent with Article 19(2). The objective component of 'insult', therefore, must be found in 19(2)'s morality clause. In the next section, I shall

---

[46] The point was nicely summed up by the European Court of Human Rights, when it noted that 'a legal system which applies restrictions on human rights in order to satisfy the dictates of public feeling—real or imaginary—cannot be regarded as meeting the pressing social needs recognised in a democratic society, since that society must remain reasonable in its judgement....[This] would mean that freedom of speech and opinion is subjected to the heckler's veto' (*Vajnai* v. *Hungary*, (2010) 50 EHRR 44 (hereinafter *Vajnai*)).

argue for an interpretation of 295A that is informed by an under-standing of constitutional morality under Article 19(2).

Let us now turn to the question of *whom* to protect. In *Rupawate*, the Court ultimately lifted the ban because the government failed to show which the hostile 'groups' were, within the meaning of Section 153A. Section 295A similarly identifies as its subject a 'class' of citizens. This brings us to the crucial issue of cultural authority. What does it mean to say that a particular book offends *Marathas*, or the *followers of Basaveshwara*, as a class? What does it mean to say that Wendy Doniger's book is insulting towards *Hindus*? The very framing of the issue in those terms betrays two crucial assumptions: that the culture, religion, or set of beliefs at stake are monolithic, uniform, and fixed for all time, and that the people claiming to be insulted or offended speak for the entire group that they are part of. As a historical matter, both assumptions are demonstrably false. As a normative matter, they are extremely hostile towards the basic purposes of a system of free expression because they deny the possibility of cultural dissent.

As Madhavi Sunder points out, 'cultures now more than ever are characterized by cultural dissent...today, more and more individuals are claiming a right to dissent from traditional cultural norms and to make new cultural meanings—that is, to reinterpret cultural norms in ways more favourable to them'.[47] Thus, cultures are not autonomous, bounded, and homogenous systems. Their boundaries and their con-tents are constantly being contested, modified, and renegotiated. Nor is this unique to modernity: anthropologists have long argued that 'any complex human society at any point in time, is composed of multiple material and symbolic practices with a history'.[48] Therefore, as the cul-tural critic Marina Warner eloquently puts the point, 'the notion of a pure tradition should be met with derision wherever it is raised: tradi-tion must be impure, or it cannot thrive...when I choose an old casket [of tradition] I do not want it made of stable gold, but of something changeable, like copper, turning different colours with time'.[49]

---

[47] Sunder (2001: 498).
[48] Benhabib (2002: 60).
[49] Warner (2006: 83).

In addition to this, political societies are invariably highly stratified and hierarchical. Consequently, what we commonly understand as 'public culture' is often little more than the expression of the extant dominant group in society. That does not mean, however, that the rest of society is silenced. As James Scott has argued, for every public transcript of the dominant, there exists a parallel 'hidden transcript' of the oppressed, that occurs 'off-stage'.[50] The problem with taking the *visible* public culture as the culture of *all* society, involves therefore, a double-silencing of certain voices: an initial silencing at the time of the production of culture, and a contemporary silencing when, in court, the dominant public culture is taken to include all of society.

Therefore, when Dinanath Batra argues for a ban on Wendy Doniger's book, the claim is more than just outraged feelings. It is a claim to cultural authority, a claim against cultural dissent, and a claim that *one* view of Hinduism, produced and generated by one group at one particular time, *must* be the view adopted by all those who call themselves Hindus at all times (the 295A 'class'). What makes this view so dangerous is precisely that it denies all persons an equal participation in the production of culture. As Jack Balkin points out, 'dissent is central to...free speech, [and] dissent is cultural as well as political. People may disagree with what the government is doing...but they can also disagree with the aesthetics and mores of others, and they can dissent by borrowing from and subverting what they borrow. And just as democratic culture undergirds democracy in the narrow sense without being identical to it, cultural dissent is an important source of political dissent without being subsumed by it.'[51]

Thus, when the court upholds a ban on a book, it is taking sides in the debate on culture, and agreeing with one group's definition of what culture must be for everyone else. It is that which violates both the equality of all persons to shape their culture, and their right to express themselves about a culture, from the public production of which they might well have been historically excluded.

---

[50] Scott (1990).
[51] Balkin (2004: 44).

'CONSTITUTIONAL MORALITY' AND THE TRUE HARM IN HATE SPEECH

What, then, should hate speech really be about? Who should it protect and what should it proscribe? In 2014, perhaps for the first time, the Court subjected the issue to close, analytical scrutiny, and provided a reasoned answer. In *Pravasi Bhalai Sangathan* v. *Union of India*,[52] the Court was asked to issue orders or guidelines for the general curtailment of hate speech (especially in the context of elections). It declined to do so on the ground that existing legislation was adequate to deal with the issue. This means that the Court's judgment would have no precedential value. Nonetheless, the Court also decided to explicate its understanding of hate speech laws, and their place in a democratic republic committed to the freedom of speech and expression.

The tone of the judgment was set by the petition itself, which asked the Court to declare, inter alia, that hate speech violated Articles 14 (equal protection of laws) and 15 (non-discrimination). Taking up the petitioners on their suggestion, the Court cited the Canadian decision in *Sasketchewan* v. *Whatcott*[53] (which we shall discuss later in this chapter), before incorporating the Canadian Supreme Court's observations into its own judgment:

> Hate speech is an effort to *marginalise individuals based on their membership in a group.* Using expression that exposes the group to hatred, hate speech seeks to *delegitimise group members* in the eyes of the majority, reducing their social standing and acceptance within society. Hate speech, therefore, *rises beyond causing distress to individual group members.* It can have a societal impact. Hate speech lays the groundwork for later, broad attacks on [the] vulnerable that can range from discrimination, to ostracism, segregation, deportation, violence and, in the most extreme cases, to genocide. *Hate speech also impacts a protected group's ability to respond to the substantive ideas under debate, thereby placing a serious barrier to their full participation in our democracy.*[54]

---

[52] AIR 2014 SC 1591 (hereinafter *Pravasi Bhalai Sangathan*).
[53] *Saskatchewan (Human Rights Commission)* v. *Whatcott*, [2013] 1 SCR 467: [2013] SCC 11 (hereinafter *Whatcott*).
[54] *Pravasi Bhalai Sangathan*, para 7; emphasis mine.

Notice that the Supreme Court made it clear, by quoting this paragraph, that the offence of hate speech is not about causing distress to an individual, but about targeting the *social standing* of persons, *qua* their membership of groups, in a way that opens them up to hostility, discrimination, or even violence. These are arguments founded not upon protecting people's feelings, but upon *equality*.

In making this shift, the Supreme Court was echoing the most recent, comprehensive attempt at a theoretical treatment of the issue, undertaken by the legal philosopher Jeremy Waldron.[55] According to Waldron, hate speech damages two basic values that underlie modern democracies. The first is the value of *inclusiveness*. In pluralist societies, there is a multiplicity of races, religions, philosophies, and ways of life (call them 'groups'). An inclusive community is one that guarantees to each person, both as an individual and as a member of any group or groups, an assurance that she can lead her life without facing 'hostility, violence, discrimination or exclusion...'[56] by the rest of society. Everyone, Waldron argues, ought to have a 'sense of security in the [common, public] space that we all inhabit.'[57] Naturally, this sense of security is created and cultivated through daily interactions, and it is easy enough to see how it might be undermined: think of street graffiti that calls on all Muslims to go back to Pakistan, for example.

The second basic value that hate speech implicates is that of *dignity*. Waldron understands dignity as equal citizenship: an affirmation of everyone's 'basic social standing...as a proper object of society's protection and concern.'[58] It is evident that, at a deeper level, both inclusiveness and dignity stem from the basic idea of equal moral membership in the polity, or what Dworkin calls the principle of 'equal respect and concern': no person should be treated in a way that denigrates their basic moral worth or status—*qua* person or member of group—in society.[59]

---

[55] Waldron (2012). Siddharth Narrain draws the same connection. See Narrain (2014: 41).
[56] Waldron (2012: 4).
[57] Waldron (2012).
[58] Waldron (2012: 5).
[59] See Dworkin (1996).

Waldron draws the link between hate speech and these values by couching it in the language of group defamation. He takes as his example the American case of *Beauharnais* v. *Illinois*, which involved a statute that prohibited any portrayal of the 'depravity, criminality, unchastity, or lack of virtue of a class of citizens of any race, color, creed or religion'.[60] Just like individual defamation laws are aimed to protect the reputation of an individual, and preserve her standing in society, group defamation laws aim to 'uphold against attack a shared sense of the basic elements of each person's status, dignity, and reputation as a citizen or member of society in good standing—particularly against attacks predicated upon the characteristics of some particular social group'.[61]

At this point, the similarity with the feminist critique of pornography, which we discussed in the previous chapter, ought to become evident. The analogy has been drawn before: much like a pornography-soaked environment contributes to the silencing and drowning out of women's voices, an atmosphere pervaded with hate speech suffocates and silences targeted groups.[62] Along with the feminists, Waldron also believes that speech, in a sense, is constitutive of social reality. Words are not merely descriptive labels that attach onto how the world really is, but they actually do things. Specifically, he argues that the permanence of certain forms of expression—such as the written word—ensures an 'apparently ineradicable presence [that] makes a massive difference to the *environment* in which [we] live our lives'.[63] In a society soaked with hate speech, therefore, its message of exclusion and insult becomes part of its very look, thus breaking down the guarantee of inclusiveness and equal respect that a democracy ought to extend to all its members.

With this established, there looms an acute problem of the slippery slope: how do we separate 'dignity' from other ways in which free speech affects people? Waldron responds by distinguishing 'dignity'

---

[60] *Beauharnais* v. *Illinois*, 343 U.S. 250 (1952).
[61] Waldron (2012: 47).
[62] See Chapter Five.
[63] Waldron (2012: 74); emphasis mine.

from 'offence'. 'Offence' is limited to entirely subjective feelings of hurt, shock, or anger, while 'dignity' refers to a person's *objective* standing vis-à-vis society. The aim of hate speech codes is not to protect people from an 'effect on their feelings', but to preserve 'the assurance of their decent treatment in society'.[64] In a real-life situation, for instance, this would be reflected by a distinction between attacking a set of religious beliefs ('How can people be naïve enough to believe that Jesus Christ was resurrected three days after his death?'), and attacking the civic status of a religious group as a group ('Christians are scum!'). It is only the latter kind of speech that undermines the environment in which the equal moral membership of all citizens can be preserved.[65]

The similarities with the Court's reasoning in *Pravasi Bhalai Sangathan* are evident, and this, I suggest, is the best interpretation of Sections 153A and 295A. The textual hook is the use of words such as 'insult' and 'enmity', which suggest an objective component that goes beyond anger or hurt. The objective component must be found in Article 19(2), in particular, in the morality clause. Reading 19(2) morality as 'constitutional morality', we must ground the values that hate speech regulations protect within the Constitution itself. As the petitioners in *Pravasi* argued, Articles 14 (equality), 15 (non-discrimination), and 21 (liberty), as well as Article 25 (freedom of conscience) are just a few of the constitutional provisions that reflect the principle of equal concern and respect, which can be further concretized into the principles of inclusiveness and dignity. 153A and 295A legitimately proscribe forms of expression that violate these principles and undermine the equal moral membership of targeted groups—much like Section 292's obscenity prohibition legitimately proscribes sexually explicit material that undermines the equal moral status of women in society.

Furthermore, recall once again our discussion in the previous chapter, about the anti-subordination principle as part of the bedrock of constitutional morality. As we shall see in our examination of the

---

[64] Waldron (2012: 107).

[65] For variants of the argument, see Altman (1993); Lawrence III (1990); Delgado (1982).

Scheduled Castes and Scheduled Tribes (Prevention of Atrocities) Act and the Sati Prevention Act, hate speech is best understood not merely as a description, or representation, of individuals or groups, but as part of historical *practices* of subordination, practices that include exclusion from social and physical infrastructure, hostility, and outright violence. Put this way, the connections between hate speech and constitutional values grow much stronger, and the regulation of such speech (closely and narrowly defined) becomes constitutionally justifiable under Article 19(2)'s 'decency and morality' prong.

The analysis detailed here underscores the importance of context in interpreting Section 153A or 295A. Whether a form of expression qualifies as hate speech depends, ultimately, on context: the identity of the speaker, the identity of the target, the historical and cultural associations carried by the words used, the prevailing social situation, and so on. For instance, minority groups are far more vulnerable to hate speech than the dominant majority. Words that have been historical markers of subordination (nigger, Yid, *chamar*) are more suspect than words which carry no such baggage; and a society that is rife with other forms of discrimination against certain groups is more prone to the undermining effects of hate speech against those groups. Once again, for a society stratified in multiple and complex ways, such as ours undoubtedly is, it becomes impossible to come up with a determinative test for all situations, and places a substantial burden of interpretation upon the judges. But that, as we have seen, seems ultimately to be a feature of all free speech law.[66]

---

[66] An interesting application of these principles is to be found in the case of *Babu Rao Patel* v. *State*, AIR 1980 SC 763 (hereinafter *Babu Rao Patel*). The facts of the case bear a marked similarity to *Beauharnais* v. *Illinois*. The appellant wrote two articles, proposing that militant minority communities thrive on communalism. He then applied the proposition to Muslims, calling them 'a basically violent race', with a 'racial tradition of rape, loot, violence and murder'. The Supreme Court found that while the appellant was entitled to propose a link between minorities and communalism, he was guilty under Section 153A because of his 'vilification' of a particular community. *Babu Rao Patel* is a good example of the use of hate speech legislation as a tool to preserve the equal moral standing of all members of society, as against its use as a weapon to protect outraged feelings.

OTHER HATE SPEECH CODES

The basic idea that hate speech legislation is not about hurt feelings or offended sentiments, but about maintaining the equality and dignity of all persons in pluralist and inclusive societies, is latent in the free speech laws of other jurisdictions. The International Covenant for Civil and Political Rights, for instance, prohibits 'any advocacy of national, racial or religious hatred that constitutes incitement to *discrimination, hostility* or violence'.[67] This fits neatly within Waldron's scheme. 'Discrimination' threatens the target group's dignity and equality, while 'hostility' damages the social good of having an inclusive community.

Similarly, *R* v. *Keegstra* was a Canadian case that involved the conviction of a school-teacher for anti-Semitic statements insinuating that Jews had invented the holocaust to gain sympathy.[68] He was prosecuted under Canadian legislation that criminalized 'willfully promoting hatred against an identifiable group'. This law was challenged on free speech grounds. Upholding the restriction, the Canadian Supreme Court expressly referred to the Canadian *Constitutional* principles of equality (under Section 15) and multiculturalism (under Section 27).[69] Consequently, the Court defined 'hatred' narrowly, and in contradistinction to 'offence', as 'an emotion that, if exercised against members of an identifiable group, implies that those individuals are to be *despised, scorned, denied respect and made subject to ill-treatment on the basis of group affiliation*'.[70]

More recently—in 2013—the Canadian Supreme Court expressly distinguished hate speech from expression that is 'repugnant' or 'offensive'.[71] In *Saskatchewan* v. *Whatcott*, which constituted the basis of our Supreme Court's opinion in *Pravasi*, hate speech was defined as speech which caused the level of 'abhorrence, delegitimization and rejection that risks causing discrimination or other harmful effects'.[72]

---

67 Article 20, International Covenant for Civil and Political Rights; emphasis mine.
68 [1990] 3 SCR 697 (hereinafter *Keegstra*).
69 *Keegstra*.
70 *Keegstra*; emphasis mine.
71 *Whatcott*.
72 *Whatcott*, para 57.

Thus, for the Court, the crucial point was not the 'repugnancy of the ideas' expressed, but to 'reduce or eliminate *discrimination*'.[73] In its analysis, the Court noted—in a paragraph which, as we saw, was incorporated in *Pravasi*—that the effect of hate speech was twofold: to marginalize individuals based upon their membership of targeted groups (thus affecting inclusiveness and dignity); and to impair their ability to respond 'to the substantive ideas under debate...thereby placing a serious barrier to their full participation in...democracy'[74] (the drowning out effect, which we discussed before in the case of pornography). It was not, ultimately, about protecting targeted groups from emotional distress, but about guaranteeing the Canadian Charter's 'commitment to equality and respect for group identity and the inherent dignity owed to all human beings'.[75]

Similarly, European nations have hate speech codes that make holocaust denial a punishable offence. *Faurisson* v. *France* involved the challenge of France's holocaust denial law before the United Nations Human Rights Committee. The Committee rejected the challenge by expressly invoking Waldron's public good of inclusiveness: 'since the statements made by the author...' it observed, 'were of a nature as to raise or strengthen anti-semitic feelings, the restriction served the respect of the Jewish community to *live free from fear in an atmosphere of anti-semitism*'.[76]

It is the European Court of Human Rights that most famously distinguished hate speech from speech that might '*offend, shock or disturb*'.[77] Consistently, the European Court has upheld national hate speech legislation on the ground that while it is a curtailment of speech, it is nonetheless justified because it is aimed at protecting *other* basic

---

[73] *Whatcott*, para 58; emphasis mine.

[74] *Whatcott*, para 75. The Court added: 'It does this not only by attempting to marginalize the group so that their reply will be ignored: it also forces the group to argue for their basic humanity or social standing, as a precondition to participating in the deliberative aspects of our democracy.'

[75] *Whatcott*, para 66.

[76] *Robert Faurisson* v. *France*, Communication No. 550/1993, U.N. Doc. CCPR/C/58/D/550/1993(1996); emphasis mine.

[77] *Handyside*.

human rights that the European Convention guarantees: in particular, non-discrimination and tolerance (holocaust denial laws are often justified on this ground). In *Gunduz* v. *Turkey*, for instance, the European Court expressly noted that 'tolerance and respect for the *equal dignity of all human beings constitute the foundations of a democratic, pluralist society*. That being so, as a matter *of principle*, it may be considered necessary in certain democratic societies to sanction or even prevent all forms of expression which spread, incite, promote or justify hatred *based on intolerance*'.[78] Nonetheless, in *Tatlav* v. *Turkey*,[79] which involved the prosecution of a journalist for writing a critical book called *The Reality of Islam*, the European Court drew a distinction between 'abuse' and 'insult' on the one hand, and 'offence' on the other. It ruled that 'caustic commentary' about Islam could certainly cause offence to Muslims, but that *in itself* was not a good enough ground for curtailing the freedom of speech and expression.

The distinction between causing offence and causing harm via group-based hostility and discrimination was also made by the South African Constitutional Court in *Islamic Unity Convention*, a case that we have discussed before.[80] In that case, Langa J. defined harm in light of specific constitutional values: that of 'building the non-racial and non-sexist society based on human dignity and the achievement of equality'.[81] Leading on from this, the South African Human Rights Commission in *Freedom Front*—which was a case about an anti-Afrikaaner song with the lyrics '*Kill the Boer*'—referred to the Preamble of the South African Constitution. It held that the social goods of inclusivity and protecting minority communities against marginalization—grounded within the Constitution—provided

---

[78] *Gunduz* v. *Turkey*, (2005) 41 EHRR 5, para 40, 4 December 2003: (no. 35701/97), 4 December 2003; *Erbakan* v. *Turkey*, (no. 59405/00), 6 July 2006; emphasis mine; but see, for a contrary opinion, *Otto-Preminger-Institut* v. *Austria*, (no. 13470/87), [1994] ECHR 26 (20 September 1994); *Wingrove* v. *UK*, (1996) 1 BHRC 509, 25 November 1996.

[79] (no. 50692/99), 2 May 2006.

[80] *Islamic Unity Convention* v. *The Independent Broadcasting Authority*, 2002 (5) BCLR 433 (CC) (hereinafter *Islamic Unity Convention*).

[81] *Islamic Unity Convention*, para 31.

adequate justification for hate speech regulation.[82] In that case, it found that the song conveyed a message to the Afrikaner people that they were enemies of the dominant majority, and 'less deserving of respect and dignity.'[83]

Interestingly, in addition to constitutional restrictions on the advocacy of hatred, South Africa has a separate legal provision for the regulation of hate speech, which is found in the 'Equality Act.'[84] The placement of hate speech within a legislation expressly committed to equality and non-discrimination is striking. The legal provision proscribes speech that can be reasonably construed to be intentionally hurtful, harmful, or advocating hatred, on the basis of certain 'prohibited grounds', that have been the historic sites of discrimination and oppression: race, sex, ethnic origin, sexual orientation, and so on. 'Prohibited grounds' are specifically understood to be where discrimination perpetuates 'systemic disadvantage', 'undermines dignity', or 'adversely affects...the equal enjoyment of rights and freedoms.'[85] The connections with dignity and equality, and the ability to exercise one's rights and freedoms on parity with everyone else, are therefore expressly set out in the legislation itself. In *Afriforum v. Malema*, the question was whether the song '*Shoot the farmer, shoot the Boer!*', which had been a Black liberation song during the time of apartheid, constituted hate speech within the meaning of the Equality Act. The song in question had been sung by a political leader during a rally. After a detailed analysis into the history of the song, its present meaning in society, the intended and actual audience, and the impression it would convey to the targeted group, the Equality Court held that 'the entirety of the message *dehumanizes* the enemy by referring to it as dogs and describing

---

[82] *Freedom Front* v. *South African Human Rights Commission*, 2003 (11) BCLR 1283 (SAHRC) (hereinafter *Freedom Front*).

[83] *Freedom Front*.

[84] The Promotion of Equality and Prevention of Unfair Discrimination Act No. 4 of 2000.

[85] Section 10, The Promotion of Equality and Prevention of Unfair Discrimination Act, 2000.

its conduct in unsavoury terms…those words are *derogatory, dehumanizing* and hurtful'.[86]

The common thread running through all these cases, evidently, is that the ultimate *raison d'être* of hate speech laws—to repeat—is not located in subjective feelings or in sentiment, but in objective notions of dignity, equality, and participation. Hate speech legislation is constituted upon the understanding that words can have consequences, that words cannot be separated from broader practices of subordination and inequality in divided societies, and that words can actually impede equal enjoyment of rights, and equal access to social and physical infrastructure.

Our own hate speech legislation exists on the statute books. It is its interpretation that needs to undergo a fundamental shift in purposes and values.

HOW OUGHT WE TO READ THE SCHEDULED CASTES AND SCHEDULED TRIBES (PREVENTION OF ATROCITIES) ACT?

The Scheduled Castes and Scheduled Tribes (Prevention of Atrocities) Act, 1989, is an attempt at remedying India's long and continuing history of caste oppression. Out of a number of punishable actions against members of Scheduled Castes or Scheduled Tribes, one is of particular relevance to us: 'intentionally insult[ing] or intimidat[ing] with intent to humiliate a member of a Scheduled Caste or a Scheduled Tribe in any place within public view'.[87] In *Swaran Singh* v. *State*,[88] the Supreme Court found that the word 'chamar' came within the purview of this Section. The Court noted:

> …the word 'Chamar' is often used by people belonging to the so-called upper castes or even by OBCs as a word of insult, abuse and derision…in fact, the word 'Chamar' when used today is not normally used to denote

---

[86] *Afriforum* v. *Malema*, 2011 (6) SA 240 (EqC), paras 102, 107; emphasis mine.
[87] Section 3(1)(x), The Scheduled Castes and Scheduled Tribes (Prevention of Atrocities) Act, 1989.
[88] (2008) 8 SCC 435 (hereinafter *Swaran Singh*).

a caste but to intentionally insult and humiliate someone...[the Act] was obviously made to prevent *indignities, humiliation and harassment* to the members of SC/ST community, as is evident from the Statement of Objects & Reasons...hence, we have to take into account the *popular meaning of the word 'Chamar'* which it has acquired by usage, and not the etymological meaning...*this is the age of democracy and equality. No people or community should be today insulted or looked down upon, and nobody's feelings should be hurt*...in such a country like ours with so much diversity—so many religions, castes, ethnic and lingual groups, etc.—all communities and groups must be treated with respect, and *no one should be looked down upon as an inferior*.[89]

Subsequently, in 2010, the Supreme Court broadly reaffirmed this interpretation. In *Arumugam Servai* v. *State of Tamil Nadu*,[90] it held that

the word 'pallan' no doubt denotes a specific caste, but it is also a word used in a derogatory sense to insult someone (just as in North India the word 'chamar' denotes a specific caste, but it is also used in a derogatory sense to insult someone)...*it is just unacceptable in the modern age, just as the words 'Nigger' or 'Negro' are unacceptable for African-Americans today* (even if they were acceptable 50 years ago)...*in the modern age nobody's feelings should be hurt*. In particular in a country like India with so much diversity...we must take care not to insult anyone's feelings on account of his caste, religion, tribe, language, etc.[91]

In light of our previous discussion, we are now in a position to understand that part of the Court's reasoning is entirely accurate, but that another part of it is seriously flawed. The Court is correct to hold that the Scheduled Castes and Scheduled Tribes (Prevention of Atrocities) Act is about preventing indignity, humiliation, and harassment, and to connect its objectives with those of democracy and—crucially— equality and anti-subordination. It is correct to analyse the cases as being about one group treating another as fundamentally inferior,

---

[89] *Swaran* Singh, paras 21–23; emphasis mine.

[90] (2011) 6 SCC 405: (2011) 2 SCC(Cri) 993 (hereinafter *Arumugam Servai*).

[91] *Arumugam Servai*, paras 10–12; emphasis mine.

and to examine this in the context of the diverse, pluralist society that India is. It is correct to hold that certain forms of speech constitute an inextricable part and parcel of longstanding caste-based practices of subordination and social exclusion. It is correct to make the enquiry a contextual one, and examine the historical baggage as well as the present use of the words in question. It is correct to make the connection with African–Americans and 'nigger'.

It is incorrect, however, to make the issue ultimately one about *hurt feelings*. Hate speech codes, as we have argued, ought not to be about protecting peoples' feelings, but their dignity and equal moral standing in society. 'Nigger' is an unacceptable word not merely because it annoys African–Americans, but because, when located in context, it is a 'badge of inferiority', inextricably connected to a history of slavery, violence, and oppression (much like the Indian caste system). The examination of words like 'chamar' and 'pallan' ought to be undertaken within a similar framework (which the Court, for the most part, does), leaving aside the issue of subjective hurt feelings.

It remains an open question, however, whether certain words will *always* fall within the ambit of the Scheduled Castes and Scheduled Tribes (Prevention of Atrocities) Act, or whether words have permissible and impermissible uses depending on the situation in which they are used. The equation of 'chamar' with 'nigger' in *Arumugam Servai* suggests the former. It is difficult to imagine any situation in which the word 'nigger' may be justified (barring the narrow exception of scholarly articles tracing the development of the word, or something similar). This is because the social meaning carried by the word 'nigger' is almost exclusively one of denigration and insult, notwithstanding whatever descriptive associations it might have had at some point of time. The Federal Court of Australia affirmed this, holding that the use of the word 'nigger' would 'almost certainly' be a violation of the Racial Discrimination Act.[92]

On the other hand, in *Vajnai v. Hungary*, the European Court of Human Rights was called upon to decide whether Hungary could

---

[92] *Hagan v. Trustees of the Toowoomba Sports Ground Trust*, [2000] FCA 1615, para 7.

prohibit all displays of the 'red star'. It was argued that because of its association with the Soviet Union, the red star was a symbol of totalitarian tyranny, one that Hungary was entitled to prohibit. The Court found, however, that totalitarianism was not the *only* association that could be reasonably drawn from the red star. Rather, for significant sections of the Hungarian population, it represented working-class solidarity and social justice. Consequently, the Court found the prohibition invalid on grounds of overbreadth.[93] These two cases demonstrate the importance of social meaning in determining when certain forms of expression constitute hate speech under the Scheduled Castes and Scheduled Tribes (Prevention of Atrocities) Act. For example, is 'chamar' more like 'nigger', or closer to the red star? That question can only be answered by a historical and sociological analysis of what possible meanings that word has in society.

The contextual enquiry that separates insult from offence, or subjective hurt feelings, is multifaceted. It must take into account the identity of the speaker, the target group at whom the speech is directed, the historical context within which the expression is placed, the surrounding atmosphere, and so on. For example, the Scheduled Castes and Scheduled Tribes (Prevention of Atrocities) Act only criminalizes insulting expression used by a *non-Scheduled Caste/Scheduled Tribe person* against the Scheduled Caste/Scheduled Tribe constituency.[94] This embodies a concern with the structural context within which Scheduled Caste/Scheduled Tribe discrimination and oppression was perpetrated within the hierarchical Indian caste system. Other countries have developed similar principles. In Australia, for example, the Racial Discrimination Act was held not to apply to an aborigine woman who called a white prison guard 'a fucking white piece of shit'. The Federal Magistrate held that the purpose of the Act was to 'protect vulnerable minority groups'.[95] In the context of the historical and cultural dominance enjoyed by white people in Australia, and especially their position of power *relative* to aborigines, the Act was inapplicable

---

[93] *Vajnai.*
[94] S. 3(1), SC/ST (Prevention of Atrocities) Act.
[95] *McLeod v. Power,* (2003) 173 FLR 31.

to the present situation. This judgment—and the aforementioned provision in the Scheduled Castes and Scheduled Tribes (Prevention of Atrocities) Act—takes us back to Waldron's original arguments about inclusiveness and dignity. Ultimately, it is historically (and currently) oppressed minority groups who are most vulnerable to assaults upon their dignity, and who stand most to lose from a hostile public culture and environment. Hate speech codes—and judicial interpretation—ought to be sensitive to this fact.

THE CONUNDRUM OF THE SATI ACT

The 1987 Commission of Sati (Prevention) Act, which was passed in the immediate aftermath of a high-profile *sati* incident in the Rajasthani village of Deorala,[96] is an interesting legislation. The Preamble to the Act states that the commission of sati (that is, the burning alive or burying of widows or women along with the bodies of their deceased husbands or relatives) is 'revolting to the feelings of human nature', and is 'nowhere enjoined…as an imperative duty' by any religion. The Act goes on to punish the 'glorification' of sati. Glorification is defined extraordinarily broadly: 'supporting, justifying or propagating the practice of *sati* [as well as]…arranging of any function to eulogise the person who has committed *sati*'.[97] Both the Preamble of the Act, which refers to revolting feelings, as well as the definition, should make it clear that the prohibition upon glorifying sati has nothing to do with public order. It would be stretching things to a breaking point to argue that every instance of justifying sati, no matter what the context, bears any kind of proximate relationship with public order. Not can it seriously be argued that sati violates 'public morality': its ubiquity until the late nineteenth century, and its prevalence even today would refute any such facile presumption. In any case, the Act does not only ban the practice, but even its *support*.

What argument could be advanced to support the constitutionality of the speech-restricting provisions of the Sati Act? I do not think that

---

[96] Rajalakshmi (2004).
[97] Section 2(b), The Commission of Sati (Prevention) Act, 1987.

such an argument exists. Yet what is important to note is that the only justification for the Act must draw upon constitutional morality, in a manner analogous to the Scheduled Castes and Scheduled Tribes (Prevention of Atrocities) Act. Propagation of sati—so the argument would go—is not an isolated speech act, to be considered in vacuum. Rather, it is an integral part of an entire set of practices that were used to dominate and subjugate women over centuries. Advocating that a woman ought to commit suicide upon the death of her husband is one strand in a complex web, which would also include, for instance, female infanticide and bride-burning, and at the heart of which is a denial of the equal rights, dignity, and autonomy of women. If chamar—as we have argued—is 'hate speech' against certain groups *because* it denies their equal moral membership in the polity, then 'glorifying' sati is hate speech against women, of a similar sort. Once again, we can see that the underlying vision that supports some of our important speech-regulating enactments—insofar as they *can* be supported on constitutional, 19(2) grounds—is not public morality or individual morality, but constitutional morality.[98]

ADDENDUM I: SECTION 123, REPRESENTATION OF THE PEOPLE ACT, CONSTITUTIONAL 'DECENCY', AND THE *BAL THACKERAY* CASE

The Representation of the People Act, and its interpretation in the *Bal Thackeray* case, provides an interesting bookend to our discussion of 'morality' in the last two chapters. Section 123(3) of the Representation of the People Act states that a person canvassing for votes on the basis of 'religion, race, caste, community or language'[99] will be guilty of a corrupt electoral practice. In *Bal Thackeray*, it was argued that Section 123(3) violated Article 19(1)(a), and that its constitutionality was limited to appeals directly prejudicial to public

[98] See also the Protection of Civil Rights Act, 1955, which proscribes encouraging or inciting people to practice untouchability. Section 7(1)(c), Protection of Civil Rights Act, 1955.

[99] Section 123(3), The Representation of the People Act, 1951.

order, as required by 19(2).[100] The Court rejected this contention, and held that public order was not the relevant 19(2) category at all. Rather, it upheld the Section under the *decency* clause. Refuting the appellant's contention that 'decency or morality' was only about sexual morality, the Court held:

> The ordinary dictionary meaning of 'decency' indicates that the action must be in conformity with the current standards of behaviour or propriety, etc. In *a secular polity*, the requirement of correct behaviour or propriety is that an appeal for votes should not be made on the ground of the candidate's religion which by itself is no index of the suitability of a candidate for membership of the house.[101]

And:

> The fact that the scheme of separate electorates *was rejected in framing the Constitution and secularism is the creed adopted in the Constitutional scheme* are relevant considerations to treat this as a reasonable restriction on the freedom of speech and expression, for maintaining the standard of behaviour required in conformity with the decency and propriety of the societal norms.[102]

Here is a direct invocation of constitutional morality to interpret Article 19(2). If decency (*per Udeshi*) meant 'public decency', then the decision makes no sense. Because this much, at least, is uncontroversial: out of all the methods that exist today, the ballot box is the best way of gauging public opinion and public sentiment. If I invoke religion in my election speeches to persuade the people to vote for me,

---

[100] In *Jamuna Prasad Mukhariya v. Lacchi Ram*, AIR 1954 SC 686 (hereinafter *Jamuna Prasad Mukhariya*), the Supreme Court had held that Article 19(1)(a) was irrelevant to the speech-restricting provisions of the Representation of the People Act. This was because the right to vote and the right to run for office were only statutory rights. Therefore, the legislature could control the conditions under which those rights might be exercised, and regulate election speech accordingly. In *Bal Thackeray's* case, the Court agreed with the holding of *Jamuna Prasad Mukhariya*, but nonetheless subjected the provisions of the Act to detailed 19(1) (a) scrutiny. It is not clear why (*Dr Ramesh Yeshwant Prabhoo v. Prabhakar Kashinath Kunte*, (1996) 1 SCC 130 (hereinafter *Bal Thackeray's* case)).

[101] *Bal Thackeray's* case, para 29; emphasis mine.

[102] *Bal Thackeray's* case, para 31; emphasis mine.

and I am successful, on what ground can it be argued that the *public* considers such an approach contrary to decency?

So what does 'decency' mean? What standards is the Court referring to when it talks about *'current standards of behaviour or propriety'*? The Court's response is to invoke the Constitution—first impliedly, and then expressly. In the first instance, it talks about proper behaviour in a 'secular polity'. Secularism, however, is a *constitutional* ideal (and as history demonstrates, not always a popular ideal). The Court then makes it explicit by talking about the creed adopted in the Constitutional scheme, which makes the restriction reasonable in maintaining the behaviour in conformity with decency and propriety. Thus, the society whose norms are the touchstone for measuring decency and propriety is the society established and envisaged by the *Constitution*. Ultimately, restrictions on free speech must be justified only on the basis of the principles located within the Constitution itself.

Ranjit Udeshi—with which we began the previous chapter—and *Bal Thackeray*—with which we end this one—represent two contrasting stands in our 'decency and morality' jurisprudence. In between the two, we have tried to argue that as a matter of constitutional text, structure, and philosophy, it is the latter that can ultimately justify placing reasonable restrictions upon the freedom of expression.

ADDENDUM II: AUTONOMY AND THE REPRESENTATION OF THE PEOPLE ACT

The Representation of the People Act provides us with another bookend to our discussion of Article 19(2) restrictions. Recall our discussion, in the public order chapter, of autonomy as a ground and a limiting principle for regulating free speech in cases of threats to public order. The principle of autonomy has figured prominently in another area: judicial interpretation of Section 123(2) of the Representation of the People Act. Section 123(2) lists as a 'corrupt electoral practice', exercising 'undue influence' upon anyone's free exercise of an electoral right. Under Section 123(2)(a)(i), a threat of social ostracism or of excommunication from any caste or community is treated as undue influence.[103] More interestingly, Section 123(2)(a)(ii) stipulates that 'induc[ing] or attempt[ing] to induce a candidate or an elector to believe that he, or any person in whom he is interested, will become or will be rendered an object of divine displeasure or spiritual censure',[104] counts as an interference with the free exercise of an electoral right.

In interpreting these provisions, the courts have taken recourse to the language of autonomy, holding that a command or interdict from a religious or spiritual leader effectively overrides the free and independent will of the members of that religious group.[105] Similarly, while examining Section 123(3), which we discussed above, the Supreme Court appeared to accept the argument that , apart from the principle of secularism that underlay it, Section 123(3) was designed to ensure that 'powerful emotions generated by religion should not be permitted to be exhibited during election and *that decision and choice of the people are not coloured in any way*'.[106] Commenting upon these cases, Mehta correctly points out that 'the courts assume throughout that citizens are, when it comes to receiving religious speech, or speech about religion, incapable of managing the impressions they receive... we are incapable of receiving the expression on our own terms; incapable of managing our own responses; condemned to receiving these expressions unfreely and helplessly; incapable as it were, of self-discipline'.[107]

While there is much to disagree with in terms of the Court's substantive framing of the issue, the structure of the argument is identical to

---

[103] Section 123(2)(a)(i), Representation of the People Act, 1951.

[104] Section 123(2)(a)(ii), Representation of the People Act, 1951.

[105] See *Ram Dial* v. *Sant Lal*, AIR 1959 P&H 240; see also in the context of an anti-conversion law, the words of the Orissa High Court in *Yulitha Hyde* v. *State of Orissa*, AIR 1973 Ori 116: 'Threat of divine displeasure numbs the mental faculty; more so of an undeveloped mind and the actions of such person thereafter are not free and according to conscience.'

[106] *S. Harcharn Singh* v. *Sajjan Singh*, AIR 1985 SC 236, para 26; emphasis mine.

[107] Mehta (2009: 335); this marks a colonial continuity dating back to Macaulay, who headed the Law Commission that was drafting the Penal Code. According to the Law Commission, 'there is perhaps no country in which the Government has so much to apprehend from religious excitement among the people' (see Narrain (2014: 9).

the argument from autonomy in the public order cases.[108] Regulation of the freedom of speech is justified in cases of diminished autonomy, where—for some reason—individuals are impaired from evaluating speech on its own terms, and deciding for themselves whether or not they wish to be persuaded by its message.

Again, the idea that religion and autonomy are somehow conceptually incompatible seems to stretch the idea of autonomy to breaking point. As we have argued here, arguments from autonomy should be limited to a circumscribed range of public order cases, and the restrictions on speech in the Representation of the People Act are better understood as issues of constitutional decency. Nonetheless, as a conceptual template, the Representation of the People Act cases reaffirm the point that restrictions upon free speech must ultimately be grounded and justified not by appeals to public sentiment, hurt feelings, or stormy emotions, but by constitutional values.

[108] Due to the decision in *Jamuna Prasad Mukhariya*, these cases do not invoke Article 19(1)(a).

CHAPTER SEVEN

Film and Internet Censorship

. . . .

W hen the First Amendment, with its newly minted free speech restrictions in the interests of 'friendly relations with foreign States' was being debated by the Parliament, Shyama Prasad Mookerjee asked, perhaps rhetorically, whether the amendment would preclude criticism of foreign countries.[1] Sometimes, rhetoric becomes reality. In early 2014, the Indian Film Certification Board refused to certify the documentary film *No Fire Zone* before its release. *No Fire Zone*, a film about the Sri Lankan civil war, had won a series of awards at film festivals around the world, including—ironically enough—at many human rights film festivals. It also contained some strongly negative commentary about the Sri Lankan army's role in the killing of civilians and unarmed combatants during the war.

The Board refused to issue it a certificate on the stated ground that it would prejudice friendly relations between India and foreign States.[2] Was the Board concerned that the Indian public would develop a negative view about Sri Lanka, after watching its army involved in various atrocities? Or was it concerned that Sri Lanka would take a dim view

---

[1] Menon (2004: 1817).
[2] Seervai (2014).

of the film being shown in India? Either way, there is something troubling about banning a film on a hugely controversial civil war, which is critical of the acts of a State, on the ground that *just* for that reason, it would affect the reputation of that State. Would this reasoning extend to *Schindler's List* and *The Pianist*, for detailing German atrocities during the Second World War? Or to *Bury My Heart at Wounded Knee* for its unflinching retelling of the Native American genocide in 1860s and 1870s United States?

The *No Fire Zone* episode exhibits many of the symptoms that have dogged Indian film censorship since the time of Independence: an extreme form of prior restraint, minimal judicial scrutiny, and the banning of films dealing with core political issues at the very heart of the constitutional guarantee. While there is no separate constitutional provision dealing with films, and the standard principles of Article 19(1)(a) and 19(2) apply, judicial history bears some unique features worth studying separately.

Like most forms of speech regulation, film censorship has its antecedents in the colonial era. The British established the Central Board of Film Certification in 1918, and 'perceived threats to the reputation of *white women* as well as any allusion to self-governance, the Indian nationalist movement, or Indian independence were heavily censored by the colonial authorities'.[3] The heavy-handed British approach to film censorship reflected a larger worry that contemporary imperial powers faced about the rapid spread of cinema in their colonies: the impact that the new medium would have upon the allegedly excitable, irrational, and underdeveloped natives because of its direct appeal to the senses and the way it bypassed 'reasoned judgment' for the emotions.[4] In the words of a 1926 article in the *London Times*: 'the simple native, very deficient in the sense of proportion, was being subjected to wholly unprecedented provocations'.[5]

---

[3] Ganti (2009: 87); emphasis mine.
[4] Mazzarella (2009: 71).
[5] Mazzarella (2009: 68).

K.A. ABBAS AND PRIOR RESTRAINT

In independent India, the regime of film censorship was established by the Cinematograph Act of 1952. Section 5B of that Act vested the power of pre-release censorship in a Board of Censors (now known as the Central Board of Film Certification), a non-judicial administrative body. The Board was authorized to refuse to clear a film for exhibition if it felt that any of the sub-clauses of Article 19(2) would be violated (with an appeal from its decision lying to the Central Government, which was subsequently replaced by a tribunal). Section 5B also authorized the government to frame directions that would guide the censoring authority in making its determinations.[6] The government's directions, based upon similar British recommendations from 1918, were extraordinarily broad, informing the Board that 'no picture shall be certified for public exhibition which will *lower the moral standards of those who see it*...standards of life...shall not be so portrayed as to *deprave the morality of the audience*...the prevailing laws shall not be so ridiculed as to create sympathy for violation of such laws'.[7] Censorship guidelines also included multiple sub-categories dealing with 'vice and immorality', 'relations between the sexes', and so on, placing a prohibition on 'lowering the sacredness of the institution of marriage' and on 'indecorous and sensuous postures'.

Such a regime clearly suffered (and continues to suffer) from two of the most acute free speech problems that we have discussed in this book. The Cinematograph Act and its guidelines establish a system of prior restraint, which vests in the government and its administrative authorities, the power to choke off the marketplace of ideas at its source. Furthermore, the guidelines were—and continue to remain, despite some modifications—both overbroad *and* vague. For instance, one of the guidelines directs the Board to ensure that 'dual meaning words as obviously cater to baser instincts are not allowed'.[8] What a

[6] Section 5-B, Cinematograph Act, 1952.

[7] *K.A. Abbas* v. *Union of India*, AIR 1971 SC 481: [1971] 2 SCR 446 (hereinafter *K.A. Abbas*); emphasis mine.

[8] 'The Principles for Guidance in Certifying Films', http://cbfcindia.gov.in/html/uniquepage.aspx?unique_page_id=1 (accessed on 2 April 2015).

'baser instinct' is, of course, is something that no community has ever really agreed upon.

In 1969, the Cinematograph Act was challenged before the Supreme Court. A documentary film called *A Tale of Four Cities* depicted grinding poverty and inequality in the metropolises of Calcutta, Madras, Bombay, and Delhi, including shots of Bombay's red light districts. The Board refused to grant the film a 'U' certificate (unrestricted exhibition), a decision affirmed on appeal to the Central Government, on the ground that it 'depict[ed] immoral traffic in women and soliciting, prostitution or procuration'.[9] K.A. Abbas challenged the Government's decision, but by the time the case came up before the Supreme Court, the government had agreed to grant a U certificate without the cuts. Consequently, he amended his petition to directly challenge the constitutional validity of the Act and the directions.

In the previous chapter, we discussed some of the unique problems that are attendant upon a regime of prior restraint in the context of Section 95 of the Code of Criminal Procedure, which shares some of its features. To recapitulate, the initial censorship decision is made by an administrative body in non-judicial proceedings, placing the burden upon the artist to approach a court and have it overturned. Given the nature of Indian legal proceedings, that is an onerous burden indeed. It involves far more pervasive governmental involvement in censorship than a regime of post-speech punishment. Furthermore—to return to a concept we discussed in Chapter Two—when the material involved is critical of the government, or of an otherwise subversive nature, it is likely that like all other imperfect and biased bodies, the government will overestimate the nature of the threat, and come down on the side of censorship.

A regime of *complete* prior restraint makes the problem far worse because it ensures that certain ideas can never even enter the marketplace. For post-publication punishment, the material in question has at least been placed before the public, and has entered the public sphere. Prior restraint allows the government immense powers of

[9] *K.A. Abbas*, para 5.

controlling the public sphere by determining what the public will have *access* to in the first place. Therefore, it is not at all surprising that prior restraint—which arose out of the draconian printing-licence regime in monarchical England—was severely castigated by British jurists as far back as the eighteenth century,[10] held unconstitutional (subject to extremely narrow exceptions) by the American Courts,[11] and is expressly prohibited in the American Convention on Human Rights.[12]

In addition, prior restraint was the weapon of choice for the most repressive colonial strictures upon the freedom of speech and the press during the British era. We have discussed the 1823 Press Ordinance, which established a regime of prior restraint, requiring a (revocable) licence from the Governor-General-in-Council as a prerequisite for publishing any newspaper or periodical.[13] In his Memorandum, Rammohun Roy made an impeccably Blackstonian argument against this policy, arguing for unrestrained liberty of publication, *subject* to the law of the land.[14] While the 1823 Ordinance was repealed, the Vernacular Press Act of 1878 and the numerous Press Acts between 1908 and 1931 imposed severe prior restraint upon newspapers and periodicals, and their debilitating impact upon the functioning of the press has been well-recorded.[15]

Despite all this, the Supreme Court in *K.A. Abbas* nonetheless blandly held—in the teeth of the *Brij Bhushan* decision,[16] which had followed the American courts in holding prior restraint unconstitutional—that 'pre-censorship is but an aspect of censorship and bears

[10] Blackstone (1765–1769).

[11] *Near* v. *Minnesota*, 283 U.S. 697 (1931).

[12] Article 13(2), American Convention on Human Rights, 1969.

[13] See Chapters One and Three. Colonial censorship, formalized through law, had begun as early as the eighteenth century.

[14] Collett (1914).

[15] See Chapters One and Three; The Press (Objectionable Matters) Act of 1951 established a post-Independence regime of prior restraint, but was eventually repealed in 1957. Prior restraint was a staple feature of Indira Gandhi's Emergency as well.

[16] *Brij Bhushan* v. *State of Delhi*, [1950] SCR Supp. 245.

the same relationship in quality to the material as censorship after the motion picture has had a run. *The only difference is one of the stage at which the State interposes its regulation between the individual and his freedom.* Beyond this there is no vital difference.'[17]

The Court then noted that 'it has been almost universally recognised that the treatment of motion pictures must be different from that of other forms of art and expression...the instant appeal of the motion picture, its versatility, realism (often surrealism), and its coordination of the visual and aural senses...the motion picture is able to stir up emotions more deeply than any other product....'[18] The implication is clear: the excitable natives of the British colonial imagination have become the excitable citizens of the independent, democratic, and constitutional Indian State, neither of whom can be trusted to responsibly handle a medium of communication as 'realistic' as that of films. The continuity is striking, and has been a common feature of post-Independence free speech law in the context of cinema.[19] So much so, that a scholar recently noted:

> Film censorship in India exemplified the distinction and tension between citizen and population that is a characteristic feature of contemporary

[17] *K.A. Abbas*, para 20; emphasis mine. With respect to non-literary media, prior restraint is a staple feature of the Dramatic Performances Act of 1876, which was enacted by the British to regulate socially subversive Indian theatre, and is yet another legislation that—inexplicably—simply continued to exist after Independence, in various guises in the states. As late as 2013, the High Court of Madras struck down some of the more draconian prior restraint provisions of the Tamil Nadu Dramatic Performances Act of 1954, which mirrored large parts of the central legislation (*N.V. Sankaran* v. *State of Tamil Nadu*, 2013 (1) CTC 686). In the years after Independence, various High Courts held the provisions of the Dramatic Performances Act to be unconstitutional because of the absence of procedural safeguards (not, it may be pointed out, because of its substantive provisions). See, for example, *Comrade Chanan Singh* v. *Union of India*, 1961 Cr LJ 851 (Punjab & Haryana High Court); *The State* v. *Baboo Lal*, AIR 1956 All 571. The Act has been repealed in a few states, like West Bengal and Delhi. In its 248th Report, the Law Commission recommended its repeal. See Law Commission of India (2014).

[18] *K.A. Abbas*, para 21.

[19] For an outstandingly detailed, book-length treatment of this phenomenon, see Mazzarella (2013).

democracy...though the discourse of democracy is predicated on the
figure of the citizen and its corollaries of autonomy, equal rights, and
self-representation, the modernizing agendas of postcolonial nation-
states like India *presume 'populations' which are the objects of government
policy*, rather than citizens....[20]

The express reference in *K.A. Abbas* to the role of the State as *'parens
patriae'*,[21] passing legislation for the welfare of its subjects in its role as
the universal parent, buttresses this point. Nowhere in *K.A. Abbas* do
we find any reference to the idea that autonomous individuals have
the right to shape their own moral convictions as they see fit. Instead,
the Court invoked *Ranjit Udeshi*,[22] talked about the 'interests of the
society'[23] in good, wholesome cinema, and ultimately upheld all the
guidelines while requiring for exceptions in the interests of art that
is for the public good. The Court subsequently affirmed this opinion,
holding in *Rangarajan* that 'since it caters for mass audience *who are
generally not selective about what they watch*, the movie cannot be
equated with other modes of communication. It cannot be allowed
to function in a free market place just as does [*sic*] the newspapers
or magazines. Censorship by prior restraint is, therefore, not only
desirable but also necessary.'[24] Or, in other words, newspaper- and
magazine-readers, being persons of taste and discernment (not among
the 'masses') could presumably be trusted with the material they are
being given, but movie-goers could not.

What is also noteworthy about the *Rangarajan* quote is its similarity to *Udeshi* and *Baragur Ramachandrappa*.[25] In *Udeshi*, the Court
took upon itself the task of protecting those sections of the society

---

[20] Ganti (2009: 90); emphasis mine. The original idea belongs to the postcolonial thinker, Partha Chatterjee.

[21] *K.A. Abbas*, para 41.

[22] *Ranjit Udeshi v. State of Maharashtra*, AIR 1965 SC 881: [1965] 1 SCR 65.

[23] The flawed nature of that argument in *Ranjit Udeshi* has been discussed
before.

[24] *S. Rangarajan v. P. Jagjivan Ram*, (1989) 2 SCC 574: [1989] 2 SCR 204, para
10 (hereinafter *Rangarajan*); emphasis mine.

[25] *Sri Baragur Ramchandrappa v. State of Karnataka*, (2007) 3 SCC 11.

that were—supposedly—most vulnerable to corrupting and degrading influences. In *Baragur Ramachandrappa*, the Court focused on those communities that were most likely to be hurt by the offending text (as we have seen, both those tests were subsequently replaced by a reasonableness standard). Similarly, *Rangarajan* zoned in upon that constituency which the Court believed was specifically in need of protection (the non-selective mass audience), and held that the guarantee of free speech must be calibrated keeping in mind the weaknesses and vulnerabilities of that constituency.

Between *K.A. Abbas* and *Rangarajan*, and subsequently, the film censorship rules (amended in 1983, and with further government notifications) have been left untouched by the courts, and other film censorship cases have followed more or less expected lines. In *Ramesh v. Union of India*, for instance, the Supreme Court dismissed a challenge to the serial *Tamas* (based on Bhisham Sahni's novel), holding that an unflinching depiction of a historical tragedy (the partition riots) was not, in itself, a ground for a public order ban, without further evidence.[26] *Bobby International* v. *Om Pal Singh Hoon* involved the controversial film *Bandit Queen*, with its scenes of frontal nudity and rape. Rejecting a challenge to the screening of the film, the Court held—following its obscenity jurisprudence—that 'the object of [those scenes] was [not] to titillate the cinema-goer's lust but to arouse in him sympathy for the victim and disgust for the perpetrators.'[27] Finding that, ultimately, the scenes were an essential part of the film's socially useful 'message', the Court allowed its screening with an 'A' certificate. Readers will notice the similarities with obscenity jurisprudence, where seemingly obscene literature or cinema is 'saved' if the 'obscene' bits are integral to the communication of a broader, socially useful or beneficial message.

The structure of the Cinematograph Act and its attendant directions is mirrored in the context of television, by the Cable Television Networks (Regulation) Act of 1995, and its 'Programme Code'. Under

---

[26] AIR 1988 SC 775.
[27] *Bobby International* v. *Om Pal Singh Hoon*, (1996) 4 SCC 1.

Section 5 of the Act, cable operators may not transmit any programme that violates the Code.[28] Much like the Cinematograph Act guidelines, the Code vaguely proscribes 'slandering, ironical and snobbish' attitudes in the portrayal of ethnic, linguistic, and regional groups; material that is offensive to 'good taste'; 'criticism of friendly countries', and others, over and above anything that contravenes the Cinematograph Act.[29] The overbreadth is concerning. More worryingly, under Section 11 of the Act, the determination of violations of the Code, in the first instance, is left to an 'authorised officer' (which, under Section 2(a) of the Act, includes the commissioner of police), who is vested with the power of seizing the cable operator's equipment and holding it for a period of ten days before obtaining the approval of a district judge.[30] This is in addition to Section 20 of the Act, which allows the Central Government to prohibit the operation of cable television networks 'in the public interest' (recall that public interest is not a 19(2) ground), and on the basis of 19(2) grounds.[31]

The dangers associated with allowing non-judicial authorities—especially the police—to become the primary interpreters of Article 19(2) are evident. In *USA Cable Networks* v. *State of Maharashtra*, for example, an Assistant Commissioner of Police (who was an 'authorised officer' by virtue of a state gazette notification) sealed and closed down the control room of the premises of the petitioners, on responding to a complaint that certain programmes were 'defamatory'.[32] This was upheld by the Court which, arguably, had little choice, given the wording of the Act.

Removing such powers of censorship from the hands of executive authorities is a first and essential step, but as we have seen elsewhere, the deeper problem lies with the overbroad and vague wording of the substantive law, which allows a free rein to the personal proclivities of judges, and ensures that the courts become unpredictable engines of censorship themselves. In November 2014, for instance, the Delhi High

---

[28] Section 5, Cable Television Networks (Regulation) Act, 1995.
[29] Programme Code, Rule 6, Cable Television Network Rules, 1994.
[30] Section 11, Cable Television Networks (Regulation) Act, 1995.
[31] Section 20, Cable Television Networks (Regulation) Act, 1995.
[32] (2011) 113 Bom LR 867.

Court upheld a ten-day ban on the Comedy Central channel on the ground that it met the 'collective cry of society' while quoting Cricket Association of Bengal's[33] dictum of India being a 'nascent republic', where stability was all-important.[34] This idea that India is perpetually a 'nascent republic'—an eternal guest in the waiting room of history,[35] never quite ready to receive subversive speech with engaged detachment, in the manner of other, more mature democracies—occurs and recurs, as we have seen, throughout free speech law.[36]

It is reported that Viacom has since mounted a constitutional challenge, although in the light of *K.A. Abbas*, it is difficult to see how it will succeed.

RANGARAJAN AND THE SPARK IN THE POWDER KEG

Throughout this book, we have discussed how Supreme Court cases divide along two lines of free speech jurisprudence. One set of cases treats citizens as subjects, denies their capacity for autonomy and self-determination, and vests in the government-wide authority to decide what forms of expression the people can or cannot be trusted with having exposure to. *K.A. Abbas* belongs to this line of cases. However, certain parts of *S. Rangarajan* v. *P. Jagjivan Ram* (which is otherwise a conflicted and ambiguous case, including in its endorsement of prior restraint) represent the opposite line.

In *Rangarajan*, the grant of a 'U Certificate' to a film about caste-based reservations (a particularly touchy topic) was revoked by the Madras High Court. The revocation was challenged before the Supreme Court. Despite echoing *K.A. Abbas'* opinions on the impact of films upon the excitable masses, the Supreme Court's opinions on public order and the heckler's veto are striking. The State argued that a film criticizing reservation policy dealt with so incendiary a topic

---

[33] *Secretary, Ministry of Information and Broadcasting* v. *Cricket Association of Bengal*, (1995) 2 SCC 161.

[34] *Viacom Media 18 Pvt Ltd* v. *Union of India*, 216 (2015) DLT 222.

[35] Chakrabarty (2007).

[36] The trope is explored at length by Mazzarella (2013).

that it was, by that reason, bound to be prejudicial to public order.[37] Rejecting this contention, the Court held that 'our commitment to freedom of expression demands that it cannot be suppressed unless the situations created by allowing the freedom are pressing and the community interest is endangered....*The expression of thought should be intrinsically dangerous to the public interests. In other words, the expression should be inseparably locked up with the action contemplated like the equivalent of a "spark in a powder keg".*'[38] This, as we have discussed before, reflects the 'speech-brigaded-with-action' formulation of Justice Douglas in *Brandenburg v. Ohio.*[39] Crucially, it is autonomy-respecting inasmuch as it limits itself to situations of diminished responsibility (inciting an already excited mob to imminent violence) or absent responsibility (shouting 'fire' in a crowded theatre).

It was then argued before the Supreme Court that certain groups in Tamil Nadu had threatened direct violence if the film was to go ahead—a classic case of the heckler's veto. Firmly rejecting the contention, the Court asked 'what good is the freedom of expression if the State does not take care to protect it...freedom of expression cannot be suppressed on account of threat of demonstration and processions or threats of violence...that would be tantamount to negation of the rule of law and a surrender to blackmail and intimidation'.[40] The Court's answer to the heckler's veto, therefore, was not to silence the speaker, but to require the State to carry out its constitutional responsibility of maintaining law and order, and ensuring that there is a safe space for freedom of expression without concomitant violence. This is exactly as it should be. The judgment is in stark contrast to cases like *Virendra*[41] and *Baragur Ramachandrappa.*

The Court upheld *Rangarajan*'s view on public order, while departing from it in other respects, in *D-G, Doordarshan v. Anand*

[37] *Rangarajan*, para 6.

[38] *Rangarajan*, para 42; emphasis mine.

[39] 395 U.S. 444 (1969).

[40] *Rangarajan*, para 48.

[41] *Virendra v. State of Punjab*, [1958] 1 SCR 308.

Patwardhan.[42] Patwardhan's film, *Father, Son and Holy War*, about sexual violence and communalism in India, had been given an 'A' certificate (in part). Doordarshan refused to telecast it. Before the Supreme Court, apart from arguing that Patwardhan had no vested right in having his film telecast by Doordarshan, it was also argued that the film would give rise to 'communal riots and violence', because it was going to be viewed by 'illiterate and average persons who would be largely affected by its screening'.[43] The Court rejected this contention, holding the standard to be that of the 'reasonable person', with an 'average, healthy and common sense point of view'.[44] Thus, it departed from the vision of the illiterate and vulnerable Indians that we find in *K.A. Abbas* and *Rangarajan* (and, arguably, undermined the very basis on which the Court had upheld prior restraint in *K.A. Abbas* and *Rangarajan*). The Court found that as a matter of fact, the film was neither obscene, and nor was its portrayal of social evils a threat to public order. It directed Doordarshan—as a State institution, and therefore subject to Article 19(1)(a)—to screen it.

RANGARAJAN AND THE MYTH OF CULTURAL PURITY

For all its progressiveness on the public order exception, *Rangarajan* contains many of the problematic aspects that have characterized the Court's jurisprudence when it comes to morality, or the amorphous category of 'social interest'. 'Moral values in particular', the Court held in *Rangarajan*, 'should not be allowed to be sacrificed in the guise of *social change or cultural assimilation*'.[45] (Contrast this with *Khushboo's*[46] admission that all cultural values must be open

---

[42] D-G, *Directorate-General of Doordarshan* v. *Anand Patwardhan*, (2006) 8 SCC 433 (hereinafter *Directorate General of Doordarshan*).

[43] *Directorate General of Doordarshan*, para 7.

[44] *Directorate General of Doordarshan*, para 11. This view has a pedigree stretching back to 1947. See *Bhagwati Charan Shukla* v. *Provincial Government*, AIR 1947 Nag 1.

[45] *Rangarajan*, para 21; emphasis mine.

[46] *Khushboo* v. *Kanniamal*, 2010 (4) SCALE 467.

to challenge and dissent.) The Court then listed a number of 'great sages and thinkers', literary works like Thirukkural, and—what it called—'Indian' concepts like '*dharam*', before going on to note that 'these are the bedrock of our civilization and should not be allowed to be shaken by unethical standards'.[47] Readers will note echoes of Lord Devlin's justification for using 'public morality' to limit individual freedom, with all its attendant problems—discussed before—of cultural dissent and cultural democracy. Here, the Court invoked a homogeneous Indian identity (which historians will have much to say about), stretching back into antiquity, defined by a permanent and unchanging set of 'values', and then insisted on insulating that set of (hypothetical) values against dissent.

The Court's actual analysis of the film is also questionable. Analysing a scene that allegedly sent out a 'poisonous message' to the 'depressed classes' against education, the Court found that as a matter of fact, its message was the opposite. Another issue was whether one of the characters in the film accused Dr. Ambedkar of being anti-egalitarian. Here, working with the niceties of Tamil translation, the Court found that the heroine had actually said the opposite. The implication, however—and stated as much by the Court on both occasions—was that if indeed the 'poisonous message' or the anti-egalitarian depiction of Ambedkar had existed, the film could have been censored—because, in the opinion of the Court, it was a matter of fact that nobody worked as hard as Dr. Ambedkar for equality.[48]

What is particularly disturbing about these passages is that the Court—much like in the above case of cultural purity—arrogates to itself the power to decide upon an orthodoxy ('Dr. Ambedkar was an egalitarian') and then prohibit any dissent or deviation from it. This is a classic case of directly censoring the communicative *message*, as opposed to its harmful *effects* (and goes directly counter to the idea that truth can be achieved by the exercise of free speech, not its censorship). And yet, however, in the same judgment, when it came to the

[47] *Rangarajan*, para 21.
[48] *Rangarajan*, para 27.

public order issue, the Court expressly disclaimed the idea that 'truth' has any role to play in regulating free speech:

> ...different views are allowed to be expressed by proponents and opponents *not because they are correct, or valid* but because there is freedom in this country for expressing even differing views on any issue.[49]

But if that is true, then surely that freedom extends to questioning whether Dr. Ambedkar was an egalitarian, and whether education is a necessary good for the 'depressed classes'. And immediately after that, the Court drove the point home by quoting Meiklejohn's self-governance theory of free speech, emphasizing again that 'conflicting views may be expressed, must be expressed, *not because they are valid*, but because they are relevant'[50]—arguably negating its own prior analysis.

Srishti School and the Struggle over Political Memory

Rangarajan's case has echoes in a particularly egregious instance of censorship in 2014. Just the year before, communal riots—one of the worst in recent memory—had convulsed the district of Muzaffarnagar in Uttar Pradesh, causing sixty-two deaths.[51] Shubradeep Chakravarty's documentary film on the riots, *En Dino Muzaffarnagar*, was refused screening permission on the ground that 'he had shown a political party to be responsible for the riots and that a particular caste had also been mentioned'.[52] Chakravarty's fate is nothing more than *Rangarajan's* chickens coming home to roost. Political memory, and more particularly, the freedom to *shape* political history, is made subservient to an officially sanctioned narrative of the event, whether that is government-imposed or judicially-imagined.

---

[49] *Rangarajan*, para 38; emphasis mine.
[50] *Rangarajan*, para 39; emphasis mine.
[51] Jain (2013).
[52] Butalia (2014).

The poverty of *Rangarajan's* approach appears particularly stark
when compared with the recent Delhi High Court judgment in *Srishti
School of Art, Design and Technology* v. *The Chairperson, Central Board
of Film Certification*,[53] which we discussed in Chapter One. Recall
that at issue in *Srishti* was a documentary film called *Had Anhad*,
which drew upon the writings of Kabir to challenge communal polar-
ization between Hindus and Muslims. The Central Board of Film
Certification recommended four cuts, three of which were upheld
by the Film Certification Appellate Tribunal. One of the excisions
required deleting visuals pertaining to the destruction of the Babri
Masjid in 1992, on the ground that those scenes promoted 'communal and anti-national attitudes',[54] especially because they featured an
interview with an onlooker who justified the demolition, along with
exhibiting contempt for Muslims.

Drawing upon the jurisprudence of the Israeli Supreme Court,
Justice Muralidhar struck down the excision, noting that 'the scenes
and visuals that constitute the third excision are in one sense a
recalling of the memory of an historical event. *The recall may be
imperfect.* It may contradict the collective memory of that historical
event. It may revive tensions over the events being recalled. Yet, that
by itself does not invite censorial intervention to obliterate the scenes
of recall.'[55]

This paragraph is crucial because it acknowledges the simple
fact—*contra Rangarajan*—that it is not for the Court—or the State—
to take sides in the struggle over political and historical memory. It
recognizes that the freedom to speak must involve—in Edward Said's
words—the permission to narrate.[56] Ambedkar's anti-egalitarianism,
a portrayal of the Hindu interviewee's endorsement of the destruction
of the Babri Masjid, and the documentary's film-maker's attribution of
responsibility for the Muzaffarnagar massacres, are all interpretations

---

[53] 178 (2011) DLT 337 (hereinafter *Srishti*).
[54] *Srishti*, para 18.
[55] *Srishti*, para 28; emphasis mine.
[56] Said (1984).

and constructions of the past that may or may not be invoked for present political ends, but it is not the province of the Court to advance its own competing interpretation, and then use the force of law to impose it upon everyone else.

In fact, five years before, in *F.A. Picture International* v. *CBFC*, the Bombay High Court had come to a similar conclusion, striking down the Board's refusal to certify a film about the Gujarat riots. Rejecting completely the contention that Gujarat was still a 'live issue' and a 'scar on national sensitivity', and that, therefore, the film would only 'aggravate the situation',[57] the Court declined to act as a custodian of truth, holding that 'the constitutional protection under Article 19(1)(a) that a film maker enjoys is not conditioned on the premise that he must depict something which is not true to life'.[58]

The series of High Court decisions after *Rangarajan* raises the hope that its stray observations will remain an aberration on the constitutional free speech stage. Nonetheless, as a Supreme Court case, *Rangarajan* is a microcosm of the schizophrenia that has rent Indian free speech jurisprudence ever since Article 19(1)(a) came into being. Autonomy versus paternalism; active, choosing citizens versus passive, consuming subjects; cultural democracy and dissent versus uniformity and conformity; constitutional principles versus 'public' morals—these warring ideas have pulled the Court relentlessly this way and that, sometimes—as we can see—within the same judgment. For a long time now, Indian free speech jurisprudence has been standing at a crossroads. Which path it will ultimately take continues to remain an open question.

---

[57] *F.A. Picture International* v. *Central Board of Film Certification*, AIR 2005 Bom 145, para 11 (hereinafter *F.A. Picture International*).

[58] *F.A. Picture International*, para 13. See also *Ramesh Pimple* v. *Central Board of Film Certification*, (2004) 5 Bom CR 214, where the Bombay High Court rejected the Central Board of Film Certification's argument that a film on the Gujarat riots was one-sided because it showed only the sufferings of the Muslim community; and *Anand Patwardhan* v. *Union of India*, AIR 1997 Bom 25, where the Bombay High Court rejected Doordarshan's argument against screening Anand Patwardhan's film on the Khalistan violence because it promoted a 'leftist worldview'.

INTERNET CENSORSHIP UNDER THE INFORMATION TECHNOLOGY ACT

What of online freedom of speech? Section 66A of the Information Technology Act—as pointed out before— has been under the scanner for quite some time. This is the provision under which a Goa Facebook user was issued summons for a post warning about a 'second holocaust' if Narendra Modi was elected prime minister[59] and a Karnataka MBA student arrested for an MMS that had Modi's face morphed onto a corpse.[60] And of course, the infamous Bal Thackeray Facebook arrests—apart from 295A—also involved Section 66A of the Information Technology Act. This Section criminalizes, among other things, sending information that is 'grossly offensive or menacing in character', or causes 'annoyance or inconvenience'.[61] The above instances—and countless more—should indicate that Section 66A is entirely unworkable; and the discussion over the last four chapters should also make it clear that it is unconstitutional.[62]

Recall that in the second chapter, we discussed 'overbreadth' and 'vagueness' as two specific problems with speech-curtailing legislation. A statute is overbroad when it prohibits *both* conduct that it is entitled to restrict, and conduct that it is not. When it comes to fundamental rights, as held in both *Chintaman Rao*[63] and *Kameshwar Prasad*,[64] overbroad statutes are unconstitutional. Furthermore, a statute is vague when ordinary persons find it simply impossible to tell what is allowed and what is not.[65] Vague statutes strike at the heart of any legal system, one of whose primary purposes is to allow people to plan their affairs in advance by giving them adequate and clear notice

---

[59] Nagvenkar (2014).

[60] Saikia (2014).

[61] Section 66A, Information Technology Act, 2000.

[62] Notwithstanding a Central Government advisory stipulating that no arrests could be made without the prior approval of a police officer not below the rank of an Inspector-General of Police.

[63] *Chintaman Rao v. State of Madhya Pradesh*, AIR 1951 SC 118.

[64] *Kameshwar Prasad v. State of Bihar*, AIR 1962 SC 1166.

[65] Affirmed in *Rangarajan*.

about which actions are permitted, and which are prohibited. And overbreadth and vagueness become particularly acute when it comes to free speech because of the chilling effect—the possibility of self-censorship and the consequent impoverishment of political discourse, when the boundaries of permitted and proscribed speech are broadly or hazily drawn.

It is difficult to see how anyone might argue that Section 66A does not suffer from both these problems. Evidently, speech that disturbs public order or morality will often be 'offensive', 'menacing', or 'annoying'. Equally evidently, not all offensive, menacing, or annoying speech will have a causal connection with the breach of public order, or morality, even under their broader definitions (the Modi-holocaust remark and the Thackeray Facebook posts are excellent examples). Furthermore, is there any possible way of telling in advance whether a particular communication you send or put up on Facebook is 'annoying', or even 'menacing'? Section 66A is overbroad and vague, and because of this, it also vests an unbounded discretion in the executive and lower judicial authorities to implement it in entirely unconstitutional ways.

The wording of Section 66A largely follows the British Communications Act of 2003.[66] Notably, after much public criticism of that law, its scope has been curtailed to a great extent by Prosecutorial Guidelines issued in 2012 and 2013.[67] Under the Guidelines, prosecution should be limited to messages that constitute 'credible threats of violence' (this is how the Guidelines interpret the term 'menacing'), 'specifically target an individual or individuals' (in the form of stalking or harassment), or which may amount to a breach of a court order.[68] On the other hand, messages that are simply 'grossly offensive' (with nothing more) ought only to be prosecuted when it is both necessary and proportionate to do so. One test of proportionality is whether 'the content of the communication [does] not obviously go beyond *what could conceivably be tolerable or acceptable* in an open and diverse

---

[66] Section 127, Communications Act, 2003.
[67] The Crown Prosecution Service (n.d.).
[68] The Crown Prosecution Service (n.d.: para 12).

society which upholds and respects freedom of expression'.[69] This is clearly a very high threshold requirement, and would not cover the numerous cases of Section 66A abuse that we have discussed here.

The Guidelines were amended in 2013, to take into account aggravated situations of racially or religiously motivated hate speech, as well as the age and maturity of the wrongdoer.[70] The Guidelines are a good example of how the Act might be read down in order to render it consistent with the guarantees of free speech. However, taking into account the pathological perspective and the problems of implementation, striking down the Act would appear to remain the better option.

The problems with Section 66A have also crept into the Intermediaries Guidelines Rules of 2011, which were passed under the Information Technology Act,[71] with a view to regulating the conduct of online intermediaries (like search engines, data storage websites such as Youtube, and so on).[72] Under the various headings of content deemed actionable, we find categories such as 'grossly harmful', 'disparaging', or 'harassing'. Much like those of Section 66A, these categories are also very evidently overbroad. There are, however, deeper problems with the process contemplated under the Intermediaries Rules: for instance, there is no requirement of a public notice. Furthermore, arguably,[73] the Guidelines require intermediaries to disable access to 'offending content' within thirty-six hours of it being brought to their notice by an affected person. As in other areas of free speech law, we see that speech-restricting provisions bypass the requirement of judicial sanction by placing censorial power in the hands of non-judicial bodies. What is particularly troubling about the Intermediaries Rules is that they go one step beyond other censorship provisions that we have discussed, which vest the power of censorship in administrative or executive authorities. These Rules, on the other

---

[69] The Crown Prosecution Service (n.d.: para 48); emphasis mine.

[70] The Crown Prosecution Service (n.d.: para 50).

[71] See Section 79, Information Technology Act, 2000.

[72] Information Technology (Intermediaries Guidelines) Rules, 2011; see for example, Uppaluri (2012).

[73] For the controversies surrounding this proposition, see Prakash (n.d.).

hand, both empower and obligate *private parties* (who play a crucial role as gatekeepers when it comes to online expression) to restrict or curtail the freedom of speech.[74]

The procedure, therefore, places the fate of online free speech entirely in private hands, without any mediation by organs of the State. A private party can make a complaint to the intermediary, which is then burdened with the task of deciding for itself whether the offending speech violates the Guidelines. The danger of over-regulation is even greater here because for obvious reasons, private intermediaries will prefer to avoid the possibility of legal liability, than expend time and resources fighting free speech battles before the courts.

Lastly, another instance of sweeping executive powers over online speech is the set of 'Blocking Rules' framed under Section 69A of the Information Technology Act. Section 69A authorizes the 'Central government or any of its officers specially authorised by it' to direct government agencies or intermediaries to block online content, under some of the 19(2) grounds (sovereignty or integrity of India, defence of India, public order, prevention of incitement to cognizable offences).[75] Under the Blocking Rules of 2009, directions to block may be issued by a 'designated officer' (that is, an officer not below the rank of Joint Secretary), upon either a court order, or a request from a government ministry or agency. A final decision on blocking is taken by a Committee, which consists entirely of non-judicial members. Complete confidentiality, both of blocking requests and of action taken, is mandated by the Rules.[76] As is obvious, the Blocking Rules suffer from problems of transparency,

---

[74] The United Nations Special Rapporteur on the Freedom of Speech and Expression pointed this out. See La Rue (2011: para 43): '...censorship measures should never be delegated to a private entity, and that no one should be held liable for content on the Internet of which they are not the author. Indeed, no State should use or force intermediaries to undertake censorship on its behalf.'

[75] Section 69A, Information Technology Act, 2000.

[76] See Information Technology (Procedures and Safeguards for Blocking of Access of Information by Public) Rules, 2009; in particular, Rule 16.

as well as placing powers of censorship entirely in the hands of non-judicial, executive bodies, even in non-emergency situations.[77]

Ultimately, the task of interpreting Article 19(2) and deciding when the freedom of speech may reasonably be restricted is a task for the courts. However, India's online content regulation regime, much like its film censorship and cable television regimes, places that responsibility, at least in the first instance, with executive authorities. It does so by incorporating into the parent enactment the terms of Article 19(2), and leaving implementation up to the executive. In *K.A. Abbas*, the Court rejected the argument that such a scheme amounted to unconstitutionally excessive delegation.[78] It might therefore be too late in the day to challenge the provisions of the Information Technology Act on that ground. Nonetheless, the perils of such an approach have been discussed extensively. The controversies that erupted in 2012 and 2014 over successive mass-blocking orders of twitter handles and websites indicate that this is a problem that will remain acute in the years to come.

[77] According to Pranesh Prakash, however, website blocks are subject to the provisions of the Right to Information Act, 2005. See Prakash (n.d.).

[78] *K.A. Abbas*, para 44.

PART FOUR

Other Restrictions

CHAPTER EIGHT

Defamation, Privacy, and Injunctions

In India, defamation is an offence under both, civil and criminal laws. The elements of the two offences are different, and they raise different constitutional issues. We shall consider them separately.

CIVIL DEFAMATION

More such incredible tales abound about Sahara, none that could be substantiated. A group employee in Mumbai asked me whether I had seen the 'torture chamber' in Sahara Shahar. What's that, I asked. The chamber, apparently, is where an erring employee is dumped at night in his underwear and subjected to physical abuse and humiliations by his subordinates, including his driver and guards if he's of high office. Sahara does this to shame a rogue employee and destroy his self-respect and dignity, the group employee said. A communication executive at Sahara laughed when I checked with him about the authenticity of the torture chamber.

—An excerpt from Tamal Bandyopadhyay's *Sahara: The Untold Story* cited before the Calcutta High Court, in a Rs 200 crore defamation lawsuit

What Is at Stake?

Reliance, Sahara, and Infosys are massive multinational corporations wielding economic (and political) power on an enormous scale. There is one other thing that unites them: their use of Indian defamation law to target investigative journalism. Hamish McDonald's *The Polyester Prince*, a book about the Ambanis, was pulled from Indian bookshops under threats of defamation lawsuits.[1] More recently, the same strategy was used against Paranjoy Guha Thakurta's *Gas Wars*, a book about the influence wielded by Reliance upon the nation's gas production and pricing.[2] Towards the end of 2013, Sahara filed a Rs 200 crore lawsuit against journalist Tamal Bandyopadhyay and the *Mint* magazine, for his book *Sahara: The Untold Story*, before it had even hit bookstores (the excerpt at the beginning of this chapter is from an injunction order granted by a Calcutta High Court judge).[3] In the middle of 2014, Infosys served a legal notice to three journalistic outlets, claiming Rs 200 crores for 'loss of reputation and goodwill due to circulation of defamatory articles'.[4]

Let it not be thought, however, that corporations are the only ones using defamation law as a weapon. In January 2014, under threat of a defamation lawsuit, Bloomsbury withdrew a book called *The Descent of Air India*, which was highly critical of former Aviation Minister Praful Patel's role in the economic collapse of Air India.[5] It is difficult to blame Bloomsbury for capitulating. Not too long before, a Pune court had awarded damages of *Rs 100 crore* to former Justice P.B. Sawant, against the Times Media Group, which had accidentally shown his photograph next to the name of a (different) judge accused in a scam, as part of a fifteen-second clip.[6]

When we add a former aviation minister and a former Supreme Court judge to a list that already includes Reliance, Sahara, and

---

[1] Dalal (2000).

[2] *Livemint* (2014).

[3] *Sahara v. Tamal Bandyopadhyay*, T.A. No. 122 of 2013 (High Court of Calcutta).

[4] Kurup (2014).

[5] Balakrishnan (2014).

[6] Ranjan (2011).

Infosys, a clear pattern begins to emerge. Plaintiffs are entities or persons in positions of power and influence. Defendants are members of the media. And the theme is investigative journalism about those entities. In technical terms, these are called SLAPP lawsuits. 'SLAPP' stands for 'Strategic Litigation Against Public Participation', and refers to using the law in order to prevent the public from knowing about, or participating in, important affairs.[7]

Civil defamation law is uniquely suited to be pressed in service of SLAPP. There are two reasons for this. First, standards and burdens of proof: Indian law is based on the common law of defamation,[8] where to prove a prima facie case, the plaintiff need only show that the impugned statement has been 'published' (made to a person other than the plaintiff and the defendant), that it refers to him, and that it is 'defamatory'—that is, that it tends to lower the reputation of the plaintiff in the eyes of right-thinking members of society.[9] At this stage—as happened in the Calcutta High Court—the judge can grant an interim injunction restraining further distribution (of the book, in case it is a book) until the case is settled on merits. Injunctions of this sort have been described as prior restraints, and the similarities (with prior restraint) are obvious. For instance, in the case of Tamal Bandyopadhyay's book on Sahara, had the case not been eventually settled out of court, the book could not have reached the general public until the injunction had been lifted. Given the pace of Indian courts, an injunction is effectively a death sentence.

We shall return to injunctions later in this chapter. Now, once the plaintiff has proved his prima facie case for defamation, the defendant must then invoke one of the established defences in order to avoid paying damages. 'Truth' is a defence to civil defamation, as is 'fair comment'. But, proving the 'truth' of an allegedly defamatory statement will often be beyond the power of the journalist. Sometimes the statement will have come from a confidential source, which the

---

[7] Donson (2000).

[8] For a recent case affirming this proposition, see *Brig. B.C. Rana v. Ms. Seema Katoch*, 198 (2013) DLT 35.

[9] Divan (2013).

journalist has promised not to reveal. Sometimes the statement will be
the culmination of a chain of inferences, the truth of which is impossible to demonstrate as one would demonstrate a logical syllogism.
And sometimes, tight deadlines, the complexity of the issues involved,
or just simple human error will mean that, despite all due diligence,
errors will creep in. Nonetheless, the common law of defamation
establishes a regime of strict liability: it is not enough for the journalist to argue that he took all reasonable care in establishing the truth of
the allegedly defamatory statement because defamation law makes no
allowance for absence of fault or negligence.

If the standards and burdens of proof are onerous, the quantum of
possible damages is prohibitive. The damages claimed by the corporations and judges that we discussed at the beginning of this chapter all
ran into hundreds of crores. These are sums of money that individual
journalists cannot possibly pay, and that will bankrupt all but the rich-
est of publishing houses. Again, defamation law makes it possible for
entities to claim these amounts. In allowing damages for 'reputational
loss', it does not require plaintiffs to demonstrate any *actual* harm that
they have suffered, but to claim on the basis of potential loss that they
argue they *will* suffer because of their reputation having been lowered.
Furthermore, not only is 'reputational loss' impossible to quantify at
the best of times, it permits judges a great degree of discretion in fixing
amounts. The situation is exacerbated by the possibility of punitive or
exemplary damages—that is, damages calibrated not towards compensating the plaintiff for the (reputational or other) loss suffered, but
towards punishing the defendant for particularly outrageous conduct.[10]
Admittedly, Indian courts are not known for granting punitive or
exemplary damages. It is the *threat* of massive liability, however, that
in itself casts a significant chilling effect upon investigative journalism.

The combination of onerous burdens and standards of proof,
which ensure that the journalist cannot escape liability even for innocent errors made despite due care, and the ruinous extent of possible

---

[10] Under common law, exemplary damages are restricted to specific circumstances, and treated as a remedy of the last resort. See, for example, *Kuddus* v.
Chief Constable, [2002] 2 AC 122.

liability itself, makes defamation law one of the most potent weapons to silence criticism and dissent. By now, the free speech issues should be evident. Investigative reporting into the affairs of Reliance, Sahara, Infosys, and those of politicians and judges, lies at the very heart of the democratic justification of free speech: the right of the public to know—and to criticize—the functioning of the powerful and influential entities in society, those whose actions have an effect on the lives of countless citizens. Silencing this kind of journalism entails a particularly grievous impoverishment of the public discourse.

It is therefore surprising that (apart from its landmark judgment in *R. Rajagopal*), the Supreme Court is yet to seriously consider defamation law on the touchstone of Article 19(1)(a).[11] Of course, Article 19(2) expressly allows for reasonable restrictions upon the freedom of speech in the interests of defamation, but it is an open question whether the common law of defamation, as it stands, is consistent with the guarantees of Article 19(1)(a). It is all the more surprising because the use of defamation litigation to silence political and other forms of public criticism is not unique to India.[12] World over, constitutional democracies have taken notice of this, and have tried to respond. Let us first look at how other countries have dealt with this problem.

New York Times v. Sullivan and the Idea of 'Breathing Space'

In 1960, the American civil rights movement was at its peak, and was met by a wave of repression in the deep South. In this context, the *New York Times* published a full-page advertisement (drafted and paid for by certain anti-segregation activists) titled 'Heed their Rising Voices', which detailed the struggle of the civil rights activists in Montgomery, Alabama. The advertisement spoke of the violence faced by unarmed protesters and students at the hands of the Montgomery police, but also contained some factual errors. For instance, it stated that Martin Luther King Jr had been arrested seven times (he had actually been

---

[11] An argument urging the Court to do so is made by Sathe. See Sathe (2003).

[12] For instance, the use of defamation law by politicians against the media in Singapore has been well-documented. See, for example, *BBC News* (2008).

arrested four times), and that the police had padlocked certain black students into the school dining hall in order to 'starve them into submission' (this had not happened). On the basis of these factual mistakes, Sullivan, the police commissioner of Montgomery, sued the *New York Times* for libel. The Alabama courts awarded him 500,000 dollars in damages. The *New York Times* appealed to the Supreme Court.[13]

Before the Supreme Court, the stakes could not have been higher. After Sullivan, there were numerous other plaintiffs who had similar claims of libel. The total liability that the *New York Times* was looking at was three million dollars—in those days, enough to potentially drive it out of business. The case, however, was about far more than just the *New York Times*. As Anthony Lewis recounts in his magisterial history of *New York Times* v. *Sullivan*, the civil rights movement in the South depended upon swaying national sympathy by bringing the brutality and the violence to the attention of the rest of the United States.[14] This could only be done through the media. But if the fate of the *New York Times* was a three-million-dollar liability, no newspaper would dare report on the events, for fear of going down the same track. What was ultimately at stake was the fate of the civil rights movement itself, and defamation law was the South's strategy to suffocate it.

New York Times v. *Sullivan* became a path-breaking case, which changed the future course of defamation law all over the world. In an opinion that has gone down in the annals of free speech, Justice Brennan began his substantive discussion by noting the 'profound national commitment to the principle that *debate on public issues should be uninhibited, robust, and wide-open*, and that it may well include vehement, caustic, and sometimes unpleasantly sharp attacks on government and public officials'.[15] What Justice Brennan understood was that in order to survive, free speech needed '*breathing space*'—that is, the space to make mistakes. 'Erroneous statement', he

---

[13] For a book-length historical and legal treatment of the events leading up to the *Sullivan* case, see Lewis (1992).

[14] Lewis (1992).

[15] *New York Times* v. *Sullivan*, 376 U.S. 254, 270 (1964) (hereinafter *New York Times*); emphasis mine.

pointed out, 'was inevitable in free debate'[16]—and therefore, the very existence of free debate required the protection of such statements. On the other hand, under Alabama's (common law) defamation regime, 'the pall of fear and timidity imposed upon those who would give voice to public criticism [creates] an atmosphere in which the First Amendment freedoms cannot survive'[17] (a classic exposition of the chilling effect). And under the burden of proving truth, 'would-be critics of official conduct may be deterred from voicing their criticism, even though it is believed to be true and even though it is, in fact, true, *because of doubt whether it can be proved in court or fear of the expense of having to do so.* They tend to make only statements which 'steer far wider of the unlawful zone'.[18] Thus, Justice Brennan found that both the burden (proving truth) and the standards (no-fault liability) imposed upon defendants, were incompatible with a robust free speech regime. Consequently, he propounded an 'actual malice' test for defamation: liability could be imposed only if the maker of the statement either *knew* it was false, or published it with *reckless disregard* for its truth or falsity.

By a unanimous, 9–0 decision, the American Supreme Court reversed the decision of the Alabama courts, saved the *New York Times* and (according to Lewis) played a major role in saving the civil rights movement. Since 1964, the Press has not lost a defamation lawsuit in the United States.

A Bridge Too Far? Experiments with a Fault Standard

The verdict in *New York Times* v. *Sullivan* was limited to public officials. In the years following that case, however, it was gradually expanded into a general shield law for the media (with some modifications), no matter who was being reported upon, and what the topic was.[19] There

---

[16] *New York Times*, p. 271.

[17] *New York Times*, p. 278.

[18] *New York Times*, p. 279.

[19] See, for example, *Curtis Publishing Co.* v. *Butts*, 388 U.S. 130 (1967) (expanding the test, with minor modifications, to 'public figures'); *Gertz* v. *Robert Welch*,

are some who argue that the United States has gone too far in its protection of the media, sacrificing public and private reputations upon the altar of the Fourth Estate, which is a highly powerful, organized, and often hostile entity in its own right. People do have legitimate interests in their privacy and their reputation, which are often under attack from an unaccountable media. The two interests—that of reputation and privacy, and of a free press—must be balanced against each other.

The South African courts have certainly thought so. Soon after the South African Interim Constitution was passed, Justice Cameron began the process of constitutionalizing defamation law. In *Holomisa* v. *Argus Newspapers*, he held that an alleged defamatory statement that relates to 'free and fair political activity' must not only be false, but also *unreasonable*, in order to attract liability.[20] Reasonableness would be determined by whether the publisher had initiated a 'due enquiry' into the facts that he had relied upon. Furthermore, and crucially, the burden of proving unreasonableness lay upon the party alleging defamation.[21]

The South African Constitutional Court followed up in *Khumalo* v. *Holomisa*. Justice O'Regan noted that the traditional common law of defamation was incompatible with free speech in a democratic society, and would have to be modified accordingly. Expounding upon a variant of the checking theory of free speech, she observed that 'the media are important agents in ensuring that government is open, responsive and accountable to the people.'[22] Following Justice Brennan, she too expressed the worry about the chilling effect in requiring

---

418 U.S. 323 (1974) (hereinafter *Gertz*) (holding that strict liability for defamation was unconstitutional, and anything short of an actual malice standard would permit courts only to award *actual* damages); *Hustler Magazine* v. *Falwell*, 485 U.S. 46 (1988) (holding that intentional infliction of emotional distress was covered by the First Amendment); *Time Inc.* v. *Hill*, 385 U.S. 374 (1967) (hereinafter *Hill*) (shielding the press from an infringement of privacy claim brought by private individuals).

[20] 1996 (2) SA 588.

[21] But see, for a contrary approach, *National Media Ltd.* v. *Bogoshi*, 1998 (4) SA 1196.

[22] *Khumalo* v. *Holomisa*, 2002 (8) BCLR 771, para 23 (hereinafter *Khumalo*).

journalists to prove the truth of everything they said. Nonetheless, she was not willing to go as far as the American Supreme Court did, noting that under the South African Constitution, the values underlying free speech would have to be balanced against the individual right to dignity. Consequently—following the prior case of *Bogoshi*—she incorporated a 'reasonableness standard' into defamation law:

> ...if a publisher cannot establish the truth, or finds it disproportionately expensive or difficult to do so, the publisher may show *that in all the circumstances the publication was reasonable.* In determining whether publication was reasonable, a court will have regard to the individual's interest in protecting his or her reputation in the context of the constitutional commitment to human dignity. It will also have regard to the individual's interest in privacy. In that regard, there can be no doubt *that persons in public office have a diminished right to privacy, though of course their right to dignity persists.* It will also have regard to the crucial role played by the press in fostering a transparent and open democracy. The defence of reasonable publication avoids therefore a winner-takes-all result and establishes a *proper balance between freedom of expression and the value of human dignity.* Moreover, the defence of reasonable publication will encourage editors and journalists to act with due care and respect for the individual interest in human dignity prior to publishing defamatory material, without precluding them from publishing such material when it is reasonable to do so.[23]

Justice O'Regan's opinion seeks a middle ground between the strict-liability common law regime and the American undue malice standard. It recognizes that journalists ought to have fact-checking obligations and duties of due care, but also that to hold them to an absolute standard of accuracy is unjustified. It recognizes the checking value of free speech that the press is in a unique position to serve, but also the interests of individuals in privacy and dignity. A balancing of these interests comes under the ambit of a compendious test of 'reasonableness'.

Justice O'Regan also put her finger on an important point when she pointed out that persons in public office have a 'diminished right

---

[23] *Khumalo*, para 43; emphasis mine.

to privacy'. This is one reason why there ought to be differential standards of defamation when it comes to public and private individuals. To have a more exacting standard in the former case is not—as might initially appear—to accord special privileges to the press. Rather, there are a number of principled reasons for it. First—as Justice O'Regan pointed out—public persons have diminished privacy interests because they have voluntarily thrust themselves into the public eye. Second—and this is connected with the checking value—there is a public interest in knowledge of and discussion about public persons that is absent in the case of the private lives of private people. Third, public persons are in positions of power and influence that allow them access to the infrastructure of free speech with much greater ease than private people. A defamed politician, for example, can easily have access to the editorial pages of newspapers or prime-time TV channels to put out her reply in a way that will reach a large number of people, an avenue that is not normally open to private persons.

While the case for differential standards is clear, the American experience shows that a watertight and principled distinction between public and private individuals is difficult to make in practice. A possible alternative is to focus not on the identity of the person targeted, but upon the *issue*. If the issue is one of public interest (for instance, the economic affairs of Reliance as opposed to the personal life of Mukesh Ambani), then the heightened standards for defamation ought to apply.

The Australian High Court adopted the issue-based approach in *Lange v. Australian Broadcasting Corporation*.[24] Like its South African counterpart, the Court noted that the common law of defamation must be brought in line with the constitutional provisions. While the Australian Constitution did not have a free speech guarantee, the Court made an impeccably Meiklejohnian argument, reasoning from the Constitution's text and structure to hold that it contemplated a 'representative government', at the heart of which lay the need for free political discussion. Consequently, the Court held that a 'qualified

---

[24] (1997) 189 CLR 520 (hereinafter *Lange*).

privilege' extended to dissemination of information, opinions, and arguments concerning *government and political matters* affecting the people of Australia.[25] Within this framework, the publisher would be exonerated from liability for defamation as long as he could prove *reasonableness of conduct*. And he was deemed to have acted reasonably as long as he had 'reasonable grounds for believing the imputation was true, took proper steps, *so far as they were reasonably open*, to verify the accuracy of the material and did not believe the imputation to be untrue'.[26]

The problem, of course, is that in our era of expansive private power (of corporations and other entities), expanded protection only to speech about 'government and political matters' is insufficient. Thus, when the English House of Lords was invited to adopt this approach in *Reynolds* v. *Times Newspapers Ltd.*,[27] it declined to do so. The House of Lords refused to incorporate a blanket privilege for all communications of a certain type, arguing that it was futile to try and distinguish between 'political' matters, and matters that were nonetheless of important and serious public concern. Instead, it made the enquiry a case-by-case one (something similar to Justice O'Regan's position in South Africa): the Court would decide, based upon the context and circumstances of the publication, whether it had a qualified privilege *because of its value to the public*. Indeed, Section 4 of the UK Defamation Act of 2013, which replaced the 'Reynolds Defence', provides a specific exemption for statements on a 'matter of *public interest*'.[28]

The *Reynolds* approach was broadly affirmed by the Canadian Supreme Court in its 2009 decisions in *Grant* v. *Torstar Corp.*[29] and *Quan* v. *Cusson*.[30] Like its counterparts in the United States, South Africa, and the United Kingdom, the Canadian Supreme Court

---

[25] *Lange.*
[26] *Lange*; emphasis mine.
[27] [2001] 2 AC 127.
[28] Section 4, Defamation Act, 2013.
[29] [2009] 3 SCR 640: [2009] SCC 61 (hereinafter *Grant*).
[30] [2009] SCC 62.

acknowledged that the common law of defamation could cast a chill on the freedom of expression. Chief Justice McLachlin therefore recognized a 'new' defence of 'responsible communication on matters of public interest',[31] in order that defamation law remain consistent with the guarantees of freedom of speech and expression in the Canadian Charter. In so doing, the Chief Justice specified that the publication need not be restricted to 'public figures', or to 'government and political matters'. Rather, 'public interest' included subjects 'inviting public attention, or about which the public, or a segment of the public, has some substantial concern because it affects the welfare of citizens, or one to which considerable public notoriety or controversy has attached'.[32] 'Responsibility'—as in other jurisdictions—was a holistic enquiry, that would take into account the seriousness of the allegations, the reliability of the source, the urgency of the matter, whether the defamed person's point of view was solicited, and so on.

Likewise, the European Court of Human Rights expressly rejected the argument (made by Iceland) that 'political speech' could be distinguished from non-political speech otherwise in the public interest in the context of defamation proceedings. Referring to the watchdog role of the press, it held that when it came to protecting the freedom of speech and expression in a democracy, matters of 'public concern' were entitled to as much protection as 'political discussion'.[33] The watchdog role of the press has had an important impact on the European Court of Human Rights' judgments on defamation law and the media. In *Bladet Tromso*, for instance, it held that when contributing to public debate, the press ought to be allowed to rely on the content of official reports *without* independent research, if it was to maintain its public watchdog function.[34]

This survey demonstrates that jurisdictions all over the world are acutely aware of the free speech issues with the common law of defamation. Over the last three decades, there has been a gradual

---

[31] *Grant*.

[32] *Grant*, para 105.

[33] *Thorgeirson* v. *Iceland*, (1992) 14 EHRR 843, para 64.

[34] *Bladet Tromso* v. *Norway*, (2000) 29 EHRR 125, para 68.

and incremental move towards bringing defamation in line with the constitutional guarantee of free speech and expression. Issues of burdens and standards of proof, the role of the press, and the problem of the chilling effect have all been considered by the courts, which have tried to work out a balanced approach that also takes into account the importance of public reputation. Since much of this jurisprudence has emerged relatively recently, it is to be hoped that India follows suit soon enough.

Harm and Damage in the European Law

We have discussed before the interesting irony that England—the country from which we have derived most of our problematic free speech laws—has found them to be unworkable, and has changed them via legislation. We have seen this already in the context of *Reynolds*, and the Defamation Act. The English parliament has also addressed the issue from the side of *damages*. Recall that defamation claims are invariably speculative. On what basis do corporations claim Rs 200 crores as damages for loss of reputation and goodwill? On what basis does a retired judge claim Rs 100 crore for a fifteen-second TV clip wrongly putting his photograph next to another judge accused in a scam case? The English parliament attempted to address this issue of exploding claims in its Defamation Act of 2013. Apart from the general public interest exception, it must also be shown that there is likely to be 'serious harm' to the plaintiff's reputation.[35] Crucially, the legislation also defines serious harm for corporations, stating that 'harm to the reputation of a body that trades for profit is not "serious harm" unless it has caused or is likely to cause the body serious financial loss'.[36]

Proving harm is one way of dealing with the problem. The other way, of course, is limiting the quantum of damages itself. This has been the approach of the European Court of Human Rights. In *Tolstoy Miloslavsky* v. *United Kingdom*, it found a 1.5 million pound award

---

[35] Section 1(1), Defamation Act, 2013.
[36] Section 1(2), Defamation Act, 2013.

to be disproportionately large—so large, in fact, that it violated the European Convention's free speech guarantee, and did not meet the standard of being a restriction that was necessary in a democratic society.[37] The foundation of the judgment, of course, is the chilling effect on free speech that ruinously large damages awards inevitably have.

The Delhi High Court on the Chilling Effect

The constitutionalization of defamation law in India is an unfinished endeavour. In *R. Rajagopal v. State of Tamil Nadu*, the Court came tantalizingly close to developing a 19(1)(a)-based jurisprudence, but left the task half-done. In *Rajagopal*, the factual matrix was complex. Simply put, a Tamil magazine wanted to publish the autobiography of Auto Shankar, a convicted and imprisoned serial killer, ostensibly without his consent. It was also claimed that the autobiography contained defamatory statements about the police and IAS (Indian Administrative Service) administrators, alleging that there was a nexus between them and the criminals. There were, therefore, two claims before the Court: Auto Shankar's privacy claim, and the defamation *and* privacy claims of government officials, who wanted to impose prior restraint upon the publication of the book. The Court cited a series of American decisions on the right to individual privacy and defamation laws vis-à-vis the freedom of the press, including the 'celebrated' decision of *New York Times* v. *Sullivan*, before observing:

> Our system of Government demands as do the systems of Government of the United States of America and United Kingdom *constant vigilance over exercise of governmental power by the press and the media among others...* at the same time, we must remember that our society may not share the degree of public awareness obtaining in United Kingdom or United States. The sweep of the First Amendment to the United States Constitution and the freedom of speech and expression under our Constitution is [*sic*] not identical though similar in their major premises.[38]

---

[37] (1995) 20 EHRR 442, para 51.
[38] *R. Rajagopal* v. *State of Tamil Nadu*, (1994) 6 SCC 632, para 23 (hereinafter *Rajagopal*); emphasis mine.

When it came to spelling out the principles, the Court expressly prohibited the government from imposing prior restraints upon publication. It then held:

> [in] the case of public officials, it is obvious, right to privacy, or for that matter, *the remedy of action for damages* is simply not available with respect to their acts and conduct relevant to the discharge of their official duties. *This is so even where the publication is based upon facts and statements which are not true, unless the official establishes that the publication was made (by the defendant) with reckless disregard for truth.* In such a case, it would be enough for the defendant (member of the press or media) to prove that he acted after a reasonable verification of the facts; it is not necessary for him to prove that what he has written is true.[39]

This is a very curious paragraph. Although the Court expressly incorporates the language of *New York Times* v. *Sullivan*, it makes no mention of libel or defamation. It seems to limit itself to privacy or an action for damages—without clarifying whether that action for damages *must arise* out of a privacy breach, or whether it is *any* action for damages, including one arising out of a libel suit. It then goes on to adopt two contrary standards within a sentence of each other—*Sullivan's* reckless disregard test first, and the Canada/South Africa/United Kingdom 'reasonable verification test' immediately afterwards.

So what is the holding of *Rajagopal*? It is unclear, although the express invocation of *Sullivan*, and the language of *Sullivan*, seems to suggest that the Court was veering towards an actual malice standard. Furthermore, subsequently, it expressly stated that government and other institutions exercising governmental power cannot maintain a claim for defamation. Of course, as we have seen in our survey of comparative constitutional jurisprudence, much turns on the interpretation of the word 'relevant', in the phrase 'conduct *relevant* to the discharge of their official duties'. Presumably, any activity that bears a reasonable relation to official duty would fall within this category. Nonetheless, the act must be that of a *public official*. Consequently, we seem to be closest to the Australian test in *Lange*, which provides

---

[39] *Rajagopal*, para 28; emphasis mine.

heightened protection to speech about 'government and political matters'. For reasons discussed here, this is unsatisfactory because it does not address the fact that issues of public concern need not be restricted to the explicitly political.

Finally, in concluding, the Court complicated matters further by specifying that it was not ruling on whether the government could maintain a prosecution for *criminal* defamation under Sections 499 and 500 of the Indian Penal Code in the context of Articles 19(1)(a) and 19(2)—that (according to the Court) would have to wait another day.[40] *Rajagopal*, therefore, leaves the law in a welter of confusion when it comes to claims of privacy and civil defamation vis-à-vis Articles 19(1)(a) and 19(2). At the very least, it seems to hold expressly that government officials cannot sue for defamation for speech that relates to the performance of their official functions, unless a high threshold is met.

Over the last ten years, however, the Delhi High Court has begun to craft a 19(1)(a)-defamation law jurisprudence. In *Ram Jethmalani* v. *Subramaniam Swamy*, for instance, in the course of court proceedings involving the assassination of Rajiv Gandhi, Subramanian Swamy accused Jethmalani of receiving money from the LTTE. Jethmalani sued for libel. The Delhi High Court cited *New York Times* v. *Sullivan* as an 'important decision'[41] rendered in the context of libel claims and the constitutional right to freedom of speech, and noted the *Rajagopal* court's reliance upon it. It then expressly acknowledged:

> Since law of defamation, by making actionable certain utterances, runs counter to another widely accepted legal tenet—the right to freedom of expression, the two have been harmonised by judicial process so that an individual's right of privacy and protection of honour and reputation is preserved and at the same time the public interest in free speech is also protected...the pendulum between reputation and expression has swung back and forth through history, but a body of positive jurisprudence evidenced by the decision in Sullivan's case has developed...*the aim of the law was to see that there was no chilling effect*. If a person is

---

[40] *Rajagopal*, para 25.

[41] *Ram Jethmalani* v. *Subramaniam Swamy*, 126 (2006) DLT 135, para 78 (hereinafter *Ram Jethmalani*).

under a fear of being sued, he may not express himself freely on public issues and this would chill the public debate.[42]

Having acknowledged this, the Court then read *Rajagopal* as having incorporated the *Sullivan* test into the Indian law—that is, public officials could not succeed in a defamation claim unless they demonstrated actual malice. Subsequently, in 2009, in the case of *Petronet*, the Delhi High Court again cited *Rajagopal*, this time holding even more clearly:

> Because the result may be damaging self-censorship by the media to the impoverishment of political discourse—libel's so-called 'chilling effect'—[it] was deemed contrary to the public interest to continue to allow government to sue in defamation. *Nonetheless, defamation is now unavailable to such agencies, though they are free to sue for malicious falsehood.* It was also held that given that plaintiffs must prove falsity, malice, and loss, actions in malicious falsehood are perhaps less likely to chill political speech.[43]

Interestingly, *Petronet* clarified the *Rajagopal* holding by adding that the burden of proving loss, in addition to that of proving malice, is upon the plaintiff. It, therefore, went one step beyond the strict holding of *Rajagopal*.

It is important to note that technically, *Petronet* was not a defamation case, but a case about injunction (which the Court declined to grant). The question in the case was whether Petronet could claim an injunction prohibiting a website from reporting certain 'confidential matters' about its transactions. Crucially, however, immediately after citing *Rajagopal* and the defamation cases, Justice Ravindra Bhat noted that although Petronet was a private company, it was nonetheless

> a company with an equity base of Rs.1200 crores, of which 50% is subscribed by Central Government Public Sector Undertakings...equally, the negotiations conducted for the purpose of gas and allied products,

---

[42] *Ram Jethmalani*, para 94; emphasis mine.

[43] *Petronet LNG Ltd.* v. *Indian Petro Group*, 158 (2009) DLT 759: [2009] 95 SCL 207 (Del) (hereinafter *Petronet*); emphasis mine.

are meant to service the needs of the community and the consumer base in India. *Understood in a broad sense, therefore, it is engaged in a vital public function*...therefore, the claim for confidentiality has to be necessarily from the view of the plaintiff's accountability to such extent as well as its duties which have a vital bearing on the availability and presence of gas in the country.[44]

There is a crucial move made by the Court here, from public *official* to public *function*. The Court justified it by noting that

> wherever the *general public* or public agencies have a stake in companies or corporations...their right to be informed about matters that concern the functioning of such corporations, is vitally important...some may even argue that the press could sensationalize the facts in presentation of such information, *yet the right to disseminate these view* [sic] *is at the core of freedom of speech and expression and any restraint would have a chilling effect on its exercise.*[45]

These remarks, of course, are made in the context of injunctions. But notice that the Court's observations are not limited to injunctions. According to Justice Bhat, '*any* restraint...would have a chilling effect [on free speech]'. In this context, it is important to understand that the principle which undergirds the Court's decision—that is, 'the right to disseminate' information about entities involved in public functions being at the core of the freedom of speech and expression—is threatened just as much by defamation law as it is by injunctions. Therefore, *Petronet* establishes two propositions: first, that the common law of defamation can have a chilling effect on the freedom of speech, and especially upon investigative journalism; and second, that the 'core' of the freedom of speech and expression applies with equal force to information about entities performing public functions, as it does to public officials. If we accept these two propositions, we have a solid legal and jurisprudential foundation for extending the *Rajagopal* principle of high defamation thresholds from public officials to public functions.

---

[44] *Petronet*, para 64; emphasis mine.
[45] *Petronet*, para 69; emphasis mine.

Civil Defamation: Conclusion

After *Rajagopal*, government officials cannot sue for civil defamation when the offending speech is related to their official functioning, unless they can demonstrate actual malice. This is a positive development, but it is insufficient. It is crucial to protect the press not only when it comes to commenting on public *officials*, but on matters of public *concern*. That is, the scope of protection should be determined not on the basis of the identity of the subject, but on the basis of the issue. In addition, the standard should be applied for all forms of prior restraint. The rationale for these extensions is provided by the Delhi High Court in *Petronet*, and ought to be adopted.

This does not necessarily mean that the *New York Times* v. *Sullivan* standard need necessarily be extended to all such cases. There are a number of alternatives that are available. Australia accords a qualified privilege to political communication, one that is based upon showing that the publisher acted reasonably, given the circumstances. South Africa, Canada, and England[46] adopt (slightly different) tests of reasonableness and public interest, which take into account the watchdog function of the press, the problem of the chilling effect, and the need for uninhibited public criticism, in their defamation standards. The basic objective is to ensure journalistic accountability and responsibility without unduly chilling speech. A separate way of accomplishing this—in addition to tweaking the standards for defamation—is to require proof of actual harm as well as to limit the extent of damages. The varieties are endless: it is now for the Supreme Court to develop its jurisprudence on the point.

RELATED ISSUES: SEDITION, PRIVACY, AND INJUNCTIONS

Sedition in Light of *Rajagopal*: A Second Look

In an earlier part of this book, we devoted a full chapter to the law of sedition. *Rajagopal*, of course, is not a case about sedition, and makes

---

[46] The Reynold's Defence was cited with approval by the Bombay High Court in *Kokan Unnati Mitra Mandal* v. *Bennett Coleman*, (2011) 6 Bom CR 475, although as part of the fair comment defence, which is not entirely correct.

no mention of sedition. Nonetheless, its logic and its result have some interesting implications for that area of law.

The key lies in the three foreign judgments that *Rajagopal* relies upon: *New York Times* v. *Sullivan*, the English House of Lords' decision in *Derbyshire Council* v. *Times*, and the advice of the Judicial Committee of the Privy Council in *Hector* v. *Attorney General of Antigua and Barbuda*.

To understand the connections between *New York Times* v. *Sullivan*, the decision in *Rajagopal*, and the law of sedition, we need to undertake a brief excursion into American legal history. The law of seditious libel was introduced into the United States during a particularly bitter political dispute in the late 1790s, between the followers of John Adams and Thomas Jefferson. Adams, who had won the Presidential election of 1796, used the newly enacted sedition law to persecute and imprison his Jeffersonian opponents. The widespread abuse of the law met with great public opprobrium and backlash, and in the Presidential election of 1800, Jefferson campaigned on the promise of its repeal. While he did not repeal the law upon his victory, he nonetheless pardoned the individuals who had been imprisoned under it, and the law itself was not used again.[47]

The lawyers for the *New York Times* used this piece of history, 160 years later, to argue against the Alabama defamation law. They contended that, in substance, defamation against public officials was nothing more or less than the crime of sedition. What was defamation but bringing an individual into ill-repute? What was sedition but bringing *government* into ill-repute? What was defamation against government but sedition in another guise? And the historical rejection of sedition by the American people clearly indicated that defamation against the government, too, was something proscribed by a guarantee of free speech.

In his majority opinion, Justice Brennan accepted the argument, and his judgment for the *New York Times* expressly drew the link between defamation of government officials and the discarded sedition law. He noted:

[47] See, for instance, Jenkins (2001).

...the great controversy over the Sedition Act of 1798...first crystallized a national awareness of the central meaning of the First Amendment... Although the Sedition Act was never tested in this Court, the attack upon its validity has carried the day in the court of history... *What a State may not constitutionally bring about by means of a criminal statute is likewise beyond the reach of its civil law of libel. The fear of damage awards under a rule such as that invoked by the Alabama courts here may be markedly more inhibiting than the fear of prosecution under a criminal statute.*[48]

In other words, libel statutes protecting the government from criticism were simply an attempt to bring about indirectly what the Sedition Act tried to accomplish directly, by imposing penal sanctions. The basic point—which was noted by the Punjab and Haryana High Court case that we discussed earlier—is that the idea of 'defaming the government', or 'bringing it into disrepute', as constituting an offence, is simply incompatible with a democratic system based on periodic elections and rotating governments.

The second case that *Rajagopal* cited was *Hector* v. *Attorney-General for Antigua and Barbuda*, which we have discussed previously in the chapter on public order. Recall that the Constitution of Antigua and Barbuda is almost identical to ours. It guarantees a right to freedom of speech, and permits reasonable restrictions in the interests of public order. *Hector* involved a law that criminalized the making of statements that would '*undermine public confidence in the conduct of public affairs*'. In oral argument, counsel admitted that 'undermining public confidence in the conduct of public affairs' stemmed directly from the law of sedition.[49] The Privy Council, in holding that the provision was unconstitutional, noted that 'the very purpose of criticism leveled at those who have the conduct of public affairs by their political opponents is to *undermine public confidence in their stewardship* and to persuade the electorate that their opponents would do a better job of it than those presently holding office.'[50] *Hector*

---

[48] *New York Times*, p. 277; emphasis mine.
[49] *Hector* v. *Attorney-General*, [1990] 2 AC 312, 315 (hereinafter *Hector*).
[50] *Hector*, p. 318; emphasis mine.

clearly makes the point that 'disaffection' towards the government (which sedition proscribes) and 'criticism' of it (which is supposedly prohibited) are virtually impossible to distinguish in democratic society, where the whole point is to bring about changes in government *by* undermining the public confidence in it.

While *Hector* takes us a little far afield, *Derbyshire Council v. Times*, the last case cited by *Rajagopal*, brings us back to the heart of the issue. *Derbyshire*, like *New York Times*, was about a libel claim made by a government authority (the Derbyshire Council). The House of Lords had to answer the knotty question of whether a corporation could sue for libel or defamation. The Court held that while theoretically, there was no objection to a corporation doing so (since there were actual harms that could accrue to it from a damaged reputation), the case was different when it was a *government* entity:

> It is of the highest public importance that a democratically elected govern-mental body, or indeed any governmental body, should be open to unin-hibited public criticism. The threat of a civil action for defamation must inevitably have an inhibiting effect on freedom of speech...what has been described as 'the chilling effect' induced by the threat of civil actions for libel is very important.[51]

Thus, in reasoning that is almost identical to that of *New York Times*, the House of Lords held that government organs could not maintain claims for defamation. Interestingly, the House of Lords also cited the Illinois Supreme Court decision of *City of Chicago v. Tribune*,[52] which had held that statements criticizing government must be 'absolutely privileged.'[53] The word 'privilege' is a term of art, and suggests a conceptual argument in support of the above contentions. 'Parliamentary privilege' refers to the absolute immunity enjoyed by statements made within parliament.[54] Such statements cannot be punished for defamation. This privilege—which is a staple feature of

---

[51] *Derbyshire Council v. Times*, [1992] UKHL 6 (hereinafter *Derbyshire*); emphasis mine.
[52] (1923) 139 NE 86.
[53] *Derbyshire*.
[54] See, for example, Article 105, Constitution of India.

commonwealth democracies—goes back to a time in England when ultimate governing power was deemed to reside in a (very partially elected) Parliament. Post-Independence, however, ultimate governing power shifted from governing bodies to the *people* themselves (with Parliament acting as a delegate). Consequently, the absolute immunity accorded to parliamentary proceedings should now vest in the people themselves, as long as the speech in question is about matters of government, or of public importance.[55] This explains *Derbyshire Council's* holding that when it comes to elected and democratically elected bodies, 'uninhibited public criticism' is the norm.[56]

Let us return to *Rajagopal*. After citing these three cases, all of which effectively hold that the government's reputation, or goodwill, is not something to be protected as an *end in itself* (which is the basic point of sedition), *Rajagopal* held that public bodies *and* public officials cannot sue for defamation. This raises the basic question: if government cannot sue for speech that lowers its reputation in the eyes of the public (whether justifiably or unjustifiably) because of the principle that public criticism must be uninhibited, then where does that leave the law of sedition? Or, in other words, how do you differentiate being *defamed*, and being brought into *contempt* or *disaffection*?

The principles of *Rajagopal* have not been subsequently established in Supreme Court jurisprudence (although, as we saw, the Delhi High Court has affirmed them). But if the arguments above are correct, then the impact of *Rajagopal* surely undermines the foundations of the law of sedition, notwithstanding the 1962 decision of *Kedar Nath Singh*,[57] which upheld Section 124A.

Only, nobody has noticed just yet.

---

[55] For a version of this argument in the American context, see Amar (2012).

[56] *Die Spoorbond* v. *South African Railways*, 1946 AD 999 is a South African case that held a governmental body could not sue for defamation. Milo et al. expressly make the link with sedition, arguing that a contrary judgment would essentially be equivalent to establishing a regime of seditious libel (Milo et al. 2008). See also Kalven (1964).

[57] *Kedar Nath Singh* v. *State of Bihar*, [1962] SCR Supp. (2) 769.

Privacy and the Free Press in *Rajagopal*

Rajagopal also raises another issue (often linked to defamation) that has vexed jurisdictions all over the world: the clash between individual privacy and the freedom of the press. Recall that in *Rajagopal*, the question was whether the newspaper could publish Auto Shankar's supposed autobiography without his consent. By the time *Rajagopal* came to be decided, the Supreme Court had read a constitutional right to privacy under Article 21, albeit in the context of governmental surveillance.[58] The Court used this fact, along with a right to privacy in tort law, to hold that 'a citizen has a right to safeguard the privacy of his own, his family, marriage, procreation, motherhood, child-bearing and education among other matters. None can publish anything concerning those matters without his consent...if he does so, he would be violating the right to privacy of the person concerned and would be liable in an action for damages'.[59]

Immediately after this, however, the Court substantially weakened its strong defence of privacy rights by carving out three exceptions that substantially complicate matters. The position might be different, it noted, if the defamed person had 'voluntarily' thrust himself into a controversy, or invited or raised a controversy. Second, a defamation claim could not lie if the information was based on public records (subject to a decency exception for preserving the anonymity of rape victims, and so on).[60] And third—as we have seen before—government officials had no claim to privacy for their public functions.

The problem with the first exception is its indeterminacy. What does it mean to have voluntarily 'invited' controversy? Presumably, it is not wide enough to cover cases such as *Time Inc.* v. *Hill*, which *Rajagopal* quoted from extensively, and where Justice Brennan had held that 'one need only pick up any newspaper or magazine to comprehend the vast range of published matter which exposes persons to public view, both

---

[58] *Kharak Singh* v. *State of UP*, [1964] 1 SCR 332; *Gobind* v. *State of Madhya Pradesh*, (1975) 2 SCC 148.

[59] *Rajagopal*, para 28; emphasis mine.

[60] Specifically departing, with this exception, from the American case of *Cox* v. *Cohn*, 420 U.S. 469 (1975).

private citizens and public officials.'[61] *Time Inc.* v. *Hill* involved a sensationalized magazine account of the ordeal suffered by one family when they were held hostage in their own house by armed robbers. Arguably, one cannot say that that involved '*voluntarily* inviting controversy'. Yet what about film and sports celebrities, whose private lives are regularly discussed in the pages of tabloids? More importantly, what happens when something that falls clearly within the Court's delineated domains of privacy—family and procreation—is a matter of clear public interest: for instance, the disputed marital status of a prominent politician? Is it fair to say that the politician, *qua* a politician, has 'voluntarily invited controversy' about his marital status? Or is that a fact-based enquiry, limited to specific situations where, for example, his previous denial of the fact reflects poorly upon her moral character and thereby her fitness for office, which is a clear issue of public concern? What about lawyers handling a high-profile civil rights case, or defending accused terrorists? Have *they* invited controversy upon themselves?[62] These are just some of the sensitive issues that could potentially arise before the court, and the controversy test is too blunt an instrument to deal with them.

A better way might well be to take a leaf out of defamation law's book, and look to attaining a balance between the privacy interests of the person in question and the public value or interest that lies in disseminating the news or information that is alleged to violate privacy. Consider, for instance, the South African decision in *Prinsloo* v. *RCP Media Ltd.*[63] The question was whether photographs depicting activities of an intimate sexual nature could be published by a newspaper, given that the subjects of the photographs were two advocates who had—to an extent—achieved some notoriety in the public eye. Van der Westhuizen J. held that whatever the public status of the advocates, there was no public interest in publishing photographs that 'represent[ed] a view...into the most intimate privacy of the persons involved'.[64] This line of reasoning focuses the enquiry on whether

---

[61] *Hill*, p. 388.
[62] *Gertz.*
[63] 2003 (4) SA 456 (hereinafter *Prinsloo*).
[64] *Prinsloo.*

the *issue* is in the public interest, as opposed to whether the *person* has thrust themselves into the public eye. Of course, the distinction may become blurred at times. For instance, in *Tshabala-Msimang*, The High Court of Gauteng in South Africa held that reports about a minister's alcoholic binges while in hospital were 'relevant…to the performance of her constitutional and ministerial duties'.[65]

This shows that even revelations about the private and intimate details about a person's life could—potentially—be in the public interest, depending upon the context. The decision in *Tshabala-Msimang* can be profitably contrasted with *Von Hannover v. Germany*, where the European Court of Human Rights drew a distinction between 'imparting information and ideas about matters of public interest' (where the press exercised its watchdog function), and mere personal or intimate information about a public figure.[66] In that case, the Court found that the publication of various paparazzi-style photos of Princess Caroline von Hannover infringed her right to privacy, even though she was a 'contemporary public figure *par excellence*'.

Injunctions for Privacy Claims

Previously, we discussed the unique free speech problems raised by prior restraint. One other way in which information is blocked before it can reach the public is not through a government ban, but through a court *injunction*. A court injunction differs from a government ban in that it requires the government (or private party) to come before the court and prove its case in adversarial proceedings, thus also allowing the opposite party a chance to be heard. It is a controversial issue whether injunctions ought to be classified with prior restraints. Like prior restraints, they can often choke off the marketplace of ideas at its source (this is especially true in India, where interlocutory injunctions, which subsist for years, are the norm). However, unlike prior restraints, they require a judicially-trained mind to apply the law to the facts of the case. In *Rajagopal*, nevertheless, the Supreme Court seemed to conflate the two. It held:

---

[65] *Tshabala-Msimang v. Makhanya*, [2007] ZAGPHC 161.
[66] *Von Hannover v. Germany*, (2005) 40 EHRR 1.

We may now consider whether the State or its officials have the authority in law to impose a prior restraint upon publication of material defamatory of the State or of the officials, as the case may be? *We think not.* No law empowering them to do so is brought to our notice. As observed in New York Times v. United States... 'any system of prior restraints of (freedom of) expression comes to this Court bearing a heavy presumption against its constitutional validity' and that in such cases, the Government 'carries a heavy burden of showing justification for the imposition of such a restraint'. *We must accordingly hold that no such prior restraint or prohibition of publication can be imposed by the respondents upon the proposed publication of the alleged autobiography of 'Auto Shankar' by the petitioners. This cannot be done either by the State or by its officials.* In other words, neither the Government nor the officials who apprehend that they may be defamed, have the right to impose a prior restraint upon the publication of the alleged autobiography of Auto Shankar. *The remedy of public officials/public figures, if any, will arise only after the publication and will be governed by the principles indicated herein.*[67]

The Court's citation of *New York Times* v. *United States*—the Pentagon Papers case—is particularly interesting because that was a case involving injunctions as well (we will return to it in a moment). When we combine the Court's statement here with its ruling on privacy, we get the conclusion that approaching the court for an injunction against the publication of material is *not* open to the State or to State officials, but *might* be open to individuals claiming a breach of privacy.

The tension latent within the *Rajagopal* decision came to a head in two cases at the Delhi High Court, separated by a span of eight years. Soon after *Rajagopal* was decided, a single judge of that High Court acted upon the above principle by awarding a (temporary) injunction in *Phoolan Devi* v. *Shekhar Kapoor*.[68] Although the Court held that Phoolan Devi was a 'public figure' within the *Rajagopal* sense, it also held that a film depicting rape and sexual assault upon her person, without her consent, was an unjustifiable invasion of her privacy. The Court then gave a narrow interpretation to the term 'public records'

---

[67] *Rajagopal*, para 24; emphasis mine.
[68] 57 (1995) DLT 154 (hereinafter *Phoolan Devi*).

as used in *Rajagopal*, distinguishing between materials in the *public domain* (that is, newspapers, video clippings, and so on), and public *documents*, as defined under the Evidence Act (records of official bodies, tribunals, public officers and so on).[69] Consequently—and perhaps paradoxically—the upshot of *Phoolan Devi* (subsequently upheld by other High Courts) was that writing a book or an article, or making a film, out of materials wholly available in the public domain is no protection against an injunction for privacy violations.

In *Khushwant Singh* v. *Maneka Gandhi*, however, the Delhi High Court—speaking, this time, through a division bench—vacated an injunction upon the publication of Khushwant Singh's autobiography *on the ground* that the impugned parts of the book (dealing with the relationship between Maneka Gandhi and her family, including Indira Gandhi) drew upon materials already present in the public domain.[70] It then went even further, and held that the *Rajagopal* dictum on privacy did not authorize pre-publication injunctions, but was limited to a *suit for damages*. This was because insofar as the privacy right was invoked by a private party against other private parties, it took the form of a *tort* (and not a constitutional right), and consequently, the appropriate remedy was damages.[71] Thus, the 'balance' that needed to be struck between the freedom of speech on the one hand, and the rights of privacy and reputation on the other, would have to be struck not at the pre-publication stage (in a claim for injunction), but at the post-publication stage (in a claim for damages).[72] Soon afterwards,

---

[69] *Phoolan Devi*, para 37.

[70] AIR 2002 Del 58 (hereinafter *Khushwant Singh*).

[71] Indian privacy jurisprudence is an extremely complicated tangle. In early cases, the Court evolved a classic constitutional right to privacy against State surveillance, grounding it in Article 21. In *Rajagopal*, on the other hand, the Court invoked what was a right to privacy against *other private parties* under tort law, and *also* located that within Article 21. This has led to much confusion, because principles of tort, an aspect of private law, fit uneasily within the constitutional scheme, which is quintessentially public.

[72] The Delhi High Court also warned against a too-facile distinction between 'public' and 'private' lives of public figures, noting correctly that 'there is no doubt

the Madras High Court strongly affirmed *Rajagopal's* refusal to allow defamation claims by public officials, and vacated an injunction placed on certain critical reporting upon the actions of Jayalalitha, the Chief Minister of Tamil Nadu.[73]

Khushwant Singh is a bold judgment, but was it correctly decided? A close reading of *Rajagopal* seems to indicate that it was. Let us go back to the crucial paragraph of the Supreme Court judgment:

> A citizen has a right to safeguard the privacy of his own, his family, marriage, procreation, motherhood, child-bearing and education among other matters. None can publish anything concerning the above matters without his consent whether truthful or otherwise and whether laudatory or critical. *If he does so, he would be violating the right to privacy of the person concerned and would be liable in an action for damages.*[74]

The confusion is caused by the fact that the second sentence is framed as a prohibition ('None can publish...'). Nonetheless, immediately after that, the Court seems to make it clear that the *remedy* is an action for damages (while, admittedly, not ruling out injunctions expressly). And in the last sentence, the Court suggests that the public/private distinction is blurred for public figures (who voluntarily invite controversy). This is supported by the concluding paragraph, where the Court holds:

> Applying the above principles, it must be held that the petitioners have a right to publish, what they allege to be the life story/autobiography of Auto Shankar insofar as it appears from the public records, even without his consent or authorisation. But if they go beyond that and publish his life story, they may be invading his right to privacy and *will be liable for the consequences in accordance with law.*[75]

Once again, the stress is not on *preventing* publication, but on clarifying that publishers will be *liable for the consequences* of what they

---

that even what may be the private lives of public figures become mattes [sic] of public interest'. (*Khushwant Singh*, para 73).

[73] *R. Rajagopal v. J. Jayalalitha*, AIR 2006 Mad 312.

[74] *Rajagopal*, para 26.

[75] *Rajagopal*, para 29; emphasis mine.

publish. This is precisely the understanding that *Khushwant Singh* cleaves to, and on this reading of *Rajagopal*, pre-publication injunctions are not to be awarded.

Other High Courts have, however, differed. In cases after *Rajagopal* and *Phoolan Devi*, judges have awarded injunctions on the basis of an attempted *Von Hannover* distinction between a public figure, and a public figure's private life that is divorced from their public role. In *Shilpa S. Shetty* v. *Magna Publications*, for instance, the Bombay High Court injuncted newspapers from publishing articles about the multiple—and possibly adulterous—sexual relations of a noted film actress.[76] And in a particularly extraordinary decision, the Madras High Court in 2012 injuncted the publication of a biography of Jayalalitha, holding that it contained 'purely personal details', which had not been verified with the subject. Going back to *Phoolan Devi*—and ignoring the relevant portions of *Khushwant Singh* while ostensibly distinguishing it—the Court held, once again, narrative accounts based on materials in the public domain were not protected by *Rajagopal's* public records exception, and would be subject to a pre-publication injunction.[77] It stands to reason that any biography—or long, narrative account—about a public figure will contain *some* details about their private life, or at least, aspects of their private life covered by *Gobind's* definition of privacy (family, the home, marriage, procreation, child-rearing and so on). The Madras High Court decision—going against its own precedent—places a near-impossible burden upon journalists and writers by reading *Rajagopal's* 'reasonable verification' standard to require what effectively amounts to an express permission and authentication by none other than the subject of the impugned piece. For obvious reasons, such permission will not always be easy to come by.

The relationship between injunctions, privacy, and the freedom of speech and expression remains in a state of flux today. The source of the ambiguity is *Rajagopal*, which—as we have seen here—permits two equally plausible interpretations. It permits a broad and

---

[76] AIR 2001 Bom 176.

[77] *Selvi J. Jayalalitha* v. *Penguin Books India*, 2013 (54) PTC 327 (Mad).

speech-restrictive reading that limits 'public records' to official documents, 'reasonable verification' to verification with the subject, allows
a wide scope to the private in a public/private distinction, and allows
pre-publication injunctions under a regular balance-of-convenience
analysis. But it also permits a narrow and speech-protective reading,
which focuses not on official documents but on materials in the public
domain, understands reasonable verification contextually, rejects a
facile public/private distinction, and requires the balancing enquiry
to be undertaken at the stage of damages, and not in the form of a
pre-publication injunction.

Injunctions for (Corporate) Defamation Claims

What of injunctions granted to corporations, in the context of disclosure of confidential information, or—more importantly—of defamation? It is in this context that the Delhi High Court's judgment in
Petronet becomes particularly fascinating. In that case, the High Court
seemed to extend the limited dictum of the Supreme Court against
injunctions to *private* companies performing *public* functions. In that
case, Petronet LNG, a joint venture company, asked the High Court
for an injunction preventing the defendants from 'publishing confidential and/or misleading information relating to the plaintiff's nego-
tiations and contracts' on their website. Petronet claimed that there
was a 'duty of confidence'—stemming from the common law—upon
the defendants not to publish information of that nature. After citing a
copious amount of English and European jurisprudence, Justice Bhat
noted that the enquiry required a balancing between a corporation's
legitimate interest in preserving confidential information, and the
right of the press to publish, and the public to know, information in
the public interest. He then cited *Rajagopal* and the classic American
cases on prior restraint—*Near* v. *Minnesota*,[78] *Patterson* v. *Colorado*,[79]
and *Nebraska Press Assn.* v. *Stuart*[80]—before observing that in view of

[78] 283 U.S. 697 (1931).
[79] 205 U.S. 554 (1907).
[80] 427 U.S. 439 (1976).

the important public function performed by the plaintiff, 'the claim for confidentiality has to be necessarily from the view of the plaintiff's accountability to such extent as well as its duties which have a vital bearing on the availability and presence of gas in the country'.[81] Giving a heightened importance to the need for free flow of information, the Court declined to grant the injunction, holding:

> The news or information disclosure of which may be uncomfort-able to an individual or corporate entity but which otherwise fosters a debate and awareness about functioning of such individuals or bodies, particularly, if they are engaged in matters that affect people's lives, serve a vital public purpose....*In the case of a corporate entity, unless the news presented is of such a sensitive nature that its business or very existence is threatened or would gravely jeopardize a commercial venture, the Courts would be slow in interdicting such publication.* The Constitution's democratic framework, depends on a free commerce in ideas, which is its life blood.[82]

In cases of information that is of heightened public interest, there-fore, the Court held that the corporation must show an existential threat in order to succeed in a claim for injunction. Three important conclusions follow.

The first is that although the Court's judgment is restricted to quasi-public companies, its reasoning extends to all individual or cor-porate entities that 'are engaged in matters that affect people's lives'. In an era of increasing influence enjoyed by private corporations, which are coming to manage greater and greater aspects of the economy, its logic—clearly—extends to corporations such as Reliance, Sahara, Jindal, and so on.

Second—and keeping the first point in mind—under this stan-dard, injunctions of the sort that the Calcutta High Court passed against Tamal Bandyopadhyay's book on Sahara cannot happen. Sahara can sue Bandhopadhyay and Mint for defamation *after* the publication of the book, but to succeed in an injunction, they must

---

[81] *Petronet*, para 64.
[82] *Petronet*, para 73; emphasis mine.

demonstrate that what the book contains is so incendiary that their very existence will be threatened. Needless to say, that burden will be very difficult to discharge, and ensures that defamation law is not used as a method of enforcing prior restraint.

This is also extremely important because on many occasions, news in the public interest will be time-sensitive. For example, incriminating information about a public official's corrupt dealings will lose much of its relevance after that official leaves office. In such a situation, an injunction can become a tool for robbing important information of much of its efficacy and value. Recognizing this, the South African Constitutional Court noted in *Lieberthal* that 'even though the applicant seeks only a temporary relief at this stage the effect will be to stop 702 [the radio station accused of making defamatory remarks] broadcasting on this matter until the defamation action is completed. *This could conservatively take more than two years*'.[83] In South Africa, therefore, there is a presumption against granting injunctions unless it can be demonstrated clearly that the 'disadvantage of curtailing the free flow of information outweighs its advantage'.[84] In India, where cases typically drag on for years or even decades, an interim injunction—for all practical purposes—has the effect of a final disposal. Consequently, the South African approach has much to recommend itself.

Third, the standard that the Delhi High Court uses for corporations is very similar to the standard used by *New York Times* v. *United States* for the State. In *New York Times* v. *United States*, which involved the leak of the Pentagon Papers, the Court refused to injunct newspapers from publishing them, notwithstanding the government's claims that confidential information about the Vietnam war would gravely harm national security. The Court restricted the scope of injunctions to extreme situations, such as cases of 'publication of the sailing dates of transports or the number and location of troops' during times of

---

[83] *Lieberthal* v. *Primedia Broadcasting (Pty) Ltd.*, 2003 (5) SA 39; emphasis mine.

[84] *Midi Television (Pty) Ltd* v. *Director of Public Prosecutions*, 2007 (5) SA 540 (SCA), para 19.

war[85]—or, in other words, cases of imminent existential threat to the nation. *Petronet*, as we have seen, employed a similar existential-threat test with respect to corporations.

In this context, it is important to note that in *Rajagopal*, after holding that prior restraints were generally impermissible, the Supreme Court noted that its holding would not apply to the provisions of the Official Secrets Act. The Official Secrets Act does not directly deal with injunctions. It criminalizes disclosure of information 'which is likely to affect the sovereignty and integrity of India, the security of the State or friendly relations with foreign States'.[86] In case the principles of the Act are invoked in a claim for injunction, the case would probably turn upon the interpretation of the phrase 'which is *likely* to affect', and the burden and standards of proof that a court will require the government to show. The judgment of the Court in *Rajagopal*, with its reliance on *New York Times* v. *United States*, and the judgment of the Delhi High Court in *Petronet*, with its emphasis that corporations must demonstrate an 'existential threat' before they can prevent disclosure of information in the public interest, provide a strong point of departure for a speech-protective interpretation of judicial injunctions based on national security justifications, in a manner that will not allow the government to suppress critical speech by invoking national security as a matter of right.

Beyond the context of national security, the correct legal standard for granting a speech-restricting injunction to corporations remains open, especially in the context of a claim for defamation. This is because the Bombay High Court has followed a markedly different route. In *Shree Maheshwar Hydel Power Corporation* v. *Chitroopa Palit*, the plaintiff corporation was implementing a high-stakes and controversial hydel power project. A group of activists issued a press note accusing the corporation of conniving and conspiring to siphon off and loot public money while 'unleashing senseless terror'. Unlike the Delhi High Court, the Bombay High Court expressly refused to view

---

[85] *New York Times* v. *United States*, 403 U.S. 713, 726 (1971) (concurring opinion of Brennan J.).

[86] Section 5, Official Secrets Act, 1923.

defamation law through the prism of Article 19(1)(a).[87] Furthermore, in his judgment, Justice Radhakrishnan also chose to depart from the century-old, established common law rule in *Bonnard* v. *Perryman*.[88] In *Bonnard*, the English Court of Appeal had held that unless the court was convinced that the defence of justification would fail at trial, it would refrain from granting an interlocutory injunction. This decision was expressly based on the importance of the freedom of speech to the public, despite the absence of any such constitutional guarantee in England. Justice Radhakrishnan, however, relied upon four previous unreported judgments of the Bombay High Court itself, to hold that under the 'Indian law of defamation', *even at the interlocutory stage,* the Court would scrutinize the materials to examine whether or not the defamatory statements were true, made *bona fide,* and in *the public interest* (which effectively meant placing an extraordinary burden upon the defendant to prove those aspects).

It is unclear how exactly this strange beast, an 'Indian law of defamation', arose, untethered from the Constitution or from any foundations in common law, solely out of four previous unreported judgments of the Bombay High Court. It is unclear on what legal basis an extra requirement of 'public interest', in addition to truth, was thrust upon the defendants as a necessary defence to defamation, to be proven at the interlocutory stage. And then, in an extraordinarily attenuated chain of reasoning, the Court delivered its verdict, granting the injunction, because:

> The above expressions would totally damage the credibility and reputation of the Appellant Company *and in fact would jeopardise the entire Maheshwar Hydro-Electric Project and would in fact prevent the financial institutions from further advancing any loan or even granting any facility to the Appellant Company, whereby if the said project does not take off, the same will be very much against public interests, affecting the people of Madhya Pradesh, who are in the dire need of power.* Because of such defamatory statements of the Defendants, not only the Appellant

---

[87] According to the Court, Article 19(1)(a) bore no relevance to the common law of defamation, which operated between private parties.

[88] *Bonnard* v. *Perryman*, [1891] 2 Ch 269.

Company but also the very project which has been conceived for the benefit of the people of the[sic] Madhya Pradesh would get completely affected.[89]

Readers will note that this decision is directly at odds with *Petronet*, both in its categorical refusal to constitutionalize defamation law, as well as its cavalier approach to stifling free speech in the name of considerations that—most generously—can be described as hypothetical. Indeed, a few years afterwards, in *Tata Sons* v. *Greenpeace*, a case with somewhat similar facts, the Delhi High Court refused to follow *Chitroopa Palit*. In protest against Tata Sons' involvement in a mammoth port project and its allegedly devastating impact upon the habitat of the Olive Ridley Turtle, Greenpeace devised an online game, provocatively titled '*Turtle vs TATA*', which involved heroic turtles saving their homes by vanquishing 'the demons of development'. The Tatas were not amused, and filed for a permanent injunction, as well as damages worth Rs 10 crores. The Court rejected their application for a temporary (pre-trial) injunction, holding that 'courts, the world over, have set a great value to free speech and its salutary catalyzing effect on *public debate and discussion on issues that concern people at large*...the issue, which the defendant's game seeks to address, is also one of *public concern*'.[90] Carrying on from his decision in *Petronet*, and relying upon *Bonnard* v. *Perryman*, Justice Bhat reiterated an expanded Meiklejohnian understanding of the necessity for free and unrestricted discussion in the public sphere (going beyond directly political matters, or the conduct of political officials). He went on to ground the grant of injunctions firmly within the contours of Article 19(1)(a). Consequently, he held that '[a pre-trial] injunction would freeze the entire public debate on the effect of the port project on the Olive Ridley turtles' habitat. That, plainly would not be in public interest; it would most certainly be contrary to established principles.'[91]

[89] *Shree Maheshwar Hydel Power Corporation* v. *Chitroopa Palit*, AIR 2004 Bom 143, para 50; emphasis mine.

[90] *Tata Sons Limited* v. *Greenpeace International*, 178 (2011) DLT 705, para 43 (hereinafter *Tata Sons*); emphasis mine.

[91] *Tata Sons*.

We therefore have two distinct and opposed lines of jurisprudence, followed by the Bombay and Delhi High Courts. At the heart of the disagreement is the extent to which individuals may critically interrogate the policies and actions of (private and public) entities that have a lasting impact upon their lives. The battleground is the interlocutory injunction, and the procedural requirements that plaintiffs must satisfy for a grant of injunction. The Bombay High Court's judgments not only subordinate Article 19(1)(a) to the common law of defamation, but go one beyond, by placing burdens of justification upon the defendants/speakers that even common law does not require.[92] The Delhi High Court, on the other hand, insists on understanding defamation and injunctions through the lens of common law, moulded to fit the contours of Article 19(1)(a). What path the law will ultimately take remains open.

Addendum: A Note on Super-Injunctions and John Doe Orders

On 29 July 2014, Wikileaks revealed a Court-issued gag order that prohibited any reporting on 'a multi-million dollar corruption case explicitly naming the current and past heads of state of Indonesia, Malaysia and Vietnam, their relatives and other senior officials... [invoking] "national security" grounds to prevent reporting about the case, by anyone, in order to "prevent damage to Australia's international relations"'.[93] In free speech parlance, this is known as a 'super-injunction'. A super-injunction not only keeps the details of a case under wraps, but also prohibits the media from reporting on the proceedings of the case *itself*. Super-injunctions came to the fore in the United Kingdom around the turn of the decade. For example, in 2009, the oil company Trafigura was briefly granted a super-injunction, that prevented the Guardian newspaper (and 'others') from making public a leaked report about its toxic waste dumping, including a prohibition

---

[92] As Justice Bhat noted in *Tata Sons*, the common law of defamation, when it comes to the grant of interlocutory injunctions, is extremely speech-protective.

[93] Wikileaks (2014).

on reporting *parliamentary proceedings*.[94] Super-injunctions have been most frequently used to prohibit the media from reporting libel cases, or cases about scandalous allegations against footballers, although, as the Trafigura case and the Australian super-injunction demonstrate, they can also be used to suppress journalistic reporting about important political matters. Super-injunctions are not yet frequent in India, and it is to be hoped that the free speech implications shall be taken into account when the courts are asked to incorporate them into Indian law.

One anti-free speech tool that certainly has caught on in India is the 'John Doe' order—or, as its domestic avatar is known—the 'Ashok Kumar' order.[95] John Doe orders are *ex parte* injunctions that are passed against 'unknown entities' who might be involved in copyright infringement. John Doe orders achieved notoriety in mid-2014 when the Delhi High Court ordered the blocking of more than 400 websites which were allegedly infringing MSM Satellite's broadcast rights for the 2014 FIFA World Cup, including Google Docs! The list was later narrowed to 219 websites.[96] In that case, the Court authorized the Internet service providers to implement the order, by taking down the infringing websites.

John Doe orders of this sort present a grave threat to the freedom of speech and expression. To start with, they exhibit some of the more pernicious features of prior restraint. Although the blocking of websites takes place pursuant to a judicial order, it is, for most of the parties, an *ex parte* order—thus removing the important safeguard of an adversarial proceeding in a court of law. Furthermore, if the implementation of the order does not take place under judicial supervision, it places the power of censorship in the hands of private parties such as Internet service providers (going one step beyond prior restraint, where speech-regulation is undertaken by administrative bodies). And lastly, because John Doe orders are often issued to prevent 'anticipatory infringement' (as the Delhi High Court order was), they can

[94] Leigh (2011).
[95] For a summary, see Gupta (2011).
[96] Vallianeth (2014).

lead to the blocking of websites even before infringement has actually taken place. John Doe orders have been proliferating in India of late, and courts have—thus far—failed to exhibit due sensitivity towards the free speech implications of acceding to the demands of copyright enforcers in such desultory fashion. It remains to be seen whether the trend, at some point, will be arrested.

CRIMINAL DEFAMATION

The question of criminal defamation came to the fore recently when a case was filed against Arvind Kejriwal, the leader of the Aam Aadmi Party, for calling BJP politician Nitin Gadkari 'corrupt'.[97] Criminal defamation falls within Sections 499 and 500 of the Indian Penal Code. Section 499 criminalizes statements written or published, that are with the intention of harming the reputation of an individual, or with the knowledge that they are likely to harm his reputation, subject to numerous exceptions.[98] Section 500 makes criminal defamation punishable with imprisonment up to two years, or with a fine, or both.

A full account of the interpretation of Sections 499 and 500, *qua* defamation, is beyond the scope of the book.[99] With respect to Article 19(1)(a), however, notice that defamation, thus, is *both* a civil and a criminal offence. Why is this so? The reason lies deep in English history. Originally, defamation in its two forms served two different purposes. As a *civil* offence, it was aimed at compensating a person for loss of reputation. As a criminal offence, it was closely connected to breaches of the peace, or violations of public order: criminal penalties were imposed to deter people from making statements that would lead to fights or disorder. As is true for many free

---

[97] PTI (2015).

[98] Section 499, Indian Penal Code, 1860.

[99] For examples of cases explicating the scope of Section 499 and its attendant exceptions and explanations, see *Sahib Singh* v. *State of UP*, AIR 1965 SC 1451 (Exceptions 3 and 9); *G. Narasimhan* v. *T.V. Chokkappa*, AIR 1972 SC 2609 (Explanation 2); *Harbhajan Singh* v. *State of Punjab*, AIR 1966 SC 97 (Exception 9); *Chaman Lal* v. *State of Punjab*, AIR 1970 SC 1372 (Exception 1).

speech penalties, there was no need to demonstrate that a breach of peace had actually been caused—just that the statement had a *tendency* to do so.[100]

If this was the original purpose of criminal defamation, then it is more than evident that Section 499 is overbroad. While it is true that *some* statements that harm an individual's reputation will lead to immediate public disorder, it is equally true that not all will—in fact, most will not. For this reason, the United States' analogous restriction is an extremely narrowly defined category known as 'fighting words': 'those that by their very utterance inflict injury or tend to incite an immediate breach of the peace'[101]—words that, essentially, amount to 'an invitation to brawl'. Other jurisdictions have only incitement statutes, and in 2009, England abolished its own criminal defamation law (along with sedition).[102]

It seems clear, in this background, that criminal defamation law is an anachronism. It also goes much further than civil defamation. The verdict of a criminal prosecution can deprive a person of her liberty. In any event, it places a stigma of public and social disapproval that sticks for life. It is also a more potent weapon to use for silencing criticism in the press, because whereas a civil claim for compensation will often be directed against newspapers, who have deeper pockets, greater influence, and will often be in a position to settle a compensation case without necessary financial ruin, a criminal case is one against the journalist directly, and places him under a threat of imprisonment. It is hardly surprising, then, that the United Nations Commission on Human Rights referred to laws criminalizing expression as 'one of the most reprehensible practices employed to silence people…and a

[100] See, for instance, Walker (2005–06). In common law, the public order component of the offence was dispensed with in *Gleaves* v. *Deakin*, [1980] AC 477 (H.L.).

[101] *Chaplinsky* v. *New Hampshire*, 315 U.S. 568 (1942).

[102] Section 73, Coroners and Justice Act, 2009. The offence of criminal libel has, however, been upheld in other jurisdictions. See, for instance, the judgment of the South African Supreme Court of Appeal in *Hoho* v. *State*, [2008] ZASCA 98; the judgment of the Privy Council in *Worme* v. *Police Commissioner of Granada*, [2004] UKPC 8.

serious violation of human rights'.[103] Furthermore, in May 2014, the Constitutional Court of Zimbabwe held criminal defamation to be an unconstitutional violation of the freedom of speech and expression. In doing so, it expressly invoked the chilling effect of a possible prison term, as well as the superfluity of tacking on a criminal remedy to an already-existing civil offence.[104]

Criminal defamation law is additionally an anachronism because—as we have discussed exhaustively before—we already have a 'public order' exception under Article 19(2), which has been subject to detailed interpretation by the courts. Consequently, if the objective is to compensate people for loss of reputation, that function is performed far better by the existing civil law of defamation. And if the objective is to deter breaches of public order, there exists a whole different category of free speech restrictions dealing with that.

While criminal defamation is thus superfluous, it is difficult to argue that it is unconstitutional. Article 19(2), after all, expressly permits reasonable restrictions in the interests of defamation. Arguing for the unreasonableness of criminal defamation *per se* seems to be a difficult task. This, it would seem, is one of those provisions that, ultimately, Parliament must take responsibility for by repealing.

---

[103] Quoted by the Constitutional Court of Zimbabwe in *Nevanji Madanhire* v *Attorney-General*, Judgment No CCZ 2/14 (hereinafter *Nevanji Madanhire*).

[104] *Nevanji Madanhire*. See also The Committee to Protect Journalists (2014).

CHAPTER NINE

Contempt of Court

. . . .

The courts, as Alexander Hamilton pointed out at the dawn of constitutionalism, are the weakest of the three branches of government. They have control over neither the 'sword [n]or the purse... [they have] neither force nor will, but only judgment'.[1] Much of the courts' effectiveness depends upon voluntary compliance with their decisions. To compel obedience in situations where it is not otherwise forthcoming, courts are vested with the power to punish people for failing to adhere to their directions.[2] 'Contempt of court', when understood in this context, is relatively uncontroversial.

There is, however, another, vexing form that contempt of court often takes, and which shall be the focus of this chapter. This idea of contempt is predicated upon the belief that the efficacy of the courts rests not only upon compliance, but also upon favourable public perception. Statements that might adversely affect the public's opinion about the courts are also punishable.

The Constituent Assembly Debates reveal a marked uncertainty among the framers about the understanding of contempt they were inserting into the Constitution. Contempt of court was a late addition

---

[1] Hamilton (1788).

[2] For instance, for refusal to appear when summoned.

to the restrictions encapsulated in Draft Article 13(2) (what became Article 19(2)). It was introduced by T.T. Krishnamachari in October 1949, during the last reading of the Constitution, and justified as necessary to deal with situations where a person might 'speak on a matter which is *sub judice* and thereby interfere with the administration of justice'.[3] Readers will notice that this category of contempt falls somewhere between the two we discussed here. It is not disobedience of a court order, but neither is it *criticism* of the court. It refers to a narrowly circumscribed set of cases where the interests of justice might require that a matter pending before the court not be made the subject of media spotlight: a high-profile murder trial, for instance, or the sentencing of a convicted terrorist.

In his opposition to the amendment, Pandit Thakur Das Bhargava argued that contempt wasn't about the freedom of speech or expression at all. It was, rather, about individual *conduct*, such as the refusal to produce a document, the refusal to answer summons, and so on— all of which was already made punishable under the Code of Criminal Procedure (this is the first understanding of contempt discussed here). As for what he called 'technical contempt', or 'contempt not in the face of the Court', he expressed both the doubt whether it was actually covered within contempt of court law, and the fear that if so, it would be abused just like the British had abused the Judicial Officers Protection Act.[4] Concurring with this, Sri R.K. Sidhva expressed the particular concern that judges would—quite literally—be made judges in their own cause under sweeping contempt power. Citing numerous cases of abuse, he pointed out that 'judges have not got two horns; they are also human beings. They are, liable to commit mistakes.'[5] The President's response was to invoke the second version of contempt, by asking why, when laws against the defamation and libel of private

---

[3] Speech of T.T. Krishnamachari, 17 October 1949. Indian Constituent Assembly (Vol. X).

[4] Speech of Pandit Thakur Das Bhargava, 17 October 1949. Indian Constituent Assembly (Vol. X).

[5] Speech of R.K. Sidhva, 17 October 1949. Indian Constituent Assembly (Vol. X).

individuals were permitted, the same could not be done for courts as well.[6] And Mr Naziruddin Ahmad's speech brought the issue back to the administration of justice:

> ...the trial in a case must be conducted in an atmosphere of calm without any prejudice, on the evidence alone. If there is no power to proceed for Contempt of Court, any one may start a newspaper trial of a case pending in a Court or it may be that he indulges in public harangues about the merits of a case and thereby seriously prejudice[s] the fair and impartial trial of a case....[7]

The Debates indicate that there was no clear consensus on what the 'contempt of court' restriction was really trying to achieve. As it turned out, the fears of its critics proved to be prescient. Over the years the contempt power has been taken so far that in May 2014, the Supreme Court was able to not only require a 'contemnor' to apologize, but also to reject his apology because it wasn't truly 'contrite'—and, in the process, lay down the requirements, in terms of timing, tone, and tenor, of a sufficiently contrite apology.[8]

The statutory regime governing contempt law is the 1971 Contempt of Courts Act. In that Act, contempt is a civil offence, and refers to the willful disobedience of a court order. It is also, however, a criminal offence, and is defined as any act or expression that 'scandalises or tends to scandalise, or lowers or tends to lower the authority of, any court; or prejudices, or interferes or tends to interfere with, the due course of any judicial proceeding; or interferes or tends to interfere with, or obstructs or tends to obstruct, the administration of justice in any other manner.'[9]

The wording of the law is open to two interpretations. The use of the word 'other' in the last sub-clause suggests that the first two sub-clauses are also to be understood in terms of obstructing the

---

[6] Speech of the President, 17 October 1949, Indian Constituent Assembly (Vol. X).

[7] Speech of Naziruddin Ahmad, 17 October 1949, Indian Constituent Assembly (Vol. X).

[8] Mahapatra (2014).

[9] Section 2(c), Contempt of Courts Act, 1971.

administration of justice. If something does 'a', or 'b', or otherwise accomplishes the result 'c', then presumably, doing 'a' or 'b' is relevant only insofar as it is a means to 'c'. The other possibility, of course, is that 'scandalizing' or tending to scandalize the authority of the court is an offence in itself, regardless of its relationship to the obstruction of justice.[10] As we shall see, the courts have chosen the second interpretation.

'SCANDALIZING THE COURT': NOTES FROM ABROAD

'Scandalizing the court' has its origins in the common law. The term was used in the 1900 case of *R* v. *Gray*, which remains the classic English case on point. The basis of the offence—in language that the Contempt of Courts Act later adopted in substantial part—was 'any act done or writing published calculated to bring the Court into contempt, or to lower its authority'.[11] The similarities with sedition, including the term 'bringing into contempt', are not accidental. 'Scandalizing the court' is to the court what sedition is to the government. Both are based on the idea that if the institutions of the State are to survive, the public must have a good impression of them.

It is hardly surprising, therefore, that the American courts did away with the offence a very long time ago. In *Bridges* v. *California*, a labour leader called a court decision 'outrageous', and threatened a strike if it was upheld. Reversing his conviction by the lower courts, the Supreme Court focused on the (democratic) social value in statements of this sort, holding that 'public interest is much more likely to be kindled by a controversial event of the day than by a generalization, however penetrating, of the historian or scientist'.[12]

Two arguments were made in favour of overriding this public interest: preserving respect for the judiciary, and the orderly administration of justice. On the first, the Court found that contempt powers

---

[10] A 2006 amendment to the Contempt of Courts Act clarifies that the court may impose punishment for contempt only when it is satisfied that it substantially interferes, or tends to substantially interfere with the due course of justice.

[11] *R* v. *Grey*, [1900] 2 Q.B. 36.

[12] *Bridges* v. *California*, 314 U.S. 252, 268 (1941) (hereinafter *Bridges*).

simply would not achieve that objective, because 'an enforced silence, however limited, solely in the name of preserving the dignity of the bench would probably engender resentment, suspicion, and contempt much more than it would enhance respect'.[13] On the second, since carrying out a strike was a legal activity, the threat of a strike could not be classified as an illegal act of intimidation against a judge, which could wrongfully subvert justice.[14] In finding for Bridges, the Court repeated throughout the case that unfettered discussion of public affairs could only be curtailed in cases of a clear and present danger to the administration of justice.[15]

Subsequently, in *Garrison* v. *Louisiana*, the Court adopted the *New York Times* v. *Sullivan* defamation rule for criticism of judicial officials as well. An attorney was convicted after calling certain judges lazy and inefficient. Reversing, the Supreme Court held that there was a 'paramount public interest in a free flow of information to the people concerning public officials, their servants...few personal attributes are more germane to fitness for office than dishonesty, malfeasance, *or improper motivation*, even though these characteristics may also affect the official's private character'.[16] Therefore, only statements made with the knowledge of their falsity, or with reckless disregard for the truth, could be punished.[17] The Court's incorporation of the *Sullivan* standard drives home the connection between scandalizing the court, standards of defamation, and of seditious libel. The analogy rests upon equating scandalizing the court with defamation of public officials (hence, the *Sullivan* standard), and both with the idea of sedition.

The Court made its strongest statement in *Landmark Communications* v. *Virginia*, where after affirming that the operation of courts and the conduct of judges were matters of 'utmost public concern', it endorsed Justice Frankfurter's prior opinion that 'speech

---

[13] *Bridges*, pp. 270–71.
[14] *Bridges*, p. 278.
[15] *Bridges*, p. 273.
[16] *Garrison* v. *Louisiana*, 379 U.S. 64, 77 (1964) (hereinafter *Garrison*); emphasis mine.
[17] *Garrison*, p. 67.

cannot be punished when the purpose is simply "to protect the court as a mystical entity or the judges as individuals or as anointed priests set apart from the community and spared the criticism to which in a democracy other public servants are exposed".[18] In other words, if the standards of criticism for other government officials were protected by the *Sullivan* rule, then there was no good reason for making an exception for judges. *Their* conduct was just as much a matter of public interest as the conduct of government officials, and precisely the same issues vis-à-vis the checking value and the chilling effect applied to the judges as much as they did to the rest of government. What stands out with particular clarity is the unequivocal rejection of the idea that the 'authority' and repute of the judicial institution is to be protected *as an end in itself*, and that for some reason, judges are to be shielded, by using the force of criminal law, from political and other forms of criticism that we otherwise think are so crucial to a functioning democracy.

The rejection of protecting judges as an end in itself is, of course, to be contrasted with origins of 'scandalizing the court' in England, whose objective was precisely that. Nonetheless, in England, the last successful prosecution for scandalizing the court occurred as far back as 1931, and in 2012, the Law Commission expressly recommended abolishing the offence.[19]

In its paper recommending abolition, the Law Commission traced the roots of the offence to eighteenth century Britain, and to its original purpose of maintaining a 'haze of glory' around the courts. The idea was that whatever the manner in which the courts *actually* functioned, it was essential that the public *perceive* them to be just and impartial. To be impartial, and to be thought impartial, are two different things, and the Commission noted that in differentiating them, it seemed that the 'purpose of the offence is not confined to preventing the public from getting the wrong idea about judges... [but] that where there are shortcomings, *it is equally important to prevent the public from getting the right idea*'.[20] Observing the deeply

---

[18] 435 U.S. 829, 842 (1978).

[19] The Law Commission (2012).

[20] The Law Commission (2012: 8); emphasis mine.

problematic nature of this proposition in a functioning democracy, the Commission then went on to make familiar arguments about the chilling effect upon legitimate criticism, which was exacerbated by the vagueness of the offence, and its essentially self-serving nature (permitting judges to decide when their own dignity has been lowered). It ended by expressly drawing the link between scandalizing the court and seditious libel, and argued that with the phasing out of the latter, there was little reason for the former to remain.[21]

The Law Commission's recommendations were accepted, and the British parliament abolished the offence of scandalizing the court, via statute, in 2013.[22] Many commonwealth nations continue to have the offence on their statute books. In 2014, however, the Privy Council gave it a highly circumscribed interpretation, while deciding a case on appeal from the courts of Mauritius. In words that are reminiscent of the American 'clear and present danger' test, it held that there must be a 'real risk of undermining public confidence in the administration of justice'[23]—and that the accused must either intend to do so, or act in reckless disregard of whether or not he was doing so.

The close proximity between speech and the undermining of justice has figured in the judgments of numerous constitutional courts. For instance, in *R* v. *Kopyto* (a Canadian decision), a lawyer was convicted for scandalizing the court after stating that a particular decision was 'a mockery of justice...it stinks to high hell'.[24] The Court of Appeal for Ontario unanimously reversed his conviction. Three judges out of five held that the offence of scandalizing the court, as it stood, was overbroad, and inconsistent with the free speech guarantee contained in the Canadian Charter. Two judges upheld the offence, but interpreted it narrowly, limiting it to cases where there was 'a serious risk that the administration of justice would be interfered with...the risk or prejudice must be serious, real or substantial'.[25] The South African

---

[21] The Law Commission (2012: 17). A point also made in Milo et al. (2008: 42–132).

[22] Section 33, Crimes and Courts Act, 2013.

[23] *Dhooharika* v. *The Director of Public Prosecutions*, [2014] UKPC 11, 16.

[24] *R* v. *Kopyto*, 1987 CanLII 176 (ON CA) (hereinafter *Kopyto*).

[25] *Kopyto* (Dubin J.A., dissenting in part).

Constitutional Court adopted a similar (although not identical) standard in *S* v. *Mamabolo*, limiting the offence to 'egregious cases' where the offending conduct 'really was likely to damage the administration of justice'.[26] Successful prosecutions after *Mamabolo* have been in cases where, for instance, racist slurs were passed against a judge, or racist motivations were attributed to a judge.[27]

We can see that—cognizant of free speech concerns—courts have limited the application of the contempt of court offence to a range of narrow cases—for example, cases where public discussion of *sub-judice* matters might exercise a prejudicial influence upon the outcome of a case, or cases where there is a proximate connection between adverse speech and the undermining of justice. What is unambiguously *off* the table is the idea that the 'reputation' of the courts, *qua* courts, needs to be protected. Just like other branches of government, courts should be open to the most searching scrutiny, in order to sustain democratic legitimacy.

CONTEMPT AND SCANDALIZING IN INDIA

The English Law Commission expressly linked scandalizing the court and the offence of sedition. Recall, for a moment, our discussion of sedition in Chapter Four. In *Kedar Nath Singh* v. *State of Bihar*,[28] the Court restricted the scope of Section 124A to within the bounds of Article 19(2)'s public order clause. Notwithstanding the broad reading of the public order restriction in *Ramji Lal Modi*[29] and *Virendra*,[30] we noted that post-*Lohia*,[31] the trend has been to read public order narrowly, consistent with autonomy concerns, in cases such as *Rangarajan*[32] ('spark in a powder keg') and *Arup Bhuyan*[33] (incitement to imminent lawless

---

[26] *S* v. *Mamabolo*, 2001 (5) BCLR 449 (CC): 2001 (3) SA 409 (CC), para 45.

[27] *S* v. *Bresler*, 2002 (4) SA 524; *S* v. *Moila*, 2006 (1) SA 330 (T).

[28] [1962] SCR Supp. (2) 769.

[29] *Ramji Lal Modi* v. *State of UP*, [1957] 1 SCR 860.

[30] *Virendra* v. *State of Punjab*, [1958] 1 SCR 308.

[31] *The Superintendent, Central Prison, Fatehgarh* v. *Dr Ram Manohar Lohia*, [1960] 2 SCR 821.

[32] *S. Rangarajan* v. *P. Jagjivan Ram*, (1989) 2 SCC 574: [1989] 2 SCR 204.

[33] *Arup Bhuyan* v. *State of Assam*, (2011) 3 SCC 377.

action). In other words, the Court has rejected the argument that it is permissible to criminalize speech simply because its *content* might persuade people to think less of the government, which in turn would lead them to disrespect law and order and the authority of the State, and eventually cause breaches of public order.

What is sauce for the goose would ordinarily be sauce for the gander. One would, therefore, expect a similar standard to be applied when the authority in question is not the government, but the courts. Nonetheless, in 1953, in *Aswini Kumar Ghose v. Arabinda Bose*, the Court held that 'if an impression is created in the minds of the public that Judges in the highest Court in the land act on *extraneous considerations in deciding cases*, the confidence of the whole community in the administration of justice is bound to be undermined and no greater mischief than that *can possibly be imagined*.'[34]

At this point, recall the shift in sedition law during the British times, from Justice Petheram's original stress on disobedience, to Justice Strachey's expansion of sedition to cover any statement about the government 'dwelling on its foreign origin or character, *or imputing to it base motives*, or accusing it of hostility or *indifference to the welfare* of the people'.[35] Using similar language, *Aswini Kumar Ghose* fails to demonstrate a conceptual connection with the obstruction of justice, focusing instead on the equivalent of attributing base motives (accusing judges of deciding cases on extraneous considerations). Justice Strachey's sedition formulation, we argued earlier, came close to establishing a thought-crime regime. *Aswini Kumar Ghose* does little better.

'Thought-crime' is a strong term, but there is perhaps no other phrase that accurately describes what the Court sought to punish in *E.M. Sankaran Namboodiripad v. T. Narayanan Nambiar*.[36] While he was Chief Minister of the state of Kerala, Namboodiripad delivered a speech that, invoking Marxist ideology, labelled the judiciary as an 'instrument of oppression', and argued that judges were 'guided and

---

[34] AIR 1953 SC 75, para 2; emphasis mine.

[35] *Queen-Empress v. Bal Gangadhar Tilak*, (1897) ILR 22 Bom 112, p. 151; emphasis mine.

[36] [1971] 1 SCR 697 (hereinafter *Namboodripad*).

dominated by class interests, class hatred and class prejudices'.[37] Before the Kerala High Court, and then the Supreme Court, Namboodiripad argued that he had done nothing more than give expression to the core tenets of Marxist philosophy, which fell well within the freedom of speech and expression under Article 19(1)(a). He also clarified that at no point had he argued that judicial decisions should not be respected or enforced, or cast aspersions or attributed motives to any individual judge. Justice Hidayatullah, writing for the Court, went into a detailed exposition of the development of Marxist philosophy through the nineteenth and twentieth centuries, in order to prove that Namboodiripad had either 'misunderstood', or 'distorted' the teachings of Marx, Engels, and Lenin, mistaking an attack upon the State for an attack upon the judiciary.[38] He then vigorously denied the accusation that the judiciary was an instrument of class oppression, and held that 'an attack upon judges...which is calculated to raise in the minds of the people a *general dissatisfaction* with, and distrust of all judicial decisions...*weakens the authority of law* and law courts'.[39]

Marxist critiques of the judiciary are not new. Punishing them for their tendency to 'raise a *general* dissatisfaction' with the judiciary, which in turn might '*weaken* the authority of law' certainly is, and effectively amounts to outlawing an ideology (which perhaps explains the Court's painstaking efforts to 'prove' that Namboodiripad had misunderstood Marxism).[40] The situation is

---

[37] *Namboodiripad*, para 2.

[38] *Namboodiripad*, para 28.

[39] *Namboodiripad*, para 31; emphasis mine.

[40] As Sathe trenchantly points out, 'the Court could have told Krishna Menon that they were interpreting the Indian Constitution and not Marx, Engels or Lenin. Whether they had learnt about communism only by reading Middleton Murray was irrelevant because they were not supposed to be experts on Marxism-Leninism, etc. If [what] Namboodiripad had said amounted to contempt of court, he had to be punished, no matter whose views he was voicing. However, the Court seems to have spent a good deal of time on understanding Marx and then proving that Namboodiripad had either not understood Marx, or that he had intentionally distorted Marxist writings. The Court need not have undertaken such an inquiry. An interpretation of Marx or Engels' work may form a good subject for a

akin to punishing me for writing an article advocating the anarchist philosophies of Bakunin. It is possible that some people, on reading my article, might be persuaded to come around to my views, and begin to hold the government in contempt. If enough people come around to my views and start holding the government in contempt, then maybe someday the actual working of the government will be undermined. The chain of causation is not only highly attenuated, but also, of course, disrespectful of autonomy, since it attributes responsibility for an act (that is, presumably, the act of obstructing justice) not to the actor, but to the person who has persuaded him, through words and arguments, to act in that way, as though the actor himself is not an autonomous, choosing being. To quote Scanlon again: 'the harm of coming to false beliefs is not one that the autonomous man could allow the State to protect him through restrictions on expression.'[41]

In *Namboodiripad's* case, the Court was still operating within a framework that linked attacking the judiciary with undermining the administration of justice. Subsequently, in *D.C. Saxena* v. *Chief Justice of India*, the Court appeared to separate even these two concepts. It held that 'any criticism about [the] judicial system or judges which hampers the administration of justice *or* which erodes the faith in the objective approach of the judges and brings administration of justice to ridicule must be prevented.'[42] But if the entire point of preserving faith in the objectivity of judges is not to ensure the unhindered administration of justice, then what *is* the point? The Court went on to say that 'judgments can be criticised. Motives to the judges need not be attributed. It brings the administration of justice into disrepute. *Faith in the administration of justice is one of the pillars on which democratic institution functions and*

---

doctoral dissertation in politics or philosophy but is not appropriate in a Supreme Court judgment. Apart from the fact that it sidetracks the main legal issues it unnecessarily involves the Court in a political controversy' (Sathe 1970: 1742).

[41] Scanlon (1972).

[42] *D.C. Saxena* v. *Chief Justice of India*, (1996) 5 SCC 216, para 33 (hereinafter *D.C. Saxena*); emphasis mine.

sustains'.[43] Notice: *not* the administration of justice, but *faith* in the administration of justice. Faith is a 'strong belief', or a 'trust'[44] in something, regardless of whether warranted or not. Effectively, the result is to close off speech that might persuade people to *think* in a certain way, without bothering to explicate the actual harm that might result from thinking in that way.

Presumably, as in *Namboodiripad*, the harm is that if enough people lose their faith in the administration of justice, then the actual administration ultimately will suffer. This was exactly the kind of argument that the Court *rejected* in *Lohia*, when the issue was public order: that Ram Manohar Lohia persuading some people to break a tax law *could* lead to a general disrespect for law in the country, which in turn *could* lead to an eventual revolution. What is sauce for the goose (government) is not—as it turns out—sauce for the gander (the courts).

Recognizing this dichotomy, Sathe points out, in his critique of *Namboodiripad*, that the courts should have taken a leaf out of the *Kedar Nath Singh* book (upholding while narrowing the scope of sedition to bring it in line with Article 19(1)(a)), and restricted the scope of the offence to 'actual or threatened interference with the administration of justice'.[45] Unfortunately, that suggestion remained buried in the annals of the *Economic and Political Weekly*, while in *D.C. Saxena*, the Court then widened the scope of the offence even further, holding it to include 'all acts which bring the court into disrepute or *disrespect* or which *offend its dignity or its majesty or challenge its authority'.*[46] This goes even further than sedition, in criminalizing not merely causing dis*affection* (which translates to disloyalty or enmity, as per the Explanation), but dis*respect*. In other words, it places an affirmative obligation upon citizens to say nothing that could persuade their fellow citizens to stop *respecting* the courts! Again, in making no reference to the

---

[43] *D.C. Saxena*; emphasis mine.

[44] Merriam-Webster Dictionary, available at http://www.merriam-webster.com/dictionary/faith (accessed on 27 July 2015).

[45] Sathe (1970).

[46] *D.C. Saxena*, para 36; emphasis mine.

actual obstruction of justice—that is, in simply equating disrepute/ disrespect with obstruction of justice, the Court failed to consider the individual agency that is involved in crossing the bridge from disrespecting to disobeying, the agency which is *not* that of the original speaker. All it said was that slandering the court creates a 'general disaffection or dissatisfaction' with the judiciary, and 'indisposes[sic] in [the peoples'] minds to obey them'.[47] It is unfortunate how, in its public order cases, the Court has gone out of its way to require a proximate relationship between speech and disorder, but has done nothing of the sort for speech and obstruction of justice when it comes to contempt of court.[48]

Furthermore, the Court affirmed that the requirement of *mens rea* (or intent), which is basic to criminal liability, did not form an ingredient of the offence. It held that the only thing that matters is the *effect* of the words, regardless of the intention or recklessness with which they were uttered.[49] The absence of *mens rea* along with no meaningful proximity requirement establishes a boundlessly manipulable and discretionary test, with almost no guidelines to prevent abuse.

At the heart of it all, of course, is the assumption—also made by the Court in the film censorship cases, religious speech cases, and some of the earlier public order cases—that the people simply cannot be trusted to hear certain thoughts or ideas, because they are incapable of rationally making up their minds about them. This thought—an undercurrent of which is visible in *D.C. Saxena*—came to the fore in Arundhati Roy's contempt of court case, where the outspoken writer had accused the Court of stifling dissent. After observing that confidence in the judiciary could not be 'tarnished' at any cost, the Court accused Roy of trying 'to cast[sic] an injury to the public by creating an impression in the mind of the people of this *backward country* regarding the integrity, ability and fairness of the institution of [the]

---

[47] *D.C. Saxena*, para 38.

[48] And very unfortunate indeed that the Court adopted pre-democratic, eighteenth-century England's 'blaze of glory' formulation at one point in *D.C. Saxena*. *D.C. Saxena*, para 37.

[49] *D.C. Saxena*, para 40.

judiciary.'[50] According to the Court, the *raison d'être* of the scandaliz-ing provision was to maintain the confidence of that (apparently back-ward) public in the judiciary, keeping in mind 'the ground realities and prevalent socio-economic system in India, the vast majority of whose people are *poor, ignorant, uneducated, easily liable to be misled. But who acknowledly [sic] have the tremendous faith in the dispensers of justice'.*[51] In fact, the poor and the ignorant were so easy to mislead, that there was no need for any evidence that they actually had been taken up the garden path with respect to the 'integrity, ability and fairness' of the judges:

> ...the well-known proposition of law is that it punishes the archer as soon as the arrow is shot no matter if it misses to hit [sic] the target. The respondent is proved to have shot the arrow, intended to damage the institution of the judiciary and thereby weaken the faith of the public in general and if such an attempt is not prevented, *disastrous consequences are likely to follow resulting in the destruction of rule of law, the expected norm of any civilised society.*[52]

We have discussed, previously, Vincent Blasi's 'pathological per-spective' of free speech. According to Blasi, free speech protections should be designed for the worst of times, because historically, in any time of crisis, the government's response has been to overestimate the threat to itself, and overregulate free speech that it perceives to be hostile towards it. The pathological perspective need not simply apply to emergency situations, and it need not apply only to government. The Court's contempt jurisprudence demonstrates that when *any* body is given the power to regulate conduct critical of it, it succumbs to overregulation. The Supreme Court—composed, as R.K. Sidhva presciently observed in the Constituent Assembly Debates, of human beings like us—has been no exception. While the 2006 amendment to the Contempt of Courts Act clarifies that punishment for contempt

---

[50] *In Re Arundhati Roy*, (2002) 3 SCC 343, para 18 (hereinafter *Arundhati Roy*); emphasis mine.

[51] *Arundhati Roy*, para 26; emphasis mine.

[52] *Arundhati Roy*, para 40; emphasis mine.

may be imposed only in cases where an act substantially interferes, or tends substantially to interfere with the due course of justice, it is yet unclear whether this will make any tangible difference in the Court's jurisprudence.[53] This is because, as we have seen, the courts have equated the act of 'scandalizing' with interfering with the administration of justice, through a chain of reasoning that involves imputations of possible public loss of faith in the judiciary, followed by potential disrespect for its actions, and culminating in an anticipated disregard of its orders.

OBSTRUCTION OF JUSTICE IN *SUB-JUDICE* MATTERS: THE MEDIA GUIDELINES CASE

In our discussion of the scandalizing offence, we noted that the origins of the contempt of court exception—when it was first introduced in the Constituent Assembly—lay in preventing the obstruction of justice not by speaking ill of the judiciary, but by commenting on *sub-judice* matters. Of course, this too is an exercise of balancing: balancing the freedom of speech against the legitimate interest in preserving the integrity of the judicial process and the right of the accused to a fair trial. In cases such as *Mirajkar*[54] and *Reliance Petrochemicals*,[55] the Court had noted that temporary injunctions on reporting certain aspects of *sub-judice* matters are in the interests of a fair trial, but had rarely addressed its conceptual foundations in any great detail.

Subsequently, in 2012, in *Sahara v. SEBI*,[56] the Supreme Court was asked to clarify the state of law by providing guidelines on media reporting of *sub-judice* matters. In that case, the Court held:

[53] For a detailed analysis of the history of the amendment, and the tensions that it raises, see Venkatesan (2014: 240–67).

[54] *Naresh Sridhar Mirajkar v. State of Maharashtra*, [1966] 3 SCR 744.

[55] *Reliance Petrochemicals v. Proprietors of Indian Express*, [1988] SCR Supp. (3) 212.

[56] *Sahara India Real Estate Corpn. Ltd. v. SEBI*, (2012) 10 SCC 603 (hereinafter *Sahara*).

Given that the postponement orders curtail the freedom of expression of third parties, such orders have to be passed only in cases in which *there is real and substantial risk of prejudice to fairness of the trial or to the proper administration of justice*...however, such orders of postponement should be ordered for a limited duration and without disturbing the content of the publication. They should be passed only when *necessary* to prevent real and substantial risk to the fairness of the trial (court proceedings), if reasonable alternative methods or measures such as change of venue or postponement of trial will not prevent the said risk and *when the salutary effects of such orders outweigh the deleterious effects to the free expression of those affected by the prior restraint.*[57]

The twin concepts of necessity (that the restriction on expression be necessary to accomplish the goal (of a fair trial)) and proportionality (that the expression be restricted no more than required to achieve the goal) are borrowed from Canadian and European Court of Human Rights jurisprudence. The test itself—'real and substantial risk'—is more or less borrowed from the English Contempt of Courts Act[58] and the judgment of the Canadian Supreme Court in *Dagenais*.[59]

The Court's actual free speech analysis is somewhat ambiguous. It refers repeatedly to Article 21 and the right to a fair trial, the 'social interests' that 19(2) seeks to protect, and the contempt of court exception. One possible interpretation is that restraints on reporting are justified by reference to the contempt of court restriction, while their reasonableness in a particular case depends upon whether or not they are necessary and proportionate towards achieving the Article 21-grounded right of fair trial. Another interpretation is that the contempt of court restriction itself is to be understood in light of Article 21, and the necessity/proportionality test flows from there. Whatever its method, the test itself is reasonably clear, although rather

---

[57] *Sahara*, para 42; emphasis mine.

[58] Section 2(2), Contempt of Courts Act, 1981. This was brought in as a response to the judgment of the European Court of Human Rights in the *Sunday Times* case. See *The Sunday Times* vs *The United Kingdom*, (1979) 2 EHRR 245.

[59] *Dagenais* v. *Canadian Broadcasting Corporation*, [1994] 3 SCR 835; the South African Supreme Court of Appeal adopted a similar test in *Midi Television (Pty) Ltd* v. *Director of Public Prosecutions*, 2007 (5) SA 540 (SCA).

open-ended. Some critics point to precisely this aspect, and warn that it leaves the door open for the High Courts to effectively create a 'gag writ'.[60] It, therefore, remains to be seen whether, post-*Sahara*, courts will apply it in a sufficiently speech-protective manner.

[60] Gupta (2012). For another critique, which equates the test to an imposition of prior restraint, see Muralidharan (2012); for a defence of the decision, see Shankar (2012). The fears of the critics seemed to have been partially realized when the Delhi High Court gagged major newspaper and television channels from publishing the photographs of a retired Supreme Court judge, who was accused of sexual harassment by a former intern. In its analysis, the Court noted that allegations upon a public figure not only affected his reputation, but would also shake public faith and confidence in the institution that he was affiliated with. See *Swatanter Kumar* v. *The Indian Express*, 27 (2014) DLT 221: I.A. No. 723/2014 in CS(OS) No. 102/2014. For a critique of the High Court's order, see Yadava (2014).

PART FIVE

The 'Freedom of Speech and Expression'

. . . .

CHAPTER TEN

The Meaning of 'Speech and Expression'

• •

Expressive conduct includes a range of activities that go beyond 'speech', conventionally understood. How does the Constitution apply to such activities? Does 'the freedom of speech and expression' include conduct with clear political significance, such as the flying of a flag? Correspondingly, does it *exclude* 'speech' with no such significance, such as commercial advertising?

Additionally, meaningful expressive acts necessarily imagine at least two parties: a speaker and an audience. Some free speech provisions are sensitive to this. The International Covenant on Civil and Political Rights, for instance, protects the right to '*seek, receive* and impart information'.[1] Similarly, the South African Constitution protects the freedom to '*receive* or impart information'.[2] The German Constitution guarantees everyone the right to 'freely inform himself...from generally accessible sources'.[3] India's own free speech clause, by comparison, is sparsely worded. 'All citizens shall have the right to freedom of speech and expression' does

[1] Article 19, International Covenant on Civil and Political Rights; emphasis mine.

[2] Section 16, Constitution of the Republic of South Africa; emphasis mine.

[3] Article 5, Basic Law of Germany.

not, by itself, cover both speaker and audience, or distinguish between kinds of speech. That task has been left to the courts.

These questions and others, which lie at the heart of understanding Article 19(1)(a) itself, will be considered over the next two chapters.

COMMERCIAL SPEECH

Are certain kinds of speech more valuable and deserving of protection than others? Does the free speech clause contain an inbuilt hierarchy? In deciding to exclude certain forms of speech from First Amendment protection, the American courts have certainly held so, noting that obscenity, fighting words, and the like 'are no essential part of any exposition of ideas, and are of such slight social value as a step to truth that any benefit that may be derived from them is clearly outweighed by the social interest in order and morality'.[4] The South African Constitutional Court followed suit in *De Reuck* v. *DPP*, holding that child pornography amounted to 'expression of little value which is found on the periphery of the right and is a form of expression that is not protected as part of the freedom of expression in many democratic societies'.[5]

As we have discussed before, a hierarchies-of-speech model is inevitable under a democracy-based theory of free speech, although its exact structure depends upon the theory itself. The question, however, is whether that hierarchy is *already* in place under our constitutional scheme. The debate has played out most vividly in the courts' decisions on the constitutional status of commercial speech.

---

[4] *Chaplinsky* v. *New Hampshire*, 315 U.S. 568 (1942).

[5] 2004 (1) SA 406, para 59 (hereinafter *De Reuck*). In the United States, the hierarchies operate to exclude certain kinds of speech from constitutional protection altogether. In South Africa, however, the Constitutional Court has noted that the presence of express constitutional limitations implies that at the threshold stage of determining whether or not a particular form of expression deserves prima facie constitutional protection, nothing should be excluded. Hierarchies of speech play a role—as they did in *De Reuck*—when the Court asks whether the speech-regulating statute is a justifiable restriction. Article 19(1)(a) is structurally more similar to the South African Constitution.

In 1959, the Court was called upon for the first time to decide whether commercial advertisements were protected under Article 19(1)(a). In *Hamdard Dawakhana* v. *Union of India*, the constitutionality of Sections 3 and 8 of the Drugs and Medical Remedies Act was challenged. The objective of the Act was to prevent misleading advertisements for medicines, which claimed 'magical' or other similar properties for certain remedies. It arose out of a concern that many people were relying upon such advertisements, and using fake drugs for self-medication. The Court accepted the government's contention that there was a causal connection between misleading advertisements and actual physical harm caused due to self-medication.[6] It then had to consider the 19(1)(a) claims of the advertisers, which it rejected in the following language:

> An advertisement is no doubt *a form of speech* but...when it takes the form of a commercial advertisement which has an element of trade or commerce it no longer falls within the concept of freedom of speech for the object is not propagation of ideas—*social, political or economic or furtherance of literature or human thought*; but as in the present case the commendation of the efficacy, value and importance in treatment of particular diseases by certain drugs and medicines. In such a case, advertisement is a part of business...and...[has] no relationship with what may be called the *essential concept of the freedom of speech*.[7]

Thus, while the Court admitted that advertisements were a 'form of speech', it also held that 19(1)(a) was inapplicable to that particular form. The 'essential concept of the freedom of speech', for the Court, was the propagation of ideas. Commercial advertisements were simply part of a business' profit-making drive, and, therefore, unprotected under 19(1)(a). The phrase 'propagation of ideas' is considerably broader than Meiklejohn's idea that speech must be of 'governing importance', and reflects the German courts' protection of anything that contributes to the 'intellectual struggle of opinions'.[8]

---

[6] [1960] 2 SCR 671, para 12 (hereinafter *Hamdard Dawakhana*).
[7] *Hamdard Dawakhana*, para 17; emphasis mine.
[8] *Luth* Case, BVerfGE 7, 198 (1958).

Notice that the terms 'essential concept' and 'hav[ing] no relationship with' both suggest the idea of gradation. Implicit in the idea of an essential concept of free speech is the further idea that different kinds of speech bear different degrees of relationship with the 'essential concept' (explication of ideas?), and the degree of protection accorded to a particular form depends upon its proximity with the essential concept. This has been the approach of the American Supreme Court. While obscenity, fighting words, and other kinds of speech that we have discussed before get no protection at all, there are other, 'low-value' forms of speech that get *some* protection, but allow the government greater leeway to regulate than it would otherwise have. In such cases, the Court is more likely to defer to the government's conclusions about the harm that might result from such speech, and provide the government greater discretion to devise regulatory regimes that deal with the identified harm. Indeed, commercial speech is a classic example of such 'low-value' speech.[9]

At the same time, the Court's formulation in *Hamdard Dawakhana*—that free speech is essentially about the 'propagation of ideas'—is very difficult to define. Commercial advertisements, after all, are dedicated to the propagation of an idea—the idea that the advertiser's product beats all competition in the market, and ought to be purchased. The Court attempted to get around that problem by focusing on the commercial motivation underlying advertising. Yet newspapers are also profit-making enterprises, and nobody would imagine denying *them* the benefit of Article 19(1)(a). The difficulty in drawing a line between profit-making and the propagation of ideas is illustrated in the European Court of Human Rights case of *Market Intern* v. *Germany*, which involved regulating the speech of a magazine that published *criticisms* of commercial products (in a sense, anti-advertising). While upholding an injunction granted by the local courts, the European Court nonetheless held that 'in a market economy an undertaking which seeks to set up a business inevitably

---

[9] *44 Liquormart, Inc* v. *Rhode Island*, 517 U.S. 484 (1996) (hereinafter *Liquormart*).

exposes itself to close scrutiny of its practices by its competitors... in order to carry out this task, *the specialised press must be able to disclose facts which could be of interest to its readers and thereby contribute to the openness of business activities*.[10] But if that is true, then surely companies should also be allowed to contribute to the openness of business activities by publicizing their products via commercial advertising.

Furthermore, we do not normally accord blanket protection to all ideas. Pornography—as we have seen before—is also dedicated to propagating ideas, as is hate speech. In fact, hate speech is centrally about propagating ideas—ideas about the inferiority of one group of people in society. 'Propagation of ideas' as a mark of identifying protected speech, therefore, seems to have been incorrectly applied by the Court in *Hamdard Dawakhana*, and also seems to provide no justification for speech that we might think *ought* to be regulated.

Perhaps unsurprisingly, in 1995, the Supreme Court quietly abandoned the *Hamdard Dawakhana* test. *Tata Press* v. *MTNL*[11] involved Rule 458 of the Telegraph Rules, 1951, which prohibited anyone from publishing lists of telephone subscribers without permission from the Telegraph Authority. Tata Press's 'Yellow Pages', a directory of advertisements issued by businessmen, merchants, and other professionals, was alleged to contravene Rule 458 because it was akin to a telephone directory. Before the Supreme Court, Tata Press argued that the rule violated their 19(1)(a) right. It contended that *Hamdard Dawakhana* had relied upon American jurisprudence to exclude commercial advertisements from the scope of 19(1)(a), but that in the intervening thirty-six years, American law itself had moved on, and now *did* protect commercial speech under the First Amendment.

The Court agreed, and held that while commercial speech was, in general, protected by Article 19(1)(a), 'deceptive, unfair, misleading and untruthful' advertisements *would be hit by Article 19(2)*

---

[10] *Market Intern* v. *Germany*, (1989) 12 EHRR 161, para 35; emphasis mine.
[11] (1995) 5 SCC 139 (hereinafter *Tata Press*).

(presumably, the morality clause).[12] Being a smaller bench than *Hamdard Dawakhana*, the Court had to distinguish contrary precedent, which it did by limiting *Hamdard Dawakhana* only to the specific facts of that case—misleading advertisements for drugs.[13]

This is not entirely satisfactory, because recall that *Hamdard Dawakhana* excluded such speech from the scope of 19(1)(a) altogether, while *Tata Press* holds that it would be protected under 19(1)(a), but reasonably restricted under 19(2). In other words, under the *Tata Press* reading of *Hamdard Dawakhana*, misleading advertisements could be legitimately prohibited by the government because 19(1)(a) did not apply to them at all, much like it would not apply to commercial fraud, for instance. On the other hand, on the logic of *Tata Press* itself, prohibition of misleading advertisements would be justified as a reasonable 19(2) restriction upon otherwise protected commercial speech. The distinction is important because it very obviously affects both the scope of 19(1)(a), and the interpretation of the morality clause, although the Court in *Tata Press* appears not to have noticed the distinction.

In *Tata Press*, the Supreme Court invoked three reasons for protecting commercial speech. Advertisements, it held, were an important source of revenue for newspapers. And a free and independent media (reliant upon the revenue that would *keep* it independent), in turn, was the lifeblood of democracy. Second, advertisements were necessary for ensuring low prices in a market economy. And third, advertisements ensured a free flow of information, which would enable consumers to make an informed choice about products.[14]

---

[12] *Tata Press*, para 17.

[13] *Tata Press*, para 18. *Tata Press*, in turn, has been quietly contravened by the Delhi High Court in *Mahesh Bhatt* v. *Union of India*, 147 (2008) DLT 561. In that case, the Delhi High Court upheld a ban on tobacco advertising on the ground that only speech 'in the public interest' could claim the protection of Article 19(1)(a). Since tobacco caused proven health hazards, tobacco advertising did not amount to disseminating ideas in the public interest (unlike the case of *Tata Press*, which involved providing Yellow Pages to the public). The slippery slope implications of this are dangerous (advertising alcohol? chocolates?), as is the Court's strange observation that 19(1)(a) did not envisage people 'disturb[ing] social norms'.

[14] *Tata Press*, paras 19–23.

There is something curious about this reasoning. While the Court grounds all its justifications in democracy, it is not simply democracy that is doing the work. Rather, it is a particular form of *market-liberalism* that is implicated in the Court's arguments. At the heart of this vision is the autonomous consumer, who comes into the market with her preferences fully constituted, needing only to be informed about the options on offer. The idea that the 'free flow of information' put out by private players in an unregulated marketplace should be the basis for all private economic decisions is a politically and ideologically charged view of society and of democracy. The marketplace in planned or socialist democracies, for instance, would function very differently. Whatever its merits, it is in no way a view required—or even endorsed—by the Constitution, or by the free speech clause. During the debates, the framers were explicit about this point.[15]

The Court's reasoning in *Tata Press* is directly imported from American commercial speech jurisprudence, and perhaps reflects the dangers of lifting arguments brick-by-brick without adequate regard to context. There is also, however, an interesting implication. As we have discussed, the basic idea is based upon a vision of the autonomous consumer who must be allowed unrestricted access to information flows so as to make her economic decisions in the marketplace. The result of this is that American courts, despite giving significant leeway to the legislature to regulate commercial advertising, are hostile to regulation that is motivated by paternalistic concerns. If the objective of commercial speech regulation is to prevent the consumers from accessing certain information on the ground that they might—in the government's opinion, make wrong or undesirable choices—then the American courts strike it down.[16] In the American context, this is understandable, because of the similar focus on autonomy in other areas of free speech law, such

---

[15] See, for instance, Ambedkar's point about 'economic democracy' vs 'political democracy', that we have referenced earlier in this book. See Chapter One.

[16] See, for example, *Liquormart*.

as hate speech and subversive speech restrictions, which we have discussed here.[17]

The idea that autonomy in the political sphere (the justification for a high level of protection accorded to political speech) must translate into autonomy in the marketplace has also found favour with the Canadian Supreme Court. In *Ford* v. *Attorney-General of Quebec*, the Court held that 'commercial expression...plays a significant role in enabling individuals to make informed economic choices, an important aspect of individual self-fulfillment and personal autonomy'.[18]

In India, however, we have seen that the Supreme Court has, more often than not, adopted a contrary vision: restricting the films that people can watch, the books that they can read, and the things that they can say (especially about the courts), on the ground—sometimes implied, sometimes explicitly stated—that they cannot be trusted to make up their own minds in a responsible and autonomous way. In unquestioningly adopting American jurisprudence on *commercial* speech, it seems that the Court has ignored the deep tensions that this creates in 19(1)(a) interpretation. We are, it would appear, autonomous consumers, but not autonomous citizens! The government, on this paradoxical view, can be paternalistic everywhere *but* in the marketplace.

Furthermore, there are divisions even within the marketplace. For instance, under the Bar Council of India Rules, lawyers are not

---

[17] As Redish points out: 'If the individual is to achieve the maximum degree of material satisfaction permitted by his resources, he must be presented with as much information as possible concerning the relative merits of competing products. After receiving the competing information, the individual will then be in a position [to] rationally decide which combination of features best satisfies his personal needs...[moreover] *the theory of political self-government derives to a large extent from the belief in the intelligent free will of the individual, who is capable [of] making his personal decision as to how he should be governed*...informational commercial speech [thus] furthers legitimate [free speech] purposes. When the individual is presented with *rational grounds* for preferring one product over another, he is encouraged to consider the competing information [and to] exercise his abilities to reason and think; *this aids him towards the intangible goal of rational self-fulfillment*' (see Redish 1971; emphasis mine).

[18] *Ford* v. *Attorney-General of Quebec*, [1988] 2 SCR 712, para 59.

permitted to advertise or solicit.[19] This stems from the traditional belief that the law is a 'noble' profession that ought not to be soiled by commercializing it.[20] But that seems entirely irrelevant to a 19(1)(a) enquiry. After all, the legal profession—whether noble or ignoble—works on the same principles as the rest of the marketplace: it entails the performance of a service for a fee. If advertisements are constitutionally protected because they enable autonomous consumers to make informed choices in the grand marketplace, then on what basis is the legal profession alone put in a separate domain?

The contradiction was recognized by the United States Supreme Court in *Bates* v. *State Bar of Arizona*, where it observed that 'habit and tradition are not in themselves an adequate answer to a constitutional challenge',[21] and struck down the ban on legal advertising. There was simply no principled reason, it held, to prohibit commercial speech in the context of the legal profession, while it was allowed everywhere else on the basis that advertisements were essential to autonomous choice in a market economy. Nonetheless, the contradiction seems to have been ignored in India, even though—as noted here—American jurisprudence and reasoning on commercial speech has been imported wholesale. Once again, the logic of some of the Court's decisions seems to be in tension with the outcomes of others.

ELECTIONS

A democratic and republican form of government has long been held by the courts to constitute part of the unamendable, basic structure of the Constitution.[22] Perhaps surprisingly, voting—the primary mechanism for ensuring that—finds no mention in Part III's list of fundamental rights. Article 326 of the Constitution guarantees the

---

[19] Bar Council of India Rules, under Section 49(1)(c), Advocates Act, 1961.

[20] *Bar Council of Maharashtra* v. *M.V. Dabholkar*, [1976] 1 SCR 306.

[21] *Bates* v. *State Bar of Arizona*, 433 U.S. 350, 371 (1977).

[22] *Kesavananda Bharati* v. *State of Kerala*, (1973) 4 SCC 225 (hereinafter *Kesavananda Bharati*).

universal suffrage rule for elections to the House and the Assembly, but does not guarantee elections themselves.[23] Beyond that, it is the Representation of the People Act that establishes a statutory regime governing the procedures and conduct of elections.

The constitutional status of elections came up before the Supreme Court in *Union of India* v. *Association for Democratic Reforms*. Faced with complaints about the widespread criminalization and opacity of politics, the Delhi High Court passed an order directing the Election Commission to make it mandatory for election candidates to reveal any prior criminal record, assets, and educational qualifications. The Union appealed to the Supreme Court, arguing that since the conduct of elections was governed by the Representation of the People Act, the appropriate remedy was to approach the *legislature* to amend the law and introduce the Court's disclosure requirements, and not to vest in the Election Commission the power to enforce requirements that had no statutory basis.

Rejecting this contention, the Court held that Article 324 of the Constitution granted wide powers to the Election Commission, which enabled it to impose any requirements related to elections that were not expressly or by necessary implication *excluded* by the legislature from the Representation of the People Act.[24] This solved the problem of demarcating the Election Commission's power in the instant case. However, as the history of Indian politics demonstrates, politicians have not been reticent to amend the Representation of the People Act (with retrospective effect), specifically to overturn adverse Supreme Court opinions.[25] Had the Court stopped here, its decision upholding disclosure requirements would have rested on very weak legal footing, vulnerable to being undone by a simple amendment to the Representation of the People Act.

The Court's response was to invoke Article 19(1)(a):

---

[23] Article 326, Constitution of India.

[24] *Union of India* v. *Association for Democratic Reforms*, (2002) 5 SCC 294, para 29 (hereinafter *Association for Democratic Reforms*).

[25] *Indira Nehru Gandhi* v. *Raj Narain*, [1975] 3 SCR 333 (hereinafter *Indira Nehru Gandhi*).

Under our Constitution, Article 19(1)(a) provides for freedom of speech and expression. Voters' speech or expression in case of election would include casting of votes, that is to say, [the] voter speaks out or expresses by casting [their] vote. For this purpose, information about the candidate to be selected is [a] must.[26]

There are two crucial points here. The first is that voting is a protected form of expression under Article 19(1)(a). Of course, a voter is not 'speaking' in the traditional sense of the word, but at the same time, voting is an example of an expressive activity par excellence. What makes voting an expressive activity as opposed to, say, driving a car through a red light? Clearly, it cannot be only about the subjective intent with which the activity is performed, but must also be about the *objective social meaning* that it has acquired.[27] The act of entering the voting booth and pressing a button on the Electronic Voting Machine (EVM) is treated, in our society, as an expression of the voter's political will. That is what imbues it with expressive and communicative content—and, more specifically—expressive content of a political nature.

The decision in *Union of India* v. *Association for Democratic Reforms* did not say, however, whether 19(1)(a) protection is limited to expressive acts of a political nature, or whether it extends its net wider. We have here our familiar clash between Meiklejohn's narrow view of free speech and his successors' gradual broadening of its ambit, only now on the unfamiliar terrain of non-speech conduct.

Second, not only did *Union of India* v. *Association for Democratic Reforms* ground the freedom to vote as a species of the freedom of expression, but it went one step further by including ancillary aspects that are prerequisites for making that freedom effective, or meaningful. In political theory, John Rawls has distinguished between *liberties*, and the *worth of liberties* (the freedom of speech, for instance, is of no worth if one has been physically gagged).[28] Similarly, the Court held that the things which make a freedom worth having in the first

---

[26] *Association for Democratic Reforms*, para 54.
[27] Post (1995).
[28] Rawls (2005).

place are as much a part of the constitutional scheme as the freedom itself. So, if the voter is 'speaking out' by voting, it is essential that she be provided with the information that makes her speaking out a meaningful exercise of her democratic will. Consequently, the 19(1)(a) freedom to vote is meaningful only if voters are informed about their candidates' antecedents.

At the heart of the Court's judgment is a vision of democracy as a process of *informed* decision-making. The Court cited cases such as *Indian Express Newspapers*,[29] *Romesh Thappar*,[30] and *Cricket Association of Bengal*[31] to hold that Article 19(1)(a) is central to democracy, before noting:

> Public education is essential for functioning of the process of popular government and to assist the discovery of truth and strengthening the capacity of an individual in participating in [the] decision making process.[32]

This completes the link with voting. If 19(1)(a) is about democracy, and voting is the expressive embodiment of democratic governance, then the inescapable conclusion must be that voting is protected under 19(1)(a).

This distinction between the *right* to vote (which is a statutory right, governed by the Representation of the People Act) and the *freedom* to vote (which is a constitutional, 19(1)(a) freedom) is a subtle one, and has consistently informed the Court's election jurisprudence over the last decade. When we say that the right to vote is only a statutory right, we mean that the conduct and modalities of voting, how the process of voting is to be organized, and so on—are governed by a statute, and can be changed or modified by the legislature. When we refer to the *freedom* to vote, however, we are talking about voting as

---

[29] *Indian Express Newspapers (Bombay) Pvt Ltd* v. *Union of India*, (1985) 1 SCC 641: [1985] 2 SCR 287.

[30] *Romesh Thappar* v. *State of Madras*, [1950] 1 SCR 594.

[31] *Secretary, Ministry of Information and Broadcasting* v. *Cricket Association of Bengal*, (1995) 2 SCC 161.

[32] *Association for Democratic Reforms*, para 35.

an essential aspect of democracy and self-governance, protected by 19(1)(a). The difference is illustrated in cases such as this one, where an aspect of voting not included under the Representation of the People Act (disclosure of antecedents) is nonetheless considered to be so essential to any meaningful conception of the freedom to vote, that it falls within Article 19(1)(a). To take an extreme example, if the government repealed the Representation of the People Act altogether, or introduced grossly discriminatory voting provisions into it, the remedy would then lie not within the statute itself (how could it?), nor within Article 326 (which is conditional), but 19(1)(a).

Another example of the distinction is to be found in the recent judgment of the Supreme Court in *PUCL* v. *Union of India*, popularly known as the NOTA case.[33] The combined effect of Rules 41(2), (3), and 49-O of the 1961 Conduct of Election Rules was that persons who did not vote in elections were *recorded* as having not voted. PUCL challenged these rules on the ground that the secret ballot was protected by Article 19(1)(a). The Union argued that the petition was not maintainable because (voting being only a statutory right) no constitutional issue was raised.

Rejecting the contention, the Court reiterated the distinction between the *right* to vote (statutory) and the *freedom* of voting (constitutional).[34] It cited cases such as *Indira Nehru Gandhi* v. *Raj Narain* and *Kihoto Hollohan* v. *Zachilhu*[35] for the uncontroversial proposition that an effective democracy, functioning through free and fair elections, is part of the basic structure of the Constitution.[36] It then observed that secrecy was essential to free and fair elections (since that is the only way of preventing bribery, coercion, and post-election reprisals).[37] Since the freedom to vote naturally included the freedom not to vote (which was as much a positive exercise of political will as voting), it was arbitrary to guarantee secrecy for the first but not for

---

[33] *PUCL* v. *Union of India*, (2013) 10 SCC 1 (hereinafter *PUCL*).
[34] *PUCL*, para 20.
[35] AIR 1993 SC 412.
[36] *PUCL*, para 45.
[37] *PUCL*, para 54.

the second. The Court therefore directed the Election Commission to introduce a 'None of the Above' [NOTA] option into the EVMs.[38] Just as an informed electorate was essential to make the 19(1)(a) freedom to vote meaningful (and hence, disclosure requirements) so was secrecy (and hence, NOTA).

We can see that ideas of representative democracy, the freedom of speech, and voting as an expression of democratic will, are all bound together to create 19(1)(a) protections for effective and meaningful voting. These ideas are not unique to India. The American scholar Charles Black locates the freedom of speech guarantee in the idea of a *responsive* government, which the people can petition for the redressal of their grievances.[39] Responsiveness and accountability of government to people—the cornerstones of democracy—can only be guaranteed if the channels of communication are kept open at all times. Black does not, of course, extend the argument to institutional guarantees of effective voting, but the chain of argument is clear.

A potential battleground for the future might be restrictive voting provisions. For instance, in December 2014, the state of Rajasthan amended—via ordinance—its Panchayati Raj Act, imposing educational qualifications upon people who wish to run for local elected office. This seems to be a clear example of an Article 19(1)(a) violation, since the Ordinance entirely disenfranchises a class of (uneducated) people.[40]

Democracy, 19(1)(a), and the Right to Information

What of the right to information outside the specific context of elections? Much before the passage of the Right to Information Act, the Supreme Court had occasion to consider the issue in *State of UP* v. *Raj Narain*. *Raj Narain* involved the interpretation of Section 123 of the Evidence Act, which prohibits the giving of evidence 'derived from unpublished official records relating to *any affairs of State*, except with

---

[38] *PUCL*, para 61.
[39] Black (1969).
[40] For readers interested in a more detailed argument, see Bhatia (2015c).

the permission of the officer at the head of the department concerned.'[41] In deciding upon whether or not a certain 'Blue Book' was a privileged document dealing with 'affairs of State' within the meaning of Section 123 of the Evidence Act, Justice Mathew observed that Section 123 must be interpreted harmoniously with Section 162, which requires the production by witnesses of any document when summoned, 'notwithstanding any objection which there may be to its production or to its admissibility. The validity of any such objection shall be decided on by the Court.'[42] Reading the two sections together, Justice Mathew held that the interpretation of the term 'affairs of State' in Section 123 (a prerequisite for withholding disclosure) was subject to judicial review. He noted that

> in a government of responsibility...where all the agents of the public must be responsible for their conduct, there can [be] but few secrets. The people...have a right to know every public act, everything, that is done in a public way, by their public functionaries...the right to know, which is derived from the concept of freedom of speech, though not absolute, is a factor which should make one wary, when secrecy is claimed for transactions which can, at any rate, have no repercussion on public security.[43]

Yet what Justice Mathew gave with one hand, he took away with the other, holding at the same time that determinations of public security were within the sole domain of the executive, and the Minister's certificate (of non-disclosure) would be taken as conclusive. And although he cited *New York Times* v. *United States*, the extent of his deference to the executive in matters of public security is at variance with that famous judgment. In *New York Times*—which was a case about injunctions, and not about required disclosure—the American Supreme Court stipulated that an overriding public security risk would have

---

[41] Section 123, Indian Evidence Act, 1872; emphasis mine.

[42] Section 162, Indian Evidence Act, 1872.

[43] *State of UP* v. *Raj Narain*, AIR 1975 SC 865, para 74 (concurring opinion of Mathew J.; hereinafter *Raj Narain*). Note that this is the epitome of the democratic justification for free speech.

to be demonstrated by the government before an injunction could be granted—such as, for instance, the publication of troop movements during wartime.[44] Justice Mathew, on the other hand, seemed to suggest that a simple statement that a matter related to public security would be enough to exclude the jurisdiction of the courts.

Similarly, in *S.P. Gupta* v. *The President of India* the Court declaimed, in ringing phrases, that

> the concept of an open government is the direct emanation from the right to know which seems to be implicit in the right of free speech and expression guaranteed under Article 19(1)(a). Therefore, disclosure of information in regard to the functioning of Government must be the rule and secrecy an exception justified only where the strictest requirement of public interest so demands.[45]

In *S.P. Gupta*, the Court rejected out of hand the proposition that certain classes of documents were granted immunity under Section 123 of the Evidence Act simply because they related to policy-making. Such an argument, the Court held, was antithetical to the very conception of open government. Accordingly, in the context of the case, it refused to grant immunity to the correspondence between the Chief Justice of India, the Chief Justice of the Delhi High Court, and the Law Minister.[46]

Notwithstanding the promise of *Raj Narain* and *S.P. Gupta*, the Court's approach since then has been circumspect. In *Dinesh Trivedi* v. *Union of India*, the Court refused to order the disclosure of the various preparatory reports and correspondences that had gone into the writing of the *Vohra Committee Report*, about the links between politicians and organized crime. Stressing upon that part of Justice Mathew's opinion in *Raj Narain* which stated that the right to information was not absolute, the Court held that the harm that would be

[44] *New York Times* v. *United States*, 403 U.S. 713 (1971).

[45] *S.P. Gupta* v. *The President of India*, AIR 1982 SC 149, para 66 (hereinafter *S.P. Gupta*).

[46] In this context, see also Article 361A of the Constitution, which protects publication of proceedings of Parliament and the State legislatures, subject to certain conditions.

caused to intelligence agencies, and to the conditions of secrecy and confidentiality under which they functioned, outweighed the public interest in disclosure.[47]

Similarly, in *PUCL* v. *Union of India*, Section 18 of the Atomic Energy Act of 1962 was at issue. Under Section 18, the government was authorized to restrict the disclosure of any information relating to existing or proposed nuclear plants, their operations, or processes. A report published by the Atomic Energy Regulatory Board apparently contained information about 130 possible safety defects in nuclear installations and power plants across India. When PUCL sought access to the report, it was denied under Section 18. Before the Supreme Court, PUCL argued that it had a right to access the document, and that Section 18 was unconstitutional due to the absence of any guidelines canalizing the government's discretion in denying disclosure. Rejecting the contentions, the Court held that Section 18 was a reasonable 19(2) restriction, since 'the operation and functioning of a nuclear plant is…sensitive in nature. Any information relating to the training features processes [*sic*] or technology cannot be disclosed as it may be vulnerable to sabotage'.[48]

Apart from judicial pronouncements, the Official Secrets Act tears a gaping hole into the democratic 'right to know'. The Act criminalizes, for instance, disclosure or communication of information that '*might be*…directly or *indirectly*…useful to an enemy'.[49] Readers will immediately note that this term is wide enough to cover most investigative reporting, and is certainly wide enough to cover whistleblowing/journalism such as that of Wikileaks.[50] Of course, presently, the statutory framework governing the disclosure of public

---

[47] *Dinesh Trivedi* v. *Union of India*, (1997) 4 SCC 306, para 63.

[48] *PUCL* v. *Union of India*, (2004) 2 SCC 476, para 63. See also *Indira Jaising* v. *Registrar-General*, (2003) 5 SCC 494, where the Court held that a report on judicial misconduct did not even raise a right to information interest.

[49] See Section 3(c), Official Secrets Act, 1923; Section 5, Official Secrets Act, 1923; emphasis mine.

[50] The Court has tended to broaden, rather than constrict, the operation of the Act. See, for example, *Sama Alana Abdulla* v. *State of Gujarat*, AIR 1996 SC 569.

documents is the Right to Information Act, which expressly overrides the Official Secrets Act.[51] The Right to Information Act, in turn, however, contains inbuilt exceptions, including a series of security-based ones, which the government can invoke to deny information.[52] The Supreme Court's right to information jurisprudence would suggest that great deference will be accorded to the government in security-based exceptions, while holding it to a high standard in other cases.

Democracy, the Freedom of Speech, and Parliamentary Privileges

Although the Court has repeatedly held that democracy, responsive government, and the freedom of political information constitute the central meaning of Article 19(1)(a), these ideas run into a significant hurdle in the form of parliamentary privileges. A full exposition of the doctrine of parliamentary privileges shall take us far beyond the scope of this book.[53] Suffice it to say that under Article 105 (and its analogous provision for the states, Article 194), absolute freedom of speech is guaranteed in Parliament, and no member may be held liable in court for anything said or published in the course of parliamentary proceedings.[54] The original constitutional text[55] also stipulated that the 'powers, privileges and immunities' of the House would be the same as those enjoyed by the House of Commons at the time of the commencement of the Constitution. In *M.S.M. Sharma* v. *Sri Krishna Sinha*, the Supreme Court entered into a detailed historical analysis of the House of Commons (much of it relating to pre-democratic times), and held that the power to prohibit reporting of proceedings was a privilege enjoyed by the House of Commons. The Court then held that when this privilege clashed with the freedom of speech under Article 19(1)(a), in the interests of 'harmonious construction',

---

[51] Section 22, Right to Information Act, 2005.
[52] Section 8, Right to Information Act, 2005.
[53] See Seervai (2005: 2156–204).
[54] Articles 105(1) and (2), Constitution of India.
[55] Subsequently amended, but without affecting the nature of this argument.

Article 19(1)(a) would have to give way.[56] Consequently, Parliament could prohibit, if it so desired, even fair and accurate reporting of proceedings by the press, or any other person.

Readers will immediately note that harmoniously construing Articles 19(1)(a) and 105/194 need not have led to the Court's result. As Justice Subba Rao pointed out in his dissenting opinion, an equally legitimate reconciliation of the conflicting provisions would be that the Parliament would retain all its privileges and immunities *except insofar as they were in conflict with fundamental rights*.[57] In fact, the first two clauses of Articles 105 and 194, which confer an absolute right to free speech, thus contravening Article 19(2), suggest that where the framers wished to subordinate fundamental rights to parliamentary privileges, they expressly did so.[58] In any event, it is very difficult to see how principles of republican democracy are consistent with secrecy of parliamentary proceedings (except, arguably, in a narrow set of cases dealing with public emergencies or national security).

Under Article 361A of the Constitution, introduced via the Forty-Fourth Amendment, nobody may be subjected to civil or criminal liability for a 'substantially true' report of parliamentary proceedings, unless it is proved that the publication was made with malice.[59] Nonetheless this would not affect the *M.S.M. Sharma* position, that is, that the Parliament retains the privilege to *prohibit* publication of its proceedings, and punish for contempt in case of a breach. But while *M.S.M. Sharma* was subsequently referred to with approval by the Supreme Court in *P.V. Narasimha Rao v. State*,[60] it is arguable that the Supreme Court's focus on the importance of the political process in the context of Article 19(1)(a) over the last decade, in the context of its election cases, might mark the beginning of the erosion of this position.

---

[56] *M.S.M. Sharma v. Sri Krishna Sinha*, AIR 1959 SC 395, para 37 (hereinafter *M.S.M Sharma*). This is known as the 'Searchlight' case.

[57] *M.S.M Sharma*, para 57 (Dissenting opinion of Subba Rao J.).

[58] A point made by the Court in *In the matter of: Under Article 143 of the Constitution of India*, AIR 1965 SC 745 (Keshav Singh's case), but not taken to its logical conclusion.

[59] Article 361A, Constitution of India.

[60] *P.V. Narasimha Rao v. State*, AIR 1998 SC 2120.

In a fascinating essay, however, Shivprasad Swaminathan argues that *M.S.M. Sharma* is no longer good law—in light of the Forty-Second and Forty-Fourth Amendments, which *reversed* the hierarchy between Articles 105/194 and 19(1)(a).[61] According to Swaminathan, *M.S.M. Sharma's* principle of harmonious construction rested upon the premise that Articles 19(1)(a) and 105/194 were of equal constitutional weight. Whatever the validity of that claim in 1959, when *M.S.M. Sharma* was decided, Indira Gandhi's Emergency saw the passage of the Forty-Second Amendment, which *replaced* the existing Articles 105/194, with new provisions expanding the scope of privileges to those that the Parliament or legislatures '*might evolve from time to time* [emphasis mine]'. The Forty-fourth Amendment, aimed at rolling back much of the gross overreach that characterized the Emergency, also undid the changes made to Articles 105/194, and restored them to their original wording, with one change: the scope of parliamentary privileges was to be reckoned not by reference to the House of Commons at the time of the commencement of the Constitution, but to the position *immediately* before the coming into force of the Forty-Fourth Amendment.

Swaminathan contends that after the Forty-Second—and then the Forty-Fourth Amendments, the status of Articles 105/194 changed from being part of the original Constitution, to being introduced into the Constitution *via* an amendment. And *unlike* the original Constitution, all amendments are subject to the basic structure doctrine.[62] Articles 14, 19, and 21 are part of the basic structure.[63] Consequently, notwithstanding *M.S.M. Sharma*, the basic structure applies to Articles 105/194, and renders them subject to the freedom of speech and expression under Article 19(1)(a).

Swaminathan's ingenious argument rests upon grounding *Article 19(1)(a)* within the basic structure, which is a difficult task. Notwithstanding *I.R. Coelho*'s observations about Articles 14, 19,

---

[61] Swaminathan (2010).
[62] *Kesavananda Bharati.*
[63] *I.R. Coelho v. State of Tamil Nadu*, AIR 2007 SC 861 (hereinafter *I.R. Coelho*).

and 21 being part of the basic structure, courts have refrained from according basic structure status to specific, concrete constitutional provisions. What courts *have* held, of course, is that republican democracy is part of the basic structure.[64] And what we have seen in the courts' judgments about elections and the right to information is an understanding that one *aspect* of 19(1)(a) is essential to the republican–democratic project: that is, freedom of political speech, and politically expressive action. Publication of parliamentary proceedings falls as much within *this* ambit of 19(1)(a) as does voting. Consequently, Swaminathan's argument may be slightly modified: Articles 105/194 are subject to the basic structure. Freedom of political speech *as an aspect of Article 19(1)(a)* is part of the basic structure. Consequently, the freedom to publish parliamentary proceedings, which falls within the basic-structure aspect of Article 19(1)(a), overrides parliamentary privileges under Articles 105/194.

OTHER EXPRESSIVE ACTIVITIES

While voting is not speech, we have seen strong reasons, grounded in 19(1)(a) jurisprudence, for why—as politically expressive conduct—it ought to be constitutionally protected. Matters become somewhat more knotty, though, once we move beyond the realm of the directly political. In *Union of India* v. *Naveen Jindal*, for example, the Court held that flying the national flag (as long as it was done with 'respect' and 'dignity', and subject to the provisions of the Emblems and Names (Prevention of Improper Use) Act, 1950 and Prevention of Insults to National Honour Act, 1971) was a form of protected expression under Article 19(1)(a).[65]

Flying the flag is certainly a couple of steps removed from voting in its centrality to the democratic process, but arguably, it too is politically expressive conduct (the Court certainly understood it as such, referring repeatedly to patriotism, national sentiment, and the like).

---

[64] *Kesavananda Bharati; Indira Nehru Gandhi.*
[65] *Union of India* v. *Naveen Jindal*, (2004) 2 SCC 510: AIR 2004 SC 1559.

In *NALSA* v. *Union of India*, however, a case about the rights of the transgender community, decided by the Court in early 2014, it was held:

Article 19(1)(a) of the Constitution states that all citizens shall have the right to freedom of speech and expression, *which includes one's right to expression of his self-identified gender.* Self-identified gender can be expressed through dress, words, action or behavior or any other form. No restriction can be placed on one's personal appearance or choice of dressing, subject to the restrictions contained in Article 19(2) of the Constitution....*Principles referred to above clearly indicate that the freedom of expression guaranteed under Article 19(1)(a) includes the freedom to express one's chosen gender identity through varied ways and means by way of expression, speech, mannerism, clothing etc....Gender identity, therefore, lies at the core of one's personal identity, gender expression and presentation and, therefore, it will have to be protected under Article 19(1)(a) of the Constitution of India.* A transgender's personality could be expressed by the transgender's behavior and presentation. State cannot prohibit, restrict or interfere with a transgender's expression of such personality, which reflects that inherent personality.[66]

This raises a conundrum. If expressing one's gender identity through certain ways of dressing is a 19(1)(a) freedom, then it is difficult to see what expressive conduct is *not* protected by 19(1)(a). I might consider my daily game of football central to expressing my identity, but surely I cannot claim a 19(1)(a) freedom to play football. At the same time, it is easy to see where the Court is coming from. Dress and mannerisms have been the sites of historic discrimination and violence against the transgendered community. In fact, often, it is because of discrimination and violence that certain forms of clothing or mannerisms become definitive of a group's identity. There is, in such cases, a double reason to protect them: to combat violence and to protect vulnerable identities.

How then do we interpret 19(1)(a) to include expressive conduct such as that which was at stake in *NALSA*, while ensuring that it does not—*à la* Article 21—become a multipurpose, boundlessly wide,

---

[66] *NALSA* v. *Union of India*, (2014) 5 SCC 438, para 66; emphasis mine.

empty vessel? There are two ways to move towards a disciplined and principled interpretation. The first is a clear understanding of what constitutes expressive conduct falling within Article 19(1)(a). If Robert Post is right that democratic legitimacy depends upon the free and unhindered flow of information in the public sphere, then here is one possibility: expressive conduct is to be understood as that which is both subjectively intended—and will objectively be understood—to be a contribution to the public discourse.[67] This explains why, for example, we do not consider regulating doctor–patient communications, consumer protection laws, or prohibitions upon insider trading, as raising free speech concerns. While being 'speech' in its ordinary sense, a doctor–patient communication is not intended to be—and nor is it taken to be— any kind of communicative contribution to the public sphere.

Of course, much depends upon the understanding of 'public discourse' and 'public sphere', and it is impossible to spell out an iron-clad definition. In cases like *NALSA*, however, where dress/mannerisms have acquired a social meaning that is definitive of a discrete and identifiable group's identity and way of life, public expression of such identity is evidently a contribution to the public discourse in a way that playing football is not. The advantage with this approach is its flexibility. Social meanings are in a constant process of interrogation, negotiation, and contestation by the groups and individuals who create and recreate them at any given time (it could be that at some point, football does become—and come to be recognized—as publicly expressive of someone's identity). The flip side, of course, is that it vests substantial discretion in the hands of the courts.

Second, not every regulation of expressive conduct constitutes a 19(1)(a) abridgment. American courts conceptualize this issue by asking whether a regulation is directed at the *expressive* part of the conduct (in which case, it is a free speech issue), or whether at the non-expressive part.[68] To take a crude example: my burning down a house to express my endorsement of anarchism is prohibited not

---

[67] Post (1995).
[68] *United States* v. *O'Brien*, 391 U.S. 367 (1968).

because of the government's hostility towards the political philosophy of anarchism (the expressive content of my act), but because of the government's legitimate interest in preventing arson and ensuring public safety (which is unconnected to the *ideas* of anarchism). Of course, the line is not a crystal-clear one, and often time/place/manner or other ostensibly content-neutral regulations of speech turn out—on further interrogation—to be motivated by governmental hostility towards ideas, or the communicative content of an expressive act. That enquiry, ultimately, is for the courts to make.

* * *

The crucial point to take away from our reading of the cases on commercial speech, voting, and other forms of symbolic expression is that ultimately, what should matter for the threshold enquiry of whether something is protected by 19(1)(a) is not whether it constitutes 'speech', in some intuitive sense, but whether—objectively speaking— it is a communicative contribution to the public sphere, or to social discourse. This line helps us understand why we consider direct, speech-based regulation in the context of the doctor–patient relationship, insider trading, and consumer protection laws as raising no free speech issues at all. At the same time, it also helps us to understand why we do think that flying a flag, or expressing one's beleaguered identity through clothes and mannerisms—conduct that has nothing to do with speaking—*does* raise 19(1)(a) concerns.

With *NALSA*, the Supreme Court has opened up a fascinating set of free speech issues that revolve around the regulation of expressive conduct that, as we can see, is often every bit as central to a system of freedom of speech and expression as 'speech' itself. What direction the jurisprudence will now take is an open question.

CHAPTER ELEVEN

The Meaning of 'Freedom'

Free Speech and Economic Structure

W hen we think of the freedom of speech, we often imagine the lonely orator speaking to the hostile crowd, or the dissident artist who sees her book banned or her film censored, or even the intrepid journalist whose investigative work is threatened by hostile governments or corporations. We think of the State—or other powerful actors—gagging expression that they find uncomfortable or dangerous. Amidst all this, one point stands unexamined: speech today is no longer (if it ever was!) about standing up in a park and holding forth to a massed crowd. Speech today is *mediated* by an entire infrastructure that comprises of newspapers, television, the Internet, and so on. To 'speak' in any meaningful way requires access to this infrastructure (which often means access to the gatekeepers who control it—that is, newspaper editors, television channels, and others). Access is invariably determined, or at least influenced, by the prevailing economic and social arrangements in society. Consequently, questions of free speech and questions of social and economic justice are inextricably bound up with each other. It is here that some of the most fascinating questions arise under free speech law.

SAKAL PAPERS RE-EXAMINED

Recall *Sakal Papers* v. *Union of India*,[1] which we had discussed at the very beginning of this book. The government issued price-per-page regulations that tied the price of a newspaper to its size. To maintain lower prices, the newspapers would have to reduce their size (and, thereby, content), and vice versa. The government also regulated Sunday supplements, and the amount of permissible advertising. The newspapers raised a 19(1)(a) challenge. The government countered by characterizing its measures as anti-monopolistic, aiming to counter the economies of scale that allowed established newspapers to keep their prices so low that they effectively blocked the entry of other newspapers into the market.[2] The Court, in turn, characterized this measure as a 'public interest' regulation, found that Article 19(2) did not allow for restricting free speech in the general interests of the public, and upheld the claims of the newspapers by striking down the regulations.[3]

Here is the conundrum. In the circumstances of *Sakal*, if an individual wished to establish a newspaper, the prevailing economic climate (specifically, the low prices in the existing market acting as a barrier to new ventures which did not have the benefit of economies of scale) made it impossible—or at least, prohibitively expensive—for her to do so. The State's regulations were simply facilitating her in *her* attempt to speak, through the establishment of a newspaper. Why, therefore, did the Court regard this as a clash between the freedom of speech of the established newspapers and the interests of the general public, instead of between the freedom of speech of the established newspapers, *and the freedom of speech of aspiring new entrants into the newspaper market*?

The answer lies in the meaning of the word 'freedom'. Consider the following example. My bone structure and physiology dictates that I cannot fly unaided. Yet there is something odd in my saying that

---

[1] [1962] 3 SCR 842 (hereinafter *Sakal Papers*).

[2] *Sakal Papers*, para 11–16.

[3] *Sakal Papers*, para 40.

my *freedom* is restricted because of my inability to fly, or that 'I am not *free* to fly' (the more intuitively correct usage is 'I am *unable* to fly'). On the other hand, if somebody has imprisoned me, we can say with perfect propriety that my *freedom* to go out has been curtailed. In ordinary language, we seem to draw a distinction between *inability* and *unfreedom*.[4]

Let us draw the distinction in another way. There is a difference between an *interference* with freedom, and a *background condition* under which freedom is to be exercised. The distinction depends upon a choice of baseline, or an understanding of what is normal in the world. My being imprisoned amounts to an interference with my freedom because we imagine a world in which everyone is—speaking generally—'free' to move around as they wish. On the other hand, perhaps because we do not yet have a world of regularized genetic modifications, we take our bone and body structure (that constrain our ability to fly) not as a limitation upon our freedom, but simply as part of the world that we take as we find, and within whose existing framework we exercise our freedom. Notice that both cases involve a *constraint* upon our activities, but we characterize that constraint differently, depending upon how we characterize our world and our expectations of it. Therefore, we need a coherent principle that allows us to distinguish between unfreedom and inability, between interferences with freedom and background conditions that define and shape it.

The philosopher Friedrich Hayek understood the distinction to be grounded in whether or not a particular state of affairs that constrained my activity was brought about through *intentional human agency*. Hayek defined freedom as the absence of coercion, and coercion as control by the 'arbitrary will of another'.[5] Being free was to act in accordance with one's own decisions and plans. Crucially, Hayek argued that what choices were *actually* open to an individual around which to shape her decisions and plans had nothing to do with freedom. The only question was whether one could 'expect to shape his

---

[4] This argument broadly tracks points made by the philosopher G.A. Cohen, throughout his writings (Cohen 2011, 1983).

[5] Hayek (1978: 12).

course of action in accordance with his present intentions, or whether *somebody else* has power so to manipulate the conditions as to make him act according to that person's will'.[6] And the only refuge from some persons being at the mercy of the arbitrary will of others was to construct a legal system that was limited to a set of abstract, general, and impersonal rules, so that 'in most instances an individual need never be coerced unless he has placed himself in a position where he knows he will be coerced'.[7]

In the economic sphere, this naturally meant an unregulated marketplace, subject to impersonal and general market forces, and free from government tinkering. Only in such an environment could people be truly 'free' to plan their affairs without coercion. Of course, some might use the absence of regulation to 'alter the social landscape' in such a way that 'the alternatives before me may [become] distressingly few and uncertain'[8] (think of the options before a factory worker in nineteenth-century industrial Europe or twenty-first-century India). Hayek, however, saw nothing wrong with that, because that was simply a function of market forces, as opposed to coercion:

> ...even if the threat of starvation to me and perhaps to my family impels me to accept a distasteful job at a very low wage...I am not coerced... so long as the act that has placed me in my predicament is not aimed at making me do or not do specific things, *so long as the intent of the act that harms me is not to make me serve another person's ends, its effect on my freedom is not different from that of any natural calamity.*[9]

Thus, for Hayek, my impoverishment in an unregulated marketplace is just the same as being trapped by an avalanche or a flood. None of those situations involves 'coercion', properly understood, and so freedom remains unaffected. We are now in a position to understand the relevance of this worldview to *Sakal Papers*. The aspiring newspapers cannot argue that their exclusion from the marketplace is a constraint

---

[6] Hayek (1978: 13); emphasis mine.
[7] Hayek (1978: 21).
[8] Hayek (1978: 137).
[9] Hayek (1978: 137); emphasis mine.

upon their freedom because the economic impact of the marketplace is just like a 'natural calamity'. In other words, market exclusion is analogous to my inability to fly (as opposed to my being imprisoned). The market is to be understood as a background condition under which freedom is exercised, and not an interference with it. On the other hand, government *intervention* in the market by imposing regulations upon the newspapers *is* an example of direct coercion, and raises issues of freedom.

Are Hayek's arguments convincing? Intuitively, a market and an avalanche seem entirely dissimilar. It is important to remember that the market does not exist as a free-floating, abstract entity. On the contrary, it is created and maintained, shaped and structured, by human agency. It is the legal system, with its arrangement of rights, duties, powers, and privileges, which constructs the form of the market. After that, it is individual action that determines the positions occupied by actors within it. How, then, is it possible to argue that the impact of the marketplace upon my life is not determined by human action?

Hayek's response was to argue that while individual action (and an aggregation of individual actions) is relevant to the workings of the market and its impact upon people's lives, none of those acts are *specifically aimed or intended* to make anyone do or abstain from doing something ('coercion'). The market, on the other hand, is a 'spontaneous order'.[10] The entire argument, therefore, is based upon the perceived moral difference between an act that is 'aimed' at a particular outcome, and an act that achieves that outcome without 'aiming' directly at it. If I put a gun to your head and order you to do work for me, then—evidently—I 'aim' at making you work for me (and this is coercion). But if I exploit a depressed wage market and a legal system that consciously has no provisions for a minimum wage to offer you employment on subsistence terms that I *know* you have no realistic choice but to accept, I do not coerce you.

Even if we accept the difference in terminology, is there a genuinely significant *moral* difference in the situations? Remember that

[10] See, for example, Hayek (1991).

in our society, the environment that we grow up in (for example, the presence or absence of State-sponsored free primary education), the opportunities that are open to us (for example, the availability of roads and public transport for those living in remote areas), and so on, are not really determined by *active* human agency in the Hayekian sense. To exclude that from moral consideration—or to use terminological arguments to claim that none of this is about our 'freedom', properly called—seems to ignore reality.

In any case, even if we find Hayek's arguments persuasive in the abstract, it is rather clear that the Indian Constitution is not committed to this vision of society and the marketplace. *Contra* Hayek, who rejects State regulation of the market, both the Constituent Assembly Debates (especially the ones over landowning and property) as well as the Constitution itself (especially Article 31A and the Ninth Schedule) are definitive on the point that one guiding constitutional principle was precisely to *reverse* the iniquitous economic relations that had come about through force and fraud during a long period of colonial rule. Hayekian freedom, therefore, is an incorrect lens with which to approach Article 19(1)(a), or the decision in *Sakal*.

What other reasons might be invoked to justify *Sakal's* narrow understanding of 'freedoms'? Consider the following three possible arguments. First, liberal philosophers such as Berlin and Rawls—as we discussed in the last chapter—draw a distinction between 'freedom' and the 'value of freedom'. According to Berlin, for instance, 'if a man is too poor or too ignorant or too feeble to make use of his legal rights, the liberty that these rights confer upon him is nothing to him, but it is not thereby annihilated'.[11] Thus, the aspiring newspapers in *Sakal* were unable to meaningfully exercise their freedom of expression. It was of no worth to them. But the *freedom* still existed, and therefore, while the *status quo* raised serious concerns about social and economic justice, it still did not infringe upon their freedom of speech or expression. Since Article 19(1)(a) protects the *freedom* of speech and expression, and not *effective exercise* of the freedom of speech and expression, there was no constitutional violation.

[11] Berlin (1969: liiii).

If we set aside—again—the fine terminological distinctions, the basic question boils down to whether, if we understand freedom as the absence of interference by others, the absence of money qualifies as a lack of freedom. The philosopher G.A. Cohen argues that it does.[12] Money, according to Cohen, 'structures' freedom. If, for instance, I want to get from place X to place Y by train, I will need to pay for the ticket. If I do not pay and still board the train, I shall be apprehended and physically removed under sanction of law. Thus, without money, I shall be subject to actual interference by other persons that will prevent me from accessing what I could otherwise have accessed *with* the money. Or, to put it another way, money removes an interference that would otherwise have been placed upon my actions. In this way, via interference in one's action by law enforcement officials, Cohen makes the link between not having money to use the train, and not being *free* to go from place X to place Y. Hence, he argues:

> ...*money confers freedom*, rather than merely the ability to use it, even if freedom is equated with absence of interference.[13]

Even if Cohen is wrong in equating the lack of money to unfreedom, there is a further question that the Rawls/Berlin formulation pushes us to ask: is there any point of guaranteeing liberties without also guaranteeing their value to the rights-bearers? More concretely, does the freedom of expression imply an ancillary right of reasonable access, even if access is not an issue of 'freedom', strictly defined? The election cases, which we discussed in the previous chapter, answer the question in the affirmative. Recall that in those cases, the Court essentially held that the freedom to vote (an aspect of the freedom of expression) was effectively meaningless without secret ballots or disclosure requirements. The Court was protecting not merely the formally defined scope of the *right*, but all that went into making it meaningful—or, to put it another way, all that justified the existence of the right in the first place.[14]

---

[12] Cohen (2011: 166); see also Cohen (1983).

[13] Cohen (2011: 178); emphasis mine.

[14] See Chapter Ten.

Let us now consider a third argument justifying the decision in *Sakal Papers*. Every legal system must, as a matter of course, settle upon an initial distribution of liberties that protect some freedoms—and the freedom of some—at the cost of others. This is entailed in the very concept of a coercive legal system. For instance, my right to physical security excludes your freedom to assault me at will. Similarly, enshrining the right to private property in the legal system confers upon property holders the freedom to use and dispose off their property according to their choice, and *in doing so*, excludes the freedom of everyone else to trespass or in any other way use that property without the holder's permission. Private enjoyment necessarily excludes common use. The freedom of speech, too, is subject to these initial distributional decisions. According to the logic of *Sakal*, freedom of speech and expression is *actually* freedom of speech and expression *under prevailing market conditions and economic arrangements*. Thus, the government is prohibited from intervening into the market with the objective of changing (or, redistributing) the initial arrangements that determine the scope of everyone's freedom.[15]

But there seem to be no good reasons, in philosophy or in constitutional law, to justify this definition of the freedom of speech. Whatever the desirability of governmental intervention into the market, it is agreed, at least, that the government is *entitled* to do so. Indeed, certain observations of the Supreme Court cut in precisely the opposite direction. In *Cricket Association of Bengal*, a case about broadcast frequencies, the Court noted:

> It is true that to own a frequency for the purposes of broadcasting is a costly affair and even when there are surplus or unlimited frequencies, *only the affluent few will own them* and will be in a position to use it to subserve their own interest by manipulating news and views. *That also poses a danger to the freedom of speech and expression of the have-nots by denying them the truthful information on all sides of an issue which is so necessary to form a sound view on any subject.*[16]

---

[15] See, generally, Sunstein (1998).

[16] *Secretary, Ministry of Information and Broadcasting* v. *Cricket Association of Bengal*, (1995) 2 SCC 161, para 17 (hereinafter *Cricket Association of Bengal*); emphasis mine.

Consider these observations in light of the Courts' repeated insistence that free speech is about sustaining democracy, and the further point that democracy depends upon the free flow of information from 'diverse and antagonistic sources'.[17] Consider them also in light of the Dworkinian idea that every person ought to have an equal opportunity to shape the moral, social, and cultural environment of society.[18] These provide us with strong reasons to reject reading the right to free speech as a right operating within the (untouchable) contours of prevailing market conditions, and places issues of social justice squarely within the domain of free speech.

Interestingly, in *Cricket Association of Bengal*, the Court also distinguished broadcast media from print media in the context of governmental control over the former and the prevalence of market forces for the latter. This takes us to the last point about *Sakal Papers*: in that case, even if there was interference with the freedom of speech, it was by private entities using market conditions, *not* by the government. Conceptually, however, this ignores the basic fact that the structure of the market, far from existing in a vacuum (as we have already pointed out before) is *constituted* by the government through its legal system. The market is not free of human—and, in particular, governmental—agency, like my inability to fly is, which depends entirely on my physiology, and has nothing to do with any human act. Hence, if the unfreedom of aspiring newspapers is attributable to market conditions, then—given that the market is a creature of the legal system—it is, at the very least, indirectly attributable to the government itself. And this, in turn, makes it at least *permissible*, for the government to ameliorate the situation, if not obligatory. As the free speech scholar, Owen Fiss puts the point, sometimes 'the state may have to act to further the robustness of public debate in circumstances where *powers outside the state are stifling speech*. It may have to allocate public resources—hand out megaphones—to those whose voices would not otherwise be heard

---

[17] *Red Lion* v. *FCC*, 395 U.S. 367 (1969) (hereinafter *Red Lion*).
[18] See Chapter One.

in the public square. It may even have to silence the voices of some in order to hear the voices of the others.'[19]

None of this should be taken to suggest that *Sakal Papers* was wrongly decided. Certainly, the impugned law restricted the freedom of established newspapers, and it would take a balancing exercise of some ingenuity to decide upon the ultimate validity of the law. What is important to note, however, is that the Court's decision rested upon a whole host of political and philosophical assumptions about the meaning of 'freedom'. I have tried to argue that these assumptions are ill-founded, and that the Court was incorrect in classifying the issue as free speech versus public interest, and dismissing it out of hand. Issues of market exclusion and equitable access to the infrastructure of speech centrally impact the freedom of speech and expression, and any system of free expression must take them into account. *Sakal Papers* was about the government abridging the freedom of speech of some (by direct regulation) to facilitate the freedom of speech of others (who had been excluded by the operation of a legally-constituted, legally-enforced market). That is the framework within which it ought to have been examined.[20]

'ABRIDGE'

The Supreme Court's decision in *Express Newspapers* v. *Union of India*, three years before *Sakal Papers*, presents an interesting contrast. *Express Newspapers* involved a challenge to the statutorily determined minimum wage that had to be paid to all working journalists. It was argued that the minimum wage had been pegged so high that it would drive newspapers out of business. After examining American cases such as *Grosjean* to derive the proposition that the press was subject— like every other entity—to general policies of taxation and labour welfare, the Court noted:

---

[19] Fiss (1998: 4); emphasis mine.
[20] For similar arguments in a different jurisdiction, see Barron (1967); Emerson (1981); Fiss (1986).

It would certainly not be legitimate to subject the press to laws which *take away* or *abridge* the freedom of speech and expression or which *would curtail circulation and thereby narrow the scope of dissemination of information*, or fetter its freedom to choose its means of exercising the right or would undermine its independence by driving it to seek Government aid. Laws which single out the press for laying upon it excessive and prohibitive burdens which would restrict the circulation, impose a penalty on its right to choose the instruments for its exercise or to seek an alternative media, prevent newspapers from being started and ultimately drive the press to seek Government aid in order to survive, would therefore be struck down as unconstitutional.[21]

In *Express Newspapers*, however, the Court found that neither the intention, nor the 'proximate effect' of the minimum wage was to abridge the freedom of speech—rather, it was about improving the economic lot of journalists.[22] The arguments that the eventual result would be a fall in circulation, or the seeking of State aid, and so on, were dismissed as being incidental, remote, neither direct nor inevitable, and dependent upon a number of contingent factors.[23] Hence, the regulations were upheld.

How do we distinguish between *Express Newspapers* and *Sakal Papers*? In one, the Court holds that the relationship between a fixed minimum wage and a drop in circulation is not 'proximate', while holding in the other that the one between a price-per-page policy and circulation *is* proximate. In one, the Court decides that improving labour conditions is constitutionally permissible (even though the result might be a fall in circulation), whereas in the other it decides that opening up the market is constitutionally suspect (even though the result would be exactly the same). Adverse market impact because of decreased revenue from advertisements (*Sakal*) is treated as an impediment upon the freedom of speech, but adverse market impact because of diverted financial resources to paying journalists (*Express Newspapers*) is not. Why?

---

[21] *Express Newspapers Pvt Ltd v. Union of India*, AIR 1958 SC 578, para 150 (hereinafter *Express Newspapers*); emphasis mine.
[22] *Express Newspapers*, para 161.
[23] *Express Newspapers*, para 160.

As we argued previously, the difference cannot turn upon mere statistical likelihood. No evidence is available to show that a price-per-page or regulated advertisement policy has a greater chance of impacting circulation than a minimum wage. Thus, much like our discussion in the public order cases, the language of 'proximity' and 'remoteness' used by the Court in *Express Newspapers* contains an inbuilt set of moral assumptions about the meaning of 'direct impact', 'external factors', and so on. Once again, we are led back to Cohen's argument. 'Freedom' is not a neutral word, referring simply to facts about people's ability to do things, and other people's interference with that ability, but about a set of political and moral choices. Judicial decisions, in turn, endorse one set of political choices about what 'freedom' is, and reject another. In *Sakal Papers*, the Court treated the governmental intervention into the existing market as an interference with freedom. In *Express Newspapers* (more recently affirmed in *Express Publications* v. *Union of India*[24] and *ABP Pvt. Ltd.* v. *Union of India*[25]), it treated intervention in the form of labour legislation simply as a background condition under which freedom is exercised (much like my physiology is a background condition determining whether or not I can fly). These political choices are masked by value-neutral words such as 'proximity', 'remoteness', and 'intent and effect'—which is the test that the law officially subscribes to—but ultimately, it is those choices that must be interrogated.

The decision in *Express Newspapers* can be contrasted, in turn, with the famous case of *Bennett Coleman* v. *Union of India*.[26] *Bennett Coleman* involved a challenge to the Newsprint Order of 1962, and the Newsprint Policy of 1972. The Newsprint Order restricted the conditions under which newsprint could be imported. Newspapers could only be published using newsprint—think of it, in today's conditions, as a rationing of broadband. The Newsprint Policy prohibited 'common ownership units' from starting newspapers, limited the number of pages to ten, but also permitted a 20 per cent increase in page level to newspapers that had fewer than ten pages.

---

[24] *Express Publications (Madurai) Ltd* v. *Union of India*, (2004) 11 SCC 526.
[25] AIR 2014 SC 1228.
[26] (1972) 2 SCC 788: [1973] 2 SCR 757 (hereinafter *Bennett Coleman*).

While the Court found that it did not need to decide upon the constitutionality of the Newsprint Order,[27] the Policy, on the other hand, was defended on *Sakal Papers* grounds (preventing monopolies, promoting the growth of small newspapers) and struck down for the same reasons (that an effect on circulation, *ex hypothesi*, amounted to a restraint upon the freedom of speech, which was not saved by any 19(2) category).[28] Notice, once again, the assumptions that operate. The availability of newsprint is considered to be a background condition under which freedom is exercised. Restrictions upon newsprint are, therefore, not deemed to be an infringement of freedom. On the other hand, intervention into the existing market in the form of price-and-page controls *is* deemed to affect freedom. As always, the issue is couched in neutral language. In *Bennett Coleman*, the key test was whether the 'direct effect' of a law is to abridge the freedom of speech.[29] Of course, it is obvious the 'direct effect' is not value-neutral: there is nothing to show—considering pure probabilities—that restricting newsprint and curtailing pages have differential effects on content and circulation.

In his dissenting opinion, Justice Mathew made the point clearly by basing his judgment on a distinction between abridging *speech*, and abridging the *freedom of speech*. He argued that the newsprint quota did abridge speech (in the crude, factual sense that if you have less newsprint, you can 'speak' less), but not the *freedom of speech*.[30] This drives home the basic argument—once more—that 'freedom' depends upon prior political values that have been chosen, and endorsed, by a particular legal system. 'Human agency' as the distinguishing factor does not, in itself, answer the question. In *Bennett Coleman*, for instance, the scarcity of newsprint (which, at the time, used to be imported from abroad) depended as much upon governmental action (in particular, budgetary priorities) as did an imposed restriction on the number of pages a newspaper could have. What is needed is a *principle* that draws the line between what counts as an infringement

---

27 *Bennett Coleman*, para 86.

28 *Bennett Coleman*, para 75.

29 *Bennett Coleman*, para 39.

30 *Bennett Coleman*, para 103 (dissenting opinion of Mathew J.).

upon freedom, and what counts as a background condition under which freedom is to be exercised.

One plausible attempt was made in *Indian Express Newspapers* v. *Union of India*.[31] That case involved a challenge to an import duty placed upon newsprint. The Court distinguished between *general* taxes or duties that placed upon newspapers a burden similar to that placed upon other individuals or businesses in a similar position, and those that placed a fiscal burden *over and above* such contribution. *Indian Express Newspapers* partially upheld the claims of the newspapers, directing the government to reconsider its levy.[32] On a combined reading of these five newspaper cases, perhaps this is the lesson to be drawn: the 'direct effect' test is an attempt by the Court to distinguish between interferences and background conditions. Two background conditions seem to be an unregulated marketplace and *general* legislative provisions dealing with taxation and labour, applicable across the board. Anything else is a potential infringement. Whether this gives us a coherent *principle* to distinguish between the two remains, at best, unclear.

BENNETT COLEMAN: JUSTICE MATHEW'S DISSENT

Justice Mathew's dissenting opinion in *Bennett Coleman* represents the line of argument rejected in *Sakal Papers* and by the majority in *Bennett Coleman*, and illustrates the choices before the Court. The crucial difference lies in the treatment of the Newsprint Policy. While the majority took the existing market conditions as given, as an immutable background feature of the environment, and examined the Policy as a governmentally imposed departure from the market, Mathew J. treated the market itself as constituted by government policy. Analysing it from a historical perspective, he found that before the 1972 Policy, allocation of newsprint was based on the average page level of 1957, and circulation levels of 1962. As a factual matter,

---

[31] *Indian Express Newspapers (Bombay) Pvt Ltd* v. *Union of India*, (1985) 1 SCC 641: [1985] 2 SCR 287 (hereinafter *Indian Express Newspapers*).

[32] *Indian Express Newspapers*, para 110.

the disadvantaged newspapers were (mostly) established after 1962, and it was to remedy this disadvantage that the 1972 Policy had been drafted.[33] In other words, Mathew J. understood that it is futile to speak of governmental policy as a 'departure' from the existing market because invariably, the shape and form that the market takes at any given point is *itself* the result of past human decisions, often consciously directed towards shaping it that way.

In the context of this history, Mathew J. then discussed the philosophical underpinnings of free speech. Echoing agreement with the general judicial view expressed in *Sakal Papers* that the basic function of free speech was to sustain and maintain democracy, Mathew J., however, arrived at a different conclusion. For democracy to be meaningful, he observed, there must be a multiplicity and a diverse variety of ideas, viewpoints, and arguments available to the public, in order to achieve the ideal of the informed, aware electorate.[34] He then observed:

> It is no use having a right to express your idea, unless you have got a medium for expressing it.[35]

Much depends, of course, on the meaning of the phrase 'no use'. There are two ways to read it. One is an endorsement of the Cohen view, that the very meaning of freedom includes (economically determined) access to the infrastructure that constitutes that freedom. The other is an acceptance of the Berlin/Rawls distinction between a right/ freedom and the worth/value of that freedom, while simultaneously accepting that as far as the *Constitution* goes, it guarantees both the freedom and the fulfilment of the conditions that make it worthwhile or valuable. In either event, regulating market conditions to guarantee access is entirely in line with the requirements of Article 19(1)(a). Therefore, Mathew J. concluded:

> What is…required is an interpretation of Article 19(1)(a) which focuses on the idea that restraining the hand of the government is quite useless

[33] *Bennett Coleman*, para 112 (dissenting opinion of Mathew J.).
[34] *Bennett Coleman*, para 122 (dissenting opinion of Mathew J.).
[35] *Bennett Coleman*, para 123 (dissenting opinion of Mathew J.).

in assuring free speech, *if a restraint on access is effectively secured by private groups.* A Constitutional prohibition against governmental restriction on the expression is effective only if the Constitution *ensures an adequate opportunity for discussion....*Any scheme of distribution of newsprint which would make the freedom of speech a reality by making it [*sic*] possible the dissemination of ideas as news with as many *different facets and colours as possible would not violate the fundamental right of the freedom of speech of the petitioners.* In other words, a scheme for distribution of a commodity like newsprint which will subserve the purpose of free flow of ideas to the market *from as many different sources as possible* would be a step to advance and enrich that freedom. If the scheme of distribution is calculated to *prevent even an oligopoly ruling the market* and thus check the tendency to monopoly in the market, that will not be open to any objection on the ground that the scheme involves a regulation of the press which would amount to an abridgment of the freedom of speech.[36]

Justice Mathew went on to ground this opinion in the Directive Principles of State Policy, which require the State to work for the common good and to ensure that resources are not concentrated in a few hands.[37] With the Directive Principles and American scholars such as Meiklejohn and Emerson in hand, he argued that the freedom of the free speech clause was not merely the freedom of the individual to express herself, but also the freedom of *society* to be informed and have access to a wide range of ideas.[38] Since the Newsprint Policy, in its anti-monopolistic objectives, was aimed at ensuring that such a wide range of ideas was available to the general public, Mathew J. held it to be constitutionally valid.

In Mathew J.'s dissenting opinion, we find a rich and complex substantive vision underlying Article 19(1)(a). On this view, there are three separate—and complementary—political ideals that characterize and justify the free speech clause. First, free speech guarantees the right of the individual person to express herself. Second, it is also the right of the community to hear and to be informed.

[36] *Bennett Coleman*, paras 126–27; emphasis mine.
[37] Article 39, Constitution of India.
[38] *Bennett Coleman*, paras 134–36 (dissenting opinion of Mathew J.).

And third, it is a social good, contributing to a thriving democratic community. Mathew J., however, further deepens each of those ideas. The individual freedom includes not just freedom from State interference, but an ancillary right of reasonable access to the infrastructure of speech, in the teeth of an exclusionary market. The community is not just an aggregation of passive consumers, but—in the tradition of civil republicanism—a set of engaged and active citizens who must have access to a multiplicity of viewpoints in order to effectively exercise their responsibilities of citizenship. And democracy itself is treated as requiring an environment in which the public discourse consists of a *genuinely* rich and diverse set of ideas circulating in the public sphere. Nonetheless, for now, his opinion remains just that: a dissent.

OTHER CASES

It turns out, however, that the view of the majority in *Sakal Papers* and *Bennett Coleman*, treating the unregulated marketplace as an *a priori* background condition within which the right to freedom of speech operates, and not something that may itself be subject to change or modification in the interests of free speech, has been rejected elsewhere. These cases are an interesting foil to the Court's newspaper regulation jurisprudence.

   Union of India v. *Motion Picture Association* involved a challenge to various government notifications and rules, and to provisions of the Cinematograph Act that allowed the government to 'issue directions to…[cinema] licensees that scientific films, films intended for educational purposes, films dealing with news and current events, documentary films or indigenous films *have to* be exhibited by the licensee along with the other films which the licensee is exhibiting.'[39] This, therefore, was a clear case of content-based government-imposed compelled speech. The Court rejected the 19(1)(a) challenge, holding that:

[39] (1999) 6 SCC 150, para 10 (hereinafter *Motion Picture Association*); emphasis mine.

...the best way by which *ideas* can reach this large body of uneducated
people is through the entertainment channel which is watched by all—
literate and illiterate alike. To earmark a small portion of time of this entertainment medium for the purpose of showing scientific, educational
or documentary films, or for showing news films has to be looked at in
this context of *promoting dissemination of ideas, information and knowl-*
edge to the masses so that there may be an informed debate and decision
making on public issues. Clearly, the impugned provisions are designed to
*further free speech and expression and not to curtail it....*In the context of
Article 19(1) what we have to examine is whether the categories of films
so required to be carried promote dissemination of *information and*
education or whether they are meant to be propaganda or false or biased
information. The statute quite clearly specifies the kinds of films which
promote dissemination of knowledge and information.[40]

Notice that the Court does not frame the issue as one of justified
19(2) restrictions on the 19(1)(a) freedom of speech (as it did in
Sakal). Rather, it treats the issue as turning upon 19(1)(a) *itself.* This
is possible because of applying the understanding of free speech not
as an individual right, but as a social good. The goal, according to the
Court, is to ensure an informed debate on public issues. Public access
to ideas, information, and knowledge is meant to serve the purpose of
this informed debate, which is a prerequisite of thriving democracies.

The Court also rejects—expressly—the principle of content neutrality.
The very idea of diversity is opposed to content neutrality, since striving
towards a diversity or multiplicity of views is, by definition, a form of
content regulation. What, however, the Court does seem to subscribe
to is something that we may call *ideological neutrality* (or 'viewpoint
neutrality', as it is labelled in the United States), when it distinguishes
between 'information' and 'propaganda'.[41] Regulation in the interests of
ensuring a diversity of ideas is permissible, as long as it is not designed
to promote an ideology, or one specific point of view on a disputed issue.

Something similar was at stake in the case of *LIC* v. *Manubhai*
D. Shah, decided a few years before *Union of India* v. *Motion Picture*

---

[40] *Motion Picture Association*, para 18; emphasis mine.
[41] Admittedly, a slippery distinction, as scholars like Gramsci have pointed out.

Association. The Respondent had published a paper criticizing certain aspects of LIC's insurance schemes. An LIC officer published a response in *The Hindu,* to which the Respondent countered with a rejoinder, also in *The Hindu.* The LIC officer's piece was published in LIC's in-house magazine as well, but when the Respondent requested his rejoinder be published there, it was rejected. The Court held:

> Such an attitude on the part of the LIC can be described as both unfair and unreasonable; unfair because fairness demanded that both view points were placed before the readers, *however limited be their number, to enable them to draw their own conclusions and unreasonable* because there was no logic or proper justification for refusing publication...the respondent's fundamental right of speech and expression clearly entitled him to insist that his views on the subject should reach those who read the magazine so that they have a complete picture before them and not a one sided or distorted one....[42]

There is a slight error in the Court's reasoning. It is unclear how it could be my *right* that *you* get a balanced picture about something. Abstracting, however, from the specific wording of the judgment, it becomes clear that the Court was endorsing the community goal of ensuring that the public be provided a balanced account of contentious issues. The question of balance—and relatedly, ideological neutrality—is a slippery one. In these relatively straightforward cases involving a direct right of reply, it is easy enough to decipher. In more complex cases, however, it is a far more difficult question.

The most important case in this context remains *Secretary, Ministry of Information and Broadcasting* v. *Cricket Association of Bengal,*[43] which we discussed earlier. Put simply: Section 4 of the 1885 Indian Telegraph Act vested in the government a monopoly over the transmission of airwaves, of maintaining the associated infrastructure, and authorized

---

[42] *LIC* v. *Manubhai D. Shah,* [1992] 3 SCR 595, para 12. Another interesting case is that of *Dainik Sambad* v. *State of Tripura,* AIR 1989 Gau 30, where the Gauhati High Court invalidated the Government of Tripura's advertisement policy, in accordance with which a newspaper critical of government policy would not be allotted government advertisements.

[43] *Cricket Association of Bengal.*

it to issue licences for utilization. The government refused to allow the Cricket Association of Bengal to telecast certain cricket matches. The Board argued that the denial of a licence violated its 19(1)(a) right to broadcast, as well as the viewers' 19(1)(a) right to watch. The government countered by arguing that airwaves were a scarce resource, which it was empowered to selectively distribute for the public good (something similar to the newsprint argument in *Bennett Coleman*). Finding that this argument was incorrect as a matter of fact (there was, as it turned out, no scarcity in the present case), the Court then observed, in a detailed comment, that deserves to be quoted in full:

> There is no doubt that since the airwaves/frequencies are a public property and are also limited, they have to be used in the best interest of the society and this can be done either by a central authority by establishing its own broadcasting network or regulating the grant of licences to other agencies, including the private agencies...the right to use the airwaves and the content of the programmes, therefore, needs regulation for balancing it and as well as *to prevent monopoly of information and views relayed, which is a potential danger flowing from the concentration of the right to broadcast/telecast in the hands either of a central agency or of few private affluent broadcasters. That is why the need to have a central agency representative of all sections of the society free from control both of the Government and the dominant influential sections of the society*...if the right to freedom of speech and expression includes the right to disseminate information to as wide a section of the population as is possible, the access which enables the right to be so exercised is also an integral part of the said right....When, however, there are surplus or unlimited resources and the public interests so demand or in any case do not prevent telecasting, the validity of the argument based on limitation of resources disappears. *It is true that to own a frequency for the purposes of broadcasting is a costly affair and even when there are surplus or unlimited frequencies, only the affluent few will own them and will be in a position to use it to subserve their own interest by manipulating news and views. That also poses a danger to the freedom of speech and expression of the have-nots by denying them the truthful information on all sides of an issue which is so necessary to form a sound view on any subject.* That is why the doctrine of fairness which is evolved in the U.S. in the context of the private broadcasters licensed to share the limited frequencies with the central agency like the FCC to regulate the programming. *But this phenomenon occurs even in the case of the print media of all the countries. Hence the body*

like the Press Council of India which is empowered to enforce, however imperfectly, the right to reply.[44]

Ultimately, the Ministry's arguments were rejected, but what is crucial is the characterization of airwaves as 'public property', and the consequences that follow. Public property and scarcity are two very different things, and independent of each other. The responsibility of the government to use airwaves in a manner that was 'representative of all sections of society' does not stem from their scarce availability, but—as the case demonstrates—their nature as the essential infrastructure of free speech. If we understand the judgment in *Cricket Association of Bengal* in this context, we see that the infrastructure of speech is inextricably linked with the freedom of speech as well, and the control and utilization—of that infrastructure directly raises free speech issues.

These cases finally turn upon the second and third conceptions of free speech that were latent in Justice Mathew's *Bennett Coleman* dissent: free speech as a community right to be informed, and a social good aimed at promoting a rich conception of democracy, based on a thriving public sphere. It is easy enough to see why this is entirely at odds with the unregulated-marketplace viewpoint in *Sakal*, and the *Bennett Coleman* majority opinion. Unregulated marketplaces possess no safeguards against monopolies (in fact, some would argue that they tend towards monopolies), and a monopoly over ideas is something neither a vision of substantive democracy, nor the idea of community rights, can abide. Ultimately, the goal of these justifications is a state of affairs in which there is a variety of ideas accessible in the public domain. The market is an instrument (as opposed to an end in itself) that is used to bring about that state of affairs, often through intervention of regulation.

Reading *Manubhai D. Shah* and *Motion Picture Association* together with *Sakal Papers and Bennett Coleman* reveals the tensions between an (often libertarian-leaning) individual-rights view of free speech, and the social good-cum-community interests ideas of free speech. As

---

[44] *Cricket Association of Bengal*, para 17; emphasis mine.

with most areas of free speech law that we have examined in this book, we find that, ultimately, the jurisprudence is conflicted, and there are many potential paths that the Court could take in the coming years.

TWO APPROACHES TO FREE SPEECH: DISCURSIVE DEMOCRACY AND NOTES FROM THE FIRST AMENDMENT (AND ELSEWHERE)

The relationship between free speech and the market, between a system of free expression and social and economic justice, has raised issues that are not unique to India. For example, the controversy has raged with particular bitterness in the United States, and revolves around two sets of cases: those dealing with campaign finance regulation, and with broadcasting.

Citizens United v. *FEC*[45] and *McCutcheon* v. *FEC*[46] were cases that involved constitutional challenges to the legal regulation of campaign spending. On the assumption that money is speech, these regulations limited corporate and individual speech by placing various caps on different kinds of campaign spending. In *Citizens United*, the free speech rationale advanced by the government was the anti-distortion principle:[47] namely, the '...distorting effects of immense aggregations of wealth....' In rejecting this argument, the Court noted that '...political speech is indispensable to decision-making in a democracy'.[48] It cited *Buckley* v. *Valeo* for the proposition that: '[T]he concept that government may restrict the speech of some elements of our society in order to enhance the relative voice of others is wholly foreign to the First Amendment.'[49] The argument that corporations obtain an unfair advantage in the political marketplace by using funds amassed in the economic marketplace was rejected, again, by invoking *Buckley*. The Court held it impermissible to 'equaliz[e] the relative ability of

[45] 558 U.S. 310 (2010) (hereinafter *Citizens United*).
[46] 572 U.S. ___ (2014) (hereinafter *McCutcheon*).
[47] I bracket the anti-corruption argument.
[48] *Citizens United*.
[49] *Buckley* v. *Valeo*, 424 U.S. 1, 48–49 (1976).

individuals and groups to influence the outcome of elections', and that 'the First Amendment's protections do not depend on the speaker's "financial ability to engage in public discussion"'.[50]

Citizens United ultimately turned upon the Court's opinion that the campaign finance regulations in question were 'interfer[ing] with the open marketplace of ideas', and depriving the electorate of 'information, knowledge and opinion vital to its function'.[51] Similarly, in *McCutcheon*, the Court struck down a system of aggregate limits upon contributions, holding again that 'limiting political speech' was 'impermissible'. It began its First Amendment analysis with a quotation from *Cohen* v. *California*, invoking the spectre of governmental regulation over free speech as the greatest threat to the system of 'individual choice and dignity...upon which our political system rests'.[52] Most notably, the Court observed that the First Amendment was important to both the 'lonely pamphleteer' and to someone who 'spends substantial amounts of money in order to communicate his ideas through sophisticated means'.[53] The plurality also specifically rejected the dissent's argument focusing on the public good involved in preventing the capture of the public sphere by a few moneyed interests, and rejected the corollary that the scope and nature of free speech should be delineated in accordance with its contribution to the 'democratic process'.

The decisions in *Citizens United* and *McCutcheon* demonstrate that the Court's theory of free speech is one that is intentionally insensitive to issues of unequal resources and differential access to the infrastructure of speech. While agreeing that free speech is essential to a democratic process, it understands the connection between the two to be served by an unregulated public sphere solicitous to allowing individual and corporate entities maximal latitude to 'speak' (within the bounds of existing property laws and other legal rules), and *not* by attempting to bring about an end-state in which the public sphere is consciously *structured* so as to bring about a desirable plurality and

---

[50] *Citizens United.*
[51] *McCutcheon.*
[52] *McCutcheon.*
[53] *McCutcheon.*

diversity of ideas and opinions by affirmatively opening up—and regulating—access.

In its broadcasting cases—from a generation earlier—the Court had, however, adopted a very different theory. The case of *Red Lion*,[54] for instance, involved a challenge to the 'fairness doctrine', in accordance with which radio and television broadcasters, while covering 'public issues', were required to give 'each side…[a] fair coverage'[55] (compare with *LIC* v. *Manubhai D. Shah*). This was instantiated through various rules, such as a right of reply in case of personal attacks. The Supreme Court upheld the constitutionality of the fairness doctrine. Its decision had two bases: that broadcasting frequencies were a 'scarce resource', which the government was therefore required to license—and given the First Amendment's aim of *'protecting and furthering communication'*—was consequently authorized to ensure equitable access.[56] The scarcity rationale, however, proves too much: newsprint and paper are also scarce resources, but an analogous access principle for newspapers was expressly rejected in *Miami Herald* v. *Tornillo*.[57] Furthermore, there is no necessary reason why, *after* having chosen to auction off a scarce resource, the government should be able to regulate how the buyers (who presumably have free speech interests of their own) use it. Something more is needed.

This brings us to the second justification for the fairness doctrine. Justice White held that where the regulation of an important medium of communication is concerned, the people have a 'collective right to have the medium function consistently with the ends and purposes of the First Amendment. It is the right of the viewers and listeners, not the right of the broadcasters, which is paramount.'[58] What are these ends and purposes, and the rights of the viewers and listeners? According to Justice White, these are 'to preserve an uninhibited marketplace of ideas in which truth will ultimately prevail, rather than

---

[54] *Red Lion.*
[55] *Red Lion*, p. 369.
[56] *Red Lion*, p. 389.
[57] *Miami Herald* v. *Tornillo*, 418 U.S. 241 (1974).
[58] *Red Lion*, p. 390.

to countenance *monopolization of that market*, whether it be by the Government itself or *a private licensee*…it is the right of the public to receive suitable access to social, political, esthetic, moral, and other ideas and experiences which is crucial here'[59] (notice the similarities with Justice Mathew's dissent). The fairness doctrine was justified in order to prevent:

> station owners and a few networks [from having] unfettered power to make time available only to the highest bidders, to communicate only their own views on public issues, people and candidates, and to permit on the air only those with whom they agreed…[and thus denying] the legitimate claims of those unable without governmental assistance to gain access to those frequencies for expression of their views.[60]

Red Lion, therefore, is a case about structural regulation of access to a resource, a resource that forms part of the infrastructure of speech. *Red Lion* permitted the government to stipulate various conditions as part of its structural regulation, conditions that are consistent with the American Supreme Court's understandings of the First Amendment and of democracy. These understandings, however, are radically at odds with the understanding of the Court in *Citizens United* and *McCutcheon*. As is obvious from the excerpted passages: *McCutcheon* expressly disavows the 'collective interest' in having a public sphere structured so as to achieve a multiplicity of ideas and viewpoints; *Red Lion* affirms that collective interest. *Citizens United* and *McCutcheon* view the First Amendment as requiring government to stay out of the 'marketplace of ideas', whereas *Red Lion* views it as at least permitting—if not requiring—government to intervene and shape the marketplace of ideas to achieve the public good of a thriving and diverse public sphere, which is essential to self-government. And lastly, *Citizens United* and *McCutcheon* view the First Amendment as guaranteeing a right to speakers to be free of governmental regulation, whereas *Red Lion* understands it to guarantee a right to *listeners* as well—a right to be exposed—again—to a diverse marketplace.

[59] *Red Lion*, p. 390; emphasis mine.
[60] *Red Lion*, pp. 392, 400.

In the context of *Sakal Papers* and *Bennett Coleman* versus *LIC v. Manubhai D. Shah*, and *Citizens United* and *McCutcheon* versus *Red Lion*, recall our original discussions about the theories of free speech: the Holmesian view of the marketplace of ideas, and the Meiklejohnian view of democratic self-governance. If, in line with Holmes, we understand the goal of free speech as a quest for truth through a 'marketplace of ideas', then surely the analogy goes further: the idea that social good is achievable through a *laissez-faire*, unregulated marketplace is generally discredited. Governmental regulation of the market to achieve redistributional outcomes, ensure access, and provide goods and services in cases of market failure are all well-accepted even under capitalist theory. A direct market analogy would speak in favour of *Manubhai D. Shah* and *Red Lion*.

To this it may be objected that redistributional policies in the marketplace of goods derive their legitimacy *precisely* because they are the outcome of a free and unfettered exchange of ideas. Free speech, therefore, cannot be regulated in the same way as the economy because it constitutes the politically legitimate basis on which the latter is done. The question of political legitimacy brings us to the democratic-governance theory of free speech.

According to the Meiklejohnian vision, later refined by the likes of Dworkin, Post, and Balkin, free speech is essential to democracy.[61] Put simply, Meiklejohn argued that a thriving democracy needs an informed electorate; the electorate can only make an informed choice if the channels of political communication are kept open, and there is access to all the information that is relevant to making that choice. Dworkin, Post, and Balkin take this basic democratic argument in different directions. Dworkin argues that a democracy is legitimate only because and insofar as it accords equal concern and respect to all its citizens. One way it does that is by according to each an equal opportunity to shape the moral and political environment. Post rests the legitimacy of government upon the 'free circulation of public opinion' (what 'public discourse' is, is defined by contemporaneous

---

[61] See Chapter One.

social understandings). Balkin extends the argument to culture as a whole, defending a vision of 'cultural democracy' that expands the reach of the free speech principle beyond 'public discourse' to a more Dworkin-like understanding that encompasses the moral and cultural environment as a whole.[62]

There is common to this cluster of democratic theories a vision of the public sphere that is fundamentally based on egalitarianism. Democracy is best served by ensuring that as many people as possible get to *contribute* to the circulation of public opinion. Contribution requires access. Consequently, regulation of the infrastructure of speech to ensure access serves the fundamental goals of free speech. Again, as in *Manubhai D. Shah* and in *Red Lion*, there are two interrelated justifications at play: speakers' right to access and—consequently—listeners' right to a discourse that is shaped by a wide and diverse variety of contributions ensured *through* structural regulation of access and gatekeepers.

Theories that link democracy and speech are, at the bottom, united by a vision of democracy that is known as 'discursive democracy', expounded by the German philosopher Jürgen Habermas, which we briefly discussed at the beginning of this book. Habermas takes as his starting point the basic, intuitive idea of *self-legislation*, which has been integral to Western philosophy since Kant: we are only bound by those rules that, in a sense, we give to ourselves. According to Habermas, this translates into the Discourse Principle (D): action norms are legitimate only if they can be freely adopted by everyone, participating in a free and open discourse on equal terms.[63] Two essential conditions of legitimacy, then, are the principles of 'inclusivity' and 'egalitarian reciprocity': a Habermasian discourse forms a meaningful basis of legitimacy only if every participant has an opportunity to introduce any topic into the discourse, and that opportunity is made available on equal terms. A constitutional democracy is legitimate insofar as its institutions and system of rights approximate the ideal

---

[62] See Chapter One.
[63] See Chapter One.

discourse. As we can see, once we translate inclusivity and egalitarian reciprocity into concrete terms, we have justifications for both a right of equalizing access to the infrastructure of speech (egalitarian reciprocity), as well as structuring a discourse to represent all points of view (inclusivity).[64]

IMPLICATIONS

The relevance of the discussion in this chapter should be obvious. Corporate control over the media—exemplified by Reliance's recent takeover of Network 18—is one of the most contentious issues in India today. Corporate control over the media is basically control over the infrastructure of speech, as well as control over the gatekeepers that determine access to that infrastructure. True, we have antitrust and competition legislation, but the burden of this chapter has been to show that there are distinct free speech issues that are raised by these activities. On a view of free speech that connects it to a rich and substantive conception of democracy, with a public sphere founded on principles of egalitarianism and reciprocity, and on a view of free speech focused centrally on the community's right to have access to a diverse range of viewpoints, control over the infrastructure of speech in the form of concentration of the media in a few hands (with definite self-interests and ideologies) is troubling. Whether the answer lies in the Supreme Court, or in anti-monopolistic free speech legislation that was at issue in cases like *Sakal*, is yet unclear.

[64] See Habermas (1996).

PART SIX

New Horizons

. . . .

CHAPTER TWELVE

Surveillance, Net Neutrality, Shield Laws, and Copyright

• •

The aim of this concluding chapter is to push the boundaries of the domain of free speech and expression. I shall examine issues that are not generally considered within the framework of free speech, either because they have just appeared on the political and legal horizon, or because they tend to be analysed under other categories. I consider four such issues: surveillance, net neutrality, shield laws for journalists, and copyright. My observations in this chapter, of course, are only tentative and exploratory.

SURVEILLANCE

In the post-Snowden era, State surveillance has become an unavoidable feature of our daily lives. While international attention has focused on the dragnet spying conducted by the American NSA (the 'Prism Project') and the British GCHQ, India has its own surveillance apparatus, in the form of the Central Monitoring System (CMS), whose precise details remain controversial.[1] While it appears that the CMS has the capacity for bulk surveillance, its use will be targeted and limited. The same cannot be said about the Netra

---

[1] Prakash (2013).

system, which is designed to detect—and collect—all communication, via electronic media, that uses certain 'keywords' (such as 'attack', 'bomb', 'blast', and 'kill'), regardless of the context in which they are used.[2]

We normally think of surveillance as raising concerns about the right to privacy. Over the years, the Supreme Court has developed its privacy jurisprudence, specifically in the context of State surveillance. Grounding the right to privacy within Article 21's guarantee of life and personal liberty, it has held that interference with privacy must serve a compelling State interest, and must be narrowly tailored for serving that interest.[3] Surveillance, however, also implicates Article 19(1): in particular, the freedoms of speech and expression, assembly, and association (19(1)(a)–(c).

Recall our arguments about the chilling effect in the context of defamation law. The chilling effect is not only restricted to defamation. In fact, a few years before it decided *New York Times* v. *Sullivan*,[4] the American Supreme Court applied the same principle in the case of *NAACP* v. *Alabama*. In that case, the State of Alabama ordered the National Association for the Advancement of Colored People (NAACP) to compulsorily reveal its membership lists. The NAACP was heavily involved in the nascent civil rights movement in the deep South, in the teeth of State-sanctioned as well as private hostility. The Alabama government's step was clearly intended to try and 'out' NAACP members before an unfriendly and often violent public. Striking down the order, the Court held:

> Effective advocacy of both public and private points of view, particularly controversial ones, is undeniably enhanced by group association, as this Court has more than once recognized by remarking upon the close nexus between the freedoms of speech and assembly...inviolability of privacy in group association may in many circumstances be indispensable to preservation of freedom of association, particularly where a group espouses dissident beliefs.[5]

---

[2] Parbat (2013).
[3] See, for example, *Gobind* v. *State of Madhya Pradesh*, (1975) 2 SCC 148.
[4] 376 U.S. 254 (1964).
[5] *NAACP* v. *Alabama*, 357 U.S. 449, 462 (1958).

In short, the Court expressly linked the freedom to associate, the freedom of speech, and the adverse effect of surveillance upon both. Unless people are assured of privacy in their association with each other, they will tend to self-censor both in the domain of whom they associate with, as well as what they say. This is especially true when we are considering unpopular groups who have been historically subjected to persecution of various forms.

This manner of chilling operates in a particularly informal and insidious way, and requires heightened judicial sensitivity to appreciate. For instance, *Shelton v. Tucker* involved an Arkansas law that required publicly employed teachers to disclose all organizations that they had been part of for the previous five years, and *Local 1814 v. Waterfront Commission* was about compelled disclosure about political contributions made by labour union members. In both those cases, the courts struck down the disclosure requirements. In *Shelton v. Tucker*, the Court stressed upon the indirect way in which the chilling effect worked, noting that

> ...such interference with personal freedom is conspicuously accented when the teacher serves at the absolute will of those to whom the disclosure must be made—*those who any year can terminate the teacher's employment without bringing charges*, without notice, without a hearing, without affording an opportunity to explain...*the pressure upon a teacher to avoid any ties which might displease those who control his professional destiny would be constant and heavy.*[6]

Local 1814 echoed this reasoning with respect to the union workers.[7] The indirect way in which the chilling effect operates (and the consequent difficulty of *demonstrating* that speech has been chilled) was noted in a particularly striking way by the Supreme Court of Sri Lanka, in a case that involved the arrest and detention of certain members of a party. Holding that this would have a chilling effect upon the membership and activities of the party more generally, the Court held:

---

[6] *Shelton v. Tucker*, 364 U.S. 479, 486 (1960); emphasis mine.
[7] *Local 1814 v. Waterfront Commission*, 667 F.2d 267 (2d Cir. 1981).

There was in the matters before us no direct call to desist from expressive activities....The fact that the respondents took no direct action to restrict the right of the petitioners and members of the Ratawesi Peramuna to associate freely in orderly group activity however, does not end the matter...Freedoms such as these are protected not only against obvious and heavy handed frontal attack, but also from being smothered or stifled or chilled by more subtle interference...the arrest and detention...[must] have certainly had a chilling effect on the expressive and associational activities of those who had the temerity to continue to be members of the Ratawesi Peramuna.[8]

It is hardly surprising, therefore, that in its constitutional challenge to the American bulk surveillance programme, the American Civil Liberties Union (ACLU) made claims based not only upon privacy, but upon free speech as well.[9] The American Civil Liberties Union argued that the chilling effect of pervasive surveillance would inevitably mean that dissident and unpopular groups would limit their communications with it. The same arguments apply to the Indian surveillance regime as well.

If surveillance is a 19(1)(a) issue, then two conclusions follow. The first is that surveillance needs statutory backing (since reasonable restrictions upon Article 19(1)(a) can only be imposed by a 'law', and not by executive will). The second brings us to the reasonableness of surveillance itself. The standard justification used by governments the world over is that surveillance is essential to security. Under 19(2), therefore, the relevant categories would be 'security of the State' and 'public order'.

This, of course, raises the issue of the relevant test. Under the *Ramji Lal Modi* line of cases, with their broad understanding of the phrase 'in the interests of', the surveillance regime will be easy to justify (it is hardly deniable that it bears *some* relation to public order and security). If, on the other hand, the narrower test of *Lohia* is followed, then the burden upon the government will be much greater. Notably, this is a burden that the United States government has been singularly

---

[8] *Channa Peiris* v. *Attorney-General*, [1994] 1 SriLR 01.
[9] *ACLU* v. *Clapper*, No. 13-3994 (S.D. New York December 28, 2013).

unable to discharge, and its failure to show that its bulk surveillance programme had *actually* thwarted any terrorist attacks was a major reason why a federal judge held it to be 'likely unconstitutional' in late 2013.[10] Much, therefore, will depend upon what line of precedent a court chooses to adopt (broad or narrow), and how much deference it accords to the government's inevitable argument that surveillance is necessary to ensure security and stop terrorism.

NET NEUTRALITY

Broadly speaking, net neutrality is the idea that 'all internet traffic should be treated equally...no matter who uploads or downloads data, or what kind of data is involved, networks should treat all of those packets in the same manner'.[11] Net neutrality requires the gatekeepers of the Internet (such as service providers and broadband companies) to treat Internet traffic in an equal and non-discriminatory manner. Examples of possible discrimination include blocking certain content, or providing 'fast lanes' (differential speeds) based on a system of payment.

One practical example is the American Federal Communication Commission's Open Internet Order of 2010,[12] which was struck down by a Federal Court in *Verizon v. FCC*.[13] The Order imposed upon Internet service providers, obligations of transparency, no blocking, and no unreasonable discrimination. It was the second and third requirements that were struck down by the Court.

While the details of network neutrality remain controversial in many ways, let us assume that *some* form of neutrality is a desirable goal. In particular, manipulation of information available to Internet users (for political and/or commercial purposes) ought to be prevented.

---

[10] *Klayman v. Obama*, 957 F. Supp. 2d 1, 59 Comm. Reg. (P & F) 825 (D.D.C. December 16, 2013).
[11] Honan (2008).
[12] Federal Communications Commission.
[13] *Verizon Communications Inc. v. FCC*, 740 F.3d 623 (D.C. Cir. 2014).

In India, Internet service providers are both State-owned (BSNL and MTNL), and privately-owned (Airtel, Spectranet, and so on). There is, however, no network neutrality law. As one observer points out, 'The Telecom Regulatory Authority of India (TRAI), in its guidelines for issuing licences for providing Unified Access Service, promotes the principle of non-discrimination but does not enforce it…the Information Technology Act does not provide regulatory provisions relating to Internet access, and does not expressly prohibit an ISP from controlling the Internet to suit their business interests'.[14]

In the absence of a regulatory framework, there are two options. One is to argue that Internet service providers ought to be treated as 'common carriers'. Under common law, 'common carriers' (buses, taxis, ferries, and others) are obligated to transport everyone who pays the basic fare, and cannot discriminate against people, or refuse to transport anyone. It has long been argued that, in their function of transporting—or carrying—information packets across the Internet, Internet service providers ought to be treated as common carriers.[15]

While the law on common carriers is related to the obligation of *vehicles*, there is another way to think about the role—in particular—of telecommunications companies: as controllers of the *infrastructure* of carriage. In an early case, *Saghir Ahmad v. State of UP*, the Supreme Court was called on to decide upon the State's monopolization of road transport services.[16] The Court held that the right of the public to use roads and highways did not flow merely from statute, but existed

> anterior to any legislation on this subject as an incident of public rights over a highway. The State only controls and regulates it for the purpose of ensuring safety, peace, health and good morals of the public. Once the position is accepted that a member of the public is entitled to ply motor vehicles on the public road as an incident of his right of passage over a highway, the question is really immaterial *whether he plies a vehicle for pleasure or pastime or for the purpose of trade and business*.[17]

[14] Zulfi (2014).
[15] Something that was done by the American Federal Communications Commission in February 2015. See Morrison (2015).
[16] *Saghir Ahmad v. State of UP*, [1955] 1 SCR 707 (hereinafter *Saghir Ahmad*).
[17] *Saghir Ahmad*, para 11; emphasis mine.

Furthermore, this right was not enforceable merely against the State. According to the Court, the right of use stemmed from the nature of highways as public utilities, and not from whether they were State-owned or privately owned.[18]

Transposing analogies from the physical to the digital is a perilous exercise at the best of times, but if the Internet is now to be seen as a public utility, as important as roads and public highways, then *Saghir Ahmad* would seem to bear at least some relevance to the net neutrality debate.

There is, I would suggest, a 19(1)(a) argument to be made as well. Consider the 1946 American Supreme Court case of *Marsh* v. *Alabama*. In *Marsh*, a private company, the Gulf Shipbuilding Corporation, had established a 'company town': a township with buildings, streets, a sewage system, and a business block with rented stores and business places. Residents used the business block as a shopping centre, and accessed it via the company-owned pavement and street. The town's facilities were regularly used by travellers, and the roads were accessed by highway traffic. In the words of the Court, 'there is nothing to distinguish [Chickasaw] from any other town…except the fact that the title to the property belongs to a private corporation'.[19]

The dispute arose when Marsh, a Jehovah's Witness, was prohibited from distributing religious literature on the streets, under an anti-trespassing statute. The lower court rejected her free speech challenge, comparing the street to a private house, since it was owned by a private entity. The Supreme Court reversed. Four lines of reasoning can be distilled from its opinion. First, that streets, sidewalks, and similar public places had been historically used for the dissemination and reception of news, information, and opinions (mostly through public speaking and distribution of leaflets). Second, what mattered was not private ownership, but the function of the place itself: 'the owners of privately held bridges, ferries, turnpikes and railroads may not operate them as freely as a farmer does his farm. Since these facilities are built

---

[18] *Saghir Ahmad*, para 10.
[19] *Marsh* v. *Alabama*, 326 U.S. 501 (1946) (hereinafter *Marsh*).

and operated primarily to benefit the public and since their operation is essentially a public function, it is subject to state regulation.'[20] Third, the Court noted that living in privately-owned company towns was a staple feature of American life. It would, therefore, be perverse to deny a large number of citizens the same rights as enjoyed by those who lived in State-run towns. And lastly, it held that on balance, private rights of property were subordinate to the right of the public to enjoy the 'freedom of press and religion'.[21] Thus, a combination of factors—the historical use of streets and other places dedicatedly open to public speech, the absence of a feasible exit option, and the importance of free speech generally, as a constitutional right—led the Court to impose constitutional obligations on what was indisputably a private entity.

The analogy with net neutrality is striking. We live in a time when the traditional sites of public discourse—parks, towns, public streets—are now complemented by their digital equivalents: Twitter, Facebook, and the like. It is now a multiplicity of special and general-interest blogs that have become the equivalent of the old town squares, where speakers used to stand on the podium and make their arguments to the public. A section of the public itself now debates those arguments in the comments section. Thus, a significant part of opinion formation and communication, that once took place using open and publicly accessible *physical* infrastructure—now takes place in the virtual world, under the control of private gatekeepers. To that extent, Internet service providers are engaged in performing a public function, in the sense of *Marsh*.

What is equally important is the lack of a feasible exit option, since the Internet has become—essentially—an irreplaceable forum. In *Marsh*, it was assumed that it would be unreasonable to ask the residents of Chickasaw to pack up and move to a different town. In a similar way, the main online spaces are now owned by private parties, and access to those spaces is determined by gatekeepers—the Internet service providers.

---

[20] *Marsh*, p. 506.
[21] *Marsh*, p. 517.

The analogy is not perfect, of course, but in many ways, it is arguable that Internet service providers are private parties in control of a public good (the Internet) and performing a public function (access to the Internet). Admittedly, under the Constitution (Article 12), Part III is applicable only to State- or State-like entities under the functional, financial, or administrative control of the State.[22] From time to time, however, the Supreme Court has observed that when private entities perform public functions, they must be held to a public law standard. In his concurring opinion in *Unnikrishnan*, for instance, Justice Mohan argued (in the context of private educational institutions):

> What is the nature of functions discharged by these institutions? They discharge a public duty. If a student desires to acquire a degree, for example, in medicine, he will have to route through a medical college. These medical colleges are the instruments to attain the qualification. If, therefore, what is discharged by the educational institution, is a public duty that requires...[it to] act fairly. In such a case, it will be subject to Article 14.[23]

It is arguable, therefore, that internet service providers must be held to *some* obligations relating to the freedom of speech and expression. What are these obligations? In the last chapter, we discussed the social good theory of free speech: the idea that free speech serves the social goal of maintaining a public discourse that is open, inclusive, and home to a multiplicity of diverse and antagonistic ideas and viewpoints. The key question in cases such as *Sakal Papers*,[24] *Bennett Coleman*,[25] and *Cricket Association of Bengal*[26] was about governmental regulation of the access to the infrastructure of speech, in order to

---

[22] Article 12, Constitution of India.

[23] *Unnikrishnan* v. *State of Andhra Pradesh*, (1993) 1 SCC 645, paras 81–82 (concurring opinion of Mohan J.).

[24] *Sakal Papers* v. *Union of India*, [1962] 3 SCR 842.

[25] *Bennett Coleman* v. *Union of India*, (1972) 2 SCC 788: [1973] 2 SCR 757 (hereinafter *Bennett Coleman*).

[26] *Secretary, Ministry of Information and Broadcasting* v. *Cricket Association of Bengal*, (1995) 2 SCC 161.

ensure that participation was not skewed by inequality of resources. And if there is one thing that Internet fast-lanes threaten, it is a free and inclusive (digital) public sphere.

Therefore, a combination of these factors—the public function performed by Internet service providers as gatekeepers of the infrastructure of speech, the social-good theory underlying 19(1)(a), and the role served by network neutrality in maintaining an open online public sphere, provides us with an arguable case for imposing a constitutional obligation of net neutrality, even upon private Internet service providers.

SHIELD LAWS

A shield law—or, a 'source-protection law' is a law that exempts journalists from having to compulsorily reveal their sources when ordered to do so by the government (subject to overriding public interest requirements).[27] Exemptions of this sort already exist in Indian law. For example, under the Indian Evidence Act, communication between spouses is 'privileged'—that is, it cannot be used as evidence in court.[28] Shield laws exist in many American states, although the Supreme Court—by a narrow 5–4 majority—shied away from making it a constitutional right in the case of *Branzburg* v. *Hayes*. Nonetheless, the judges all understood the importance of source protection. Justice White, in his majority opinion, held that the government must 'convincingly show a substantial relation between the information sought and a subject of overriding and compelling state interest'.[29]

In England, journalists are protected under the statutory provisions of the Contempt of Courts Act. Section 10 permits the courts to compel disclosure only if it is 'in the interests of justice or national

[27] I do not discuss here the legality of 'sting operations' in the context of law enforcement.

[28] Privileged communications are covered by Ss. 122–29, Indian Evidence Act, 1872.

[29] *Branzburg* v. *Hayes*, 408 U.S. 665, 700 (1972).

security or for the prevention of disorder or crime.[30] In *Goodwin v. The United Kingdom*, the European Court of Human Rights found that the English judges had not interpreted the Section in conformity with the European Convention, when they ordered a journalist to reveal his sources. The European Court held that because of the important 'watchdog function' performed by the press, source protection was particularly important. If journalists could be legally compelled to reveal their sources, the chilling effect would be obvious: sources would be reluctant to reveal confidential and politically fraught information to journalists, and journalists, in turn, would be reluctant to jeopardize their sources by speaking to them about these matters. Consequently, the European Court of Human Rights held that journalists could be compelled to do so only when there was an 'overriding requirement in the public interest'.[31]

Our understanding of Article 19(1)(a)—especially as informed by the arguments in the previous chapter—demonstrates the importance of shield laws to free speech. If free speech is about the right to receive information, and about the social good of a public sphere in which information circulates freely and widely, then the vehicles of information must occupy a central position in a theory of free speech. Presently, the press is among the most important of those vehicles. Furthermore, shield laws are essentially about protecting the practice of investigative journalism, which is central to the checking value of free speech, which we discussed in Chapters One and Two. Thus, on both the community's right-to-receive-information, as well as the social-good-of-democracy justifications, shield laws—or at least, journalistic source protection of some sort—is mandated by Article 19(1)(a). Restrictions—or cases of compelled disclosure— might be those that satisfy the *Lohia* test of public order.

Indian jurisprudence on the issue is yet to take off. The Law Commission proposed a variant of a shield law,[32] but no concrete

---

[30] Section 10, Contempt of Courts Act, 1981.

[31] *Goodwin v. The United Kingdom*, (1996) 22 EHRR 123, para 39.

[32] Law Commission of India (1983). The Law Commission recommended the insertion of Section 132A into the Evidence Act, codifying journalistic privilege.

action has been taken. Various High Courts, on the other hand, have not been sympathetic to the proposition[33]—and the Supreme Court, in a challenge to the Prevention of Terrorism Act, upheld a provision that required compelled disclosure to the investigating officer.[34] At this point, therefore, one of two things is needed: either a strong shield law, or a definitive Supreme Court ruling on the point.

COPYRIGHT

Copyright over a particular work vests in the right-holder a statutorily imposed time-bound monopoly over certain key aspects of its use (such as copying it, modifying it, performing it, or so on). Copyright over any expressive work, therefore, severely curtails what other people can do with it, and evidently limits their freedom of speech and expression. It is surprising, therefore, that only very recently has copyright begun to be examined in the context of free speech.

One set of arguments—popular in the United States—hold that the existing copyright regime balances the concerns of protecting the author's interests, and those of free speech, *internally*. Through doctrines such as fair use and fair dealing, which provide limited exceptions to copyright, a balance is achieved between giving creators no rights at all (which, it is argued, will result in fewer works of art being created), and between giving them such stringent rights that everyone else's interests are sacrificed.[35] The argument is controversial; it also seems to focus entirely on the *volume* of work that is created (trying to achieve a balance that maximizes artistic (or other expressive) production), while ignoring entirely the problem of access.

The problem of access is illustrated most sharply by a recent development. In 2012, three academic publishing houses—Oxford

---

[33] See, for example, *Court on its Own Motion* v. *The Pioneer*, 68 (1997) DLT 259.

[34] *PUCL* v. *Union of India*, (2004) 9 SCC 580.

[35] See, for instance, *Harper & Row* v. *Nation Enterprises*, 471 U.S. 539 (1985).

University Press, Cambridge University Press, and Taylor & Francis—
filed a lawsuit against Delhi University, and a local photocopying shop.
They argued that by allowing students to photocopy large chunks of
academic textbooks, there was a clear and continuous violation of
copyright. The case is ongoing before the Delhi High Court. At issue
is the interpretation of the 'fair dealing' exception under the Indian
Copyright Act. Under Section 52(a)(i), 'fair dealing' with literary
works, for the purposes of private use, including research and teach-
ing, does not constitute an infringement of copyright.[36]

The problem of access is highlighted clearly by the fact that at
present prices, buying textbooks is a significant financial issue for
a large number of Indian students. This is where Article 19(1)(a) is
implicated: in the previous chapter, we discussed extensively how
State *censorship* is not the only way in which freedom of speech can
be affected or curtailed. Equally, economic exclusion from the public
sphere, shaped and structured by the existing market, affects that freedom. Once again, recall Justice Mathew's words in *Bennett Coleman*:

> ...an interpretation of Article 19(1)(a) which focuses on the idea that
> restraining the hand of the government is quite useless in assuring free
> speech, if a restraint on access is effectively secured by private groups.
> A Constitutional prohibition against governmental restriction on the
> expression is effective only if the Constitution ensures an adequate op-
> portunity for discussion.[37]

Copyright legislation provides the power to restrain access to private groups. The problem becomes particularly acute when it comes
to education because it can hardly be denied that the educational
system is *the* most important avenue for access to knowledge and
ideas, and for entry into the public sphere of opinion. Unaffordable
book prices constitute a heavy barrier to access, and these, in turn,
are determined by a statutorily enforced copyright regime. Copyright,
therefore, directly implicates the Article 19(1)(a) regime.

---

[36] See Section 52, Indian Copyright Act, 1957.
[37] *Bennett Coleman*, para 126 (dissenting opinion of Mathew J.).

This does not, of course, mean that the Delhi University copyright case should be decided one way or another: there are a host of factors to be balanced against each other. It does mean, however, that concerns about free speech should form part of the Court's analysis of the extent to which copyright ought to be enforced—something which is beginning, in an embryonic form, to enter into the legal thought of other countries. Soon, hopefully, it will in ours as well.

Conclusion

. . . .

In conclusion, it would perhaps be best to reiterate a confession that was made at the beginning of the book: the courts are not the primary battlegrounds of free speech in India. In large part, this is because of the structure of the Indian legal system, which often dispenses with the need to have judicial authorities *mediating* between coercive executive action and the citizen. Speech-restricting offences in the Indian Penal Code are cognizable, which allows the police to arrest without a warrant. While the deprivation of liberty is temporary (ordinarily, under the Code of Criminal Procedure, arrested persons must be produced before a magistrate within twenty-four hours), arbitrary arrests can, and do, have a significant chilling effect upon the freedom of speech.

Further, substantive speech-restricting provisions vest initial censorial power in the hands of executive or administrative authorities. Under Section 95 of the Code of Criminal Procedure, governments do not need judicial sanction before banning books. Films cannot see the light of day without prior clearance from an administrative certification board. Administrative authorities are vested with the power to block cable television channels as well as websites. As we have discussed extensively throughout this book, such a regime—of partial and, at times, complete prior restraint—is deeply damaging to a system of free speech. Perversely, it places the burden of approaching the court not upon the State, which has deprived a citizen of her freedom of expression, but upon the citizen herself. By doing this, it not only lowers the costs of censorship for the State, but also—considering the snail's pace at which the Indian judicial system moves—justifies the old adage, 'the process is the punishment'.

These problems have simple solutions, although they are unlikely to be achieved in the near future. Speech-based offences ought to be made non-cognizable, and prior restraint (both partial and complete) ought to be severely curtailed. The freedom of a citizen to speak and express herself ought only to be restricted by the order of a court, applying the law of the land. If the State wishes to ban a book or a film, or block a website, it should bear the burden of coming before a court and convincing it that the restriction falls within the contours of Article 19(2). Alternatively, in the event that this solution might be considered too extreme because it would—for example—prevent the police from taking immediate action to control incitements to rioting, a regime of heavy civil damages, enforceable against the police (or the State, as the case may be) and effectively implemented, ought to be in place to provide a significant disincentive for frivolous arrests.

And yet, would this solve anything? Have not the courts been as effective engines of censorship as the government and the police, upholding the law of sedition, endorsing book bans, and allowing the heckler's veto? This is a question that has no clear answer, and takes us into the realm of this book: the *jurisprudence* of Indian free speech law.

It is here that readers may be forgiven for thinking that, like Sisyphus, we have been rolling an immense boulder up a steep cliff, only for it to spill out of our grasp and roll back down from the edge of the peak. Doctrine is uncertain, judgments contradict one another, and sometimes there are contradictions within the same case. *What is the Indian constitutional law on free speech?* The answer seems to be: there are many.

At the cost of oversimplification, we can discern two broad streams of thought in Indian cases. These streams flow in opposite directions, and lead to a great tension—almost, a schizophrenia—in Indian free speech law. Let us call the first the moral–paternalistic vision of free speech. The moral–paternalistic vision holds that human beings are corruptible and corrupt, prone to violence, and cannot be trusted with too great a measure of freedom—especially when it comes to the freedom of speech, which is quintessentially corrupting. Human beings must be protected from malign influences. These influences could take the form of a pornographic novel (corruptor of morals), insulting speech (corruptor of public harmony and inter-group amity), subversive speech (corruptor of public order), contempt of court (corruptor of the public faith in the judiciary), and so on. In a series of cases, the Court has restricted what people can read, watch, or hear, how they can challenge dominant social and cultural norms, and how they can protest against judicial power, on the ground that all this is being done for the protection and improvement of the people themselves.

The second vision of free speech is the liberal–autonomous vision. This vision views individuals as thinking, deciding beings who bear the responsibility of choosing for themselves how to lead their lives; which doctrines to subscribe to and which to reject; what is good, or moral, or decent, and what isn't. It is not for the government to substitute *its* vision of the correct or good life, and impose that upon individuals by restricting what they can see, speak, or hear. To ban speech simply because of its persuasive value is to insult the autonomy both of the speaker, and of the listener. The liberal-autonomous vision countenances restricting free speech in certain, limited cases, such as incitement to imminent violence (situations of diminished autonomy), or when other, important constitutional values are implicated (hate speech, or certain kinds of violent or degrading pornography).

Our discussions during the course of this book reveal that Indian jurisprudence is evenly divided between these two approaches. Precedents abound for both points of view, and sometimes—as happened in *Rangarajan*—the same case reflects both approaches. What this means is that, going forward, Indian free speech law is in the balance. It is still open for a judge, or a group of judges, or a court, to stamp their own image upon free speech law, by definitively taking forward one line of jurisprudence at the expense of the other. At various points in this book, I have tried to show how that might be possible.

Of course, this might never happen. The Supreme Court's habit of sitting in panels, and its somewhat cavalier approach towards its own precedent, makes any kind of consistency well-nigh impossible to come by. But the hope remains that, at some point, when doctrine, text, and structure begin to matter again in Indian jurisprudence, our free speech law will attain some of the clarity that it needs. Whether it will be the kind of clarity that is desirable for free speech advocates is something that remains to be seen. The Court's prior record on civil liberties does not give ample space to hope, but until this situation of flux remains, an alternative reality is possible to imagine, and might even come true.

One other theme that has been prominent throughout the book is the deep connection between the freedom of speech and equality. Equality plays an important role in two distinct areas of free speech law. The first is an alternative justification for pornography and hate speech legislation. The argument from equality transforms both the reasons for limiting pornography and hate speech (from corrupted morals and outraged feelings to equal respect and dignity), as well as the understanding of what *is* pornography, and what is hate speech. The second role played by equality is in equalizing *access* to the 'marketplace of ideas', whether it is by breaking up newspaper monopolies, or ensuring net neutrality through legislation or adjudication. Here, the egalitarian conception of free speech comes into tension with its libertarian aspect: is the government entitled to change the structure of the marketplace, so as to guarantee access for those who cannot have it through the workings of the unregulated marketplace? Here again, we see tensions in the Court's jurisprudence over the years, and a present position that is balanced and uncertain between the two poles.

It must be added here that for all the possibilities that a divided jurisprudence leaves us, the regressive laws that continue to inhabit our penal legislation will always remain halters upon whatever the Court can achieve. Whether it is the colonial confines of Sections 153A and 295A, enacted to control a restive subject population, or the more recent Section 66A, there is only so much a court can do, bound within the contours of a restrictive text; and as we have seen, whatever the

Court does, as long as these provisions remain on the statute books, the gap between law and practice in our country ensures they will be abused—Blasi's pathological perspective writ large. Perhaps, ultimately, the only solution is for the Court to rethink its earlier decisions upholding these provisions, and make long overdue amends.

Whatever we think about the legitimate restrictions upon the right to freedom of speech in the abstract, it is clear that the contemporary scenario is undesirable. Arrests for Facebook likes and for political satire, the banning of books that challenge cultural norms, the banning of films that raise serious issues, the persecution of investigative reporting—all of this is deeply problematic for any polity that calls itself a 'democracy'. So far, this book has argued, the Courts have often failed to meet these challenges, but there is enough material in Indian constitutional history and doctrine for them to change course. Whether, in the future, they will rise to the challenge remains an open question.

Postscript

On 24 March 2015, a two-judge bench of the Supreme Court decided *Shreya Singhal* v. *Union of India*.[1] It struck down Section 66A of the Information Technology Act in its entirety, upheld Section 69 (blocking rules), and read down Section 79 (intermediary liability).

While upholding the constitutionality of Section 69 and the blocking rules, the Court also specified that blocking orders would have to be reasoned and written, and were subject to writ proceedings under Article 226.[2] Insofar as the Court has repeatedly held that Article 19(1)(a) includes the right of the public to know and to access information, there is an argument to be made that the judgment impliedly overrules the secrecy requirement, since a reader cannot challenge a blocking order unless he knows of its existence.[3]

Second, the Court read down Section 79 by clarifying that 'actual knowledge' (that would trigger intermediary liability) would be limited to cases where there was either a court order or a government notification.[4] This is not entirely satisfactory, since—yet again—it allows the executive to have a first go at censorship. At the very least,

---

[1] *Shreya Singhal* v. Union of India, (2015) 5 SCC 1 (hereinafter *Shreya Singhal*).
[2] *Shreya Singhal*, para 109.
[3] For a more detailed version of the argument, see Bhatia (2015b).
[4] *Shreya Singhal*, para 117.

though, it removes the burden of deciding upon the illegality or legality of online speech from the shoulders of private intermediaries. This, as we had discussed, was one of the most significant problems with intermediary liability under the Information Technology Act.

What deserves particular attention is the Court's holding on Section 66A. The judgment is significant for its outcome simply because, as readers would have noticed, the Supreme Court has always preferred to read down laws rather than strike them down for violating Article 19(1)(a). More than that, however, the judgment is extremely significant for its reasoning.

Justice Rohinton Nariman, writing for the Court, employed four arguments to hold Section 66A unconstitutional. First, he argued that in using terms such as 'menacing', 'grossly offensive', 'annoying', and 'inconvenient', Section 66A fails the proximity test under Article 19(2)'s public order restriction. He grounded this in a distinction between advocacy and incitement,[5] and held—following *Lohia*[6]—that under Article 19(2), incitement to public disorder can be restricted, but mere advocacy, or discussion, cannot. Importantly, he did not depart from *Ramji Lal Modi*[7] or *Virendra*,[8] but instead *reconciled* them with *Lohia* by holding that the 'tendency' to public disorder is restricted only to cases where it is to *incite* disorder.[9] Second, Justice Nariman held that Section 66A is void for vagueness;[10] third, that it is overbroad;[11] and fourth, that it is likely to exercise a significant chilling effect upon the freedom of speech.[12]

Additionally, Justice Nariman reasserted a crucial textual point that has been honoured more in the breach than observance ever since *Ranjit Udeshi*:[13] that 'public interest' cannot be a ground for restricting an

---

[5] *Shreya Singhal*, para 13.
[6] *The Superintendent, Central Prison, Fatehgarh* v. *Dr Ram Manohar Lohia*, [1960] 2 SCR 821.
[7] *Ramji Lal Modi* v. *State of UP*, [1957] 1 SCR 860.
[8] *Virendra* v. *State of Punjab*, [1958] 1 SCR 308.
[9] *Shreya Singhal*, paras 37–41.
[10] *Shreya Singhal*, para 82.
[11] *Shreya Singhal*, para 83.
[12] *Shreya Singhal*, para 90.
[13] *Ranjit Udeshi* v. *State of Maharashtra*, AIR 1965 SC 881: [1965] 1 SCR 65.

Article 19(1)(a) right. Any restriction *must* conform to the eight specific categories of Article 19(2), each of which has a defined meaning.[14] And lastly, he rejected the State's argument that the Internet, being a unique medium with greater reach and spread than other media, should be subjected to greater regulation. While admitting that there might be laws designed to capture specific offences that might be unique to specific media (such as, for instance, website blocking), he reaffirmed the fact that any such regulation must pass muster under the Article 19(2) tests.[15]

Readers who have struggled through this book will immediately see the critical importance of each of these arguments.[16] In its sharp distinction between advocacy and incitement, its collapsing of 'tendency' into proximity, and its insistence upon the requirement of proximity, *Shreya Singhal* emphatically belongs to the line of cases—*Lohia–Rangarajan–Arup Bhuyan*—that are predicated upon a vision of the autonomous, responsible, and choosing citizen. Its endorsement of proximity and its constitutionalization of both vagueness and overbreadth, further undermine the basic logic that upheld Section 295A in *Ramji Lal Modi*, and sedition in *Kedar Nath Singh*.[17] Its acknowledgment of the chilling effect—as well as its invocation in specifically striking down a legal provision—creates the legal foundation for the future constitutionalization of civil defamation, and perhaps the erasure of criminal defamation. And its affirmation that Article 19(2) scrutiny is medium-neutral knocks the bottom out of the entire justification for imposing prior restraint upon the cinema, because of its unique, medium-based affective qualities.

Whether *Shreya Singhal* will actually have an impact upon other areas of free speech law remains to be seen. But there is no doubting that more than any other judgment, it has with great clarity and lucidity, laid the foundations for a free speech jurisprudence that can reclaim the original promise of Article 19(1)(a).

---

[14] *Shreya Singhal*, para 21. He also cites *Lohia* for the narrow definition of 'public order', as opposed to the broader 'law and order'.

[15] *Shreya Singhal*, para 28.

[16] For a more detailed argument, see Bhatia (2015a).

[17] *Kedar Nath Singh* v. *State of Bihar*, [1962] SCR Supp. (2) 769.

Bibliography

Altman, A. 1993. 'Liberalism and Campus Hate Speech: A Philosophical Examination', *Ethics*, 103(2): 302–17.

Amar, A. 2012. *America's Unwritten Constitution*. New York: Basic Books.

Ambedkar, B. 2014. *The Annihilation of Caste*. New Delhi: Navyana.

Baker, C. Edwin 1978. 'Scope of the First Amendment Freedom of Speech', *UCLA Law Review*, 25: 964–1040.

———. 1989. *Human Liberty and Freedom of Speech*. New York: Oxford University Press.

Balakrishnan, S. 2014. 'Praful Patel, Descent of Air India and the Killing of a Critical Book', *DNA*, 16 January.

Balkin, J. 2004. 'Digital Speech and Democratic Culture', *NYU Law Review*, 79(1): 1–55.

Barendt, E. 2007. *Freedom of Speech*. Oxford, New York: Oxford University Press.

Barron, J.A. 1967. 'Access to the Press. A New First Amendment Right', *Harvard Law Review*, 80(8): 1641–78.

BBC News. 2008. 'Editor "Defamed" Singapore Leader', *BBC News*, 24 September.

Benhabib, S. 2002. *The Claims of Culture: Equality and Diversity in the Global Era*. Princeton: Princeton University Press.

Berlin, I. 1969. *Four Essays on Liberty*. London, New York: Oxford Paperbacks.

Bhatia, G. 2015a. 'The Striking Down of S. 66A: How Indian Free Speech Jurisprudence Found Its Soul Again', *Indian Constitutional Law and Philosophy*, 26 March, https://indconlawphil.wordpress.com/2015/03/26/

the-striking-down-of-section-66a-how-indian-free-speech-jurispru-dence-found-its-soul-again/ (accessed 31 March 2015).

Bhatia, G. 2015b. 'The Supreme Court's IT Act Judgment, and Secret Blocking', *Indian Constitutional Law and Philosophy*, 25 March, https://indconlawphil.wordpress.com/2015/03/25/the-supreme-courts-it-act-judgment-and-secret-blocking/ (accessed 31 March 2015).

———. 2015c. 'The Constitutional Challenge to Rajasthan's Panchayati Raj Ordinance', *Indian Constitutional Law and Philosophy*, 5 January, https://indconlawphil.wordpress.com/2015/01/05/the-constitutional-challenge-to-rajasthans-panchayati-raj-ordinance/ (accessed 12 January 2015).

Bhatia, S. 1997. *Freedom of Press: Politico-Legal Aspects of Press Legislation in India*. New Delhi: Rawat Publications.

Bindra, C.J.S. 1954. 'Freedom of Speech and Expression', *All India Reporter*, 62–65.

Black, Charles. 1969. *Structure and Relationship in Constitutional Law*. Baton Rouge: Louisiana State University Press.

Blackstone, W. 1765–69. *Commentaries on the Laws of England*. http://avalon.law.yale.edu/subject_menus/blackstone.asp (accessed 16 October 2014).

Blasi, V. 1985. 'The Pathological Perspective and the First Amendment', *Columbia Law Review*, 85(3): 449–514.

Bork, R.H. 1971. 'Neutral Principles and Some First Amendment Problems', *Indiana Law Journal*, 471: 1–35.

Brecht, Bertolt. 1986. *The Life of Galileo* (trans. J. Willett and H. Rorrison). London: Methuen Drama.

Burke, J. 2014. 'Outcry as Penguin India Pulps "Alternative" History of Hindus', *The Guardian*, 13 February.

Butalia, P. 2014. 'Two Laws on Censorship', *Indian Express*, 4 November.

Chakrabarty, D. 2007. *Provincializing Europe*. Princeton: Princeton University Press.

Chari, M. 2014. 'Why Many Indian States Are Using the 1923 Goondas Act to Curb Digital Piracy', *Scroll*, 6 August.

Cohen, G.A. 1983. 'The Structure of Proletarian Unfreedom', *Philosophy and Public Affairs*, 12(1): 3–33.

———. 2011. 'Freedom and Money', in M. Otsuka (ed.), *On the Currency of Egalitarian Justice and Other Essays in Political Philosophy*, pp. 166–92. Princeton: Princeton University Press.

Collett, S. (ed.). 1914. *The Life and Letters of Raja Rammohun Roy*. Calcutta: R. Cambray & Co.

Committee on Homosexual Offences and Prostitution. 1957. *Report of the Committee on Homosexual Offences and Prostitution*, CMD No. 247. London: HMSO.

Dalal, S. 2000. 'Dhirubhai Ambani and Stories that Need Telling', *Rediff*, 26 July.

Delgado, R. 1982. 'Words that Wound: A Tort Action for Racial Insults, Epithets and Name Calling', *Harvard Civil Rights—Civil Liberties Law Review*, 17: 133–81.

Desai, S. and C. Gonsalves. 1989. *Freedom of the Press*. Bombay: C.G. Shah Memorial Trust.

Devlin, P. 1959. *The Enforcement of Morals*. Oxford: Oxford University Press.

Dhavan, R. 1978. *Censorship and Obscenity*. Totowa, New Jersey: Rowman and Littlefield.

———. 1982. *Contempt of Court and the Press*. Bombay: N.M. Tripathi.

———. 2007. *Harassing Husain: Uses and Abuses of the Law of Hate Speech*. Delhi: Sahmat.

———. 2008. *Publish and Be Damned: Censorship and Intolerance in India*. New Delhi: Tulika Books.

Divan, M. 2003. 'Morality, Obscenity and Censorship', *Supreme Court Cases (Journal)*, 1: 1–16.

———. 2013. *Facets of Media Law*, 2nd edn. New Delhi: Eastern Book Company.

Donogh, W.R. 1911. *A Treatise on the Law of Sedition and Cognate Offences in British India: Penal and Preventive*. Calcutta: Thacker, Spink and Co.

Donson, F.J.L. 2000. *Legal Intimidation: A SLAPP in the Face of Democracy*. London, New York: Free Association Books.

Dworkin, G. 2014. 'Paternalism', in Edward N. Zalta (ed.), *The Stanford Encyclopedia of Philosophy*, http://stanford.library.usyd.edu.au/entries/paternalism/ (accessed 24 January 2014).

———. 2005. 'Moral Paternalism', *Law and Philosophy*, 24(3): 305–19.

Dworkin, R. 1966. 'Lord Devlin and the Enforcement of Morals', *Yale Law Journal*, 75(6): 986–1005.

———. 1978. *Taking Rights Seriously*. Cambridge, Massachusetts: Harvard University Press.

———. 1981. 'Is There a Right to Pornography', *Oxford Journal of Legal Studies*, 1(2): 177–212.

———. 1986a. *A Matter of Principle*. Cambridge, Massachusetts: Harvard University Press.

———. 1986b. *Law's Empire*. Cambridge, Massachusetts: Harvard University Press.

———. 1996a. *Freedom's Law*. Cambridge, Massachusetts: Harvard University Press.

———. 1996b. 'Why Must Speech Be Free?', in *Freedom's Law: The Moral Reading of the American Constitution*, pp. 195–214. Cambridge, Massachusetts: Harvard University Press.

Emerson, T. 1955. 'The Doctrine of Prior Restraint', *Law and Contemporary Problems*, 204: 648–71.

———. 1970. *The System of Free Expression*. New York: Random House.

———. 1981. 'The Affirmative Side of the First Amendment', *Georgia Law Review*, 15(4): 795–849.

Federal Communications Commission. 'In the Matter of Preserving the Open Internet', FCC 10-201.

Feinberg, J. 1971. 'Legal Paternalism', *Canadian Journal of Philosophy*, 1(1): 105–24.

———. 1987a. *Harm to Self (Moral Limits of the Criminal Law)*. New York, Oxford: Oxford University Press.

———. 1987b. 'Offence to Others', *Philosophy and Phenomenological Research*, 48(1): 147–53.

Fiss, O. 1986. 'Free Speech and Social Structure', *Iowa Law Review*, 71: 1405–25.

———. 1998. *The Irony of Free Speech*. Cambridge, Massachusetts: Harvard University Press.

Fraser, N. 1990. 'Rethinking the Public Sphere', *Social Text*, 25/26: 56–80.

———. 1997. *Justice Interruptus: Critical Reflections on the 'Postsocialist' Condition*. New York: Routledge.

Ganachari, A. 2009. 'Combating Terror of Law in Colonial India: The Law of Sedition and the Nationalist Response', in Marianne Vardalos and Guy Kirby Letts (eds), *Engaging Terror: A Critical and Interdisciplinary Approach*, pp. 93, 106. Boca Raton: Brown Walker Press.

Gandhi, M.K. 1958–84. *The Collected Works of Mahatma Gandhi*, Vol. 22. New Delhi: The Publications Division, Ministry of Information and Broadcasting.

Ganti, T. 2009. 'The Limits of Decency and the Decency of Limits', in W. Mazzarella and R. Kaur (eds), *Censorship in South Asia: Cultural Regulation from Sedition to Seduction*, pp. 87–122. Bloomington: Indiana University Press.

Grossman, H.M. 1956–57. 'Freedom of Expression in India', *UCLA Law Review*, 4: 64–80.

Gupta, A. 2011. 'John Doe Orders and Internet Outages', *Indian Law and Technology Blog*, 18 August, http://www.iltb.net/2011/08/internet-outage/ (accessed 18 January 2014).

———. 2012. 'The Advent of the Gag Writ', *The Hoot*, 20 September, http://thehoot.org/web/The-advent-of-the-gag-writ/6309-1-1-7-true.html (accessed 18 January 2014).

Habermas, J. 1990. 'Discourse Ethics: Notes on a Program of Philosophical Justification', in *Moral Consciousness and Communicative Action*, pp. 43–116. Cambridge, Massachusetts: MIT Press.

Habermas, J. 1991. *Moral Consciousness and Communicative Action*. Cambridge, Massachusetts: MIT Press.

———. 1994. 'Remarks on Discourse Ethics', in *Justification and Application*, pp. 19–113. Cambridge, Massachusetts: MIT Press.

———. 1996. *Between Facts and Norms: Contributions to a Discourse Theory of Law and Democracy*. Cambridge, Massachusetts: MIT Press.

Hamilton, A. 1788. 'The Federalist No. 78', *Independent Journal*, 14 June, http://www.constitution.org/fed/federa78.htm (accessed 27 July 2015).

Hart, H.L.A. 1963. *Law, Liberty and Morality*. Stanford, California: Stanford University Press.

Hayek, F.A. 1978. *The Constitution of Liberty*. Chicago: University of Chicago Press.

———. 1991. *The Fatal Conceit: The Errors of Socialism*. Chicago: University of Chicago Press.

Honan, M. 2008. 'Inside Net Neutrality: Is Your ISP Filtering Content?', *MacWorld*, 12 February.

Hornsby, J. 1995. 'Disempowered Speech', *Philosophical Topics*, 23(2): 127–47.

Indian Constituent Assembly. 1949. *Constituent Assembly Debates*. New Delhi: Lok Sabha Secretariat.

Jain, B. 2013. 'Government Releases Data of Riot Victims Identifying Religion', *The Times of India*, 24 September.

Jebaraj, P. 2011. 'Binayak Sen Among Six Charged with Sedition in 2010', *The Hindu*, 2 January.

Jenkins, D. 2001. 'The Sedition Act of 1798 and the Incorporation of Seditious Libel into the First Amendment', *American Journal of Legal History*, 45(2): 154–213.

Joshua, A. 2014. 'Revise Your Book, Orient Blackswan Tells Megha Kumar', *The Hindu*, 17 June.

Kalven, H. 1964. 'The New York Times Case: A Note on "the Central Meaning of the First Amendment"', *The Supreme Court Review*, Vol. 1964, 191–221.

Kant, I. 1784. 'What Is Enlightenment?', http://www.columbia.edu/acis/ets/CCREAD/etscc/kant.html (accessed 16 October 2014).

Khosla, G.D. 1976. *Pornography and Censorship in India*. New Delhi: Indian Book Company.

Kurup, D. 2014. 'Infosys Slams Defamation Notice on Three Newspapers', *The Hindu*, 10 June.

La Rue, F. 2011. *Report on the Promotion and Protection of the Right to Freedom of Opinion and Expression*, Human Rights Council, 17th Session, A/HRC/17/27.

Langton, R. 1993. 'Speech Acts and Unspeakable Acts', *Philosophy and Public Affairs*, 22(4): 293–330.

Law Commission of India. 1983. *Report No. 93: Disclosure of Sources of Information by Mass Media*, September, http://lawcommissionofindia.nic.in/old_reports/rpt93.pdf (accessed 27 July 2015).

———. 2014. *Report No. 248: Obsolete Laws: Warranting Immediate Repeal*, September, http://lawcommissionofindia.nic.in/reports/Report248.pdf (accessed 27 July 2015).

Lawrence III, Charles R. 1990. 'If He Hollers Let Him Go: Regulating Racist Speech on Campus', *Duke Law Journal*, 39(3): 431–83.

Leigh, D. 2011. 'Superinjunction Scores Legal First for Nameless Financier in Libel Action', *The Guardian*, 29 March.

Lewis, A. 1992. *Make No Law: The Sullivan Case and the First Amendment*. New York: Vintage Books.

Livemint. 2014. 'RNRL, Anil Ambani serve Defamation Notice to Authors of Gas Wars', *Livemint*, 22 April.

MacKinnon, C. 1988. 'Not a Moral Issue', in C. MacKinnon, *Feminism Unmodified*, pp. 146–62. Cambridge, Massachusettes: Harvard University Press.

Madison, J. 1788. 'The Federalist No. 48', *The New York Packet*, 1 February, http://www.constitution.org/fed/federa48.htm (accessed 27 July 2015).

Mahapatra, D. 2014. 'Contempt Powers Needed to Secure Respect, SC Says', *The Times of India*, 31 May.

Mathur, P. 2004. 'Exposing a Maharashtra Legend', *Asia Times*, 9 October, http://atimes.com/atimes/South_Asia/FJ09Df02.html (accessed 31 March 2015).

Mazzarella, W. 2009. 'Making Sense of Cinema in Late Colonial India', in W. Mazzarella and R. Kaur (eds), *Censorship in South Asia: Cultural Regulation from Sedition to Seduction*, pp. 63–86. Bloomington: Indiana University Press.

———. 2013. *Censorium: Cinema and the Open Edge of Mass Publicity*. Hyderabad: Orient BlackSwan.

Mazzarella, W. and R. Kaur (eds). 2009. *Censorship in South Asia: Cultural Regulation from Sedition to Seduction*. Bloomington: Indiana University Press.

Mehta, P.B. 2009. 'Passion and Constraint: Courts and the Regulation of Religious Meaning', in Rajeev Bhargava (ed.), *Politics and Ethics of the Indian Constitution*, pp. 311–38. New Delhi: Oxford University Press.

Meiklejohn, A. 1948. *Free Speech and its Relation to Self-Government*. New York: Harper.

———. 1961. 'The First Amendment is an Absolute', *The Supreme Court Review*, 1961: 245–66.

Menon, N. 2004. 'Citizenship and the Passive Revolution: Interpreting the First Amendment', *Economic and Political Weekly*, XXXIX(18): 1812–19.

Mill, J.S. 1869. *On Liberty*. London: Longman, Roberts and Green, http://www.bartleby.com/130/ (accessed 27 July 2015).

Milo, Dario, Glenn Penfold, and Anthony Stein. 2008. 'Freedom of Expression', in S. Woolman (ed.), *Constitutional Law of South Africa* 2nd edn, pp. 42–1 to 42–193. Cape Town: Juta Legal and Academic Publishers.

Morrison, K. 2015. 'Net Neutrality: FCC Reclassifies ISPs as Common Carriers', *Social Times*, 26 February, http://www.adweek.com/socialtimes/net-neutrality-fcc-reclassifies-isps-as-common-carriers/616039 (accessed 31 March 2015).

Muralidharan, S. 2012. 'A Judicial Doctrine of Postponement and the Demands of Open Justice', *Economic and Political Weekly*, XLVII(38), http://www.epw.in/web-exclusives/judicial-doctrine-postponement-and-demands-open-justice.html (accessed 21 January 2014).

Nagvenkar, M. 2014. 'Goa: Facebook User Faces Jail for Anti-Modi "Holocaust" Comment', *Firstpost*, 24 May.

Nair, N. 2013. 'Beyond the "Communal" 1920s: The Problem of Intention, Legislative Pragmatism, and the Making of Section 295A of the Indian Penal Code', *Indian Economic Social History Review*, 50(3): 317–40.

Narrain, S. 2011. '"Disaffection" and the Law: The Chilling Effect of Sedition Laws in India', *Economic and Political Weekly*, XLVI(8): 33–37.

———. 2014. 'The Constitution of Hurt: The Evolution of Hate Speech Law in India', Harvard Law School LLM Dissertation, unpublished manuscript, on file with the author.

Parbat, K. 2013. 'Government to Launch "Netra" for Internet Surveillance', *The Economic Times*, 16 December.

Popper, K. 1945. *The Open Society and Its Enemies*, Vol. 1. London: Routledge.

Post, R. 1991. 'Racist Speech, Democracy and the First Amendment', *William and Mary Law Review*, 32(2): 267–327.

———. 1995. 'Recuperating First Amendment Doctrine', *Stanford Law Review*, 47(6): 1249–81.

———. 1997. 'Equality and Autonomy in First Amendment Jurisprudence', *Michigan Law Review*, 95(6): 1517–59.

———. 2011. 'Participatory Democracy and Free Speech', *Virginia Law Review*, 97(3): 477–89.

Prakash, P. 2013. 'How Surveillance Works in India', *India Ink*, 10 July.

———. n.d. 'Visible and Invisible Censorship', unpublished article, on file with the author.

Prasad, S. 2014. 'We the Goondas', *Bangalore Mirror*, 4 August.

PTI. 2010. 'Sedition Case Registered against Arundhati Roy, Geelani', *NDTV*, 29 November.

PTI. 2012. 'Two Mumbai Girls Arrested for Facebook Post against Bal Thackeray Get Bail', *India Today*, 19 November.

———. 2015. 'Former BJP President Nitin Gadkari Slaps Defamation Notice on Arvind Kejriwal', *The Economic Times*, http://articles.economictimes. indiatimes.com/2014-02-01/news/46898012_1_bjp-president-nitin-gadkari-arvind-kejriwal-defamation-notice (accessed on 28 July 2015).

Rajalakshmi, T.K. 2004. '"Sati" and the Verdict', *Frontline*, 21(5), http://www.frontline.in/static/html/fl2105/stories/20040312002504600.htm (accessed 31 March 2015).

Ramnath, K. n.d. 'The Other Criminal Codes: Crises, Excesses and the Goondas Acts in Indian Legal Imagination', unpublished manuscript on, file with the author.

Ranjan, S. 2011. 'Cause for Defamation?', *Deccan Herald*, 25 November.

Rawls, J. 1993. *Political Liberalism*. New York: Columbia University Press.

———. 2005. *A Theory of Justice*. Cambridge, Massachusetts: Bellknap Press.

Raz, J. 1988. *The Morality of Freedom*. New York: Oxford University Press.

Redish, M.H. 1971. 'The First Amendment in the Marketplace: Commercial Speech and the Values of Free Expression', *George Washington Law Review*, 39: 429–73.

Richards, D.A.J. 1974. 'Free Speech and Obscenity Law', *University of Pennsylvania Law Review*, 123(1): 45–91.

Said, E. 1984. 'Permission to Narrate', *Journal of Palestine Studies*, 13(3): 27–48.

Saikia, A. 2014. 'The Law Spreads Its Net', *Newslaundry*, 26 May.

Sastri, Gopalakrishna. 1964. *The Law of Sedition in India*. Bombay: N.M. Tripathi.

Sathe, S.P. 1970. 'Freedom of Speech and Contempt of Court', *Economic and Political Weekly*, V(42): 1741–42.

———. 2003. 'Defamation and Public Advocacy', *Economic and Political Weekly*, XXXVIII(22): 2109–12.

Scanlon, T.M. 1972. 'A Theory of Freedom of Expression', *Philosophy and Public Affairs*, 1(2): 204–26.

Scott, J. 1990. *Domination and the Arts of Resistance: Hidden Transcripts*. New Haven: Yale University Press.

Seervai, H.M. 2005. *Constitutional Law of India*, Vol. 2, 4th edn. Delhi: Universal Law Publishers.

Seervai, S. 2014. 'India Bans Film about Sri Lanka War', *The Wall Street Journal (India)*, 22 February.

Sethi, V. 1980. 'Freedom of the Press', *Journal of Constitutional and Parliamentary Studies*, XIV: 270–89.

Shankar, R. 2012. 'Supreme Court's Decision on Reporting of Proceedings', *Economic and Political Weekly*, XLVII(40), http://www.epw.in/commentary/supreme-courts-decision-reporting-proceedings.html (accessed 21 January 2014).

Shastri, C.L.R. 1949. 'Freedom of Person and of Expression: New Presbyter but Old Priest Writ Large', *Modern Review*, 28–30.

Shiva Rao, B. 1967. *The Framing of India's Constitution: Select Documents*, Vol. 1. Delhi: Universal Law Publishing Co.

Siegel, R. 2004. 'Equality Talk: Antisubordination and Anticlassification Values in Constitutional Struggles Over Brown', *Harvard Law Review*, 117(5): 1470–547.

Sorabjee, S 1976. *Law of Press Censorship in India*. Bombay: N.M. Tripathi.

———. 2000. 'Constitution, Courts, and Freedom of the Press and the Media', in B.N. Kirpal, Ashok H. Desai, Gopal Subramanium, Rajeev Dhavan, and Raju Ramachandran (eds), *Supreme But Not Infallible: Essays in Honour of the Supreme Court of India*, pp. 334–59. New Delhi: Oxford University Press.

———. 2003. 'Palkhivala and the Constitution of India', *Supreme Court Cases (Journal)*, 4: 33, http://www.ebc-india.com/lawyer/articles/2003v5a1.htm (accessed 31 March 2015).

Stanton-Ife, J. 2014. 'The Limits of the Law', in Edward N. Zalta (ed.), *Stanford Encyclopedia of Philosophy*, http://plato.stanford.edu/entries/law-limits/ (accessed 16 October 2014).

Sudhakar, P. and S. Vijay Kumar. 2012. 'Kundankulam: 11 Protesters Held on Sedition Charges', *The Hindu*, 20 March.

Sunder, M. 2001. 'Cultural Dissent', *Stanford Law Review*, 54(3): 495–567.

Sunstein, C. 1992. 'Free Speech Now', *University of Chicago Law Review*, 59(1): 255–316.

———. 1998. *The Partial Constitution*. Cambridge, Massachusetts: Harvard University Press.

Swaminathan, S. 2010. 'The Conflict between Freedom of the Press and Parliamentary Privileges: An Unfamiliar Twist in a Familiar Tale', *National Law School of India Review*, 22(1): 123–33.

The Committee to Protect Journalists. 2014. 'Zimbabwe's Top Court Strikes Down Criminal Defamation', *The Committee to Protect Journalists*, 13 June, https://cpj.org/2014/06/zimbabwes-top-court-finds-criminal-defamation-to-b.php (accessed 27 July 2015).

The Crown Prosecution Service. n.d. 'Guidelines on Prosecuting Cases Involving Communications Sent Via Social Media', http://www.cps.gov.uk/legal/a_to_c/communications_sent_via_social_media/ (accessed 27 July 2015).

The Hindu. 2012. 'Mumbai Police Arrest Cartoonist, Slap Sedition, Cybercrime Charges on Him', *The Hindu*, 10 September.

The Law Commission. 2012. *Law Com 335: Contempt of Court: Scandalising the Court*. London: The Stationery Office.

Thiruvengadam, A.K. n.d. 'The Evolution of the Constitutional Right to Free Speech in India (1800–1950): The Interplay of Universal and Particular Rationales', unpublished manuscript on file with the author.

Times News Network. 2014. 'Hindu Sena Stonewalls Radio Mirchi's "Kiss of Love Wall"', *The Times of India*, 16 November.

Tribe, L. 1978. 'Toward a Metatheory of Free Speech', *Southwestern University Law Review*, 10: 237–86.

Tripathi, P.K. 1958. 'Free Speech in the Indian Constitution: Background and Prospect', *Yale Law Journal*, 67(3): 384–400.

———. 1972. 'India's Experiments in Freedom of Speech', in *Spotlights on Constitutional Interpretation*, pp. 255–90. Bombay: N.M. Tripathi.

Uppaluri, U. 2012. 'Constitutional Analysis of the Information Technology (Intermediaries' Guidelines) Rules, 2011', 16 July, http://cis-india.org/internet-governance/constitutional-analysis-of-intermediaries-guidelines-rules (accessed 27 July 2015).

Vallianeth, T. 2014. 'Ashok Kumar Goes on a Rampage', *SpicyIP*, 8 July.

Venkatesan, V. 2014. *Constitutional Conundrums: Challenges to India's Democratic Process*. Haryana: LexisNexis.

Waldron, J. 2012. *The Harm in Hate Speech*. Cambridge, Massachusetts: Harvard University Press.

Walker, C. 2005–2006. 'Reforming the Crime of Libel', *New York Law School Law Review*, 50: 169–203.

Warner, M. 2006. 'Saint Cunera's Scarf', in *Signs and Wonders*, pp. 86–91. London: Random House.

Wikileaks. 2014. 'Australia Bans Reporting of Multi-National Corruption Case Involving Malaysia, Indonesia and Vietnam', 27 July, https://wikileaks.org/aus-suppression-order/press.html (27 July 2015).

Yadava, R. 2014. 'Free Speech, Interim Injunctions and Media Guidelines', *Indian Constitutional Law and Philosophy*, 24 January, https://indconlawphil.wordpress.com/2014/01/27/guest-post-free-speech-interim-injunctions-and-media-guidelines/ (accessed 26 January 2015).

Zulfi, M. 2014. 'Net Neutrality: Here's Everything You Need to Know About It', *Indian Express*, 10 February.

Index
. . . .

About the Author

Gautam Bhatia is a practicing lawyer in Delhi, and visiting faculty, West Bengal National University of Juridical Sciences, Kolkata. He has been involved in contemporary constitutional cases before the Supreme Court of India, including the right to privacy judgment and the constitutional challenge to the Aadhaar programme. He graduated from the National Law School of India University, Bangalore, in 2011, and was the Rhodes Scholarship awardee. He completed the Bachelor of Civil Law degree at the University of Oxford, winning the prestigious Herbert Hart Prize in Jurisprudence and Political Theory. Subsequently, he completed his MPhil (Law) from the University of Oxford, and LLM from Yale Law School. He is a contributor to the Oxford University Press title *The Oxford Handbook of the Indian Constitution* (2016). His scholarly work has appeared in the *Max Planck Encyclopaedia for Comparative Constitutional Law*, *Global Constitutionalism*, *The Asian Journal of Comparative Law*, and *Constellations*, and he has been cited by the Supreme Court of India in its judgment on the right to privacy.